International Kierkegaard
Commentary

Volume 17
Christian Discourses
and
The Crisis and a Crisis in the Life of an Actress

International Kierkegaard Commentary

Volume 17
Christian Discourses
and
The Crisis and a Crisis in the Life of an Actress

edited by
Robert L. Perkins

MERCER
UNIVERSITY PRESS

ISBN-10 0-88146-031-1
ISBN-13 978-0-88146-031-5

MUP/H723

International Kierkegaard Commentary
Volume 17. *Christian Discourses*
and *The Crisis and a Crisis in the Life of an Actress*
Copyright ©2007
Mercer University Press, Macon, Georgia 31207 USA
All rights reserved
Printed in the United States of America
First edition, November 2007

The paper used in this publication meets the minimum requirements
of American National Standard for Information Sciences — Permanence
of Paper for Printed Library Materials, ANSI Z39.48-1984.

Library of Congress Cataloging-in-Publication Data

Kierkegaard, Søren, 1813–1855.

[Christelige taler. English]

Christian discourses ; and, The crisis and a crisis in the life of an actress /
edited by Robert L. Perkins. -- 1st ed.
    p.   cm. -- (International Kierkegaard commentary ; v. 17)
Includes bibliographical references and index.
ISBN-13: 978-0-88146-031-5 (hardback : alk. paper)
ISBN-10: 0-88146-031-1 (hardback : alk. paper)
1. Christian life--Lutheran authors. 2. Theater. 3. Heiberg, Johanne Luise,
1812-1890. I. Perkins, Robert L. II. Kierkegaard, Søren, 1813-1855. Krisen og en
krise i en skuespillerindes liv. English. III. Title. IV. Title: Crisis and a crisis in the
life of an actress.

BV4505.K3413 2007
248.4--dc22

2007039634

Contents

Acknowledgments

All the contributors to the volume would desire to make acknowledgments to family and friends, but it is a privilege reserved for the editor. Those whom the contributors would have named will be content to have served their family and colleagues.

I have the privilege of thanking a number of persons at Stetson University who have supported my work in general and the International Kierkegaard Commentary in particular: H. Douglas Lee, president of Stetson University; James R. Beasley, vice president for administration and chief operating officer; Grady Ballenger, dean of the College of Arts and Sciences; and Ron Hall, chair, Department of Philosophy.

The advisory board, C. Stephen Evans, Andrew Burgess, and Sylvia Walsh, read the contributions, and David Cain served as volume consultant. The interest of Mercer University Press and especially the efforts of Senior Editor Edmon L. Rowell, Jr. are deeply appreciated. Princeton University Press gave permission to quote from *Christian Discourses, The Crisis and a Crisis in the Life of an Actress*, and the addendum, "Phister as Captain Scipio," and other translations to which they hold copyright.

The several contributors and I also thank our families for the lost evenings and other scattered hours while we pursued these tasks. Finally, I wish to thank my wife, Sylvia Walsh, for assistance at every stage of this project and for making our life together an unutterable joy.

Robert L. Perkins

In Memoriam

Edna H. Hong
28 January 1913 – 3 April 2007

Stephen D. Crites
27 July 1931 – 13 September 2007

Sigla

AN	"Armed Neutrality." See *Point of View* (PV).
BA	*The Book on Adler*, ed. and trans. Howard V. Hong and Edna H. Hong. Princeton: Princeton University Press, 1995.
C	*The Crisis and a Crisis in the Life of an Actress*. See *Christian Discourses* (CD).
CA	*The Concept of Anxiety*, ed. and trans. Reidar Thomte in collaboration with Albert B. Anderson. Princeton: Princeton University Press, 1980.
CD C	*Christian Discourses* and *The Crisis and a Crisis in the Life of an Actress*, ed. and trans. Howard V. Hong and Edna H. Hong. Princeton: Princeton University Press, 1997.
CI NSBL	*The Concept of Irony* together with "Notes on Schelling's Berlin Lectures," ed. and trans. Howard V. Hong and Edna H. Hong. Princeton: Princeton University Press, 1989.
CUP	*Concluding Unscientific Postscript to "Philosophical Fragments,"* 2 vols., ed. and trans. Howard V. Hong and Edna H. Hong. Princeton: Princeton University Press, 1992.
COR	*The Corsair Affair*, ed. and trans. Howard V. Hong and Edna H. Hong. Princeton: Princeton University Press, 1982.
EO, 1 EO, 2	*Either/Or*, 2 vols., ed. and trans. Howard V. Hong and Edna H. Hong. Princeton: Princeton University Press, 1987.
EPW FPOSL	*Early Polemical Writings*, ed. and trans. Julia Watkin. Princeton: Princeton University Press, 1990.
EUD	*Eighteen Upbuilding Discourses*, ed. and trans. Howard H. Hong and Edna H. Hong. Princeton: Princeton University Press, 1990.
FPOSL	*From the Papers of One Still Living*. See *Early Polemical Writings* (EPW).
FSE JFY	*For Self-Examination* and *Judge for Yourself!*, ed. and trans. Howard V. Hong and Edna H. Hong. Princeton: Princeton University Press, 1990.
FT R	*Fear and Trembling* and *Repetition*, ed. and trans. Howard V. Hong and Edna H. Hong. Princeton: Princeton University Press, 1983.
JC	Johannes Climacus or "De omnibus dubitandum est." See *Philosophical Fragments* (PF).
JFY	*Judge for Yourself!* See *For Self-Examination* (FSE).
JP	*Søren Kierkegaard's Journals and Papers*, ed. and trans. Howard V. Hong and Edna H. Hong, assisted by Gregor Malantschuk. Bloomington and London: Indiana University Press, 1, 1967; 2, 1970; 3 and 4, 1975; 5-7, 1978.
LD	*Letters and Documents*, ed. and trans. Hendrik Rosenmeier. Princeton: Princeton University Press, 1978.
NA	Newspaper Articles, 1854–1855. See *The Moment and Late Writings* (TM).
NSBL	"Notes on Schelling's Berlin Lectures." See *The Concept of Irony* (CI).
OMWA	"On My Work as an Author." See *Point of View* (PV).
P WS	*Prefaces* and "Writing Sampler," ed. and trans. Todd W. Nichol. Princeton: Princeton University Press, 1998.
PC	*Practice in Christianity*, ed. and trans. Howard V. Hong and Edna H. Hong. Princeton: Princeton University Press, 1991.

PF   *Philosophical Fragments* and "Johannes Climacus," ed. and trans. Howard V. Hong
JC   and Edna H. Hong. Princeton: Princeton University Press, 1985.
PV   *The Point of View*: "On My Work as an Author"; "The Point of View for My Work
OMWA   as an Author"; "Armed Neutrality," ed. and trans. Howard V. Hong and Edna H.
AN   Hong. Princeton: Princeton University Press, 1998.
R   *Repetition*. See *Fear and Trembling* (FT).
SLW   *Stages on Life's Way*, ed. and trans. Howard V. Hong and Edna H. Hong. Princeton:
        Princeton University Press, 1988.
SUD   *The Sickness unto Death*, ed. and trans. Howard V. Hong and Edna H. Hong.
        Princeton: Princeton University Press, 1980.
TA   *Two Ages: The Age of Revolution and the Present Age. A Literary Review*, ed. and trans.
        Howard V. Hong and Edna H. Hong. Princeton: Princeton University Press, 1978.
TDIO   *Three Discourses on Imagined Occasions*, ed. and trans. Howard V. Hong and Edna
        H. Hong. Princeton: Princeton University Press, 1993.
TM   *"The Moment" and Late Writings*, ed. and trans. Howard V. Hong and Edna H.
NA   Hong. Princeton: Princeton University Press, 1998.
UDVS   *Upbuilding Discourses in Various Spirits*, ed. and trans. Howard V. Hong and Edna
        H. Hong. Princeton: Princeton University Press, 1993.
WA   *Without Authority*, ed. and trans. Howard V. Hong and Edna H. Hong. Princeton:
        Princeton University Press, 1997.
WL   *Works of Love*, ed. and trans. Howard V. Hong and Edna H. Hong. Princeton:
        Princeton University Press, 1995.
WS   "Writing Sampler." See *Prefaces* (P).

Danish editions

SKP   *Søren Kierkegaards Papirer*, second enlarged edition by Niels Thulstrup, with index
        vols. 14-16 by Niels Jørgen Cappelørn. Copenhagen: Gyldendal, 1968–1978.
SKS   *Søren Kierkegaards Skrifter*, ed. Niels Jørgen Cappelørn, Joakim Garff, Jette
        Knudsen, Johnny Kondrup, and Alastair McKinnon. Published by Søren
        Kierkegaard Forskningscenteret. Copenhagen: Gads Forlag, 1997ff.
SKS, K *Kommentar til Søren Kierkegaards Skrifter*. Published by Søren Kierkegaard
        Forskningscenteret. Copenhagen: Gads Forlag, 1997ff.

Introduction

Both Karl Marx's *The Communist Manifesto* and Søren Kierke-gaard's *Christina Discourses* were published in the fateful year 1848. Both authors were incredibly busy, deeply embroiled in their respective work.

The Second Congress of the Communist League, meeting in London from 29 November to 8 December 1847, commissioned Karl Marx (not "and Engels") to prepare a manifesto. On 26 January 1848 the Central Committee, with no little impatience, demanded that Marx finish it. About the first of February the manuscript finally arrived in London and the first edition of *The Communist Manifesto* was printed between 14 and 18 February.[1] On 24 February the proletarians of Paris toppled the bourgeois monarchy of Louis Philippe. Inspired by the events in Paris, demands for liberal reforms, including freedom of the press, trial by jury, the writing of constitutions in all German states, and the convening of a national parliament, were widespread. By early March several liberal regimes were established in Germany and by the middle of March, street demonstrations in Vienna brought down Metternich, the central figure in the Restoration who had "ruled" Austria and had been the most powerful politician in Europe since Waterloo. Uprisings in Hungary, Bohemia, Croatia, Venetia, and Lombardy weakened Austria. Although themselves challenged, Prussia and Russia remained the only reactionary bastions. After more than a week of bloody fighting in early March in Berlin, Wilhelm Friedrich IV withdrew his troops and announced that Prussia would take the lead in the unification of Germany and the modernization of the state. In Paris and now head of the Communist League, Marx and the Central Committee adapted the principles of *The Communist Manifesto* to the conditions of

---

[1] Karl Marx, *The Communist Manifesto*, ed. Frederick L. Bender. A Norton Critical Edition (New York, London, W.W. Norton and Company, 1988).

Germany and demanded a liberal and democratic platform.[2] Having neither political power, organized military support, nor a monetary base, and under constant pressure from Friedrich Wilhelm, the Communist League dispersed, and Marx moved to Cologne where in June he and Friedrich Engels founded the newspaper, *Neue Rheinische Zeitung*, which continued until 1 May 1849, in which they pursued a liberal democratic (not socialist) critique of German politics. The democrats and the liberals in the Frankfurt Parliament, threatened militarily but having no financial base, fell apart, and Friedrich Wilhelm regained control over political developments and easily put down uprisings in May 1849. Marx moved from Cologne to Paris and on 6 August 1849 he returned to London where he remained until his death in 1883. The communist revolution was history. (What later happened to "Marxism" is another story.)

Meanwhile, Denmark had its own version of the 1848 revolution, but happily it was neither bloody nor was it betrayed and destroyed by reactionary vengeance. The urban cultural elite and the emerging bourgeois demanded a constitution and the king granted it.[3] That's that! Three factors contributed massively to the success of the transition from absolute monarchy to a modern liberal state. First, Denmark's isolation from the raging struggles of the proletariat in the more industrialized countries of France, Germany, and England and its lack of coal and iron contributed to its slower and later development. Second, over many years the absolute monarchy had already developed a bureaucracy that was largely made up of sensible men. Third, there was an invisible and popularly elected reservoir of political experience in the tradition of strong local government that survived from Viking times. The new constitution, which still governs, addressed the grievances of all classes except the landless agricultural workers, but difficulties over Schleswig-Holstein involved the new democratic government in a war with Prussia in which Holstein and the southern part of Schleswig were

---

[2]This text, "Demands of the Communist Party of Germany," is implicitly the strongest critique of the Leninist, Stalinist, and Maoist regimes ever written. See Bender, *The Communist Manifesto*, 15-17.

[3]Bruce Kirmmse, *Kierkegaard in Golden Age Denmark* (Bloomington: Indiana University Press, 1990).

finally lost.[4] The political revolution was nonviolent and more of an evolution than revolution or an attack on the economic foundations of the ruling classes. Neither was the revolution an attack on the religious and moral heritage nor on the class structure, although there was still work to do primarily for the landless rural cottagers. When an organized proletariat appeared, democratic, constitutional, and bureaucratic structures were already in place to address their grievances.

Kierkegaard wrote *Christian Discourses* in the midst of these political changes in Jutland and the military challenges from Prussia, the changing urban and rural economics and class structure, and the emerging modern democratic state. In *Christian Discourses*, published 26 April 1848, Kierkegaard did not frontally attack any of the just-mentioned issues but rather stuck to his vocation as a religious writer. He examined the social, moral, and religious assumptions of the urban classes and attempted to illuminate its conceptual confusions, bad faith, and the falsetto of its self-justification. He rejected the religious presumption and the unspoken but nearly universal *apologia* of the claim that the culture was essentially Christian, the presumption that "Denmark is a Christian country." *Christian Discourses* is both an olive branch offered to and a judgment upon Christendom. When it was ignored by the reading public and, more importantly, by the religious leadership, it was succeeded by *The Sickness unto Death* (written in March-May 1848, published 30 July 1849) and *Practice in Christianity* (begun in 1848 and published 17 September 1850), by Anti-Climacus. Together these works expressed a more strident critique of the age and its religious pretensions.[5]

In 1848 Kierkegaard also wrote *A Cycle of Ethical-Religious Essays, The Lily of the Field and the Bird of the Air, Armed Neutrality, The Point of View for My Work as an Author*, and a short piece on the genius of the actor, Joachim Ludwig Phister, in "Phister as Captain Scipio"

---

[4]The Schleswig-Holstein issue was not finally resolved until the plebiscite of 1920. The mixture of languages and the alternate playing of the nationalism card by Denmark's National Liberals and by the Prussians were prominent causes of the losses. Palle Lauring, *A History of the Kingdom of Denmark* (Copenhagen: Høst and Søn, 1960).

[5]For an extended discussion of place of *Christian Discourses* in Kierkegaard's authorship, see CD, xi-xvii.

(CD, [xi]). Literarily, it was a very productive year. Kierkegaard benefitted from the peaceful transition from an absolute to a constitutional monarchy by being able to cleave to his own vocation with fewer distractions than most other Europeans at that time. Not only was he disinclined to participate in the political life, his favorable historical situation aided his determination to single-mindedly serve what he perceived to be his own vocation. His responses mix a discernment of fundamental issues of the times with an absence of public participation that amazes readers today. His frequent protest is that he wrote "without authority" (BA, 228-33), which he understood primarily in a religious sense, applies also to his relation to the political and social issues of the age.

Both Marx and Kierkegaard worked very hard that frightfully decisive year. There are tremendous ironies here, for *The Communist Manifesto* and *Christian Discourses* look in opposite directions and can scarcely be compared. Those in the twentieth century who inherited and puzzled over their conflicting views left their conflicts unresolved, and that is perhaps the only lesson that can be learned by attempting to think about them in dialogue.[6] It is interesting that the contributors to this volume ignore the ambiguities of these close distant relations. That both Kierkegaard and Marx rejected the justification offered on behalf of a bourgeois form of life in all its contemporary forms as humanly fulfilling is important. One sought revolution to achieve a new form of life in this world without transcendence; the other, in the tradition of the prophets, sought to establish the authority of the Unconditional.

I turn now to thumbnail sketches of the essays collected in this volume arranged according to the divisions of *Christian Discourses*.

The Cares of the Pagans

Merold Westphal in his essay, "Paganism in Christendom: On Kierkegaard's Critique of Religion," introduces "The Cares of the

---

[6]Gregor Malantschuk may have gone as far as anyone can in his essay, "Did Kierkegaard Read Karl Marx?" in *The Controversial Kierkegaard* , trans. By Howard V. Hong and Edna H. Hong (Waterloo, Ontario; Wilfird Laurier University Press, 1976) 76-82. For all the imaginative care and research skill Malantschuk lavished on a small detail, he earned only a "perhaps" as a reward.

Pagans" and *Christian Discourses* with his characteristic ironic style. Westphal's recent development transforms his earlier theme that Kierkegaard was a prophetic philosopher into the view that he is a philosopher of suspicion. Westphal continues to think of Kierkegaard as a critical philosopher, not in the tradition of the critics of religion but in the tradition of those who understand religion as social criticism. The theme of paganism in Christendom, found in Kierkegaard's early authorship, is continuous throughout the authorship and comes to dominance in *The Moment*. *Christian Discourses* is a stage on Kierkegaard's way, and Westphal's reading of the first three of the meditations in "The Cares of the Pagans" points the way into and through not only this part of the book but the whole text.

The essay by David Possen "On Kierkegaard's Copenhagen Pagans," provides an analysis of Kierkegaard's appeal to the text from Matthew 6:23-34 as he applies it to the lifestyle and sentiments of his contemporaries and himself. Possen reviews the tangle of concepts shared between Magnús Eiríksson, Hans Lassen Martensen, and Kierkegaard. In one of his books, Eiríksson argued that Kierkegaard is a purveyor of "superstition" and Martensen of "disbelief." In "The Care of Presumptuousness," Kierkegaard stealthily implies, without identification of course, that the charge of superstition applies especially to Martensen and that Eiríksson is simply confused. Possen argues that this passage goes to the heart of the theological of the disputes between them and then applies these issues to the critique of Martensen in *The Concept of Anxiety*, claiming that his theology is simply a travesty of the Lutheran principle of *sola gratia* while along the way Possen presents Kierkegaard's own distinctive view of grace.

In her essay, "The Genius and the Saint: The Spiritual Teaching of Kierkegaard in *Christian Discourses* and Thérèse of Lisieux in *Story of a Soul*," Louise Carroll Keeley finds the obvious contrasts, but she finds the similarities to be more interesting. Keeley analyzes seven issues emphasized by Kierkegaard in "The Cares of the Pagans" that reflect parallel themes in Thérèse's *Story of a Soul*, showing how both challenged bourgeois piety by a profound inward turn. Thérèse, however, did not ever come into the fierce open struggle with her church and society as did Kierkegaard, perhaps due for the most part to her cloistered life; that is, her life was not a lifelong engage-

ment and critique of bourgeois religiosity outside the walls of the
convent. In spite of their great differences in life and culture, the
similarities point to a common human, or at least, Christian subjectivity and inwardness.

States of Mind in the Strife of Suffering

In her essay, "Suffering and Strife: For What Can We Hope?,"
Patricia Huntington investigates the intellectual confusion created by
two concepts of suffering, the first being the notion of the release
from suffering in the afterlife, and the second being the concept of
temporal suffering in everyday life. The tension arises because the
distinction between two senses of suffering is frequently overlooked
or confused. There is a natural tendency to desire and to understand
deliverance from suffering as an overcoming of earthly ills and
troubles. However, the Christian faith understands that deliverance
from suffering will occur only in the afterlife. The confusion arises
when people confuse the categories and expect faith to deliver them
from the troubles and anxieties of existential humdrum, crises,
tragedies, and even uncomfortable trivialities. When we think in that
manner we cheat ourselves of the opportunity to profit religiously
from the strife we encounter in ordinary life; we miss the
exhilaration of spiritual growth in and through difficulty, challenge,
and even defeat.

To the question why anyone would become involved with
Christianity in the first place, Christopher A. P. Nelson replies, "The
Joy of It." But what kind of joy is offered to the Christian? As Kierkegaard describes it, Christian joy results from an intensification of
suffering. Nelson addresses this strange notion in *Upbuilding
Discourses in Various Spirits, The Lily of the Field and the Bird of the Air*
in *Without Authority* (WA, 36-45) and *Christian Discourses*. He begins
with Kierkegaard's experience of "indescribable joy," and attempts
to describe why the unutterable and the indescribable are such by
reference to the fundamental psychology of a human being as hinted
at by Johannes Climacus and worked out in detail by other
pseudonyms, most notably by Anti-Climacus. Because of the complex nature of a person, as a synthesis of time and eternity, terms
such as weakness or wealth do not possess the ordinary meaning
they have in the immanent world but are inverted so that poverty is
wealth, weakness is strength, and so forth. The concept of joy as it is

used in the everyday life in Christendom is also reversed. All worldly values are transvalued. Thus, Kierkegaard's understanding of the inverse psychology of the Christian life turns out to be another basis of his critique of Christendom in the name of Christianity.

Thoughts that Wound from Behind — for Upbuilding

In his essay, "Kierkegaard's *Christian Discourses* on Upbuilding, Mildness, and Polemic: 'A Temple-Cleansing Celebration and Then the Quiet,' " David J. Gouwens analyzes the structure of *Christian Discourses* through an interpretation of the immediate theological (or ecclesiastical), social, and political environment. Gouwens's previous studies of Kierkegaard's psychology are silently applied to enable us to better understand the basic categories and strategies of the present essay. Thus, Kierkegaard does not verbally assault his reader of the first part of *Christian Discourses* so much as he leads the reader to understand that the cares of the pagans are pervasive in Christendom. Part two advertises joy throughout, but implicitly testifies to the trial and terror of sin. But Kierkegaard finally leads to the conclusion that in the midst of the complexity of our lives, even in the midst of our sin, the supreme joy is that of forgiveness. Part three, "Thoughts That Wound from Behind — for Upbuilding" is the focus of Gouwens's essay. He shows us the order and development of Kierkegaard's indictment of the smugness of Christendom for its light-mindedness with regard to sin and discipleship as that is manifested in the unwillingness to accept the voluntary suffering that accompanies any attempt to follow Christ. Part four, "Discourses at the Communion on Fridays," comes as a quiet intimacy that is or can be experienced by those who experientially have followed the way to this time of communion, Kierkegaard's favorite church service. He fully intended to create a resounding contrast between parts three and four, and he did. Communion is an affirmation of God's gift of love through a simple but joyous worship; it confirms our desperate need for spiritual sustenance even as it provides it.

Mark A. Tietjen in his essay, "Aristotle, Aquinas, and Kierkegaard on Prudence," uses Kierkegaard's reservations about prudence (*klogskab*) to contest the sufficiency of the understanding of prudence (*phronesis*) in Aristotle. Basic to this comparison Tietjen works through Kierkegaard's presentation of *klogskab* in *Christian Discourses* and *phronesis* as discussed by Aristotle in book VI of

Nicomachean Ethics. Tietjen's wider aim is to assess Kierkegaard's relation to the classical virtue tradition and to recent claims that Kierkegaard is a major contributor to the recent revival of virtue theory. The crucial turn is, no doubt, Aquinas's adaptation of Plotinus's fourfold division of the virtues. Then appropriating the notion of infused prudence from Aquinas, Tietjen argues that the notion of prudence is subordinate to neighbor love in Kierkegaard and, given that, he can be understood "preeminently as a virtue ethicist," a claim Tietjen maintains even as he challenges, redefines, and extends it.

In his essay, "The Opposition between Objective Knowledge and Subjective Appropriation in Kierkegaard and Climacus," Thomas C. Anderson undertakes to examine the relation of the epistemological claims to their subjective and ethical appropriation because he thinks Climacus's more philosophical treatment of the issues illumine Kierkegaard's own position as expressed in *Christian Discourses*. Anderson claims that the issue has been somewhat clouded by the carelessness with which some commentators have collapsed the two positions, Climacus's and Kierkegaard's, into one, losing nuances in both. After a strenuous effort to distinguish the two views, Anderson attempts to apply the implications of the distinction by examining the four major works (the last unpublished) that followed the publication of *Christian Discourses*: *The Sickness unto Death*, *Practice in Christianity*, *For Self-Examination*, and *Judge for Yourself!* (PV, xxv-xxvi).

In his essay, "The Sickbed Preacher: Kierkegaard on Adversity and the Awakening of Faith," Ronald F. Marshall addresses a rare theme in Kierkegaard's writings: the importance of physical illness and the prospect of imminent death in the religious and Christian consciousness. In his authorship the phenomenon of physical illness and death is so subordinated to the theme of spiritual illness and death that the foreboding of physical death may not have been properly noticed. If that is the case, Marshall goes far to address any such putative one-sidedness. He penetratingly examines the issue of physical illness and death in the context of Luther's theology, in contrast to the denial of death in contemporary pop-religion and culture, and in dialogue with the signal insights of Kierkegaard's scattered views of physical death.

Discourses at the Communion on Fridays

Lee C. Barrett essay, "Christ's Efficacious Love and Human Responsibility: The Lutheran Dialectic of 'Discourses at the Communion on Fridays,'" shows how Kierkegaard comes to terms with and transforms the perennial debate within Lutheranism between synergism and monergism, adroitly holding them in tension and unity by appealing to the intense pastoral interests of both theological points as expressed in *The Formula of Concord*. In so doing Barrett shows how completely Lutheran Kierkegaard was in his sacramental and practical theology. Kierkegaard does not indulge in any metaphysical/theological speculation about the relation of God's will to human motivation but addresses the care of souls, that is, he implicitly develops the elements of both synergism and monergism that pertain to upbuilding. Kierkegaard's use of upbuilding as a criterion to evaluate the issues of the ancient, and frequently acrimonious, controversy points the way to a reevaluation of the history of theology.

According to David R. Law, in his essay, "Kierkegaard's Understanding of the Eucharist in *Christian Discourses*, Part Four," Kierkegaard was not vitally interested in many matters that have fascinated theologians for centuries, for instance, the meaning of real presence. Rather, Kierkegaard primarily emphasized the single individual's relation to God and how the Eucharist contributed to the appropriation of theological truth by the recipient and elicited worship and obedience. This concern presses Kierkegaard to reconsider the nature of the presence of Christ in communion, but not of course by revisiting the traditional debates. Law attempts to interpret the book as itself a means of preparation for communion. Law sets his essay in the context of *Christian Discourses* and finds a progression that leads the reader step by step to the communion table. For instance, he does not read parts one and three so much as social criticism but as leading to part four and, more important still, to the communicant's preparation. Not only does the authorship come to rest at the communion table, but Law shows how this specific book does.

The Crisis and a Crisis in the Life of an Actress

In his essay, "The Stage and Stages in a Christian Authorship," Hugh Pyper explores the idea of "performance" in Kierkegaard's conception of what it is to be a human being and the relationships between human beings and God. Pyper also considers performance to be a key to Kierkegaard's own understanding and practice of being a Christian author. What is the difference between the actress's effort and/or participation in various occult entities such as the character in a play and Kierkegaard's pseudonymous authorship, in which he through the various authors offers independent but related presentations, understandings, and participations in the drama of the divine/human relation? How is the actress related to the part she plays? How is Kierkegaard related to the many viewpoints and arguments expressed by the pseudonyms? Exploiting Martin Thust's idea that just as the actress animates a role, so the author, Victor Eremita or Frater Taciturnus for instance, enlivens an idea, and brings it to life in and through character. The actress takes a character in a written play and bodies it forth on the stage. Thus the idea of performance runs parallel to Kierkegaard's own sense of himself as an author.

Joseph Westfall' considers the question whether "Inter et Inter," Kierkegaard's pseudonym, is an aesthetic author or not, in his essay, "The Actress and an Actress in the Life of a Critic: Higher Criticism in 'The Crisis.' " Paying attention to Kierkegaard's seven other treatments of drama in the authorship, each of which he briefly discusses, Westfall argues that Inter et Inter's critical efforts create a new level of criticism above the ethical. He argues that if Inter et Inter is like an aesthetic author, he is such as no other. Madam Heiberg's talents are unique, for she not only can develop capabilities in different ways as her life development requires, she can also develop new potentialities as roles are replayed at different times in her life development. This position, as suggested by Inter et Inter, transcends both the aesthetic and the ethical; Westfall claims that "the development of potentiation" depends entirely upon recollection's relation to time or, more accurately, eternity.

Phister as Captain Scipio

Christopher A.P. Nelson, in his essay, " 'Drunk?' / 'Not Drunk?': The Dialectic of Intoxication in 'Phister as Captain Scipio' and 'Becoming Sober,'" discusses the figure of intoxication as "shorthand for a variety of existential impairments." Neither of the writings discussed in Nelson's essay were published in Kierkegaard's lifetime, and that in itself provokes questions. Be that as it may, the two documents have as a common theme the dialectical turn that the best indicator that one is "drunk" is the sometimes strained appearance of being sober. Thus the accusers of the apostles in Acts and Phister's "reflective" performance reveal drunkenness as a metonym of despair. And here we are back at the heart of some major issues of the authorship addressed in *Judge for Yourself!*, at which Nelson challenges us to look again.

Thus far have our authors led us. We—the contributors, the advisory board, and the editor—invite our readers to become our teachers by better research, analytic thinking, and synthetic insight.

Robert L. Perkins

1

Paganism in Christendom: on Kierkegaard's Critique of Religion[*]

Merold Westphal

The Critique before Christian Discourses

Many years ago I was invited to submit an essay projecting the direction that the philosophy of religion might take in the next decade. With appropriate apologies to Kant, I submitted an essay entitled "Prolegomena to Any Future Philosophy of Religion That Will Be able to Come Forth as Prophecy." The idea was that philosophers of religion might well take Amos and Jeremiah as models rather than Galileo and Newton. I made it as clear as I could that by 'prophecy' I meant not foretelling the future but religiously motivated social critique, concluding that "perhaps the best way to explore this possibility further would be to look more closely at that philosopher who, more than any other since Socrates, does this kind of philosophy — Soren Kierkegaard."[1] In what I have always taken to be a quite wonderful irony, the editors, who apparently wanted apologetics, rejected the essay they had commissioned.

In *The Point of View for My Work as an Author*, Kierkegaard tells us that (1) his authorship as a whole is a religious authorship; and (2) he makes this claim not on the basis of his own conscious intentions at every point but on the basis of the role played by divine Governance. He does not say so in so many words, but he might with equal right describe his authorship as a whole, not just as

---

[*]A version of this essay appears in French translation as "Le paganisme dans la chrétienté. La critique kierkegaardienne de la religion," *Nordiques* no. 10 (Printemps-Été 2006): 101-18.

[1]This essay and a short sequel, "Kierkegaard as a Prophetic Philosopher" appear as the first two chapters in my *Kierkegaard's Critique of Reason and Society* (Macon: Mercer University Press, 1987); quotation is from p. 18.

religious but, precisely because of the way it is religious, as a critique of religion. For Kierkegaard the critique is at once a critique of reason and society — of reason in the mode of Hegelian speculation and of society in the mode of Christendom. Both take themselves to be genuinely Christian, a claim Kierkegaard's critique regularly challenges.

His critique is not that of the skeptic, who challenges the epistemic grounds of faith in order to cast doubt on the truth or the rationality of religious beliefs. He insists that the central beliefs of theism in general and Christianity in particular are known by faith in response to divine revelation and not by unaided human reason, but he presents himself as a believer, not an unbeliever.[2] He aims not at the propositional content of belief but at the believer, or perhaps more precisely, the believing as the "how" rather than the "what" of faith. Thus his critique belongs to the hermeneutics of suspicion, which has been defined as "the deliberate attempt to expose the self-deceptions involved in hiding our actual operative motives from ourselves, individually or collectively, in order not to notice how and how much our behavior and our *beliefs are shaped by values we profess to disown.*"[3]

In this respect Kierkegaard's critique resembles the religion critique of Marx, Nietzsche, and Freud, whom Ricoeur has called the masters of the "school of suspicion."[4] But, of course, with one major difference: they are the enemies of faith, he its friend, though only of

---

[2]That this presentation is not a thespian performance is perhaps best seen in the prayers to be found throughout his writings. See Perry D. LeFevre, ed., *The Prayers of Kierkegaard* (Chicago: University of Chicago Press, 1956). Or, for that matter, in *Christian Discourses.*

[3]Merold Westphal, *Suspicion and Faith: The Religious Uses of Modern Atheism* (New York: Fordham University Press, 1998) 13. The words 'actual operative' are included to preclude a narrowly psychologistic interpretation. One can thus speak as freely about the actual function of beliefs and practices as their motives. Like the detectives who ask, Who benefits from this death?, suspicion asks, What work do these beliefs and practices perform for the believers and practitioners?

[4]Paul Ricoeur, *Freud and Philosophy: An Essay on Interpretation*, trans. Denis Savage (New Haven: Yale University Press, 1970) 32. Cf. his *The Conflict of Interpretations: Essays in Hermeneutics*, ed. Don Ihde (Evanston: Northwestern University Press, 1974) and *Lectures on Ideology and Utopia*, ed. George H. Taylor (New York: Columbia University Press, 1986).

the faith that doesn't sell itself.[5] They seek to discredit the beliefs by discrediting the believing, while he seeks to discredit the believing in order to preserve for the beliefs their power to call believer and unbeliever alike to repentance and faith.

It is strange that Ricoeur does not include Kierkegaard as one of the masters of suspicion, especially since he sees as clearly as anyone that it would be a genetic fallacy to infer the falsehood of the "what" from the faultiness of the "how." For example, I may believe the defendant to be guilty more out of envy than evidence, but he may be guilty all the same. Thus Ricoeur says with reference to Freud what can be said of any mode of suspicion:

> My working hypothesis . . . is that psychoanalysis is necessarily iconoclastic, regardless of the faith or nonfaith of the psychoanalyst, and that this "destruction" of religion can be the counter part of a faith purified of all idolatry. Psychoanalysis as such cannot go beyond the necessity of iconoclasm. This necessity is open to a double possibility, that of faith and that of nonfaith, but the decision about these two possibilities does not rest with psychoanalysis . . . The question remains open for every man whether the destruction of idols is without remainder; this question no longer falls within the competency of psychoanalysis.[6]

That suspicion can be the search for "a faith purified of all idolatry" means that religious motivation can give rise to suspicion just as easily as hostility to religion.

Since it is a question here of Kierkegaard's authorship *as a whole*, it should come as no surprise that to speak of Kierkegaard's critique of religion is to speak of a polyphonic, almost fugal textuality. In fact, that critique is doubly multifaceted. On the one hand, there is the plurality of pseudonyms, each of whom represents a distinctive standpoint. On the other hand, even when writing under his own

---

[5]Dietrich Bonhoeffer's concept of "cheap grace" has a distinctively Kierkegaardian ring to it. See *The Cost of Discipleship*, 2nd ed., trans. R. H. Fuller and Irmgard Booth (New York: Macmillan, 1959). Cf. Kierkegaard, FT 5, 8. The theme of getting the benefits of faith as cheaply as possible is a recurring theme in *For Self Examination* and *Judge for Yourself!* Cf. FT 5 where *Fear and Trembling* opens with this theme.

[6]*Freud and Philosophy*, 230, 235. Ricoeur adds that "Freud does not speak of God, but of god and the gods of men; what is involved is not the truth of the foundation of religious ideas, but their *function* . . . " (emphasis added).

name, Kierkegaard has more than one critical concern. Thus by 'Kierkegaard's critique of religion' I understand the complex cluster of critiques his authorship presents for our consideration, whether in his own name or pseudonymously. Since I want here to focus on one important theme, I leave aside for another time and place the debate whether the parts coalesce into a reasonably harmonious whole.

Kierkegaard's critique culminates in the explosive "attack upon Christendom" of 1854-55 (see *'The Moment' and Late Writings*). But Christendom and its piety are under attack from the very beginning. Thus, even before the authorship proper begins with *Either/Or*, the dissertation on irony develops a critique of speculative philosophy that is at least indirectly a critique of theological rationalism (liberal Protestantism) and theological orthodoxy (conservative Protestantism). In spite of the conflict between them, they share the false view (1) that the primary task of faith is good theory, having the right answers to all theological questions, and (2) that "our" theology is *the* place where those answers are to be found.[7] In terms of the history of Protestant theology, Kierkegaard belongs more nearly with the pietists, who opposed both rationalism and orthodoxy not as false, necessarily, but as having elevated the head over the heart, the "what" over the "how."

In *Either/Or*, Judge William is the epitome of Christendom, successful, upright, devout. He defends the morality of marriage against the amoral posture of the young aesthete,[8] and he talks incessantly about God and the Eternal. He is so complacent that he does not even notice, as the reader is expected to notice, how he is rebuked by the sermon from a pastor friend of his that he sends to his own young friend.[9] It is entitled "The Upbuilding That Lies in the Thought That in Relation to God We Are Always in the Wrong" (EO, 2:337-54). In more than three hundred pages of epistolary admo-

---

[7]One is reminded of Camus's definition of the world of myth as a world of all answers and no questions and of Heidegger's analysis of ontotheology as the attempt of theory to render the whole of being transparent, devoid of mystery.

[8]Just as Kierkegaard had critiqued romantic irony and especially Schlegel's *Lucinde* in *The Concept of Irony*.

[9]For helpful commentary, see John E. Hare, *The Moral Gap* (Oxford: Clarendon Press, 1996), ch. 8. Much of Nietzsche's "attack upon Christendom" is summed up in two words, "Wretched contentment"! *Thus Spoke Zarathustra*, prologue, §3.

nition to another, it seems never to have occurred to him that he might be in the wrong. The implication, in the context of the authorship as a whole, is that he only seems to be living "before God." To a dangerous degree his faith is illusory (Freud), ideological (Marx), and the product of a pharisaical interpretation of good and evil according to which, since "they" are evil, "we" (by default, as it were) must be good (Nietzsche).[10]

In *Fear and Trembling*, the Abraham story is used to challenge an all too Hegelian Christendom that reduces responsibility to *Sittlichkeit*,[11] the laws and customs of one's people. It might have borne the subtitle, "The Upbuilding That Lies in the Thought That in Relation to God the Laws of My State and Customs of My Culture Are Always in the Wrong,"[12] most especially when they function to set limits to what God can expect of me. Having been baptized, all I need to do to be a good Christian is to be a respectable citizen.[13]

Then there is the critique in *Philosophical Fragments* of the attempt to reduce revelation to recollection, ignoring the distinction so crucial again and again to Kierkegaard's critique between human understanding and divine understanding, effectively constraining

---

[10]For a more charitable reading of Judge William, suggesting that there is more Socratic self-examination in him that is suggested here, see Robert L. Perkins, "Either/Or/Or: Giving the Parson his Due," *International Kierkegaard Commentary: Either/Or, Part II*, Robert L. Perkins, ed. (Macon: Mercer University Press, 1995). For the difference between Judge William as he appears in *Stages on Life's Way* and as he appears in *Either/Or*, 2, see Paul Marten's "The Equivocal Judge William: Comparing the Ethical in Kierkegaard's *Stages on Life's Way* and *Either/Or*" in Robert L. Perkins, ed., *International Kierkegaard Commentary: "Stages on Life's Way"* (Macon GA: Mercer University Press, 2000) 91-111.

[11]Kierkegaard uses the Danish equivalent of this Hegelian term, *Sædelighed*.

[12]Cf. Derrida's argument that the laws can never be identified with justice, which is always still to come. See "Force of Law: The 'Mystical Foundation of Authority,'" in *Acts of Religion*, ed. Gil Anidjar (New York: Routledge, 2002). For this reading of *Fear and Trembling*, see my "Abraham and Hegel" in *Kierkegaard's Critique of Reason and Society*.

[13]Taking a cue from Martin Buber, who speaks of the prophetic protest against "the baalisation of YHVH Himself" in ancient Israel, we could speak of the bourgeoisification of the Holy Trinity in Christendom. See Buber's *The Prophetic Faith*, trans. Carlyle Witton-Davies (New York: Harper & Row, 1960) 118-20 and chap. 34 of *Suspicion and Faith*.

the latter by the former.[14]

Paganism in Christendom in The Sickness unto Death

Kierkegaard develops his "attack upon Christendom" under the rubric "paganism in Christendom" — two texts tangential to each other in 1848, *Christian Discourses* and *The Sickness unto Death* (hereafter, *Sickness*).[15] After a brief sketch of this theme in the latter, we can turn our attention to the former.

In *Sickness*, selfhood is essentially relational and the most fundamental relation is to God. We stand in this relation whether we know it or not, whether we like it or not. It is an inescapable fact about us just as much as, say, our corporeality and mortality. But it is not just a fact. It has normative significance. To be transparent to ourselves and thus able to become who we are is to know that we exist "before God" (SUD, 79-89). In other words, for the Christian existentialist essence precedes existence. Lacking this awareness, the pagan is by definition "without God in the world." This is a reference to Ephesians 2:12, where Paul describes the Gentiles not only as "without Christ" but also as "aliens from the commonwealth of Israel, and strangers to the covenants of promise," in other words, outside the light of biblical religion.[16]

In biblical times this would include the Egyptians, Canaanites, Babylonians, Assyrians, Greeks, and Romans, among others. For Kierkegaard, who did not see himself facing a religiously multicultural world as we might see ourselves today, the pagans would be secularists, whether the proletarians who saw the church as nothing

---

[14]In a very un-Lutheran way, reducing revelation to recollection collapses the Pauline contrast between the wisdom of the world and the wisdom of the cross. 1 Cor. 1:18-25. In effect, God can't tell me anything that human understanding can't discover for itself. Cf. "The Difference between a Genius and an Apostle" in *Without Authority*.

[15]The former was written mostly in 1847 and published in 1848, while the latter was written mostly in 1848 and published in 1849. Already in *Fear and Trembling* (1843), paganism is the reduction of responsibility to good citizenship in which there is no relation to God higher than one's relation to the nation and the state (FT, 55, 60). Thus Hegelian Christendom is a paganism that cannot coherently honor Abraham as the father of faith.

[16]Sometimes the pagan is distinguished not only from the Christian but also from the Jew.

more than a prop for the privileged or those whom Schleiermacher called "the cultured among the despisers of religion."[17] At least one other group must be included, those whom Anti-Climacus calls "disbelieving Christianity" who "wanted to get rid of the qualification *before God*" in the name of a "higher wisdom" that on close examination was simply "the old paganism" (SUD, 83). This is a thinly disguised reference to Hegel and, doubtless to both his idealist predecessors and his Danish followers.[18]

We are reminded of Johannes Climacus, who prefaced the Preface to *Philosophical Fragments* with an epigraph from Shakespeare: "Better well hanged than ill wed." Like Kierkegaard himself, he thought outright denial of biblical religion more honest than keeping its language but changing the meaning in the name of a "higher wisdom". When the category 'before God' is effectively neutralized, existentially and not merely theoretically, whether by denial or by distortion, the result is spiritlessness, the despair of being ignorant of having an eternal self (SUD, 42-47). In other words, while paganism can signify modern secularism in its various forms, it also signifies various forms of religion that can be described as "without God in the world" because their gods are idols (SUD, 8). In either case, to fail to exist "before God" is to fail to become a self.[19]

Such paganism, essentially if not transparently secular, can exist in Christendom (SUD, 45). Anti-Climacus's lament is not about those outside the (state Lutheran) church but precisely those inside, those like Judge William and Hegel who take themselves to be Christian but are self-deceived, like those who think the cheap Rolex or Viagra they bought over the internet is the real thing. He introduces us to three such characters. Of the first he writes, "In Christendom he is also a Christian, goes to church every Sunday, listens to and understands the pastor, indeed, they have a mutual understanding;

---

[17]See his famous 1799 *On Religion: Speeches to Its Cultured Despisers.*

[18]Hegel regularly presents the *Begriffe* in which he expresses his philosophy as superior to the mere *Vorstellungen* in which biblical religion and the traditional Christian theologies operate. See, e.g., chap. 7 of my *History and Truth in Hegel's Phenomenology*, 3rd ed. (Bloomington: Indiana University Press, 1998).

[19]Anti-Climacus thinks the point at which contemporary paganism fails to exist "before God" is in the failure to understand sin as a matter of the will, of defiance and disobedience (SUD, 87-96, 116).

he dies, the pastor ushers him into eternity for ten rix-dollars—but a self he was not and a self he did not become" (SUD, 52). Of the second, Anti-Climacus writes that he is one of those

> competent and dynamic men who have a sense and aptitude for real life. Charming! He has been happily married now for several years, as it says in novels, is a dynamic and enterprising man, a father and citizen, perhaps even an important man; at home in his own house the servants call him "He Himself;" downtown he is among those addressed with "His Honor;" his conduct is based on respect of persons or on the way others regard one, and the others judge according to one's social position. In Christendom he is a Christian (in the very same sense as in paganism he could be a pagan and in Holland a Hollander), one of the cultured Christians. (SUD, 56)[20]

Finally, of the third, we read that outwardly he looks every bit

> "a real man." He is a university graduate, husband, father, even an exceptionally competent public office holder, a respectable father, pleasant company, very gentle to his wife, solicitude personified to his children. And Christian?—Well, yes, he is that, too, but prefers not to talk about it, although with a certain wistful joy he likes to see that his wife is occupied with religion to her upbuilding. He rarely attends church. . . . (SUD, 63-64)

In other words, in Christendom there are those who take themselves to be Christians, but who live their lives in categories and principles that effectively erase the true seriousness of what it means to live "before God". Among these principles are the reduction of revelation to recollection and the reduction of responsibility to respectability, ideally in the mode of prominent citizenship. But this doesn't require

---

[20]In *Concluding Unscientific Postscript*, Climacus satirizes speculative thought which purports to be without presuppositions. "Yet one thing is assumed: Christianity as given. It is assumed that we are all Christians." He then introduces the man who became concerned whether or not he really could call himself a Christian, to which his wife responds, "Hubby, darling, where did you ever pick up such a notion? How can you not be a Christian? You are Danish, aren't you? Doesn't the geography book say that the predominant religion in Denmark is Lutheran-Christian? You aren't a Jew, are you, or a Mohammedan. What else would you be, then? It is a thousand years since paganism was superseded; so I know you aren't a pagan. Don't you tend to your work in the office as a good civil servant . . . " (CUP, 1:50-51).

anything beyond Plato and Aristotle.[21]

The Cares of the Pagans: Poverty and Abundance

Against this background, let us turn now to the theme of paganism in Christianity in part one of *Christian Discourses*, entitled "The Cares of the Pagans."[22] This treatise is a sustained meditation on the Gospel for the Fifteenth Sunday after Trinity in the lectionary of the Danish service book. It is from the Sermon on the Mount, Matthew 6: 24-34. Here we have seven of the fourteen discourses Kierkegaard devoted to this text.[23] To many it would be best known

---

[21]In *Philosophical Fragments*, recollection is the notion that the truth is within us, not in the narrow sense that it is a priori but in the broader sense that we can recognize it without any divine help. Thus the epistemological differences between Plato's "rationalism" and Aristotle's "empiricism" are immaterial. Similarly in "The Difference between a Genius and an Apostle," the former signifies immanence, the latter transcendence. Thus, "The genius is what he is by himself, that is, by what he is in himself; an apostle is what he is by his divine authority" (WA, 94). What distinguishes the insights of the genius, whether poet or philosopher, from those of the apostle is that the former have no essential God relation, whereas that relation is the essential mark of the apostle, who speaks by means of and on behalf of another. "If the authority is not the other (το ἕτερον) . . . then there simply is no authority" (WA, 99). This is why Climacus links the category of revelation to that of offense (PF, 49-54), and it is why Anti-Climacus can write that "the relation of personality to Christianity, is not to doubt or to believe, but to be offended or to believe" (PC, 81n.). Transcendence signifies the authority of alterity.

[22]In the earlier translation by Lowrie we find "The Anxieties of the Heathen." Kierkegaard's term is *bekymring* (whose verbal form the Hongs translate as to worry). There is an obvious link to the German *Bekümmerung*, which is a crucial term in Heidegger's early work from 1920 to 1922. See "Comments on Karl Jaspers's *Psychology of Worldviews*" (1920) and "Phenomenological Interpretations in Connection with Aristotle" (1922), both in *Supplements*, ed. John van Buren (Albany: SUNY Press, 2002), and the phenomenology of religion lectures to be found in *The Phenomenology of Religious Life*, trans. Matthias Fritsch and Jennifer Anna Gosetti-Ferencei (Bloomington: Indiana University Press, 2004), especially §10 of "Introduction to the Phenomenology of Religion" (1920-21) and §12 of "Augustine and Neo-Platonism" (1921). Theodore Kisiel notes that after 1922 this term is replaced by care (*Sorge*) and anxiety (*Angst*). *The Genesis of Heidegger's Being and Time* (Berkeley: University of California Press, 1993) 538n.19.

[23]The other seven are to be found as follows: 3 in "What We Learn from the Lilies in the Field and from the Birds of the Air" (in *Upbuilding Discourses in Various Spirits*); ; 3 in *The Lily in the Field and the Bird of the Air* (in *Without Authority*); and 1 in *Judge for Yourself!*

for verse 24, "No one can serve two masters . . . You cannot serve God and mammon," or for verse 33, "But seek first God's kingdom and his righteousness; then all these things will be added to you." For Kierkegaard, however, its special interest is the presentation of the birds of the air and the lilies of the field as our teachers.[24]

Each of the seven discourses has the same structure. With regard to each care (worry, anxiety), we are told that the bird does not have it,[25] that the Christian does not have it, and that the pagan has it. It would be a terrible misinterpretation to take this as an empirical claim about two groups of people who are called or who call themselves pagans and Christians. These are more nearly *Wesensschauen*, descriptions of essential characteristics, platonic forms, as it were. Thus Kierkegaard speaks of "the Christian" and "the pagan" in the singular.[26] The pagan, regularly described as living without God in the world,[27] is thereby without defense against these worries, while the Christian, who lives "before God," is thereby freed from these worries.

Because these are not empirical claims about different demographics, we must read them this way: just to the degree that you are free from these worries you are truly living as a Christian, and just to the degree that you are encumbered with these anxieties you are a pagan, even if you live in Christendom and take yourself and are taken by others to be a Christian. The Christian is surely presented as superior to the pagan, but the reader is not to judge the actual pagan (CD, 10) both because the pagan is an ideal type and because the purpose of this type is to prevent the careless and complacent assumption that one is a Christian.[28] Thus the text is

---

[24]Strictly speaking, they are assistant teachers to "the Gospel itself" and "*the Teacher*" who is "the Way and the Truth and the Life" (CD, 9-10). This is not theology of nature or natural theology but a heuristic for reading the Gospel text and subjecting ourselves to its authority. See note 20 above.

[25]In the fifth discourse the lily is added.

[26]In the first discourse the pagans are referred to in the plural, but in the other thirteen formulas, both Christian and pagan are referred to in the singular.

[27]For example, CD, 18-19.

[28]Nor is it appropriate to "sneeringly denounce the *so-called Christian* who does not live this [carefree] way" (CD, 10, emphasis added). Kierkegaard numbers himself among such Christians (CD, 11-12). Humble repentance is the appropriate response, not self-righteous superiority.

about paganism in Christendom, for it turns out that "we are living in the place, in a Christian country where there are only Christians," but these cares, which the pagan has and the Christian does not, "are found among people in this country; ergo, this Christian country is pagan" (CD, 11).

Just as the sermon at the end of *Either/Or* is a critique of the piety of Judge William, so this text is a critique of the religion of a certain "Christianity" in Christendom. It is written very much in the spirit of Anti-Climacus, who will write, "Christendom has abolished Christianity without really knowing it itself. As a result, if something must be done, one must attempt again to introduce Christianity into Christendom" (PC, 36). Neither baptism, nor orthodox theology, nor regular church attendance, nor civic virtue make a person truly Christian. Perhaps it was an inkling of such thinking that led Climacus to speak of "becoming" rather than "being" a Christian in *Concluding Unscientific Postscript* (hereafter *Postscript*).[29]

The first two discourses concern the care (anxiety, worry) of poverty and abundance respectively. Their common text is drawn from verses 25 and 32 of Matthew 6:

Therefore you should not worry and say, "What shall we eat?" or "What shall we drink?"—the pagans seek all these things.

The message is quite simple. The piety that coexists with worries about earthly possessions is pagan piety. True Christian faith is carefree in this regard, whether poor or rich, and in this respect the Christian is like the bird.

In the first discourse, both the bird and the poor Christian are carefree because they are content with the daily bread that they receive from God, bread that Kierkegaard assimilates to the manna the Israelites received in the wilderness after their exodus from Egypt (CD, 13; cf. Exodus 16). But there is a huge difference. The Christian knows, as the bird does not, that daily provisions come from God. The bird lives in immediacy, the Christian in a twofold reflection. Reflection, in a usage Kierkegaard borrows from Hegel, is always the relation of one thing to another. Whereas immediacy sig-

---

[29]The human being is not naturally carefree but "be becomes this as a Christian, and *the more he becomes a Christian*, the more he who has is as one who does not have" (CD, 26, emphasis added).

nifies an absence of alterity, reflection always signifies some duality.[30] There is a double reflection here, at once epistemic and ontological.

On the epistemic side, the Christian "knows that the daily bread is *from God.*" Kierkegaard spells out this knowing in a series of the Christian's beliefs, without distinguishing belief from knowledge (CD, 15-16). The duality in this case, missing from the bird's life, is the relation of the fact of God as giver to the knowledge of God as giver. Each time the Christian prays and gives thanks for daily bread "it becomes clearer to him that he exists for God and God for him" (CD, 16) This explicit awareness is perhaps what Anti-Climacus has in mind when later if 1848 he describes faith as resting *transparently* in God (SUD, 14, 30, 46, 49, 82, 131).

On the ontological side, what the knowledge knows is the relation to God and the importance of the relation. Here the category "before God" is fully operative. The self is not a substance some of whose qualities are essential but whose relations are accidental. This relation is utterly fundamental to the self's identity. But Kierkegaard does not dwell in such abstract discourse; he rather describes this relation as between a lover and a beloved. This means that the fact that the gift of daily bread comes from the lover is more important than the gift itself (CD, 15, 17, 32), which is the earthly meaning of the knowledge that "life is more than food" (verse 25). There is a heavenly meaning as well. The Christian believes (knows) that "just as he will certainly receive the daily bread as long as he has to live here on earth, he will some day live blessed in the hereafter" (CD, 16). Had Kierkegaard known the Heidelberg Catechism (1563), he might have cited the opening question and answer.

Q. What is your only comfort, in life and in death?

A. That I belong—body and soul, in life and in death—not to myself but to my faithful Savior, Jesus Christ, who at the cost of his own blood has fully paid for all my sins and . . . also

---

[30]On the Hegelian character of Kierkegaard's use of these categories, whether overtly or (as here, with a trans-academic readership in mind) tacitly, see my "Kierkegaard and the Role of Reflection in Second Immediacy," in *Immediacy and Reflection in Kierkegaard's Thought*, ed. P. Cruysberghs, J. Taels, K. Verstrynge (Leuven: Leuven University Press, 2003) 159-79.

assures me of eternal life. . . .[31]

Where such comfort is fully operative, there need be no anxiety about one's daily bread.

But what about the notion from *Fear and Trembling* that faith is a second immediacy? Does faith as freedom from the care of poverty get to reflection but not beyond this to a second immediacy? That would mean that the dualities of subject and object (knowledge and fact known) and of self and God remain dualisms, that they remain externally related, antithetical, without reconciliation. Several factors suggest otherwise.

First, the Christian does not merely know that the daily bread comes from God but prays and gives thanks to God for it, and this knowledge is so deeply embedded in prayer and thanksgiving that it could never be the quest for theoretical certainty (CD, 14, 16). With a footnote to Heidegger or Dewey, we might say that neither the daily bread nor God as its giver are "objects" out there that knowledge might or might not succeed in reaching; rather the Christian, the daily bread, and the God from whom it comes are so intimately intertwined in life that knowledge is not getting outside consciousness to contact the world but giving language to the being-in-the-world in which one is always already immersed. This immersion, this immediacy is "second" because it is not one's natural condition but must be learned. The knowledge and the life, reflection and second immediacy are mutually implicative.

Second, the alternative to this knowledge is not doubt but forgetting (CD, 16).[32] Kierkegaard is doing a phenomenology of faith rather than an epistemology of belief, and the question is not about propositions, evidence, warrant, justification, and so forth, but abut persons and what they are willing and able to keep in mind. To remember in this context is not to have an occasional thought, as to remember that it is time once again to get someone a birthday card, but to see oneself and one's world in a certain way all the time. In

---

[31]Found in the creedal and confessional books of various Reformed and Presbyterian churches; in *Creeds and Confessions of Faith in the Christian Tradition*, ed. Valerie R. Hotchkiss and Jaroslav Pelikan (New Haven, Yale University Press, 2003) 2:427-57; and at numerous sites on the internet, including http://www.rca.org/aboutus/beliefs/heidelberg/complete.html.

[32]See the reference to PC, 81n. in n. 21 above.

this sense I remember the law of gravity at all times, whether I am thinking about it or not. Belief (knowledge) is not merely a propositional attitude but the form and substance of one's being-in-the-world.

Third, in the text the Teacher commands that we not worry about what we will eat and drink. Here ontological reflection seems to prevail over any second immediacy, for, as Kierkegaard and Levinas have especially reminded us, where do we experience authentic alterity more fully than in the command of another, most especially a divine other. But to leave it at that is to forget that the one who commands and the one commanded are related (in faith) as lover and beloved. The lover commands for the sake of the beloved, and the beloved finds freedom rather than slavery in obedience partly in realizing this and partly because it is the nature of love to want to give itself.[33]

Thus there is a second immediacy here, a unity in diversity in which subject and object, self and God are united in a harmonious totality. This is not the speculative totality of which Hegel dreams. For (1) while knowledge is involved, it is not primarily a matter of theory but of attitude and affect; (2) what becomes transparent in the process is not God but the fact that I am essentially in relation to a God who is not transparent to my thought; and (3) the movement to this *second* immediacy is not necessary, either conceptually or developmentally. In terms of Christian categories, of course, this conversion is necessary. But those categories are not themselves necessary, and in any case the movement is necessary as a task, not an inevitability. Moreover, the description of the task makes it abundantly clear that like faith in *Fear and Trembling*, it is the (unfinished) task of a lifetime (FT, 6-7, 122-23).

In this first discourse the contrast between the Christian and the pagan is made more specific than the contrast between "before God" and "without God in the world." Whereas the Christian is defined as the one who prays and gives thanks for daily bread, the pagan is defined in biological and sociological terms as "man, citizen, and

---

[33]Psalm 119 and other biblical expressions of love for God's law are relevant here.

father" (CD, 19) and by the desire to be rich (CD, 20-21).[34] Onto-logically speaking, of course, the poor pagan exists before God every bit as much as the poor Christian and is as essentially defined by this relation as the poor Christian. But the former does not remember this, and so is without this knowledge although he was baptized and married in the church, will be buried by the church, and, as he notes, has had his children baptized, catechized, and confirmed in the church. The reason for this forgetting in the midst of these outward signs of Christianity is a certain contempt for Scripture.

> "If it were not out of a sense of decency," he says, "and out of respect for my children, whom according to custom one has of course had instructed in religion, I would bluntly say that there is very little to be found in Holy Scripture that answers this most im-portant question [of what we shall eat and drink], and very little at all that is of any benefit . . . We read about Christ and the apostles but find not the slightest contribution to an answer to the proper life-question, the primary question: what they lived on . . . On the whole, I miss earnestness in Holy Scripture. . . . Let the preachers prattle about such things to women and children; yet every earnest and enlightened man secretly agrees with me, and where the earnest people come together . . . there they honor only the sagacity that has an understanding of reality." (CD, 19)

Kierkegaard comments that the ungodliness of this paganism "is to be totally unwilling to know anything else, to be totally unwilling to know that this care is sinful, that Scripture therefore says that a person can burden his heart with worry about his livelihood in the same sense as he can burden it with gluttony and drunkenness (Luke 21:34)" (CD, 19).

This unwillingness has two important consequences. First, the pagan is earthbound. While the Christian "turns his gaze upward and looks away from the danger [of 'continually crav[ing] more and more'] . . . the thoughts of the one who wants to be rich are continually on the earth" (CD, 20-21). It is a matter of attention or attentiveness. This, in turn, means that instead of "*working* for the

---

[34]Perhaps the "poor" pagan does not live below the poverty line as a peasant or proletarian, but rather as someone who wants to move from the lower middle class to the upper middle class or from the middle to the upper class. On the economic side of the psychology of relative deprivation, see Thomas E. Ludwig, et al., *Inflation, Poortalk, and the Gospel* (Valley Forge, Judson Press, 1981).

daily bread, which every human being is commanded to do" and instead of "*praying* for the daily bread," the pagan's lot is "to *slave* for it — and yet not be satisfied by it, because the care is to become rich." Life becomes a matter of "despondent grief," "dark and brooding dejection," and "spiritless busyness" (CD, 20-22).[35] This reference to slavery points ahead for the Seventh Discourse, which focuses on verse 24, "No one can serve two masters . . . You cannot serve God and mammon."

The Second Discourse concerns the care of abundance, an anxiety from which the bird and the rich Christian are free. Not so the pagan. There are two key words here. 'Enough' and 'ignorant'. For the bird and the Christian the daily bread is enough.[36] But, of course, this is automatic for the bird. In its immediacy it lacks the capacity to "continually crave more and more" (CD, 20) and thereby to be anxious that it doesn't have enough but must get more. The Christian lacks this immediacy and therefore has the capacity for this craving and for the anxiety that is its flip side. Whence then the serenity of finding the daily bread, which the rich Christian has in abundance, to be enough?

It comes from ignorance. In its immediacy the bird is ignorant of its abundance and thus incapable of being anxious about it. The Christian, by contrast, must become ignorant, and , more precisely and paradoxically, "ignorant of what he knows . . . just like an absent-minded person" (CD, 26, 31).[37] And whence this ignorance? It is a matter of attention and arises from what the Christian "bears in mind" and remembers (CD, 27-29, 32).[38]

---

[35]Kierkegaard also describes this greed and a burden by which one is "weighed down" (CD, 18). Cf. Augustine's description of sin as slavery to a habit to which he is bound by links in a chain and tied down to earth by a weight. The imagery is that of a ball and chain. *The Confessions of St. Augustine*, trans. Rex Warner (New York: New American Library, 1963), 168-69 (VIII, 5).

[36]Kierkegaard would have loved John V. Taylor's little book, *Enough is Enough* (London: SCM Press, 1975), which easily reads as a critique of paganism in Christendom on the matter of wealth and possessions.

[37]Sartre's analysis of bad faith in *Being and Nothingness* is relevant here. It can best be summarized by saying that in bad faith I manage not to notice that of which I am in fact aware, and in that sense I become ignorant of it.

[38]Much of Christian spirituality is a matter of attentiveness. See, for example, *The Collected Works of St. John of the Cross*, trans. Kieran Kavanaugh, O.C.D. and

The Christian pays attention to two themes which undermine the sense of one's possessions as one's own. The first of these is the thought of death. This thought can, of course, give rise to that philosophy that is so crudely but eloquently expressed in the slogan, "whoever dies with the most toys wins." The Christian draws a different conclusion. "But when I think that I can perhaps die tonight, 'this very night,'[39] then, however rich I am, I do not own anything either. In order to be rich, I must own something for tomorrow etc., I must be secure *for* tomorrow; but in order to be rich, I must also be sure *of* tomorrow" (CD, 27-28).

"Then also in another way thought takes aim at the thought of possession. If I am to be rich, I must indeed own something, and thus what I own is mine." But the Christian "bears in mind" that "the owner is God" and "he owns nothing except what is given to him and owns what is given to him not for him to keep but only on loan, as a loan, as entrusted property" (CD, 28-31). The rich Christian is a mortal steward, and as such is free from the anxiety of abundance.

The rich pagan does not "remember" or "bear in mind" these thoughts and therefore

> is as far as possible from being ignorant of his wealth and abundance . . . Not only is he without God in the world, but wealth is his god . . . He has only one need, wealth, the one thing needful — therefore he does not even need God: But where one's treasure is, there is one's heart also, and the rich pagan's heart is with wealth on the earth . . . He is capable of disregarding everything that is lofty and noble and holy and lovely, but it has become impossible for him to disregard his wealth at any moment. (CD, 33-34)[40]

Otilio Rodriguez, O.C.D. (Washington, D.C.: Institute of Carmelite Studies, 1991), 91-92, 188-89, 193, 392, 548, 586-87, 686-87, and "The Birth of Spiritual Attentiveness," in Thomas Keating, *Open Mind, Open Heart* (Amity, NY: Amity House, 1986), 71-80. Attentiveness is closely linked to recollection in its dual sense of remembering and of deliberately drawing the mind away from its immediate being-in-the-world and into that inwardness in which attention can be focused on God.

[39]The reference is to Jesus warning against greed and the parable of the rich man who built bigger barns, to whom God says, "You fool! This very night your life is being demanded of you. And the things you have prepared, whose will they be?" Luke 12:13-21.

[40]The biblical allusions in this passage are from Eph. 2:12, Luke 10:42, and Matt. 6:21 respectively. See the discourse, "To Need God Is a Human Being's Highest

In other words, in these first two discourses paganism in Christendom consists in combining the outward marks of Christianity with a dominant mode of being-in-the-world that has given itself over to the values of a materialist, consumerist society. In the process God is pushed to the periphery insofar as God claims to be the absolute source of meaning and normativity over against which society's ethos is only relative.[41] But the god who plays second fiddle to the social mores of any society is no God at all but an idol.[42]

The Cares of the Pagans: Lowliness and Loftiness

The third and fourth discourses concern another pair, the care (anxiety, worry) of lowliness and loftiness. They are meditations on the following portion of the text from Matthew 6: "Do not worry about what you will wear—the pagans seek all these things." It is immediately clear that it is not a question of poverty, which has just been discussed. The significance of clothes is not the covering of nakedness or protection from the cold but social status. The opposite of lowliness is eminence or loftiness (CD, 37, 48). It is a matter of "power and honor and prestige" (CD, 48, 56). Thus "what you will wear" becomes the symbol for all the external signs of being Somebody, a Big Wig or a Big Wheel.

As with poverty and abundance, these are not absolute but relative terms. Thus it is a matter of comparison as to who has less and who has more of these commodities (CD, 37, 50). The fundamental question thus becomes whether one lives primarily before others, the crowd, for whom these distinctions are of great importance, or before God, for whom they are not (CD, 40-44). The lowly Christian,

---

Perfection" in EUD, 295-326.

[41]See FT, 56, 62, 68-71.

[42]It is in a Kierkegaardian spirit that Karl Barth speaks of "all those intermediary, collateral, lawless, divinities and powers and authorities and principalities ([Romans] vii.38) that obscure and discolour the light of the true God . . . Family, Nation, State, Church, Fatherland. And so the 'No-God' is set up, idols are erected, and God, who dwells beyond all this and that, is 'given up'." *The Epistle to the Romans*, trans. Edwyn C. Hoskyns (New York: Oxford University Press, 1933), 50-51. The "the baalisation of YHVH Himself" (see n. 13 above) is updated as the Americanization or the EUification of the God of the Bible.

for whom the latter is the case, is not unaware of his or her lowliness in the eyes of the others (CD, 39). So once again it would seem we are dealing with a cultivated ignorance. But instead of using that imagery, Kierkegaard here speaks of the speed with which the bird, the lily, and the Christian get started with being themselves before God. For the bird and the lily their immediacy means that they *are* themselves, while for the Christian reflection means to become oneself before God (CD, 38-40).

On this journey the Christian has God as the *prototype*. As a human being there is the fact that each was created in the *image* of God and has, as it were the model within. But as a Christian the *prototype* is the God who "has lived on earth . . . has allowed himself to be born in lowly and poor circumstances, yes, in ignominy" (CD, 41-42). Kierkegaard continues reprising the gospel narratives as the story of the lowly one who has become for the Christian the prototype. Thus "the lowly Christian's aspiration is only to dare in life and in death to appropriate his name or to be named after him . . . He believes and hopes he will ever more and more approach a likeness to this prototype" (CD, 42-43).[43] To the degree that this happens, "before God" continually trumps "before the others" and the lowly Christian is free from the care of lowliness.

It is just the opposite with the lowly pagan. Here "before the others" continually trumps "before God", and so "he is without God in the world" even if he takes himself to be a Christian.

> To be a human being—that is not anything to be, he thinks . . . because there is no distinction or advantage over all the other human beings. To be a Christian—that is not anything to be, he thinks—we all, of course, are that. But to become a councilor of justice—to be that would be something, and he must above all become anything in the world; to be nothing at all is something to despair over (CD, 44).[44]

---

[43]Anti-Climacus presents the lowliness of Christ as a possible source of offense. See PC 102-105. Here we encounter what I call Religiousness C, in which Jesus is not only the Paradox to be believed, but the Prototype, Paradigm, Pattern to be imitated. See my "Kierkegaard's Teleological Suspension of Religiousness B" in *Foundations of Kierkegaard's Vision of Community*, ed. George B. Connell and C. Stephen Evans (New Jersey: Humanities Press, 1992), 110-29.

[44]There are obvious overtones here with Anti-Climacus's analysis of "DESPAIR OVER THE EARTHLY OR OVER SOMETHING EARTHLY" which is a "pure immediacy" in

Such a person "slaves himself to death under the weight of what he is not . . . the despairing lowly one, the pagan, sinks under comparison's enormous weight" (CD, 45).

It will come as no surprise that the eminent Christian does not have the care of loftiness, which would really be a continuation of the care of lowliness. For while it would take place higher on the social totem pole, it would simply be the anxiety of feeling oneself not to be high enough. By definition the Christian does not feel this way, understanding that

> there is a God in heaven who is not a respecter of persons . . . When he speaks with God, he discards all earthly, all sham pomp and glory, but also all the untruth of illusion . . . he understands that it is an illusion to think that because at every moment of his life and in countless ways he feels this sense of life continually strengthened by his being important to all or to countless people . . . that there-fore his life would also be more important to God . . . he under-stands that it is an illusion — if someone wants to make him believe, because a word of authority from him is sufficient to set thousands in motion, indeed, almost to transform the shape of the world . . . that God would therefore also be different toward him. (CD, 51-52)

This is because the eminent Christian "allows the conception (the Christian conception) to take away from him the power and the loftiness . . ." What conception? "He believes that before this God he is a sinner and that this God is equally zealous against sin, whoever the sinner is." Thus he treats his earthly loftiness as the actor treats the king he plays on the stage or the child treats the emperor he plays in a game with his friends, because "the play and the child's game are a nonreality. But neither is it reality, in the Christian sense, to be eminent in actuality; the real is the eternal" (CD, 52-53).

The eminent pagan, of course, has the care of loftiness. "What is the care? A craving to become more and more . . . It is the care lest someone by slyness, by force, by lies, or by truth will take away his delusion" (CD, 57). This delusion is not merely a deficiency of intellect or sanity. Like despair, it is an illness of the spirit, and it can be fatal if left untreated. "Finally the care swallows its prey . . . he

---

which "there is no infinite consciousness of the self." For this "*man of immediacy* . . . his self, he himself, is an accompanying something within the dimensions of temporality and secularity" (SUD, 50-51).

exists before others. But this self does not exist; his innermost being has been consumed . . . he ceases to be a human being" (CD, 58).

There is a double tragedy here. We mustn't forget that Kierkegaard is concerned about paganism in Christendom. The first tragedy is that a human being ceases to be a human while biologically alive instead of becoming a self before God. The second tragedy is that he holds in his hands the cure to this cancer of the spirit, Christianity. But it has been so watered down that he either doesn't bother to take it or he takes it only to find that it has lost its healing power.

The final three discourses concern the cares of presumptuousness, of self-torment, and of indecisiveness, vacillation, and disconsolateness. The critique of piety, most especially Christian piety, that remains external and superficial instead of working a deep inner transformation of the self before God becomes richer and more diverse. But by now it may be possible to leave the detailed analyses of these cares as an exercise for the reader who is willing to learn from "*the Teacher*" (CD, 9-10).

2
On Kierkegaard's Copenhagen Pagans
David D. Possen

In part one of *Christian Discourses*, Kierkegaard analyzes seven "Cares [*Bekymringer*] of the Pagans": seven forms of worry [*Bekymring*] with which pagans, but not Christians, are afflicted. Kierkegaard derives his account of the pagans and their cares from Matthew 6:24-34, the excerpt from the Sermon on the Mount that serves as his epigraph. In this passage — source of the famous parable of the lilies and the birds — Jesus urges his followers to set aside all anxiety about worldly goods and security, which "the pagans seek."[1] Christians, unlike pagans, should "seek first God's kingdom and his righteousness" today; for "tomorrow will worry about itself."[2]

In his Introduction to "The Cares of the Pagans," Kierkegaard reveals that his goal is not to *interpret* the above lines in their first-century Judean context, but to *apply* them to his own nineteenth-century Danish "Christendom": a polity that conceives of itself as "a Christian country, where there are only Christians" (CD, 11). By prompting his local readers to meditate on the cares that Jesus dubbed "pagan," Kierkegaard directs these readers to make an unhappy "observation," and draw a mournful "conclusion," about their own beloved Denmark: "alas . . . these cares are found among people in this country; ergo, this Christian country is pagan" (CD, 11). Briefly put, when Kierkegaard speaks of "the pagans" in "The Cares of the Pagans," he is alluding not simply to the polytheists of Jesus' day, but to the merely nominal Christians — the Copenhagen pagans — of his own.[3]

There is even evidence that much of what Kierkegaard writes

---

[1]Matthew 6:32, as translated at CD, 7.

[2]Matthew 6:33-34, as translated at CD, 7.

[3]"The pagans who are found in Christendom have sunk the lowest," Kierkegaard remarks (CD, 12). They are even "below paganism," insofar as, "after having been lifted up, [they] have fallen once again and have fallen even lower" (CD, 12).

about "the pagans" is penned with *particular* Copenhagen pagans in mind. These references to individuals are carefully veiled (as we might expect). Yet in certain cases we have enough clues to peek behind Kierkegaard's veils; and such glimpses can be an interpretive boon for the present-day reader. In the pages that follow, I offer what I consider to be a small but significant contribution to this effort: an analysis of references to two of Kierkegaard's immediate contemporaries — the theologians Magnús Eiríksson (1806–1881) and Hans Lassen Martensen (1808–1884) — in the fifth discourse of "The Cares of the Pagans," titled "The Care of Presumptuousness."

I begin by reviewing, in §1, a complex distinction that lies at the heart of "The Care of Presumptuousness:" the distinction between true Christianity, on the one hand, and the "superstition" [*Overtro*] and "disbelief" [*Vantro*] of presumptuous pagans, on the other (CD, 67).[4] By drawing this distinction, I argue in §2, Kierkegaard deftly appropriates the terminology of Eiríksson's book *Tro, Overtro og Vantro*,[5] published two years before *Christian Discourses*. In his book, Eiríksson harnessed the schema faith/superstition/disbelief [*Tro/Overtro/Vantro*] in order to portray both Kierkegaard (a representative of "superstition") and Martensen (primarily a representative of "disbelief") as outside the bounds of "faith." Kierkegaard's response in "The Care of Presumptuousness," I show, is to redefine Eiríksson's terms ingeniously. On Kierkegaard's account, it is *Martensen*'s thought that emerges as the epitome of "superstition" — while Eiríksson's proves to be a species of sheer confusion.

In §3, I bring Kierkegaard's assault on Martensen as "the superstitious one" [*den Overtroiske*] into tighter focus. I argue that this long-neglected passage is in fact of considerable philosophical and theological significance. For unlike many of Kierkegaard's better-known attacks on Martensen, in which marginal issues or *ad hominem* jabs take center stage, *this* passage speaks succinctly to the heart of their dispute. Most fundamentally, Kierkegaard differed with

---

[4]In fact Kierkegaard enumerates *three* forms of "presumptuousness": "spiritlessness" [*Aandløshed*], "superstition," and "disbelief" (CD, 66-67). As we will see in §1 and §2 below, however, superstition and disbelief represent the two *essential* forms of presumptuousness as Kierkegaard defines it (CD, 63).

[5]Magnús Eiríksson, *Tro, Overtro og Vantro, i deres Forhold til Fornuft og Forstand, samt til hinanden indbyrdes* (Copenhagen: H. C. Klein, 1846).

Martensen on the relation between grace and reason. Whereas Martensen promised to blaze a speculative trail to Christianity's truth by taking heed, and so taking hold, of grace's power to enlighten human reason (*gratia illuminans*), Kierkegaard condemned Martensen's project as a travesty of the Lutheran principle of *sola gratia*, the monergism of grace.[6]

This basic condemnation of Martensen is nowhere more plainly articulated, to my knowledge, than in the closing paragraphs of "The Care of Presumptuousness." In §4, I highlight the significance of these paragraphs by comparing them to the fierce diatribe against Martensen in chapter IV of *The Concept of Anxiety*. Both passages, I show, diagnose Martensen with a pernicious form of *anxiety*: a *fear of grace* that manifests itself in the wish to master grace by intellectual means. Yet "The Care of Presumptuousness" takes this shared argument one step further, by pairing its diagnostic critique of Martensen with a concise account of Kierkegaard's own view. And this last account, I conclude, is of inestimable value to scholarship: it is a clear portrait, in Kierkegaard's own published, signed words, of a human being's *proper* relation to grace.

1. Kierkegaard on Faith, Superstition, and Disbelief

Kierkegaard opens "The Care of Presumptuousness" by briefly recalling the lily and bird of Jesus' parable (CD, 60-63). The problem of presumptuousness, Kierkegaard remarks, does not arise at all for such creatures as the bird or lily, which "in their relation to God . . . are like a baby when it is still as good as one with its mother" (CD, 62). For human beings, however, the situation is rather different. A human being's relation to God is not so much like that of an infant

---

[6]*Monergism* denotes the belief that God's grace is the sole force — the *monon ergon* — that is efficacious in human redemption. Because the word is often associated with Calvin and the Reformed tradition, many Lutheran writers shy away from it. Yet it has a prominent pedigree in Lutheran history — dating back to the Gnesio-Lutherans' successful campaign, in the mid-sixteenth century, to resist what they took to be an influx of "synergism" (the opposite of monergism, namely, the belief that forces distinct from grace, such as human action or the human will, can play a part in human redemption) into official Lutheran teachings. For more on the "Synergist Controversy," see *Documents from the History of Lutheranism, 1517–1750*, ed. Eric Lund (Minneapolis: Fortress Press, 2002) 183-84, 196-202.

to its mother as it is like that of an "older" child to its parents: a child who, though still enormously dependent on its mother and father, nonetheless has the power to *conceive* of itself as an entirely autonomous being (CD, 62). It is in this last capacity to imagine or declare our independence, Kierkegaard explains, that presumptuousness arises:

> Between God and a human being, there is the eternal essential difference of infinity; and when this difference is in any way encroached upon, even in the slightest, we have presumptuousness. Presumptuousness therefore is *either* in a forbidden, a rebellious, an ungodly way *to want to have God's help, or,* in a forbidden, a rebellious, an ungodly way *to want to do without God's help.* (CD, 63)

We become presumptuous when we fail to comport ourselves properly toward our need of God, and seek instead to "encroach" upon the gap that separates ourselves from our Maker. Such encroachment, Kierkegaard explains, may take one of two forms. *Either* we acknowledge our dependence on God's help, but go on to seek this help in an inappropriate way; *or* we deny, and so defy, the fact of our dependence.

The above definition marks the intellectual center of "The Care of Presumptuousness." The remainder of the discourse serves essentially to elaborate this definition's consequences and corollaries. The first of the above forms of presumptuousness—wanting to have God's help inappropriately—is soon explicated as *superstition* [*Overtro*]; while the second—wanting to do without God's help—is defined as *disbelief* [*Vantro*]. Meanwhile, the absence of presumptuousness—that is, the path of respecting (rather than encroaching upon) the difference between God and man, and of properly seeking God's help—is depicted as true Christianity.

Beyond these three possibilities, finally, a fourth is introduced: that of failing to engage with the fact of our dependence on God at all. Kierkegaard describes this last human possibility as "spiritlessness," or the "spiritless ignorance of God" (CD, 66). Kierkegaard dubs this path too a form of presumptuousness; even though, strictly speaking, presumptuousness "pertains essentially to a person's relation toward God," and the spiritless person is precisely someone who concerns himself with everything *but* his God-relation (CD, 63, 66). From Kierkegaard's perspective, however, the spiritless person's mask of indifference toward God in fact belies his deep *aggression* toward his Maker. Because he cannot kill God, the spiritless person devotes himself instead to "killing the thought of God": that is, to expunging the thought of God so thoroughly that it does not occur to him that God matters to him at all. In this manner, Kierkegaard explains, the spiritless person constitutes a kind of passive or unconscious deformation of a disbeliever, who *openly* "wants to deny God" (CD, 66-67).

If we set the spiritless person aside, we are left with three kinds of people — the "Christian," the "superstitious person," and "the disbeliever" — who are all at least minimally conscious that they are "involved with God" (CD, 67). Whereas the Christian and the superstitious person embrace their dependence on God, however, the disbeliever actively *resists* his need of God's help — by denying his need of God, by declaring his independence from God (CD, 67). Kierkegaard allows that a confident disbeliever might succeed in persuading himself that he has won such independence. Yet in his *actual* relation to God, Kierkegaard insists, this disbeliever is far more careworn and fearful than he himself realizes:

> Perhaps such a pagan does say that he is without care. But this is not so. . . . However much he hardens himself, he nevertheless carries in his inmost being the mark that God is the strongest, the mark that he *wills* to have God against himself. . . . [He] has the care that God will take everything away from him, has this care at every moment. . . . [He] is in a very real way in the power of anxiety [*Angest*], since he never really knows in whose power he is — is this not fearful [*angestfuldt*]! Although disbelieving, he scarcely knows whether he is in the power of disbelief or of superstition. . . . Abandoned by God, whom he wants to deny, overwhelmed by God, whom he wants to do without, he is in the power of evil forces, the sport [*Bold*, lit. "ball"] of disbelief and superstition. (CD, 67-68)

The disbeliever's very hostility to God is a clue to the anxiety that drives him. What is it, Kierkegaard asks, that motivates the disbeliever to deny God's power, if it is not his *fear* of that same power, his terror that, in an instant, God might rob him of everything that he loves and possesses? Disbelief, Kierkegaard explains, is not a stable point of view. It is an unceasing oscillation, like the bouncing of a ball [*Bold*], between the disbeliever's illusion of autonomy ("disbelief") and his fear of a powerful God grown monstrous ("superstition"). For this reason, while Kierkegaard's disbeliever may certainly be said to be more self-aware than his unconscious "spiritless" counterpart, it is clear that he too hardly knows himself at all.

The most self-aware of Kierkegaard's specimens of presumptuousness is "the superstitious person." Kierkegaard uses this designation to refer not to the disbeliever, who is superstitious without realizing it, nor *a fortiori* to the spiritless person, who is not even aware of his aggressive disbelief, but instead to the person who *openly* acknowledges his need of God, who "declares that it is God's help that he wants to have" — but then wants to have this help "arbitrarily" [*vilkaarligt*], that is, willfully, on his own turf and terms (CD, 68). Kierkegaard compares the latter individual to the Simon of Acts 8:18-19, who "wants insanely to buy the Holy Spirit with money or wants to make money with the help of the Holy Spirit" (CD, 68, 441n70). The superstitious person in effect hopes to appropriate God's power, to terminate his dependence on God, *precisely by means of* acknowledging his dependence on God. To rephrase this point in terms of Kierkegaard's original definition of presumptuousness: the superstitious man wants indeed to have God's help — but he wants this in "a forbidden, a rebellious, an ungodly way" (CD, 63).

The true "Christian," meanwhile, is an individual who *properly* seeks God's help. He is the superstitious person's opposite number: for whereas the superstitious person seeks Divine aid in order to evade or overcome his dependence on God, the Christian turns to God without any such pretensions. The Christian is content with his dependence on God, and hopes only to *remain* content with this dependence: "The Christian knows that to need God is a human being's perfection. . . . He craves only to be *satisfied with God's grace*" (CD, 64). Unlike the presumptuous pagans, in other words, the Christian seeks to be nothing other than what he is — a human being who stands in need of God's grace at every moment. Kierkegaard explains:

> He does not insist on helping himself but prays for God's grace. He does not insist that God shall help him in any other way than God wills; he prays only to be satisfied with his grace. The Christian has no self-will whatever; he surrenders himself unconditionally. But with regard to God's grace he again has no self-will; he is satisfied with God's grace. He accepts everything by God's grace — grace also. He understands that even in order to pray for his grace he cannot do without God's grace. (CD, 64)

These sentences affirm a central tenet of Lutheran orthodoxy: that there is nothing we can *do* in order to gain the unmerited grace that alone can save us. As Luther famously and trenchantly insisted, our actions, our will, and even our reason are of no help to us in acquiring grace.[7] Rather, grace comes of its own accord to those who have "faith."[8] However, having faith is not something we can *do* or *will* on our own devices; faith too is a gift of grace, for which we must appeal afresh to grace at every moment.[9] To put this point concisely: we need grace in order to be redeemed — but that is not all. We also need grace in order to seek and receive grace properly, i.e., to pray for grace and be satisfied with it in faith — in a word, to avoid presumptuousness; and we need grace in all of these ways *at every moment*.[10]

We will return to these matters in §3 below. For the present, let us simply note that we have now fully enumerated the *human* cast of characters in "The Care of Presumptuousness": the spiritless man, the disbeliever, the superstitious man — and the Christian. Two nonhuman characters still remain, namely, the lily and the bird of Jesus' parable. The bird, in particular, plays a prominent role as the Christian's poetic foil: "In its need, the bird is as close as possible to God; it cannot do without him at all. The Christian is in even greater

---

[7]Cf. Martin Luther, "Disputation Against Scholastic Theology," tr. Harold J. Grimm, in *Luther's Works: American Edition*, ed. Jaroslav Pelikan and Helmut T. Lehmann (Philadelphia: Fortress Press and Minneapolis: Concordia Publishing House, 1955-86), vol. 31, 9-16, 9-10. See also Martin Luther, "The Bondage of the Will," tr. Philip S. Watson and Benjamin Drewery, in *Luther's Works: American Edition*, vol. 33, 290.

[8]Martin Luther, "Preface to the Complete Edition of Luther's Latin Writings," tr. Lewis W. Spitz, Sr., in *Luther's Works: American Edition*, vol. 34, 323-338, 337.

[9]Martin Luther, "Preface to the Complete Edition of Luther's Latin Writings," in *Luther's Works: American Edition*, 337.

[10]According to Luther, we never become deserving of grace during our lifetimes; and so we are never in a position (except in Heaven) to *know* on our own devices that our place in Heaven is assured. Even the most saintly Christians, so long as they live, are at best *simul justus et peccator*: redeemed and yet in need of redemption at one and the same time. Cf. Martin Luther, "Lectures on Romans: Glosses," tr. Jacob A. O. Preus, in *Luther's Works: American Edition*, vol. 25, 258, 336. On the place of *simul justus et peccator* in Kierkegaard's theology and writings, see Andrew J. Burgess, "Kierkegaard's Concept of Redoubling and Luther's *Simul Justus*," in *International Kierkegaard Commentary: 'Works of Love,'* (Macon, GA: Mercer University Press, 1999) 39-55.

need; he *knows* that he cannot do without him. The bird is as close as possible to God; it cannot do without him at all. The Christian is even closer to him; he cannot do without—his grace" (CD, 65). The Christian, then, is a human being who is just as utterly dependent on God as is Jesus' bird of the air. He differs from the bird only insofar as he *knows* of his dependence, that is, insofar as he knows that what he needs is God's unmerited gracious aid. For this reason, we might say that the Christian both needs God more and comes closer to God than does the bird—but this is so only in virtue of the Christian's self-knowledge.

What distinguishes the Christian from the remaining characters of "The Care of Presumptuousness," then, is his *self-knowledge in his dependence.* The Christian exists in utter dependence on God and knows it; the bird simply and unknowingly exists in its dependence; but the pagan—whether he is spiritless, disbelieving, or superstitious—is *deluded* in his dependence, that is, deluded by a conscious or unconscious presumptuous wish to escape from his dependence. At the end of "The Care of Presumptuousness," Kierkegaard recapitulates this threefold contrast in a markedly ominous tone. "As much closer to God as the Christian is than the bird," Kierkegaard writes, "so much further away from God is the pagan than the bird": for the pagan suffers "eternal perdition away from the face of God" (CD, 69). In the sections that follow, we will revisit this dark warning in light of the discourse's subtle references to two of Kierkegaard's Copenhagen contemporaries. We will soon come to understand just *whom* Kierkegaard means to condemn as "pagan"—and on what grounds.

2. Eiríksson's Tro, Overtro og Vantro

Let us briefly recall Kierkegaard's definition of presumptuousness: "*either* in a forbidden, a rebellious, an ungodly way *to want to have God's help, or,* in a forbidden, a rebellious, an ungodly way *to want to do without God's help*" (CD, 63). We are now equipped to correlate this definition with Kierkegaard's fourfold taxonomy of Christians and pagans. In Kierkegaard's "*either,*" we can immediately recognize his "superstitious person"; while in his "*or*" we may plainly see his "disbeliever"—together with the "spiritless person," whose forgetting of God represents a special form of disbelief.

Opposed to this entire *either/or* of presumptuousness, finally, stands "the Christian," who is "satisfied with grace" (CD, 64). The Christian knows that he stands in constant need of God's gracious aid; and he is at peace with this predicament.

Thus a *tripartite* schema lies at the core of "The Care of Presumptuousness." True Christianity, which is abbreviated elsewhere in *Christian Discourses* as "faith" [*Tro*],[11] is here opposed to "superstition" [*Overtro*] and "disbelief" [*Vantro*], the two basic forms of presumptuousness. I will now suggest that the three resonant *terms* at the core of this schema — *Overtro, Vantro,* and (implicitly) *Tro* — are more than artifacts of Kierkegaard's penchant for wordplay. These terms also constitute a reference, I submit, to Magnús Eiríksson's provocative book *Tro, Overtro og Vantro,* which had appeared in Copenhagen shortly before Kierkegaard began work on *Christian Discourses.* As we are about to see, Kierkegaard had good reason to craft a retort to Eiríksson's book: for it rather brusquely condemns Kierkegaard's *Fear and Trembling* as a specimen of "superstition."[12]

Eiríksson was well known to Kierkegaard; all too well known, as Kierkegaard might have put the matter.[13] An Icelander by birth, Eiríksson had studied theology at the University of Copenhagen during the 1830s, the decade of Kierkegaard's own university educa-

---

[11]See, e.g., the meditation on "faith" at the close of "The Care of Loftiness," the discourse immediately prior to "The Care of Presumptuousness" (CD, 59).

[12]A superb new article on Eiríksson's career and relation to Kierkegaard is now in press as Gerhard Schreiber, "Magnús Eiríksson: an Opponent of Martensen and an Unwelcome Ally of Kierkegaard," in *Kierkegaard and His Danish Contemporaries,* ed. Jon Stewart (London: Ashgate, forthcoming 2008). I thank Schreiber for generously sharing his manuscript with me. For a brief treatment of the Kierkegaard-Eiríksson relationship, see Emanuel Skjoldager, "An Unwanted Ally: Magnus Eiríksson," in *Kierkegaard as a Person,* ed. Niels Thulstrup and Marie Mikulová Thulstrup (Copenhagen: C. A. Reitzel, 1983) 102-108. For more on the relation between the two men, see Erik Bøgh, "Magnus Eiríksson og Søren Kierkegaard," in *Søren Kierkegaard og St. Sørens-Dyrkelsen* (Copenhagen: Gandrup, 1870) 48-55, together with the anonymous reply, *Søren Kierkegaard og St. Erik og St. Magnus Dyrkelsen* (Copenhagen: Cohen, 1870). See also Hans Sofus Vodskov, "Magnus Eiríksson," in *Spredte Studier* (Copenhagen: Gyldendal, 1884) 31-40.

[13]Kierkegaard resented Eiríksson's attempts to enlist him as an intellectual ally; he refused out of hand Eiríksson's repeated requests for financial assistance; and he (privately) inveighed against Eiríksson's "bungling stupidity" (JP, 6:6597). Cf. Emanuel Skjoldager, "An Unwanted Ally: Magnus Eiríksson," 105-106.

tion.[14] Like Kierkegaard, Eiríksson had followed with alarm the rapid rise at Copenhagen of the philosopher/theologian Hans Lassen Martensen and his peculiar brand of post-Hegelian speculative theology.[15] In the mid-1840s, Eiríksson's antipathy to Martensen burst into open war. At considerable personal expense, Eiríksson published a series of book-length polemics against Martensen — including a disastrous open letter to King Christian VIII[16] — all in a futile effort to have Martensen removed from his professorship. Five major anti-Martensen volumes appeared under Eiríksson's byline between 1844 and 1850. *Tro, Overtro og Vantro* is the second of these five, and appeared in 1846.[17]

We will shortly see that Kierkegaard soon developed a close acquaintance with *Tro, Overtro og Vantro*. He had good reason to do so. The book neatly promotes Eiríksson's own theological stance — that of "faith" — as a careful path between the Scylla of Martensenian "disbelief" and the Charybdis of Kierkegaardian "superstition." Briefly, Eiríksson grounds his definitions of faith, superstition, and disbelief in terms of a further distinction between "reason"

---

[14]Eiríksson entered the University of Copenhagen in 1831, and received his degree in 1837. For more on Eiríksson's student days, see Svend Aage Nielsen, *Kierkegaard og Regensen* (Copenhagen: Graabrødre Torv, 1965) 70-75.

[15]On the term "post-Hegelian," see §3 below. Meanwhile, for a wry firsthand account of Eiríksson's early disillusionment with Martensen, see Magnus Eiríksson, *Tro, Overtro og Vantro*, 81n-82n and 88n-89n.

[16]Eiríksson's letter not only demanded that Martensen be fired, but also criticized the Danish Crown's authoritarian rule. Eiríksson was soon faced with the threat of public prosecution for insulting the Crown. See Skjoldager, "An Unwanted Ally: Magnus Eiriksson," 103.

[17]The others are Magnús Eiríksson, *Om Baptister og Barnedaab, samt flere Momenter af den kirkelige og speculative Christendom* (Copenhagen: S. L. Møller, 1844); *Dr. Martensens trykte moralske Paragrapher, eller det saakaldte "Grundrids til Moralphilosophiens System af Dr. Hans Martensen," i dets forvirrede, idealistisk-metaphysiske og phantastisk-speculative, Religion og Christendom undergravende, fatalistiske, pantheistiske og selvforguderiske Væsen, belyst og bedømt* (Copenhagen: H. C. Klein, 1846); *Speculativ Rettroenhed, fremstillet efter Dr. Martensens "christelige Dogmatik," og Geistlig Retfærdighed, belyst ved en Biskops Deeltagelse i en Generalfiskal-Sag* (Copenhagen: J. G. Salomon, 1849); and *Den nydanske Theologies Cardinaldyder, belyste ved Hjælp af Dr. Martensen's Skrifter samt Modskrifterne, tillige med 75 theologiske Spørgsmaal, rettede til Dr. H. Martensen* (Copenhagen: Chr. Steen & Søn, 1850). A comprehensive overview of these texts and their relevance to Kierkegaard is forthcoming in Gerhard Schreiber's "Magnús Eiríksson," as cited in n. 12 above.

[*Fornuften*] and "the understanding" [*Forstanden*]. "Reason," according to Eiríksson, denotes the human mind's capacity to receive Divine truth; while our "understanding" is an analytical, critical faculty restricted to processing the information that is already available to us. Armed with this distinction, Eiríksson proceeds to define "faith" as the *confluence* of reason and understanding, "disbelief" as the *exclusion* of reason by the understanding, and "superstition" as the *rejection* of both reason and the understanding:

> Where pure understanding is dominant, there is *disbelief*, namely, the absence of faith or no faith, but only assumptions and knowledge based on tangible proofs of the understanding.
> Where the inner sense, reason, is heard and respected appropriately — without the understanding *either* setting itself up as its absolute judge *or* being excluded and disparaged — there and only there can religious *faith* develop in its soundness and power.
> Where, however, the understanding is condemned and excluded; where reason's sound sense, with its immediate That and its rational Why, is not given appropriate heed — but, in some cases, dim feeling and unconstrained fantasy are cultivated and encouraged via the lower senses, or, in other cases, external authority is made the guiding principle and is followed — there *superstition* reigns infallibly.[18]

In the remainder of his book, Eiríksson expatiates at length on these definitions — and offers his readers several potent examples of *local* disbelief and superstition. Thus Eiríksson's discussion of disbelief makes continual and pointed reference to Martensen's writings, lectures, and jargon.[19] Two of Eiríksson's prime examples of superstition, meanwhile, will strike Kierkegaard's readers as familiar: "'I believe because it (something) is absurd (*credo quia absurdum est*)' — the Church Father Tertullian — or 'Faith is by virtue of the absurd' — Joh. *de silentio* in the book *Fear and Trembling*. . . . These sentences are false in and of themselves, and provide an opening for the most unrestrained superstition."[20] In these lines we

---

[18]Magnús Eiríksson, *Tro, Overtro og Vantro*, 49-50, my translation, several original emphases removed.
[19]Magnús Eiríksson, *Tro, Overtro og Vantro*, 61-64. Ultimately, Eiríksson diagnoses Martensen with a *mixture* of disbelief and superstition: see Magnús Eiríksson, *Tro, Overtro og Vantro*, 66-67, 81-82, 85-92.
[20]Magnús Eiríksson, *Tro, Overtro og Vantro*, 56, my translation.

may detect a nineteenth-century ancestor to more recent charges of irrationalism and fideism in Kierkegaard.[21]

In 1850, Eiríksson developed the above jab at *Fear and Trembling* into a book-length pseudonymous riposte.[22] The appearance of the latter book prompted a flurry of writing on Kierkegaard's part, culminating in an unpublished but priceless "Reply" attributed to Kierkegaard's pseudonym Johannes Climacus.[23] For our purposes, what is most significant about this "Reply" is that it reveals that, four years after the publication of *Tro, Overtro og Vantro*, Kierkegaard remained acutely aware of that book's critique of him — and indeed recognized the family resemblance between it and Eiríksson's new volume. Addressing Eiríksson's pseudonym Theophilus Nicolaus, Kierkegaard's own Johannes Climacus writes: "Finally, a word about your scholarly essay, which stands approximately *au niveau* with Magnús Eiríksson's *Tro, Overtro og Vantro*. . . . You have misinterpreted *Fear and Trembling* to such an extent that I do not recognize it at all" (JP, 6:6598).

We will here say no more about the details of Kierkegaard's 1850 "Reply" to Eiríksson. Our concern has been simply to document the *fact* that Kierkegaard was well-acquainted with Eiríksson's *Tro, Overtro og Vantro*. In so doing, we have established the plausibility of my working hypothesis: that the schema of faith, superstition, and disbelief that Kierkegaard employs in "The Care of Presumptuousness" — written in 1847, and published in 1848[24] — amounts to a correction and reuse of Eiríksson's 1846 taxonomy.

----

[21]For an analysis of Eiríksson's critique as a forerunner to twentieth-century charges of irrationalism, see Cornelio Fabro, "Faith and Reason in Kierkegaard's Dialectic," in *A Kierkegaard Critique*, ed. Howard A. Johnson and Niels Thulstrup (New York: Harper & Brothers, 1962) 156-206, 172, 179, 200n31.

[22]Eiríksson attributed this book to "Theophilus Nicolaus, brother of the aforementioned knight of faith." Theophilus Nicolaus [Magnús Eiríksson], *Er Troen et Paradox og "i Kraft af det Absurde"? Et Spørgsmaal foranledigt ved "Frygt og Bæven, af Johannes de silentio," besvaret ved Hjelp af en Troes-Ridders fortrolige Meddelelser, til fælles Opbyggelse for Jøder, Christne og Muhamedanere, af bemeldte Troes-Ridders Broder, Theophilus Nicolaus* (Copenhagen: Chr. Steen & Søn, 1850).

[23]"Reply to Theophilus Nicolaus" (JP, 6:6598). In a meticulous analysis of this text, Fabro extracts a prescient and thoroughgoing reply by Kierkegaard to the irrationalism charge. See Fabro, "Faith and Reason in Kierkegaard's Dialectic," 179-84.

[24]On the composition of *Christian Discourses*, see CD, xii.

In the next section, we will return to the *content* of "The Care of Presumptuousness." We will there see that Kierkegaard, like Eiríksson, employs the trichotomy faith/superstition/disbelief in order to attack Martensen and Martensenian theology. Yet where Kierkegaard criticizes Martensen, he does so under the heading of *superstition*, rather than that of disbelief. He thereby replaces Eiríksson's portrait of superstition with a radically different account: superstition is now the realm of Christian speculation, rather than the domain of faith "by virtue of the absurd."

In so doing, I submit, Kierkegaard breezily implies that Eiríksson has muddled his categories. Kierkegaard drives the last point home, moreover, when he remarks that confusion about disbelief and superstition is entirely to be expected, since "truly it is very difficult" to tell the difference between the two (CD, 65-66). As we have already mentioned, confusion about disbelief and superstition is even described as a *symptom* of presumptuousness, which bounces its victims like a "ball" [*Bold*] between the two (CD, 66). Such confusion — Eiríksson's confusion — is finally the mark of a pitiable fate. "No bird is tossed about in this manner, not even in the worst weather!" (CD, 66).

3. Martensen as Kierkegaard's "Superstitious Person"

I will now interpret Kierkegaard's critique of superstition in "The Care of Presumptuousness" as a frontal assault on Martensen. Researchers have long recognized that Martensen is a frequent target of Kierkegaard's polemical prose.[25] Indeed, a vivid 1850 notebook entry suggests that a sustained critique of Martensen suffuses Kierkegaard's *entire* pseudonymous authorship:

You will not deny it, will you, Prof. M. You do not want the embar-

---

[25]On Kierkegaard's tempestuous relation to Martensen, see Curtis L. Thompson, "Introduction," in *Between Hegel and Kierkegaard*, ed. Curtis L. Thompson and David J. Kangas (Atlanta: Scholars Press, 1997) 40-80; Jon Stewart, *Kierkegaard's Relations to Hegel Reconsidered* (Cambridge: Cambridge University Press, 2003); J. H. Schjørring, "Martensen," in *Kierkegaard's Teachers*, ed. Niels Thulstrup and Marie Mikulovà Thulstrup (Copenhagen: C. A. Reitzel, 1982) 177-207; Arild Christensen, "Efterskriftens Opgør med Martensen," *Kierkegaardiana* 4 (1962) 45-62; and Robert Leslie Horn, *Positivity and Dialectic: A Study of the Theological Method of Hans Lassen Martensen* (Copenhagen: C. A. Reitzel, 2007) 223-30.

rassment of being the only one in the kingdom to deny that from
the very beginning these pseudonyms, in a highly disturbing and
annoying manner, have had a bearing on the system. And this
whole matter of the system, again, was chiefly linked to your name.
. . . "The system" in Denmark and the pseudonyms essentially
belong together. (JP, 6:6636)

Evidently everyone in the kingdom apart from Martensen was
aware that an unceasing critique of his Hegelian (or, as Martensen
would have it, post-Hegelian) "system" pervades the writings of
Kierkegaard's pseudonyms.[26] In recent years, scholars have duly
sought — and have productively found — traces of just such a polemic
throughout the pseudonymous writings.[27] In what follows, I will
press this project in a new direction. I will argue that Kierkegaard's
polemic against Martensen is also present in "The Care of Presumptuousness," to which Kierkegaard proudly signed his own name.
Moreover, I will submit, the *root* of Kierkegaard's disagreement with
Martensen is here articulated more concisely and sharply than perhaps anywhere else in Kierkegaard's authorship.

Let us begin by reviewing the essentials of the Kierkegaard-
Martensen dispute. Martensen's fame as a philosopher and theo-

---

[26]One example of this "everyone in the kingdom" is Eiríksson, who in 1846
praised

the *Concluding Unscientific Postscript* of Johannes Climacus — or Magister S.
Kierkegaard — who at long last elaborates, in this important work, on the *authentic* theology and doctrine. Although he goes further than I do in his opposition to doctrine, tradition, and the so-called "objective," and although our
conceptions of faith are quite different (on this see my book *Tro, Overtro og
Vantro*), we are essentially in clear agreement about the character of speculative
theology — and particularly the *Martensenian* theology — to which he *plainly
alludes* in many places. (Magnús Eiríksson, *Dr. Martensens trykte moralske Paragrapher*, IVn, my translation, last emphasis mine).

Another example is Rasmus Nielsen (1809–1884), who cast himself as a champion
of Kierkegaard's cause against Martensen in his 1849 *Mag. S. Kierkegaards "Johannes
Climacus" og Dr. H. Martensens "Christelige Dogmatik": En undersøgende Anmeldelse*
(Copenhagen: C. A. Reitzel, 1849).

[27]As of this date, the most comprehensive collation of references to Martensen
in the pseudonymous authorship is the impressive effort of Jon Stewart in *Kierkegaard's Relations to Hegel Reconsidered*. I have recently learned, however, that a forthcoming book — Curtis Thompson, *A Speculative Theologian Determining the Order of
the Day: Kierkegaard's Volatile Relation to Martensen* (Copenhagen: C. A. Reitzel,
2008) — promises to cover this ground still more thoroughly.

logian was grounded in his oft-repeated and well-received claim that, by paying proper regard to the power of God's grace (theonomy), a Christian speculative thinker can overcome the variously ironic, ignorant, autonomous, and pantheistic standpoints of Socrates, Dante, Descartes, Kant, Goethe, Schleiermacher, and even Hegel, and ascend to a standpoint of higher knowledge.[28] To be specific: by opening his mind to the power of *gratia illuminans* (enlightening grace), the speculating Christian may acquire "co-knowledge" with God.[29] With the aid of God's grace, the speculating Christian can participate in "the immanent thinking" that comprehends "the mystery" of the Divine order of things, including the provenance of sin and the operations of grace, all from the point of view of eternity.[30]

In the 1840s, the above view came under harsh and repeated attack in Kierkegaard's writings. In *Concluding Unscientific Postscript*,

---

[28]On Martensen's claim to have advanced beyond Hegel, see J. H. Schjørring, "Martensen," 185. See also Hans Lassen Martensen, *Af mit Levned*, vol. 2 (Copenhagen: Gyldendal, 1882) 45, cited and translated by Curtis L. Thompson in Thompson and Kangas, eds., *Between Hegel and Kierkegaard*, 8. For another source (1836) in which Martensen claimed to have "gone beyond" Hegel, see Thompson and Kangas, eds., *Between Hegel and Kierkegaard*, 9n11. On Martensen's prescription for how a "Protestant poet" — presumably his ally Johan Ludvig Heiberg (1791–1860) — might improve upon the poetry of Goethe, see Martensen, "Betragtninger over Idéen af Faust med Hensyn paa Lenaus *Faust*," *Perseus: Journal for den speculative Idee*, 1 (1837) 91-164; see also George Pattison, *Kierkegaard, Religion, and the Nineteenth Century Crisis of Culture* (Cambridge: Cambridge University Press, 2002) 101-103. On Martensen's attempt to supersede "autonomous" Kantian and Schleiermacherian thought, see Martensen, "On the Autonomy of Human Self-Consciousness in Modern Dogmatic Theology," tr. Curtis L. Thompson, in Thompson and Kangas, eds., *Between Hegel and Kierkegaard*, 72-147. Finally, for Martensen's praise of Johan Ludvig Heiberg (1791–1860) as a poet who had superseded Dante, and had further pioneered a mode of aesthetic and ethical discernment (humor) that outstripped that of Socrates and other non-Protestants (irony), see Hans Lassen Martensen, "Nye Digte af J. L. Heiberg," *Fædrelandet* 398 (January 10, 1841) cols. 3210-12; see also George Pattison, *Kierkegaard, Religion*, 111-12.
[29]Hans Lassen Martensen, "On the Autonomy of Human Self-Consciousness," in *Between Hegel and Kierkegaard*, ed. Thompson and Kangas, 82, 147.
[30]Hans Lassen Martensen, "Rationalisme, Supernaturalisme og *principium exclusii medii* i Anledning af H. H. Biskop Mynsters Afhandling herom i dette Tidsskrifts forrige Hefte," *Tidsskrift for Litteratur og Kritik* 1 (1839) 456-473, 460, tr. Jon Stewart in *Kierkegaard's Relations to Hegel Reconsidered*, 351.

for example, Kierkegaard dispatches his pseudonym Johannes Climacus to mock Martensen's claims, jargon, and person merciless-ly. Thus Climacus parodies an unnamed but unmistakable "specula-tive" thinker who "wants to enter God's council" by comprehending Christianity's truth "with the help of immanence" or "*sub specie aeterni*," that is, "from an eternal, divine, and especially theocentric point of view" (CUP, 1:212, 1:214, 1:216-217). The *Postscript* is peppered with such passages. They attack everything from Martensen's idiosyncratic theory of *humor*—a God's-eye-view of sin, redemption, and Heaven, which we will briefly meet in §4—to Martensen's notorious attempts to take credit for "going beyond Hegel" (CUP, 1:291, 1:370). Such passages are revealing; but they are revealing only up to a point. For the most part, they concern them-selves only with Martensen's posturing, slogans, and jargon. As a result, they grant us access only to the *surface* of Kierkegaard's deep disagreement with Martensen.

The core of the quarrel between Kierkegaard and Martensen concerns the relation between grace and reason in Lutheran life. As we mentioned in §1 above, Lutheranism is grounded in its founder's doctrine of *sola gratia*, or the monergism of grace: the claim that humanity can be redeemed *only* by God's gracious intervention. For Kierkegaard and Martensen, the burning question here is whether we can *make sense* on our own of the knowledge that redemption provides. Luther, for his part, had insisted that human reason "neither knows nor understands" Christianity's truths, including the provenance of sin or the workings of grace. We can grasp such truths, he wrote, only by means of "the light of the gospel and the knowledge of grace."[31] On Martensen's interpretation, Luther's notion of *gratia illuminans* (enlightening grace) implies that Christian-ity facilitates an *ascent in knowledge* for its adherents.[32] In other words, Christian redemption allows our limited natural knowledge of the world (*autonomy*) to be replaced with a higher body of knowl-edge, furnished by grace (*theonomy*). This higher knowledge is accessible to all those who, in keeping with their Christian faith,

---

[31]Martin Luther, "The Bondage of the Will," in *Luther's Works: American Edition*, vol. 33, 290-291. See also Martin Luther, "The Disputation Concerning Justification," tr. Lewis W. Spitz, in *Luther's Works: American Edition*, vol. 34, 166.
[32]Martensen, "On the Autonomy of Human Self-Consciousness," 82.

incorporate an acknowledgment of God's gracious power into their method of speculation.[33]

Kierkegaard deplored the above claims. He countered them in a variety of texts — including the *Postscript*, mentioned above. On Kierkegaard's more traditional Lutheran line, human reason cannot make *use* of grace in order to come to terms with Christianity's truth. The best we can do, Kierkegaard claims, is to acknowledge our inability to wrap our minds around Christianity's truth — and then to "flee" to grace.[34] To boast of *knowing* Christianity's truth, or even of knowing this truth with the aid of grace, is in Climacus's words to fail "to exist" (CUP, 1:206n). It is to seek "to enter God's council" without acknowledging that one is "an existing human being, subject to the claims of existence," a mere human being who cannot outgrow or outlive one's unceasing need of grace (CUP, 1:212, 206n).

In this last context, finally, "The Care of Presumptuousness" is singularly valuable. For this discourse gives voice, more concisely than any other Kierkegaardian text that I know of (signed or pseudonymous), to precisely what irked Kierkegaard so deeply about Martensen's theory of theonomy:

> He wants by inadmissible means to penetrate the forbidden, discover the hidden, discern the future. [He] wants to make money with the help of the Holy Spirit. He wants to force himself on God ... to make himself, him the uncalled, into what only God's call can make a person. [He] wants God to serve him. What else is it, even if [he] declares that it is God's help that he wants to have — when he arbitrarily wants to have it, what else is it than wanting God to serve him? (CD, 68)

These lines describe a man who loudly proclaims his need of grace ("God's help") — yet in reality wants to *take advantage* of grace in order to storm the heavens on his own terms. Such a man seeks "to

---

[33]Martensen, "On the Autonomy of Human Self-Consciousness," 82.

[34]The concept of fleeing to grace [*at henflye til Naade*] lies at the bedrock of Kierkegaard's Christianity. For a thorough account of Kierkegaard's theology of grace, see Craig Quentin Hinkson, *Kierkegaard's Theology: Cross and Grace. The Lutheran and Idealist Traditions in His Thought* (dissertation: University of Chicago, 1993). See also Sylvia Walsh, *Living Christianly: Kierkegaard's Dialectic of Christian Existence* (University Park, PA: Pennsylvania State University Press, 2005); and my "The Voice of Rigor," in *International Kierkegaard Commentary: Practice in Christianity*, ed. Robert L. Perkins (Macon, GA: Mercer University Press, 2004) 161-85.

force himself on God," and so to discover what is "forbidden," namely, "the hidden" and "the future." It should be clear at once that these lines constitute a caricature of Martensen's thought. More specifically, they offer a deeper sketch of what the *Postscript* calls Martensen's attempt "to enter God's council": Martensen's account of how the Christian thinker may use theonomy (the power of grace) in order to attain coknowledge of God's immanent world-view.

The broader purpose of the above lines is to provide a description of "the superstitious person" [*den Overtroiske*]. When we read them with reference to Martensen, however, their further and narrower purpose comes into view: to *diagnose* Martensen as a superstitious man—indeed, as "the superstitious person" *par excellence*. We will now examine the details and implications of this diagnosis.

In §1, we learned that the root of superstition lies in its victims' hope that, by harnessing the power of grace, they might free themselves from their dependence on God. The superstitious person, in other words, is a person who fails to accept himself as he is: a human being in need of grace, who must appeal to grace on *God's* terms and not his own. Here, finally, lies the core difference between a superstitious person and a Christian: whereas the superstitious person hopes to manipulate God's aid to his own ends, the Christian "does not insist that God should help him in any way other than God wills . . . He accepts everything by God's grace—grace also" (CD, 64).

Applied to Martensen, the above lines suggest that he has deviated from Christianity by attempting to turn God's grace into a *tool* of human reason. The attraction of theonomy, after all, is that by its aid human reason is supposed to be able to pass beyond the limits of a merely human perspective—and acquire "coknowledge" with God. Yet the latter goal is, to Kierkegaard, the essence of pagan presumptuousness as he has defined it: an effort to "encroach" upon "the eternal essential difference of infinity . . . between God and a human being" (CD, 63). It follows that Martensen's talk of grace, however plentiful and reverent, in no way mitigates his superstition, his presumptuousness, or his paganism. To the contrary: it is precisely Martensen's *theory* of grace that prevents him from *accepting* grace in proper Christian fashion.

Kierkegaard closes his sketch of superstition by outlining a grim prognosis for Martensen, the prognosis of *anxiety*:

> Where are care and anxiety, pale fear, and dreadful shuddering
> more at home than in the captious kingdom of superstition? This
> anxiety no bird has known, not even the fearful, panic-stricken
> bird. . . . Just as grace comes through God to each person who as a
> Christian draws nearer to him, so too anxiety comes through
> himself to the person who presumptuously withdraws from God
> or presumptuously draws near to him. (CD, 68-69)

In the last line, we learn the fates of each of the three main human
types of "The Care of Presumptuousness": the *Christian* who draws
nearer to God (*Tro*); the *disbeliever* (and by extension the *spiritless
person*) who "presumptuously withdraws" from God (*Vantro*); and
the *superstitious person* who "presumptuously draws near" to God
(*Overtro*). The Christian, who properly flees to grace, duly receives
it; but the disbeliever and superstitious person, who do not seek
grace or who seek it improperly, reap only their own "anxiety"
thereby.[35]

Now, what does anxiety have to do with superstition? We have
already encountered Kierkegaard's explanation of the *disbeliever's*
anxiety: just beneath the disbeliever's denial of grace, we saw in §1,
there lurks a desperate fear of God's wrath. What is it, then, that
makes the *superstitious person* anxious? (More to the point: in what
way is *Martensen* motivated by anxiety?) On this issue, the discourse
is surprisingly cryptic. Kierkegaard simply *asserts*, without further
comment, that "the captious kingdom of superstition" is anxiety's
truest "home."

Even if the text of the discourse is here of little help to us,
however, another avenue of interpretive approach still lies open: we
may build on our surmise that Kierkegaard's account of superstition
is directed at Martensen. In §4, we will pursue precisely this avenue

---

[35]This should not be taken to imply that Kierkegaard believed that the provision
of grace is limited to those who seek it properly. To the contrary: Kierkegaard
means to call our attention to the *miraculous* character of grace, which is offered to
all even though none can earn it. As Kierkegaard explained in 1854: "What the old
bishop once said to me is not true—namely, that I spoke as if the others were going
to hell. No, if I can be said to speak at all of going to hell, then I say something like
this: If the others are going to hell, then I am going along with them. But I do not
believe that; on the contrary, I believe that we will all be saved, and this awakens
my deepest wonder" (JP 6:6947).

of approach. We will turn to an older, similar passage, found in Kierkegaard's pseudonymous polemic against Martensen, in which "anxiety" comes to the fore. In so doing, we will not only discover why Kierkegaard is here so quick to associate anxiety with superstition; we will also develop a closer understanding of the taxonomic *structure* of "The Care of Presumptuousness."

4. Martensen's Anxiety — and the Christian's Resort to Grace

One of the fiercest diatribes against Martensen in Kierkegaard's entire pseudonymous literature is that found at the end of chapter IV of *The Concept of Anxiety* (CA, 151-54). Here Kierkegaard has his pseudonym, Vigilius Haufniensis, characterize Martensen as a "demonic" figure in flight from Christian Heaven. In the following excerpt, Martensen appears as Vigilius's exemplar of the fourth, and presumably the worst, form of "demonic" anxiety:

> To study the demonic properly, one needs only to observe how the eternal is conceived in the individuality, and immediately one will be informed. . . . In our times, the eternal is discussed often enough; it is accepted and rejected, and (considering the way in which this is done) the first as well as the second shows lack of inwardness. . . .
>   (a) Some deny the eternal in man. . . .
>   (b) Some conceive of the eternal altogether abstractly. . . .
>   (c) Some bend eternity into time for the imagination. . . . Some envision eternity apocalyptically, pretend to be Dante, while Dante, no matter how much he conceded to the view of imagination, did not suspend the effect of ethical judgment.
>   (d) Or eternity is conceived metaphysically . . . in such a way that the temporal becomes comically preserved in it. . . . If one has reflected thoroughly on the comic, studying it as an expert, constantly keeping one's category clear, one will easily understand that the comic belongs to the temporal, for it is in the temporal that the contradiction is found. . . . In eternity, on the other hand, all contradiction is canceled, the temporal is permeated by and preserved in the eternal, but in this there is no trace of the comical.
>   However, men are not willing to think eternity earnestly but are anxious about it, and anxiety can contrive a hundred evasions. And this is precisely the demonic. (CA, 151-54)

This lengthy text describes four modes of thought about "eternity" — four theories about the reality and nature of "eternal life" (CA, 152) — that can seduce us away from an earnest relation to Christianity's Heaven and Hell. One such mode of thought is, of course, the outright denial of eternity's existence — as in mode (a), which corresponds to the "disbelief" of "The Care of Presumptuousness."[36] Yet mode (a) is by no means the only way in which we can fail "to think eternity earnestly." Instead, our very *acceptance* of Christian eternity can portend an equally dangerous lack of earnestness — depending on "the way in which this [acceptance] is done." (This corresponds to the place of superstition in "The Care of Presumptuousness": specifically, to the fact that the pagan presumptuousness of the superstitious person is in no way mitigated by his *professions* of dependence on grace.)

In modes (b), (c), and (d), accordingly, Vigilius presents three forms of thought that purport to *embrace* Christian eternity; but their nominal embrace of eternity does not make these modes any less "demonic" than the disbelief of mode (a). In mode (b), for example, I define eternity as a tranquility and permanence that surpasses anything that I have ever experienced (CA, 152). This formulation may be accurate enough as a description of Heaven, but it cannot possibly capture the *urgency* with which Christianity demands that I think of Heaven and Hell. Mode (b), in short, leaves me no room to see why I ought to concern *myself* with my eternal life *right now*.

Mode (c) conjures up a poet who mistakes his own poetic depictions of eternity for the genuine article. Vigilius's subsequent references to "apocalyptic" poetry and pretending "to be Dante" make it clear that he here has a very specific poet in mind: namely, the prominent Golden Age poet and playwright Johan Ludvig Heiberg (1791–1860). In 1841, Heiberg had published a play entitled "The Soul After Death": an "apocalyptic comedy" about a remarkably Copenhagenish Hell.[37] In a review of the play that infuriated Kierkegaard, Martensen praised Heiberg for having outshone Dante's *Divine Comedy*.[38] "The entire comic dimension is lacking in

---

[36]In a further anticipation of the psychology of disbelief in "The Care of Presumptuousness," Vigilius explains mode (a) as motivated by a "fear" of the eternal that "nevertheless . . . cannot get rid of it entirely" (CA, 152).

[37]Johan Ludvig Heiberg, *Nye Digte* (Copenhagen: C. A. Reitzel, 1841). On "The Soul After Death" and Martensen's review, see George Pattison, *Kierkegaard, Religion*, 111-12.

[38]Hans Lassen Martensen, "Nye Digte af J. L. Heiberg," in *Fædrelandet*, vol. 2, nos. 398-400 (Jan. 10-12, 1841), cols. 3205-3232: 3210-3212.

the Catholic *Inferno*," Martensen declared.[39] Inasmuch as the latter poem depicts the Christian afterlife in a dark mood of judgment and punishment, it lives up to neither the designation "comedy" nor the epithet "divine."[40] Heiberg's play, on the other hand, embodies a *higher* form of comedy, namely, the authentic Protestant "humor."[41]

In the text of (c), Vigilius scornfully dismisses Martensen's praise of Heiberg. Heiberg's supposed improvement on Dante's masterpiece, Vigilius retorts, amounts to the cheap trick of releasing his characters from "the effect of ethical judgment," by purging the terror of Hell from his comic afterlife. Yet such a view of the afterlife, Vigilius remarks, brings us no closer to true Christian eternity than does mode (b). Indeed, Heiberg's comic cosmos gives me reason to *stop* thinking earnestly about Heaven, Hell, or the Divine judgment—for in it I know that I will ultimately be saved.[42]

With this we arrive at mode (d): Vigilius's frontal attack on Martensen. At the root of Martensen's praise for Heiberg, Vigilius notes, lies a dangerously misguided attempt to conceive of eternity "metaphysically, in such a way that the temporal becomes comically preserved in it." By this Vigilius is referring to Martensen's further claim, alluded to above, that Protestantism allows *its* poets (unlike, say, the Catholic writer Dante) to comprehend eternity from a *higher* perspective—here the immanent world-view of "humor"—which understands all the vicissitudes of earthly life as incorporated, in a truly *divine* kind of *comedy*, into the eternal life of spirit.[43]

---

[39]Hans Lassen Martensen, "Nye Digte af J. L. Heiberg," col. 3210. Here and in all subsequent citations from this text, I rely on the partial translation by K. Brian Söderquist in "Irony and Humor in Kierkegaard's Early Journals: Two Responses to an Emptied World," in *Kierkegaard Studies Yearbook 2003*, ed. Niels Jørgen Cappelørn, Hermann Deuser, and Jon Stewart (Berlin: Walter de Gruyter, 2003) 143-67, 153.

[40]Hans Lassen Martensen, "Nye Digte af J. L. Heiberg," col. 3210.

[41]Hans Lassen Martensen, "Nye Digte af J. L. Heiberg," col. 3210.

[42]Needless to say, Kierkegaard's claim to "believe" that "we will all be saved," mentioned in an earlier note, is rather different from claiming or imagining that one already *knows* the same (JP, 6:6947).

[43]Martensen explains:

In a *divina commedia* which has the principle of humor within it, God would not just be depicted as the righteous judge of the world, but as the absolute spirit, which not only views people through ethical categories, but just as much through metaphysical ones; not just through tragic categories, but just as much

"Protestantism," Martensen writes, "by its philosophic nature, cannot stop with the spirit's concrete forms of actuality, but wishes to comprehend spirit in its pure metaphysical freedom, whose aesthetic expression is the comic."[44]

Vigilius's text in (d) constitutes a passionate retort to these claims. According to Vigilius, Martensen has managed to understand *neither* comedy nor eternity. Had he had any inkling of either, he would surely have acknowledged that "the comic belongs to the temporal, for it is in the temporal that the contradiction is found." In other words, Martensen has failed to see that comedy's place is in our present, human lives, and not in the hereafter. This is because "contradiction" pervades temporal life; but it is utterly absent in eternity, where "all contradiction is canceled."

To grasp Vigilius's point about comedy, contradiction, and eternity, it will help to recall Socrates's famous remark that, following his death, he planned to continue his ironic interrogations in the afterlife (Plato, *Apology*, 41b). For Vigilius, by contrast, Heaven is precisely the place where neither Socratic irony nor Protestant "humor" is necessary: there will be no contradictions left—no Sophism, and no justified sinners—for a Socrates or a Heiberg to expose. Vigilius's eternity is a place of "total recollection," where "what is essential will have the effect of a Lethe on what is unessential." In Vigilius's Christian afterlife, there is only a transparent Heaven and Hell. There are no longer living human beings, who can at once be *peccator* and *justus*; there are only the saved and the damned.

By displacing "the comic" onto the realm of eternity, then, Martensen concocts a false "metaphysical" Heaven. He thereby manages to evade all earnest thought of the Divine *judgment* that he praises Heiberg for omitting; and in so doing, he loses all contact with Christianity's actual doctrine of eternity. Vigilius closes his critique with a stern diagnosis: Martensen suffers from the "demonic" form of anxiety, namely, anxiety *about* eternity. Unwilling or unpre-

---

through comic ones. In the end, it accepts them all in grace because they are not only sinful but also finite, not only evil, but depraved, not only condemnable, but ridiculous; they are not only fallen but they belong to a fallen world. (Hans Lassen Martensen, "Nye Digte af J. L. Heiberg," col. 3210)

[44]Hans Lassen Martensen, "Nye Digte af J. L. Heiberg," col. 3210.

pared to reconcile himself to the thought (and, potentially, the terror) of Christianity's transparent afterlife, Martensen evades this thought by distorting it, by failing "to think eternity earnestly."

On my reading, this diagnosis of Martensen corresponds precisely to, and so illuminates, the attribution of anxiety to "the superstitious person" in "The Care of Presumptuousness." After all, Martensen's theory of humor (Vigilius's target in *The Concept of Anxiety*) and his theory of theonomy (Kierkegaard's target in "The Care of Presumptuousness") are clear variations on a single theme. Both theories purport to extract a body of *higher* knowledge — an immanent view of God's cosmos; a humorous God's-eye-view of Heaven, sin, and redemption — from the presumption that grace *has already been* furnished, whether in the revelation of Christianity's truth, on the one hand, or in the justification of sinners and their admission to Heaven, on the other.

From Kierkegaard's point of view, this entire mode of thought is decidedly un-Christian. It amounts to an *anxious* attempt to use the effects of grace for the ends of human reason. In the one case, Martensen is anxious, perhaps unconsciously so, about his own relation to Heaven and to justifying grace; and so he thinks of eternity and speaks about it as though it were possible for human beings to understand it (in "humor") and so master it. In the other case (and here we may fill in the blank left in "The Care of Presumptuousness"), Martensen is anxious, perhaps unconsciously so, about his own relation to Christianity's truth and to enlightening grace (*gratia illuminans*); and so he thinks of this truth and speaks about it as though it were possible for human beings to understand it (via "theonomy") and so master it. In both cases — whether what is at issue is admission to Heaven or the apprehension of God's truth — what provokes Martensen's anxiety is the thought that no living human being can *comprehend* the workings of grace except by resorting to grace. And in both cases, Martensen's anxiety manifests itself as an attempt to wrest control of grace by comprehending it.

The Christian of "The Care of Presumptuousness," meanwhile, is the opposite number to the anxious Martensen. The Christian faces squarely the exigency that Martensen cannot bear to accept, namely, that human beings cannot progress beyond our abject need of grace, for "to need God is a human being's perfection" (CD, 64). Whereas Martensen reacts to his dependence on God's grace with anxiety, the

Christian is "satisfied" with his state of dependence: he "craves only" to remain so satisfied (CD, 64). The Christian certainly does not seek grace as a means to any end *higher* than grace itself. Rather, even though it "at first glance seems so meager and humiliating," the Christian is content with grace, and indeed regards grace as "the highest and most blessed good" for a human being (CD, 65).

In all of these ways, the Christian and the "superstitious man" are disclosed as polar opposites; and thus Martensen emerges not only as one of Vigilius's demoniacs, but also as Kierkegaard's superstitious pagan *par excellence*. I conclude: When we read the discourse alongside *The Concept of Anxiety*, we find in "The Care of Presumptuousness" a thoroughgoing critique of Martensen's theological standpoint. This critique is particularly valuable, in my view, because it comes complete with a diagnosis of the *anxiety* that motivates Martensen's error—together with a constructive account of Kierkegaard's Christian alternative.

In both *The Concept of Anxiety* and "The Care of Presumptuousness," finally, Kierkegaard situates his critique of Martensen within a broad *taxonomy* of forms of deviation from Christianity. While the details and methods of these two texts' taxonomies differ, they share a common goal: each alerts us to the many ways in which *anxiety about grace* can creep into our lives and carry us away from Christianity. That this anxiety is apparently found even and especially in *Martensen*, Denmark's premier theorist of grace, ought immediately to give us pause. It ought to remind us that, as Kierkegaard saw the matter, there is a world of difference between seeking grace properly and improperly—and between calling oneself a Christian and being one.

3

The Genius and the Saint:
The Spiritual Teachings of Kierkegaard
in Christian Discourses and Thérèse of Lisieux
in Story of a Soul

Louise Carroll Keeley

Kierkegaard's spiritual teachings in part one of *Christian Discourses* (1848) bear a remarkable but unlikely resemblance to the spiritual insights of Thérèse of Lisieux in the three manuscripts which constitute her *Story of A Soul* (1897). In this essay I extract and compare their positive teachings using Kierkegaard's discourses as the spine of the analysis. Though Thérèse's reflections lack Kierkegaard's dialectical rigor and are the product of a spiritual rather than a philosophical maturity, her insights match his fairly closely. Given their astonishing differences in temperament, religious background, and circumstance, one would expect their religious views to diverge or even collide. Instead, one meets with more commonality than difference. Certainly one explanation for this commonality is their shared reliance upon central texts, notably the Gospels and *The Imitation of Christ* by Thomas à Kempis.[1] But this fact alone cannot account for their strangely consistent insight. If not, what can?

In the seven discourses which constitute "The Cares of the Pagans," Kierkegaard seems to showcase a polemical side. A closer look reveals that more positive lessons undergird Kierkegaard's architectonic of pagan cares. The birds of the air and the lilies of the field model behaviors which, when recast in the life of the Christian, offer concrete spiritual guidance and direction. Although Kierke-

---

[1] See Cornelio Fabro, C.P.S. in "Faith and Reason in Kierkegaard's Dialectic" in *A Kierkegaard Critique*, ed. Howard A. Johnson and Niels Thulstrup (Chicago: Henry Regnery Company, 1962) 199 n 29: "Kierkegaard already grasped intuitively this principle of Christian perfection, which some years later, Ste. Thérèse of Lisieux was to expound in a more serene mood, but in an analogous Christological sense, derived from the same sources, the Gospel and the *Imitation* [*of Christ*]."

gaard does not name these Christian concepts with the same specificity that he names their corresponding cares, he analyzes them with comparable rigor. These concepts, in order of appearance and tied sequentially to the seven discourses, are: *trust in God's provident care, thinking the thought of eternity, being oneself before God, becoming like a child again, being satisfied with God's grace, grasping the eternal in the present day, and perfect obedience.* Thérèse's profound insights into these same Christian teachings confirm, expand and, in my judgment, spiritually deepen the concepts which Kierkegaard examines with such care.

I begin by offering an account of the logic of the structure of part one of *Christian Discourses* and then turn to the essay's two major concerns, namely, an analysis of their seven shared spiritual teachings and a brief assessment of their challenge to bourgeois piety. Kierkegaard's rejection of Christendom's bourgeois piety is well known as is his sharpening of that critique in the years after the publication of *Christian Discourses.* Thérèse's refinement and deepening of a late nineteenth century Catholic bourgeois piety is less well known. Both elude the grip of their society's conventional piety by making a profoundly inward turn, where interiority, compelled by persistence, surrenders its truths. In both cases it is the self's encounter with God experienced as Love which yields these insights. In my view, Kierkegaard veers off this course toward the end of his life as his speech became more vitriolic, his judgment more severe, his condemnations more fierce. Thérèse, on the other hand, remains faithful to her conviction that "love is repaid by love alone,"[2] even in the twin grip of spiritual trial and imminent physical death.

Overview

Bruce Kirmmse argues in *Kierkegaard in Golden Age Denmark* that *Christian Discourses* has a polemical purpose.[3] He notes in particular that parts one and three indict the established order in Christendom.

---

[2]See *Story of a Soul: The Autobiography of St. Thérèse of Lisieux,* trans. John Clarke, O.C.D., 3rd ed. (Washington DC: ICS Publications, 1996) 195; hereafter cited as SS.

[3]Bruce H. Kirmmse, *Kierkegaard in Golden Age Denmark* (Bloomington: Indiana University Press, 1990) 340-58; hereafter cited as Kirmmse, *Golden Age* .

The title of part one, "The Cares of the Pagans," reminds Christendom's self proclaimed "Christians" that their anxieties are the cares of heathens. In effect, one is a pagan if one shares the cares of a pagan and makes no honest admission that one does. Coupled with the "dark saying(s)" (CD, 93) of part two and the "thoughts that wound from behind" (CD, 161) of part three, the tone of the text is one of urgency, peril, indictment.

But there is another side of *Christian Discourses*, part one, which in my view, though less prominent, is more important. Underlying Kierkegaard's sharp polemic against those who live like pagans in Christendom, he explores seven Christian concepts which communicate how the Christian should live. These positive teachings are the focus of the present essay.

Christian Discourses is divided into four major parts and each part in turn is divided into seven discourses. Each discourse in part one has an identical structure: (1) an analysis of why the bird (or the lily or both) does not have the care under discussion (2) an account of why the Christian does not have this anxiety (3) an acknowledgement that the pagan does have this worry and (4) a concluding admonition to study the lily and the bird.

The whole is carefully constructed. The care of poverty and the care of abundance concern the proper spiritual attitude toward external goods. In discourses three and four the focus turns toward the world's evaluation of what constitutes lowliness and what loftiness. The fifth discourse communicates the cure for all these follies: complete reliance upon the grace of God. The worry which discourse six addresses presumes that the present (and its reliance upon God's grace) has been breached: its worry is the anxiety about tomorrow, all forms of which are reducible to self-torment. Finally, in the seventh discourse the learner is urged to decide now to heed the lily and the bird whose spiritual pedagogy counsels the practice of obedience.

In each of the seven discourses of part one, Kierkegaard recounts a care or anxiety that afflicts the pagan which the Christian, by definition, avoids. He begins each discourse with a Scriptural reference cautioning against various provocations to worry, and ends each reflection by observing that "the pagans seek all these things." The seeking of the pagan originates and terminates in worry. Seeking fueled by worry exacerbates worry. Anxiety, left to itself, becomes its own best accelerant. The first point of instruction is therefore negative: do not worry. Worry demonstrates that what the pagan seeks—namely, control over one's own life and destiny, with no dependence whatsoever on Another—is doomed to fail. When worry takes action to secure its own future its failure is constantly on display since no one is really independent. I am reminded of the game that children play where all make together a tower of hands; as the hand on the bottom is withdrawn, it repositions itself quickly on top of the heap of hands, again and again until, in a frenzy of speed and laughter, the pile of hands completely collapses. The wreckage reveals what was true all along: the structure could not secure itself. Similarly, despite the pagan's best efforts and considerable worries, one can never really stand security for oneself.

The Care of Poverty / Trust in God's Provident Care

All seven cares of the pagan have this in common: an unholy bid for independence, a refusal to submit, a desire to be on one's own, a refusal to concede one's ultimate dependence. Not surprisingly, given worry's inexhaustibility, each worry has its peculiar specialty and zeal.

The pagan who has the anxiety of poverty wants to be rich. Ironically, the very effort to enrich oneself diminishes the self. Distrust is the foundational attitude of this care. The pagan refuses to believe that one's life is "the object of anyone else's care" (CD, 17), preferring the skepticism of distrust to the confidence of trust no matter how poorly the undertaking proceeds.

The worry of poverty is not merely concerned with satisfying the necessities of life, securing one's livelihood, insuring a kind of general welfare, or even maintaining a certain standard of living. Instead, fully fueled, the person in the grip of this worry seeks wealth. The logic of this anxiety is such that plenty does not suffice; one covets everything. Hence Kierkegaard observes that "the one who wants to be rich walks in temptation everywhere" (CD, 20). The goods of the world are no longer blessings that signal the presence of the Benefactor; instead, the pagan heeds them as things to be consumed or used up, like a glutton feeding without the provocation of hunger.[4]

Kierkegaard thinks that the anxiety of poverty leads to slavish-ness and the ruination of the self which had made itself so important by asking constantly about itself ("What shall I eat? What shall I drink?"). In contrast to the provisions of the bird — always "enough," no matter how substantial or meager — the pagan's bread is never thought sufficient. Unlike the miracle of the loaves and fishes where a little proves enough for all, the pagan's expectation is essentially antimiraculous: plenty is found to be inadequate even for one. "To damn oneself and one's life to this slaving" (CD, 21) is the inevitable result: because there is never enough, one must constantly procure more, as if to meet some impossibly large quota that is being used up faster than it can be replenished. Depression is the inevitable result: a slave to the getting and the keeping, who succeeds ultimately at neither, this pagan is reminiscent of Callicles in Plato's *Gorgias* whose unhappy soul is compared to a leaky sieve.[5]

In contrast to the depressive heaviness of the pagan, weighed down by the burden of acquisition, the bird is carefree and light and resourceful in discovering "enough." Most importantly, the bird points to the perfection of these attitudes in the Christian.

The Christian (who is, by definition, without the anxiety of poverty) is rich in heavenly wealth. Whereas the pagan focuses slavishly on the world, the Christian attends to God: "In connection with all danger, the main thing is to be able to get away from the thought of it. Now, you cannot get away from poverty, but you can get away from the thought of it by continually thinking about God" (CD, 21). The pagan is preoccupied with *things*; the Christian sees these things in their character as *gifts*. Thus the Christian seeks the Source of these blessings, not the things themselves. In contrast to the mistrust of the impoverished pagan, the Christian relies upon the Benefactor's provident care.

Kierkegaard assures the reader frequently that the lily and the bird are teachers, not judges. Neither the bird nor the lily have

---

[4]For interesting discussions of the relationship between obsessive, addictive, and dependent attitudes see *Addiction and Spirituality*, ed. Oliver J. Morgan and Merle Jordan (St. Louis: Chalice Press, 1999) and Gerald G. May, M.D., *Addiction and Grace* (San Francisco: Harper Collins Publishers, 1988).

[5]Plato, *Gorgias*, 493a-494b.

earned any of the privileges they enjoy; they simply find themselves on the receiving end of God's gratuitous blessing. In the Christian's case the impulse to earn God's affection must be eradicated, too. Instead, the Christian couples trust in God's provident care with a conviction that one neither can nor should try to earn God's love. This hybrid is comparable to the attitude of the well-loved child who learns to trust before the prospects of earning or repayment are ever posed. Trust trumps earning when the child's foundational experience is love. When this is absent or only partially true, the self cedes room for earning to elbow its way into place. Now the self is poised for an ongoing contest between love and fear, trust and mistrust, confidence and doubt.

If the Christian, for whatever reason, detects a trace of the desire to earn, Kierkegaard would advise him to turn away from himself altogether; after all, though one is preoccupied with earning love one's preoccupation is still with one's *own* earning. Instead, Kierkegaard urges him to meditate on the reality that God's unconditional love has brought this self into being in the first place.[6] It is perhaps surprising that this is not so easy to do; most of those who want most of all to pay the price of admission, as it were, no matter what the cost, can manage only with difficulty to give up trying to earn one's way. Why is this so hard? Because it means giving up one's sense of unworthiness which one has become accustomed to, even enamored of, as one's unclarified but foundational experience of the self. The self, though beloved by God, scorns God's judgment in favor of its own, preferring its sense of its own badness to God's goodness in loving it nonetheless. Its insistence upon its own badness is essentially a way to rebuff love, and love's "appalling and incomprehensible mercy."[7]

The Christian who "understands that one's life is the object of Another's care" (CD, 17) is emboldened by a confident expectation of being always on the receiving end of God's blessing. This daily bread, however much and in whatever form it is offered, is welcomed as an extraordinary feast because it is given by the Giver

---

[6]See David G. Benner, *Surrender to Love: Discovering the Heart of Christian Spirituality* (Illinois: InterVarsity Press, 2003).

[7]Franz Wright, "To John Wieners: Elegy and Response," poem in *Walking to Martha's Vineyard* (New York: Alfred A. Knopf, 2005) 15.

of all good gifts: after all, "does not even an otherwise humble gift, an insignificant little something, have infinite worth for the lover when it is from the beloved" (CD, 15).

Thérèse's Teaching on Trust

In Thérèse's *Story of a Soul*, trust in God's provident care undergirds everything. Proceeding from trust, the double coupling of humility and love, and surrender and mercy emerge. By contrast, while trust figures prominently in the first discourse of *Christian Discourses*, thereafter it recedes. In Thérèse's manuscript, trust is utterly pervasive.

Trust in God's provident care is evident in two ways. First, Thérèse is confident that God's abiding care sustains her in every aspect of her *ordinary daily life*. Second, in her *spiritual* ventures she manifests an absolute trust in God. Her radical trust in this second respect forms the heart of Thérèsian spirituality.

Thérèse rarely, if ever, felt stirred to worry whether or not her earthly provisions were "enough," since there was usually no prior inadequacy. But she wrote even in austerity: I "do not feel the pinch of poverty since I never lack anything" (SS, 217). Because she understood that "nothing is mine" (SS, 226), she had "no difficulty in never reclaiming them when they are sometimes taken away" (SS, 233). Thérèse's spiritual observation is reminiscent of the bird's more mundane lesson in *Christian Discourses*: "I have frequently noticed that Jesus doesn't want me to lay up provisions; He nourishes me at each moment with a totally new food; I find it within me without my knowing how it is there" (SS, 165).

Although *The Story of a Soul* is a litany of trust, that trust is not directed toward procuring the goods of the world. Instead, in Thérèsian spirituality to trust means *to confide oneself to Love, the absolutely trustworthy One*. With the abandon of a skydiver in freefall, one commends oneself to God, whole and entire, no strings attached. Thérèse excels at this, and in doing so confirms certain of Kierkegaard's insights concerning the spiritual life.

Thérèse calls this radical life of trust her "little way," the "way of spiritual childhood, the way of trust and absolute surrender" (SS, xi). Spiritual childhood, as Thérèse understands it, involves a relation of dependence which, stripped of any pejorative connotations, is really a form of humility. When humility is missing inordinate attachments multiply; when humility is present, one sees aright one's own limitations and makes every effort to resist lying about them. When humility is coupled with love, as it was in Thérèse's case, one sees aright from both sides: one knows one's own sinfulness but trusts that God's mercy surpasses it; one realizes that one's own efforts can never achieve what Love manages effortlessly. This coupling of humility and love, which characterizes Thérèsian spirituality, prompts her always to look away from herself to attend to God, confident that God will in turn attend to her. Moreover, humility and love are unfairly matched, with love being the stronger of the two.[8] Thus humility's conclusions about the *self* are trumped by love's conclusions about *God*. God can and will do for the striving self what that self cannot achieve on its own.[9]

Although Thérèse recommends "bold surrender" (SS, 198), she understands it as "the surrender of the little child who sleeps without fear in its Father's arms" (SS, 188). The child is able to manage this, without taking thought, because the parent is experienced as trustworthy. God's trustworthiness is not limited to a present sense of ease. God's love communicates "an unspeakable foresight" (SS, 84), an "anticipating Mercy" (SS, 259), and thus reassures one concerning the future. Nor does the past, no matter how vile, undermine her trust. Instead Thérèse writes, "*even though I had on my conscience all the sins that can be committed*, I would go, my heart broken by sorrow, and throw myself into Jesus' arms, for I know how much he loves the prodigal child" (SS, 259; emphasis added). But unlike the

---

[8]The primacy of love in Thérèsian spirituality is evident throughout *Story of a Soul*. In Manuscript B—she identifies her discipline as "the science of love" (SS, 187) and proclaims that "my vocation is Love" (SS, 194). In Thérèse's view, "it is only love that makes us acceptable to God" (SS, 188). These passages could be multiplied many times over without exaggerating the preeminence of love.

[9]Thérèse's confidence in this is unshakable: "I don't count on my merits, since I have none," she confides, but trusts instead in "God alone, (who) content with my weak efforts, will raise me to Himself" (SS, 72). In Manuscript C, Thérèse uses the imagery of a lift or elevator to explain how this is possible: "I am too small to climb the rough stairway of perfection" (SS, 207), but since God does not inspire desires whose realization is impossible, "the elevator which must raise me to heaven is your arms, O Jesus! And for this I had no need to grow up, but rather I had to remain little" (SS, 208).

prodigal child who was received home with much rejoicing when he expected to be greeted with disdain, Thérèse expects to be met by merciful love.

Thérèse ends Manuscript C mid-sentence, too weakened by illness to continue. Her final words are "I go to Him with confidence and love" (SS, 259). Elsewhere she says plainly: "I know too well what to believe concerning His Mercy and His Love" (SS, 259 n 353) to be moved by any manner of fear. No one, no sin, can frighten her into repudiating what she knows with absolute certainly: when humility encounters love, and surrender meets with mercy, fear is utterly defeated. Earlier Thérèse wrote: "The Lord is so good to me that it is quite impossible for me to fear him" (SS, 250). "My nature was such that fear made me recoil; with love not only did I advance, I actually flew" (SS, 174).

The Care of Abundance / Thinking the Thought of Eternity

The care of abundance that troubles the rich pagan is an anxiety that originates in the comparative. Ordinarily, the pagan worries that others have more than he has, necessitating an interminable game of catch up. The pagan who relies upon the measure of the comparative to assess the adequacy of his own wealth has yoked himself to a useless method: there is always someone whose wealth outstrips his own.

The rich pagan is exceedingly cognizant of his wealth: he "neither knows nor wants to know about anything else" (CD, 33). But when thought occupies itself exclusively with wealth it exacerbates anxiety. No matter how rich the pagan is one can never be rich enough. One wants, in addition, to go on being rich, secured against every eventuality, especially any diminishment of one's wealth. Morbidly preoccupied with money to the point of disinterest in everything else, Kierkegaard compares him to a "glutton who starves in abundance," a "squint eyed miser who never looks up from his money except to see enviously that someone else owns more" (CD, 34).

Unlike the pagan who is hunkered down with his treasure, the bird is "a traveler" (CD, 24). It seeks as it always has "enough" and no more. The bird has no need to gather in a supply of riches to offset some future lean time. It is a traveler and thus expects to abide long enough only to secure its bread of "enough." If, however, the bird finds itself in abundance its ignorance preserves it from knowing this. Thus the bird cannot be anxious on its behalf.

Ignorance prevents the Christian, too, from having the care of abundance but unlike the bird whose ignorance is simply given the Christian must *acquire* ignorance. How does the Christian achieve this? By resorting to "thought and the power of thought" (CD, 26) which "takes aim at the thought of possession" (CD, 28).

Kierkegaard believes that it is delusional to think that one can possess anything at all. He argues that we all already know this but we manage to repress our understanding in order to press ever more insistently our urgent claim upon things: "everyone really knows well enough that in the more profound sense no human being owns anything, that no one has anything except what is given to him" (CD, 28). The giver—or in Kierkegaard's surprising phrase, "the owner" (CD, 29)—is always God. Though God may entrust something to a human being "on loan" (CD, 29), the beneficiary cannot claim to possess it in any permanent sense since "the essential feature (of possessions) is their losableness" (CD, 27). Losableness can be accomplished in two ways. First, a thing can be lost, forsaken, used up, forgotten, misplaced, or recovered by someone else. But losableness can take a second direction, too—namely, the human being can be taken away from one's things by death. This variant of losableness constitutes a complete break with possessiveness. Even the body, which had seemed to be more one's own than anything else, forsakes the self in death—illustrating, in its corruption, that even it can not be permanently claimed.

The Christian understands that his wealth is "on loan" (CD, 29) by keeping the thought of one's own death before one always. Kierkegaard explains that one complies best when one concentrates faithfully on the thought of the possibility of one's own death this 'very day.' In telling oneself "I can perhaps die tonight, 'this very night,'" (CD, 27), one pulls the rug of tomorrow out from underneath oneself and reminds oneself that one's days are carefully numbered. It does this more pointedly, but with no more certainty, than the thought of one's death many years hence. If "the rich Christian bears in mind he knows it" and "renders to himself an account of his knowing" (CD, 29) he manages to have wealth while being spared wealth's anxiety.

The poor Christian does not have to take this additional step. He begins at the place where the rich Christian eventually arrives after maneuvering to get there by thinking constantly the thought of death. The Christian who has earthly wealth must take this long and terrible thought-detour. Because the poor Christian, like the bird, already understands that he is a traveler, not destined for permanent residence in this world, he is spared the rich Christian's grueling thought-exercise. Still, it is a matter of indifference whether one begins in earthly poverty or earthly wealth: the one who seeks aright seeks the Giver not the gifts.

Kierkegaard does suggest, however, that the wealthy Christian can realize a "double joy from doing good" (CD, 32) by imitating the magnanimity of the Benefactor. The wealthy Christian, who uses his riches in this way, becomes the "confidant" (CD, 33) of God.

In his analysis of the care of abundance, Kierkegaard urges the aspiring Christian to become ignorant concerning one's wealth by refusing all comparative measures, reflecting on the essential losableness of things, and thinking the thought of death. One does this best by practicing the art of remembering something else—or, more accurately, Someone Else—the source, course, and end of all that is good.

Thérèse's Teaching on Thinking the Thought of Eternity

Although Thérèse worries that she might have been an easy target for this care if she had been introduced to the world's pleasures less cautiously, this assessment seems more self-critical than accurate. She knew from her earliest days that perishable riches could not satisfy the deepest longings of the human heart: "God gave me the grace of knowing the world just enough to despise it and separate myself from it" (SS, 73). This knowledge, even if partly instinctive, flourished in an environment where contempt for the world was paramount.[10] Not only does she show virtually no attraction to material things, she is drawn from her earliest days to the eternal. In fact, thinking the thought of eternity comes so naturally to her that she exemplifies the very spiritual attitude that

[10]Ida Friederike Görres, *The Hidden Face: A Study of St. Therese of Lisieux* (San Francisco: Ignatius Press, 1959), 31; hereafter cited as Görres, *The Hidden Face*.

Kierkegaard describes. Although she does not provide a conceptual account of this, it is evident in the numerous biographical details she does provide.

Alert, too, to the danger of human relationships that vie with God for the beloved's affection, she refused to be moved by human eminence: "Close up, I saw that 'all that glistens is not gold,' and I understood the words of the *Imitation* 'Be not solicitous for the shadow of a great name, not for acquaintance with many, nor for the particular love of individuals'" (SS, 121). Although she later develops a profound understanding of charity (SS, 233-259), at this point she fixes on affections that she regards as unsuitable: "how can a heart given over to the affection of creatures be intimately united with God?" (SS, 83). Therese had no talent for making friends, especially in her youth where friendship occasioned more bitterness than sweetness. Still, she regards this incapacity as a special grace: if subsidiary love of creatures steers one's affections, she reasons, love of God can be correspondingly reduced.[11]

Although Thérèse knew that inordinate attachments entrap, she found within herself a dispositional and spiritual attraction to the eternal that made such entrapment unlikely. In her case nature and grace conspired to produce unanimity of desire and desired. At an extremely early age, without formal instruction, she practices a form of contemplative prayer that betrays something more than natural introversion. Moreover, thinking the thought of eternity is, in Thérèse's manuscript, often coupled with the thought of death. She laments those who "didn't think about death enough," who failed to see "that all is vanity and vexation of spirit under the sun, that the only good is to love God with all one's heart and to be poor in spirit here on earth" (SS, 73). This preoccupation with human finitude is not morbidity disguised as depth, nor pathology dressed up as insight. Instead, death fixes one's thought on one's eternal prospects, where it belongs. Not surprisingly, praying at the grave of her mother is memorable for personal and spiritual reasons, for no other place manages to make the argument against triviality so effectively. Kierkegaard, too, certainly understood this as his numerous

---

[11]For different views see Augustine, *Confessions*, IV.iv(7)-IV.x(15), trans. Henry Chadwick (Oxford: Oxford University Press, 1991) 56-63 and C. S. Lewis, *The Four Loves* (New York: Harcourt Brace, 1960) 168-73.

graveside reflections make clear.

The Care of Lowliness / Being Oneself before God

The lowly pagan is in despair. Despair is the condition of not being satisfied with being oneself. This care originates in his fascination with what " 'the others' make of him" (CD, 44). It terminates there, too, when he "sinks under comparison's enormous weight" (CD, 45) convinced that he is nothing at all.

The pagan's fundamental affirmation is "'I am nothing and will never become anything'" (CD, 46). But why does he detest himself so much? How does it happen that one's pronouncement concerning one's self—namely, "I am nothing"—is itself a radical negation of the self? And why, though his affirmation is a negation, does he cling "tightly to being nothing" even when "he really is not only something but is much" (CD, 46)?

Kierkegaard argues that the lowly pagan errs by adopting the comparative as the measure of the self. By establishing "the others" as the criterion for the self, one submits to being "what 'the others' make of him and what he makes of himself by being only before others" (CD, 44). The pagan credits their judgment that he does not matter, appropriating their assessment uncritically as his own. Compared to these worldly and advantaged others, one's own wretchedness stands out. What they are reminds one of what one is not. This illicit importing of the comparative as the standard for self-assessment assures the self's continual recession until one's care is "being nothing—indeed, not being at all" (CD, 44). In Kierkegaard's words, "he clings tightly to being nothing" (CD, 46) even though being nothing is precisely one's torture. Masochism amplifies despair.

The bird "is what it is, is itself, is satisfied with being itself, is contented with itself" (CD, 37). Its innocent celebration of itself is not an achievement but a given, not an outcome but a starting point. It is what it is firsthand, not subsequent to learning who "the others" are. Because the bird does not recognize the distinction lowly/eminent, the grey sparrow does not eye the golden one enviously. Instead, it revels innocently in being itself. The bird's lesson, though easy for it to achieve, takes spiritual courage to duplicate. The bird teaches that being itself matters—the very lesson that the lowly pagan, as if to spite himself, rejects.

Unlike the bird who is oblivious to the distinction between the lowly and the esteemed, the lowly Christian understands the difference but refuses to be caught in its "slyly concealed snare" (CD, 39). The lowly Christian understands that "in order to begin to be oneself, a human being first of all must be finished with what the others are and by that find out then what he himself is — in order to be that" (CD, 39). Although the lowly Christian realizes that he is counted among the lowly from the perspective of the world, he refuses the ultimacy of that perspective, privileging, instead, the true criterion of existing before God. The pagan exists in relation to others; attuned to the subtleties of grade and rank and caught up in that calculative mindset, he desecrates the very self he seeks assurance about from these others. The bird, innocently preoccupied with itself, is sweet contentment. But only the Christian exists consciously before God, where authentic being oneself becomes possible.

A person can only be oneself "by being in the one who is in himself" (CD, 40). But this is God. Because God knows in and through God's self "what each human being is in himself" (CD, 40), to be oneself is to be before God. Thus the requirement is infinitely ratcheted up.

This being oneself before God is accomplished in and through a redoubling (*Fordoblelse*) that other creatures (like the bird and the lily) cannot do. First, the lowly Christian is a human being who is made in the image and likeness of God. To exist consciously before the Creator God means to understand oneself as made. Just as the bird is what it is, in a roughly analogous way the human being is what it is, although the human being understands what the bird simply embodies. But the human being, in the present case, is also a Christian, and this requires *becoming*. This is the point of redoubling: in this regard "he is not like the bird, because the bird is what it is" (CD, 41). "But one cannot be a Christian in this way; if one is a Christian, one must have become that . . . the lowly Christian was a human being, just as the bird was a bird, but then he became a Christian" (CD, 41).

Kierkegaard describes redoubling as a two-step process: "as a human being he was created in God's image (*Billede*)" (CD, 41); in this respect one is summoned to be oneself before God. "But as a Christian he has God as the prototype (*Forbillede*)" (CD, 41), too, and *imitating* the prototype asks something more than *imaging* the

Creator. To imitate Jesus, who is the revelation of the love of God, means to embody that same love in one's life, to be in one's own person a living witness to that Love. It is, in effect, an invitation to relationship: "he believes that this prototype, if he continually struggles to resemble him, will bring him again, and in an even more intimate way, into kinship with God" (CD, 43).

Given the lure and the rigor of the invitation, it is not surprising that Kierkegaard calls the prototype an "unsettling thought . . . a summons . . . a rigorous requirement . . . an incentive . . . a promise . . . and a fulfillment" (CD, 41-42). Imitation produces intimacy, both terrifying and joyful. Neither the pagan with his constant complaint that "'I am nothing,'" nor the bird with its unreflective sense of its own mattering can live in Christian intimacy with God.

Thérèse's Teaching on Being Oneself before God

Thérèse, too, advocates consenting to be oneself before God, exactly as one is, with no provisions whatsoever for comparison. Like Kierkegaard, Thérèse understands that God alone is the criterion of the self such that to be in right relation to God "consists in doing His will, in being what He wills us to be" (SS, 14).

Although Thérèse was recognized as a Doctor of the Roman Catholic Church by Pope John Paul II in 1997, the language of Thérèse's spiritual narrative is decidedly personal and nondoctrinal; it has little of the analytical precision of Thomas, the psychological expansiveness of Augustine, or the intellectual subtlety of Teresa of Avila. Although Thérèse has a natural psychological acuteness and a sparkling, even playful, intelligence, there is something *minor* about her story that runs counter to the grand ideas and personalities of the spiritual classics. Indeed, Thérèse calls her teachings her "little way," and insists, repeatedly that it consists in becoming *small*. To the contemporary ear, this self-estimate sounds annoyingly modest, even self-denigrating and false. For Thérèse, however, it is neither. It is, instead, an attempt to articulate what it means to be oneself before God.

Thérèse's metaphors feature, without exception, ordinary, unremarkable things — the kind of things that children might notice but that adults typically overlook. She introduces her memoir as "the springtime story of a little white flower" (SS, 13). Occasionally she describes herself as Jesus' "little plaything" (SS, 136) a tiny ball that Jesus could do with as He wished. Similarly, she imagines herself as a small boat that carries the sleeping child Jesus, oblivious to the vessel's adriftedness. Finally, "I look upon myself as a weak little bird, with only a light down as covering" (SS, 198). In a letter that she wrote to herself on the occasion of her profession, she asks to "be looked upon as one to be trampled underfoot, forgotten like your little grain of sand" (SS, 275). It is "extreme littleness" (SS, 198) that she attends to when she "sees herself as she really is in God's eyes: a poor little thing, nothing at all" (SS, 206).[12] Even when Thérèse unexpectedly acknowledges some special privilege, she compares herself to a pack animal selected to carry the sacred relics: "if I think this inspiration belongs to me, I would be like 'the donkey carrying the relics' who believed the reverence paid to the saints was being directed to him" (SS, 234).

The psychologically astute contemporary reader may find these diminutives offputting; after all, their cumulative effect is one of a sort of neurotic minimizing, an anorexia of the spirit where the more slender the self is, the more credible. But I think this reading is essentially unfair to Thérèse. Her vocabulary of littleness testifies not to self-hatred but to the immense glory of God. If self-hatred underlay these claims, one would find the typical marks of self-denigration — namely, repulsion for the self, resentment for one's lot, resolve that someone else must pay, bitterness that holds fast to the very self that one despises, as if to punish oneself all the more, like the pirates' torture of belting a live prisoner face to face with a corpse as it decays. Instead, in Thérèse's case, it is important to remember that miniature things — especially birds and flowers — are the things that she always loved best. Because she understands herself in relationship to God, it is impossible to find a diminutive that errs in the direction of modesty. Although it is true that other souls may be greater than hers, this barely interests her: instead, she explains how such apparent partiality on God's part might be understood so that every soul, from the smallest to the most comprehensive, can fulfill

---

[12]There is another side of Thérèse that is less frequently remarked upon but is, in my view, compatible with the first. "I feel the vocation of the warrior, the priest, the apostle, the doctor, the martyr," (SS, 192) she writes, wondering "how can I combine these contrasts?" (SS, 192).

its spiritual potential and achieve sanctity.

In *Story of a Soul* Thérèse recalls one of her earliest lessons. When a thimble is compared to a tumbler, it is evident that the latter can contain more water but it cannot be said to be more full. The thimble and the tumbler are equally full since "it was impossible to put in more water than they could contain" (SS, 45). Similarly in the case of souls: the littlest has "nothing to envy" (SS, 45) in the greatest, since both can be as full of God's grace as it is possible for them to be. Thérèse makes the same point when she compares souls to flowers: the greatest souls are like roses or lilies, elegant beauties who compel attention and awaken desire. But even common flowers, like daisies and violets, are beautiful in their frail simplicity: "these must be content . . . to give joy to God's glances when he looks down at his feet" (SS, 14). Just as a violet should not aspire to be a rose since this would mean not wanting to be itself, so too the holy soul must consent to be itself before God.

In Thérèse's text, as in Kierkegaard's, being oneself before God and refusing to import the comparative as a measure go together. Thérèse admits that she was once troubled by the fact that God seemed partial to particular souls, a surefire way to seed unhealthy spiritual competition. She explains: "I wondered for a long time why God has preferences, why all souls don't receive an equal amount of graces" (SS, 13). In particular, the granting of great graces to great sinners — like St. Paul and St. Augustine — left her baffled. She determines that it is God's prerogative, not human worthiness, to differentiate between souls: "he does not call those who are worthy but those whom he pleases" (SS, 13). Just as a painter may select a worn out or defective brush to use, so too God may choose whomever God pleases. Besides, no soul is shortchanged, either in itself or with respect to God's attentiveness to it: "our Lord's love is revealed as perfectly in the most simple soul who resists his grace in nothing as in the most excellent soul" (SS, 14). Indeed, "our Lord is occupied particularly with each soul as though there were no others like it" (SS, 14). Given God's condescension, if there is any privilege to be had it is awarded to the littlest who is content to spend itself in love of God: "I feel that if You found a soul weaker and littler than mine, which is impossible, You would be pleased to grant it still greater favors, provided it abandoned itself with total confidence to Your Infinite Mercy" (SS, 200).

The Care of Loftiness / Becoming like a Child Again

The eminent pagan, like his lowly counterpart, assesses his stature in comparison with other human beings by using the criterion of earthly loftiness. Unlike the lowly pagan who believes himself to be diminished by the comparison, the lofty pagan is confident that the comparison proves his superiority. Low and lofty alike are mistaken in positing the earthly as the criterion for assessing the self.

Kierkegaard's view is that earthly loftiness is essentially false because it carves out distinctions within a frame of reference that is itself ungrounded: "at the base of all this lies nothing" (CD, 56). Whoever uses the sliding scale of the earthly can pinpoint one's relative earnings and status, but it is an assessment made in a vacuum, without the true grounding that only the eternal can provide.

Thus Kierkegaard describes the lofty pagan as living obliviously atop an abyss, an abyss with all the trimmings of a grave. In one's constant "craving to become more and more" (CD, 57) — to increase one's worldly stature and earnings, to add to one's holdings and influence — one protects oneself against earthly dangers and loss. But in one's vigilance to safeguard against these perceived threats, one misses the reality of the yawning abyss beneath. The lofty pagan secures his delusion against sabotage, caring only "lest someone by slyness, by force, by lies, or by truth will take away his delusion" (CD, 57), but it is precisely this success that blinds him to the precariousness of his real position — namely, his residence atop a grave. "Finally," Kierkegaard writes, "the care swallows its prey" (CD, 58). Although the esteemed pagan loses none of his earthly treasure, "in his innermost being he is as dead" (CD, 58), fit only for the grave which he has cavorted upon with such abandon these many years.

The bird, by contrast, models a "heavenly equality" which constitutes "the contact point of the instruction" (CD, 50). Unlike the pagan who "fights and struggles and hankers and aspires" (CD, 57) to secure a place above all the others, the bird teaches another lesson: the flight of one need not entail the grounding of all the rest. In fact, true loftiness cannot even differentiate between high and low because its referent, the eternal, admits of no gradations whatsoever. Because no one is thought to be more lowly, the bird is lofty without suffering the anxiety of loftiness.

The Christian understands that earthly distinctions of all sorts mean nothing to God. Only the eternal is real. Kierkegaard compares the lofty-minded person who does not know this to a youth who is assigned the role of emperor in a play. If the youth forgets himself and assumes that the prerogatives associated with being emperor extend into daily life — confounding the appearance with the reality — everyone will ridicule his thoughtless consistency. Although the eminent Christian is not required to renounce all worldly advantage, Kierkegaard cautions one to engage in "the most rigorous self-examination that none of this beguiles him" (CD, 55). The danger of being beguiled is very great: one is living with "fire and candles . . . in a powder depot" (CD, 55).

Although lowliness and loftiness are essentially equivalent, Kierkegaard prefers lowliness for two reasons. First, the prototype lived in actual earthly lowliness when He assumed human form; whoever lives similarly escapes the "detour" (CD, 55) which the person of earthly loftiness must walk. Second, Kierkegaard maintains that "no one comes to Christ except *as* a lowly person, as someone who by himself and by what he is by himself is nothing" (CD, 52). Here lowliness refers not to one's actual earthly condition but to something akin to what the Gospels commend as poverty of spirit. Kierkegaard compares this spiritual lowliness to "becoming *like* a child again" (CD, 52) and reminds us that the Gospels make it the condition for entering the kingdom of heaven. Someone who becomes like a child in this way recognizes that "by himself and by what he is by himself (he) is nothing" (CD, 52). Hence God must be relied upon for everything.

In Kierkegaard's text, the summons to become like a child again requires one to throw off certain dangerous acquisitions which one gains with the passage of time, to backtrack, as it were, to recover the more pristine and truthful perspective of innocence. The movement Kierkegaard recommends duplicates the re-doing of repentance, where one goes back in order to go forward as one ought. In particular, becoming like a child again involves two alterations: (1) one gives up one's delusional belief that earthly distinctions and privilege matter as one learns to differentiate between appearance and reality, the temporal and the eternal. Just as children are oblivious to the nuances of earthly privilege, so too Christians must *become* oblivious. (2) After trying to stand security for oneself and failing, one learns to recognize one's absolute reliance upon Another. Again, the child models this trusting and joyful dependence that the Christian is called to duplicate in spiritual maturity.

Thérèse's Teaching on Becoming like a Child Again

Although Thérèse echoes Kierkegaard's summons to become like a child again, her understanding of spiritual childhood is far more comprehensive and pervasive. It includes and surpasses the themes of grace, humility, and obedience examined in this study. Because it is her preferred way to conceptualize her cumulative spiritual wisdom, crossing all of the categories that this study distinguishes, I focus in this section on correlating Thérèse's views with Kierkegaard's two major insights, with no intention of reducing her meaning to his.

Kierkegaard suggests that with the passage of time one tends to accumulate time's biases. So long as time's momentum seems assured and eternity's horizon a distant prospect, the valuations of time become more and more weighty. To become like a child again is to critique these lies of the world and time *as lies*, to undertake a conscious backtracking to reoccupy the kingdom of the child. The child does not differentiate between loftiness and lowliness because he has not yet been initiated into these categories. No special grace enables the child to do this: he is simply blind (as of yet) to the world's estimations. The Christian is summoned to rehabilitate that perspective by consciously adopting it as one's own.

While time and worldliness are persuasive suitors, Thérèse does not succumb to their attractions. From her earliest days she has an eye only for the eternal. She knows that the offerings of time cannot satisfy, that only in eternity will one truly be at home, and she constantly keeps this in mind. One sees this in her frequent reminder to herself that "life is your barque not your home" (SS, 87). In her sister's editorial correction, the word 'life' is amended to read 'time.' In either case the point is clear: time deceives, but eternity does not.

Although loftiness and lowliness are essentially equivalent, Kierkegaard prefers lowliness, because it avoids the detour that loftiness has to take in order to arrive where lowliness begins. So, too, does Thérèse. Lowliness keeps one honest about time's constitutional proneness toward delusion. Worldly loftiness, even of the ecclesiastical variety, need not entail a corresponding spiritual development.

Despite Thérèse's partiality toward worldly lowliness, the spiritual teaching of her 'little way' does not privilege spiritual lowliness over spiritual loftiness. To do this would assume that the violet really *is* better than the rose and can take some prideful pleasure in this. Thérèse's spirituality takes its point of departure from a soul's acceptance of reality and argues that all souls, great and small alike, are called to be perfect in holiness. Thus the soul that is akin to the lily is called to a resplendence that is dazzling in its prominence, whereas the soul whose model is the tiny crocus, the first blossom to defy winter's ban, is less stately but no less beautiful. Holiness, in both cases, means consenting to be oneself.

Absolute reliance upon God is the second major feature of Kierkegaard's understanding of what it means to become a child again. Thérèse's insistence on this point saturates virtually every page of her memoir, imparting the overall impression of complete and utter reliance, even—perhaps especially—when one's own efforts fail miserably: "I should be desolate for having slept (for seven years) during my hours of prayer . . . well, I am not desolate. I remember that little children are as pleasing to their parents when they are asleep as well as when they are wide awake" (SS, 165). But unlike Kierkegaard who takes his inspiration from the New Testament, Thérèse's views on spiritual childhood originate in Old Testament sources, especially Proverbs, Wisdom, and Isaiah (SS, 188). Even amidst the grand landscapes and bold personalities of the Old Testament, it is maternal love that attracts her: "As one whom a mother caresses, so will I comfort you; you shall be carried at the breasts and upon the knees they will caress you" (Isaiah 66:12-13).

The Care of Presumption / Being Satisfied with God's Grace

Although poverty, abundance, lowliness, and loftiness each have their respective anxieties, one can be innocently poor, rich, abased, or exalted if one does not succumb to the spiritual anxiety linked to one's earthly condition. Hence Kierkegaard contends that it is ultimately a matter of indifference whether one is poor or rich, diminished or esteemed. But presumptuousness is different. Presumptuousness does not speak of one's earthly condition at all but rather is symptomatic of a spiritual condition where one's relationship to God is a misrelation. It has anxiety built right into it. Hence it is impossible to be presumptuous without having the care of presumption. With this alteration, Kierkegaard signals a deepening of anxiety, a move from the external to the internal, from simple to multifaceted anxiety.

The presumptuousness of the pagan takes three forms, spiritlessness, disbelief, and superstition. If Kirmmse's suggestion that these distinctions prefigure the anatomy of despair in *The Sickness unto Death* is correct, the presumption of spiritlessness is presumptuousness "improperly so-called."[13] The spiritless ignorant person takes no thought of God at all. He lives instead "as if he were his own master, himself the architect of his fortune, himself the one who must take care of everything but also the one who is entitled to everything" (CD, 66-67). Because this pagan kills the thought of God "and every feeling and mood that like his emissaries bring him to mind" (CD, 66), the anxiety that grips him is not necessarily conscious. Still, he is "anxious about living—and anxious about dying" (CD, 66)—though without being able to say exactly why. Because he does not think about God at all he thinks he can do without God: this is the presumption of spiritlessness.

The presumption of disbelief requires a consciousness of God sufficient to deny all involvement with God. The repressed anxiety of spiritlessness becomes, in this new form, a conscious and felt disturbance. Disbelief rejects God; it refuses to acknowledge God's governance and substitutes itself as master. Like its counterpart in *The Sickness unto Death* (in despair at not willing to be oneself), this presumption is a variant of unwillingness: unwilling to acknowledge or to submit to God's will, it ventures "in a forbidden, a rebellious, an ungodly way to want to do without God's help" (CD, 63).

The third form of presumptuousness is superstition. Unlike his predecessors who either actively repress the thought of God or reject belief in God, the superstitious pagan seeks to make God serve him. Like its corollary (in despair at willing to be oneself), this presumptuousness wants to call all the shots, to be in charge, to bend everything to its will. It desires "in a forbidden, a rebellious, an ungodly

---

[13]Kirmmse, *Golden Age*, 344.

way to want to have God's help" (CD, 63) — that is, to have God's help not as God offers it but on human terms and conditions.

By contrast, the bird and the lily "continually will as God wills and continually do as God wills" (CD, 61). But what the bird and the lily achieve effortlessly, the Christian must learn.

The Christian understands that "to need God is a human being's perfection" (CD, 64). In the world of the spirit, absolute neediness — not radical independence — corresponds to the reality that all is grace. But this hosanna of absolute gratitude toward God must be preceded by the grueling work of mastering self-will. It is true that everything is grace, but to see this truth one must begin by defeating the ego's insistence that it can provide satisfactorily for itself.

The Christian must learn "to be satisfied with God's grace, which at first glance seems so meager and humiliating" (CD, 65). To do this means to put aside all presumptuousness, all arrogance, all willfulness, every impulse toward independence and control. It is to cast one's lot with God who upholds every being in existence, the one in whom we "live and move and have our being."

Thérèse's Teaching on Being Satisfied with God's Grace

"Those souls are rare," Thérèse writes, "who don't measure the divine power according to their own narrow minds" (SS, 209). From this admission, Thérèse seems to exclude herself: God's love is like "an abyss whose depths I cannot fathom" whereas "my love . . . is not even like a drop of dew lost in the ocean" (SS, 256). But no matter. Thérèse tells us inevitably that God's love is so great that it can eradicate "this whole multitude of sins . . . like a drop of water cast into a burning furnace" (SS, 259). Human sinfulness, and certainly human imperfection, are trumped, overwhelmingly, by God's absolutely incalculable love.

Aware, as these metaphors show, of the incommensurability of God's love compared to human love and God's mercy compared to human sinfulness, it is no surprise that Thérèse shows no evidence of presumptuousness. Her recitation of the graces with which God has blessed and steered her course is so earnest in its conviction and so frequent in its repetition that one accommodates fairly quickly to what smacks of exaggeration. But Thérèse's simple chronicle of grace, which accounts for the real order of her life, presses ahead with such confidence that exaggeration loses its explanatory power. Instead, Thérèse experiences God's grace so often because she is attuned to God's offering most always, finding what others miss because she is always on the look-out for it. Moreover, to the degree that she is preoccupied with God she is less and less reliant upon herself. This shrinkage of the self, which she documents as part of her lifelong quest to achieve nothingness, is troubling in our psychological age but spiritually fairly commonplace in great souls like Saint Augustine or Simone Weil.[14] The erosion of the self makes room for God's appearance who all along has sustained, and now enlivens the self which knows better than to center itself on itself.

Thérèse came to know the incomparable power of grace first hand in what she called her "complete conversion" (SS, 98) of Christmas, 1886. Without rehearsing the details, which are so inconsequential that one might wonder at her making so much of them, it is clear that she was gripped by a formidable grace that changed her profoundly. What Thérèse experienced was the ease with which God could do what she could not do, even with extraordinary effort: "The work I had been unable to do in ten years was done by Jesus in one instant, contenting himself with my good will which was never lacking" (SS, 98). "God was able in a very short time to extricate me from the very narrow circle in which I was turning" (SS, 101). Freed from the scruples which debilitated her, her earliest and most genuine personality restored, grace transformed her instantly in the wake of effort's long and arduous failure. When Thérèse writes that "since that night I have never been defeated in any combat" (SS, 97), she can make such an astonishing claim because it is not the ferocity of human will that is being celebrated but the efficacy of God's grace.

Thérèse practices being satisfied with God's grace so patiently and thoroughly that eventually she observes that God "has always given me what I desire or rather He has made me desire what He wants to give me" (SS, 250). In Catholic tradition, Thérèse has been

---

[14]Certainly a Christian theology of creation does move in the direction from nothingness to being, and what is created is pronounced 'good.' Thérèse is not referring to a metaphysical nothingness, but to a desire more akin to 'emptying oneself.' See Augustine, *Confessions*, I.vi(6), X.ix(6) and Simone Weil, *Waiting for God*, trans. Emma Craufurd (New York: Harper and Row, 1951) 17.

sentimentalized so excessively that it is easy to forget that what she is given is very frequently suffering. This suffering is desired *because given; that is, what is given determines desire (rather than desire determining what is given) when one wishes to be perfectly satisfied with God's grace*. This accounts for Thérèse's disconcerting attraction to suffering, which one is tempted to attribute to some neurotic impulse to punish. Instead, she embraces whatever the Beloved offers, conforming her desire to God's offerings. When Thérèse says that she knows "how to draw profit from everything" (SS, 179), she testifies both to her resourcefulness in utilizing God's grace and the victory of love over fear.

There is no more remarkable testament to this than the affliction of her final days. Despite her unwavering faithfulness, Thérèse underwent a trial of faith that lasted for the last year and a half of her life. "One would have to travel through this dark tunnel to understand its darkness" (SS, 212) she writes. This invasion of her soul by "the thickest darkness" (SS, 211) imaginable was a torment so severe that at one point she confesses that it "has taken away all my joy" (SS, 214). In particular, this trial of faith deprived her of the sweetness of the thought of heaven, replacing it with the nihilistic prospect of a "night of nothingness" (SS, 213). Though she continues to sing "of the happiness of heaven and of the eternal possession of God, I feel no joy in this, for I sing simply what I want to believe" (SS, 214). Enduring, as she does, this dark night of the soul, even as her physical sufferings become progressively acute, her fortitude and resolve are extraordinary: "while I do not have the joy of faith," she writes, "I am trying to carry out its works" (SS, 213).

The Care of Self-Torment / Grasping the Eternal in the Present Day

The self-tormenting pagan's anxiety is defined simply as "care about the next day" (CD, 70). "What exactly is self-torment? It is the trouble (*Plage*) that today (which has enough trouble of its own) does not have. And what is self-torment? It is to cause this trouble oneself" (CD, 70-71). Urged on by uncertain cravings and worries which stir "the fire of passion in which anxiety dwells" (CD, 78), the pagan lives at a constant distance from himself. This distance continually recedes, as another "next day" takes the place of its predecessor, giving the tormentor an endless supply of new occasions for self-torture. The tormentor torments himself by trying to occupy the "next day" which does not yet exist. Not only is the project inherently self-defeating, since the future is inevitably "not yet," but it entails both the abandonment of the present day and the forfeiture of eternity. In short, the self-tormentor's wrong relationship to time insures that he can never be contemporaneous with himself: "the self-tormentor desouls himself by wanting to live the next day today" (CD, 79). In this hell of its own making the self uses itself up in useless worry.

Although the bird knows nothing of the next day, it symbolizes the proper attitude toward time by constantly residing in the present day. Because the bird has no self, and "the next day lies in the self," (CD, 71) the bird is essentially rid of the next day without trying.

But what is it about being a self that makes the fixation on the next day possible? Kierkegaard suggests that it has to do with the capability of the human mind to envision a future and to populate that future with its fantasies and fears. Thus the cure for self-torment is "to gain the mastery over one's mind . . . by getting rid of the next day" (CD, 71). This demands spiritual concentration wherein the mind trains itself to attend and submit to the present day, resisting any futurizing impulse. By concentrating and centering its self in its now, the mind nips in the bud its own tendency toward dissoluteness.

In Kierkegaard's psychology the curbing of self-torment is never easy because it is tied to the structure of the self as the synthesis of the temporal and the eternal: "in his becoming a self, the next day came into existence for him" (CD, 71). Once alert to the prospect of the next day, earthly or worldly cares threaten to bind a person to it. Kierkegaard reminds us that this fixation on the next day is *evil*: "The next day — it is the first link in the chain that shackles a person . . . (to) that care, which is of evil" (CD, 72). Imagine, for example, an alcoholic who wants to stop drinking but who fixes upon an endless succession of "next days" that tempt him; this method makes failure likely: the endless succession of next days is too intimidating, one's resolve too modest to insure victory. And so the alcoholic, however well-intentioned, succumbs fairly easily to the interminable parade of next days.

Kierkegaard instead urges grasping the eternal in the present day:

> The one who rows a boat turns his back to the goal toward which he is working. So it is with the next day. When, with the help of the eternal, a person lives absorbed in today, he turns his back to the next day. The more he is eternally absorbed in today, the more decisively he turns his back to the next day; then he does not see it at all. When he turns around, the eternal becomes confused before his eyes and becomes the next day. But when, in order to work toward the goal (eternity) properly, he turns his back, he does not see the next day at all, whereas with the help of the eternal he sees today and its tasks with perfect clarity. (CD, 73)

This task, then, is to live contemporaneously with oneself. In Kierkegaard's view, contemporaneity, fully developed, is faith. Whoever learns "to live in this way, to fill up the day today with the eternal and not with the next day" (CD, 75) has learned it from the prototype who leaves "a footprint so that we would learn from him" (CD, 77) how this is done. But how *is* this done? The prototype "had the eternal with him in his today — therefore the next day had no power over him" (CD, 77). When the Christian imitates the prototype, he must do likewise. Kierkegaard identifies this as dying to temporality: "if there is no next day for you, then either you are dying or you are one who by dying to temporality grasped the eternal, either one who is actually dying or one who is *really* living" (CD, 72).

Thérèse's Teaching on Grasping the Eternal in the Present Day

Thérèse, too, understands that worry is a spiritual disease. Thérèse was particularly susceptible to the kind of infinitizing worry for which there is no answer save the steady tightening of worry's grip. Although Thérèse did not tend to worry about the next day overmuch, she does import the kind of hypothetical worry (that the next day specializes in) into the present day. Her scruples and spiritual trials are perfect examples. Tortured by "what ifs" while nailed down, in effect, to herself, these scruples self-perpetuate with no possibility of relief.

Subsequent to her 1886 conversion, however, I find no occasion where she succumbs to useless worry. She becomes, in effect, a model of fearless acceptance despite innumerable objective difficulties that she had to face. How does she accomplish this? In effect, she does not: she yields to grace. Grace redirects attention away from oneself, the site of these unanswerable worries, "the narrow circle in which I was turning without knowing how to come out" (SS, 101), back to God. Once centered on God, the maturing soul begins to understand Thomas à Kempis's words from the *Imitation of Christ*: "love never finds impossibilities, because it believes everything is possible, everything is permitted" (SS, 114). The echo of Kierkegaard's observation in *The Sickness unto Death* that "God is that all things are possible" is unmistakable.

The Care of Indecisiveness, Vacillation, and Disconsolateness / Perfect Obedience

Indecisiveness, vacillation, and disconsolateness are all forms of "doubleness, the two wills, masterlessness, or what amounts to the same thing, slavery" (CD, 87). The root of all doubleness is disobedience. As disobedience progresses from indecisiveness through vacillation to disconsolateness, one's spiritual condition worsens, culminating in "the most terrible kind of disobedience"(CD, 90) — the loss of God and oneself as if neither were worth bothering about at all.

Although the pagan is the master of deliberation, he never settles confidently upon a choice. Vacillation cannot decide between competing options. It postpones resolution altogether. As the postponement stretches out forever, the tension between the options — never taut in the first place — slackens to the point of dissolution. Disconsolateness is a form of emotional oscillation. In disconsolateness one has an intimation of some good that one is missing but cannot reach, mired as one is in temporality's ambiguous offerings. Doubt, irresolution, and joylessness are the cognitive, volitional, and emotional expressions of doublemindedness. In Kierkegaard's view they originate when one undertakes to serve two masters rather than one. Hence "paganism is a kingdom divided against itself" (CD, 87).

The lily and the bird model what it means to serve one master wholly. Both are essentially unnecessary — superfluous beauties that dot the landscape of creation simply because God willed them into being: "But just because they are a superfluity in this way, the most perfect obedience is required of them. Certainly everything that exists is by grace; but the one who owes everything to grace to the degree that he understands he is a superfluity, he must be all the more obedient" (CD, 81). Although the bird and the flower neither understand nor ponder their status as superfluous, the obedience that they teach prefigures the Christian's "even more perfect obedience" (CD, 86) that arises from a kinship with the Master that the lily and the bird do not have.

The Christian undertakes to serve and to love the Master "with his whole mind and with his whole heart and with all his strength" (CD, 83-84). Possessed of mind, will, and emotion as one is, the Christian seeks to align these faculties with the master's until one's "likeness to God" (CD, 84), one's "kinship with that Master" (CD, 82) is revealed. But this is very difficult to do. Unlike the bird who "has no other will than God's will . . . the Christian has another will, which in obedience he always sacrifices to God" (CD, 84). If Kierkegaard is correct that every human being loves his own will more than anything or anyone else, this conforming of one's will to God's must be extraordinarily hard. Learning obedience "from him who is the Way" (CD, 85) banishes indecisiveness (by faith), vacillation (through resolve), and disconsolateness (in joy and gratitude). Only love can accomplish this, Kierkegaard writes: "only love unites wholly, unites the dissimilar in love" (CD, 84).

Thus the Christian becomes faithful, resolute, and joyous (rather than indecisive, vacillating, and disconsolate). But the task is not really a three-fold one at all: in Kierkegaard's spiritual shorthand what the Christian strives to realize is perfect obedience. This obedience underlies the singlemindedness of the Christian just as insubordination condemns the pagan to his doubleness.

Thérèse's Teaching on Obedience

In obedience, Thérèse had no superior: "her obedience, as all who testified during the beatification process made clear, was perfect."[15] Although Thérèse understood obedience to her religious superiors as a subset of obedience to God, and excels in this practice, "she had a clear sense of the limits of authority" too.[16] Most importantly, she knew a deeper form of obedience than the authoritarian one that compels submission to one's appointed

[15]Kathryn Harrison, Saint Thérèse of Lisieux (New York: Viking Press, 2003) 150.
[16]Görres, The Hidden Face, 236.

superiors. This form of Thérèsian obedience consists largely in breaking one's own will so as to realize an interior conformity to one's exterior achievement. Certainly it is possible to do what one is told begrudgingly, reluctantly, indifferently, etc. Thérèse seeks not just to *do* what obedience asks but to *be* as obedience requires. Although Kierkegaard's understanding of obedience is dialectically superior to hers, it is otherwise nearly identical. In Kierkegaard's version, mind, will, and emotion are unified in the service of one master, fueled precisely by that kind of singlemindedness that kept Thérèse constantly driven toward her Goal.

For Thérèse "monastic obedience calls for perfect inner submission, submission without a trace of repressed defiance, without any withholding of consent."[17] Without "pure, simple, and joyful acceptance,"[18] it is hard to distinguish mere adherence to regulation from the crassest form of authoritarian groveling, and no point to the observance of rule anyway. Thérèse, of course, understood that the goal of obedience was to effect this inward transformation. Thus in her spirituality obedience is learned in tandem with breaking one's own will. Presumably this is never easy to do but in Thérèse's case it might have been especially difficult given her "extraordinary strength of will."[19] When Thérèse speaks about living "a serious and mortified life" (SS, 143) she does not mean that she has undertaken particularly severe forms of corporal punishment. Contrary to the spirit of the age, Thérèse is suspicious of mortification: "when I say mortified, this is not to give the impression that I performed acts of penance. Alas, I never made any . . . my mortifications consisted in *breaking my will, always so ready to impose itself on others*" (SS, 143; emphasis added).

No account of Thérèsian spirituality can be complete without faith, resoluteness, and joy. Rather than pose doubt in opposition to faith (thereby inaugurating the struggle of doubleness), Thérèse interprets doubt as being within faith's purview. Thus doubt's dark night of the soul, though a classic form of spiritual desolation, attests to the presence of faith through the experience of its absence. Similarly, part of resolve is to absorb irresolution and disarm it.

---

[17]Görres, *The Hidden Face*, 233.
[18]Görres, *The Hidden Face*, 232.
[19]Görres, *The Hidden Face*, 57.

Finally, Thérèse knew that the undertone of joy is often disconsolate-ness. But unlike those whose first instinct is to separate and divide off, Thérèse's instinct is to unify and subordinate. Thérèse never yields to disconsolateness or sadness; instead, she interprets it within the wider frame of joy noting that Jesus "seems to encourage me on this road" (SS, 173). Thus Thérèse writes: "my consolation is to have none on earth" (SS, 187). This impulse, on Thérèse's part, to interpret everything as an occasion for grace shows that singlemindedness that Kierkegaard names obedience.

Conclusion

How might one account for the striking similarities in Kierke-gaard's and Thérèse's understanding of the Christian life, given their religious, psychological, and cultural differences? On the one hand, there is no coincidence at all. In both cases, serious meditation on Scripture yields authentic Christian teaching. Both advocate an un-compromising reading of Scripture, and neither flinches at those teachings' rigor. On the other hand, in a century preoccupied with the science of salvation—where rules and regulations, dogma, clericalism, authoritarianism and conservative politics characterized French Catholicism—how did Thérèse manage to discover her vocation of love and to acquire experiential certainty about it? Similarly, in a society where piety collaborated with worldliness and was in league with the political status quo, how did Kierkegaard articulate Christianity's real entailments? When cultural religiosity becomes *slavish* or *decadent* or both, it becomes ripe for critique by an individual whose *formal* religious experience takes place within that religious horizon but whose *interior* religious education far exceeds it. I think this is true for both Thérèse and Kierkegaard.

Bourgeois French Catholicism in the late nineteenth century had become fairly slavish in its attitudes. Despite her deep and abiding affection for Catholicism and the absence of any formal critique of it in her writings, Thérèse's "little way" offers a *clear existential alternative realizable within the very system that her spiritual way both corrects and serves.* Thérèse's doctrine of spiritual childhood has nothing slavish or childish about it despite language which some find juvenile, or even "the endless kitsch surrounding (her) figure."[20] Instead, her memoir celebrates the interior freedom of one who understands herself to be the child of God. The Gospels pit the slave against the child, urging the Christian to move from the compulsory small-mindedness of the slave to the free openheartedness of the child and heir. The slave anticipates condemnation; the child confidently awaits blessing. The slave's cowering defensiveness incarnates the expectation of abuse; the child's posture of trusting reliance presumes care. In her person, attitudes, and writings, Thérèse models the joyful humility of one who understands herself to be a beloved child of God. Emboldened by her long and arduous education in love, she lives in fearless intimacy with God.

Something is decadent when the life has been sucked out of it, when what looks to be a solid something is in reality a facade or prop. When fissures occur invisibly along the thing's fault lines, the facade remains propped up, but without life, like a corpse seated at a table, prepared, but unable, to eat. In Kierkegaard's view, the nineteenth century Danish Church was decadent in precisely this way: it could neither partake of nor provide spiritual nourishment. But unlike Thérèse who revivifies what she loves from *within*, Kierkegaard's diagnosis of rigor mortis presumes that he stands *outside*—not Christianity, to be sure—but its decadent cultural imposter.

I have argued that Thérèse duplicates Kierkegaard's 1848 teachings (without, of course, having read Kierkegaard at all). But their moment of intersection is extremely short-lived. Thérèse rehabilitates from within, transforming the narrow French Catholicism of her childhood, with its emigré attitude toward the world, so as to carry it forward into modernity.[21] She articulates a spirituality for ordinary souls, denying the claim that vocation is the domain solely of the ordained. Instead, all share in the vocation to love, bearing its burdens and its exquisite joys in common. Thérèse transforms an outmoded and dubiously conventional expression of religiousness into one that spoke meaningfully to a new generation of Catholics in the first decades of the twentieth century. In

[20]Görres, *The Hidden Face*, 15.
[21]Görres, *The Hidden Face*, 34-37.

particular, in the midst of the disaster of the First World War, and its wake, Thérèse's teachings of love and trust made her the best loved saint of modern times. In her advocacy of unbridled confidence and love, she embodies the spirit of Vatican II before Vatican II.

Kierkegaard, on the other hand, becomes increasingly alienated from the Church. Whereas Thérèse goes forward, Kierkegaard essentially goes backward, attempting to recover an orthodox New Testament Christianity which, he believes, is no longer salvageable in the present Danish Lutheran Church. After 1848, Kierkegaard veers off in an increasingly strident and severe direction, culminating in attitudes openly hostile to Christendom in 1854-55. Unlike Thérèse who renews and deepens from within, Kierkegaard departs from Christendom, condemning its excesses and hypocrisies.

Still, their moment of agreement, however short-lived, suggests a notable kinship. What Thérèse and Kierkegaard have in common is their profound reliance upon interiority to steer them rightly, a constant privileging of rigor over ease, and a conviction that the grace of God holds all aloft.

4

Suffering and Strife: For What Can We Hope?
Patricia Huntington

A tension pervades Kierkegaard's *Christian Discourses* that threatens to collapse into a contradiction and thereby undermine the existential aim of *upbuilding*.[1] It is the tension between salvation understood as future *release from all suffering* in the afterlife (we suffer "only once") and redemption in the here and now from within suffering (all of temporal suffering is but "a moment" when measured, from within time, by eternity).[2] The tension is not primarily ideational. That is, it consists not simply in whether the promise of perfect joy can be found only in the beyond after time as compared to the (supposed) imperfection of joy we can have now from within time. The tension lies, rather, in the way that *suffering*, here understood as a middle term, finds itself dialectically — that is, happily/unhappily — located between the ideal of perfect joy and the existential requirement to win joy now; that is, between the future promise of salvation in the afterlife (a futural relation to ideality) and the upbuilding that can and must be won from within time-bound existence (present embodiment of eternal and joyous hope).

Insofar as the dogmatic interpretation of salvation as release from all suffering — a dogma that Kierkegaard inherits — establishes an ideal of perfectibility of joy in the afterlife that is denied us in the

---

[1] In his journals, Kierkegaard distinguishes Christian from upbuilding discourses in that the former work from Christian rather than universally human categories (JP, 1:638). Nevertheless, I retain the use of the term "upbuilding" not solely because it is central to my reflections but also because it is the term Kierkegaard uses to focus part two of *Christian Discourses*, "States of Mind in the Strife of Suffering" (CD, 95-97).

[2] I will refer throughout this essay to the two phrases "only once" (CD, 97) and "one moment" (CD, 97-98) without referencing them anew. Both stem from the first discourse in part two, "The Joy of It: That One Suffers Only Once But Is Victorious Eternally." See n. 21 below for clarification of Kierkegaard's conception of "the moment" and its limitations.

here and now, it threatens to supply a false measure for the joy that can be found within suffering as if that joy would be less than eternal (impeccable or without sin in its actual realization in the now as opposed to imperfectly realized from moment to moment in the course of time).[3] More carefully stated, the promise is vulnerable to mis-appropriation according to a simple, nondialectical equation of suffering with temporal existence. This tension—signaled at the outset in *Christian Discourses* by the "only once" —thus occasions an existential fall into the mis-understanding that invests all hopes in, and thus defers Hope to, the "time" beyond now.

While not chiefly concerned with isolating in what manner time impedes or inversely occasions fortification of perfectibility in Faith, Hope, Joy, and Love, I aim to show that the very want of measuring

---

[3]In *Concluding Unscientific Postscript to 'Philosophical Fragments'*, Climacus, who illuminates religiousness A (immanent religiousness) as distinct from religiousness B (Christianity), distinguishes between nonreligious and religious suffering. Aesthetical or immediate consciousness sees time-bound existence in terms of fortune and misfortune, and yet the simple act of deriving joy from external suffering (rather than wishing it away) is no necessary sign of religious suffering (CUP, 1:452-53). Religious suffering stems from the inward discovery that one cannot escape adversity and flee into a perfected joy because, as an existing subject who must relate to the eternal, joy "must be held fast in the existence-medium" (CUP, 1:452). Because temporal existence separates us from the eternal, religious suffering "pertains specifically to [one's] being separated from the joy" (CUP, 1:453). The crucial matter, for my reflections, is twofold. On the one hand, Climacus makes life difficult for us in so far as the desire to find perfect joy in the afterlife, what we might call "the retirement home model" of hoping, could make us fall back behind religiousness A into an aesthetical mode of living. On the other hand, Climacus, even with the three intensities of existential pathos (relating to the Absolute as Absolute, suffering loss of immediacy, and guilt), cannot move us beyond the sufferings of finite existence in which we continue to imagine eternal hope as a perfectability attainable solely in the afterlife rather than now. It is my purpose to question further whether even Christian suffering, either as articulated by Kierkegaard or as we read Kierkegaard, adequately brings us to die away to all vestiges of hoping for retirement after life. See Sylvia Walsh's marvelous commentary on the difference between Climacus and Anti-Climacus on religious and Christian suffering in *Living Christianly: Kierkegaard's Dialectic of Christian Existence* (University Park, PA: Pennsylvania University Press, 2005) 114-22. For a discussion of the three intensities of pathos in Climacus, see Merold Westphal, *Becoming a Self: A Reading of Kierkegaard's 'Concluding Unscientific Postscript'* (West Lafayette, IN.: Purdue University Press, 1996) 150-79.

existence by an idealized afterlife threatens to foster what Kierke-gaard calls "a deceitful wish-connection" (CD, 122). The manner in which we hope for release from suffering runs the grave danger of confounding two orders of suffering, temporal suffering and *religious strife*. When we confound hope for release from suffering with Hope (the awareness that in God all things are possible), we treat the eternal joy found within temporal suffering as incomplete unto itself. Worse, we deny ourselves the possibility that something essential could be understood from within time about joy and suffering that would mark the full inversion, dialectically speaking, of our ordi-nary view of the promise of salvation. While seeking at best to pro-vide food for thought, I explore the imperfection in our disturbing and persistent failure to apprehend and embrace the constructive nature of strife.

I. Passing Through: Direct or Indirect?

Part two of *Christian Discourses*, "States of Mind in the Strife of Suffering," begins with a discourse that could easily lead us astray, for "The Joy of It: That One Suffers Only Once But Is Victorious Eternally" promises that if we believe in the eternal, eternity can hold down all of time with its power to steal from us, through the aid of hardship, the victorious joy that can weather every order of earthly suffering but pass through life "unscathed," without even a "mark . . . upon the soul" (CD, 101, 102). Faith in the eternal power-fully sets all worldly suffering in its place, for it alone casts the light which reveals that *"the one time of suffering is a moment"* even if "the suffering lasts seventy years" (CD, 97). The whole of temporality can neither trap us like prisoners in suffering (CD, 100) nor corrupt the soul (CD, 102), if only we realize that *"[t]he one time of suffering is a transition or a passing through"* (CD, 101). But where does the empha-sis fall in "passing through" — on the time beyond time or on quality of passage? Is passing "through" a mode of passage to be dis-tinguished from merely suffering time in immediacy as if time only passes "through" us by piercing us with hardship? (CD, 101)

It is tempting, in reading a discourse that heralds the Christian promise, to believe that only *first order faith* is required of us in order to "hold temporality down" (CD, 99) and pass through unscathed.[4] And Kierkegaard's ongoing reminders that we do already understand the Christian dogma (ideal) in some basic sense lend credence to such temptations. Yet Kierkegaard takes pains, in at least two ways, *to work against* such a sallow reading even as his text allows the reader to enter the discourse at whatever level of faith he or she has.[5] As Sylvia Walsh well clarifies, Kierkegaard understood his own dialectical practice as an author to hold forth the ideal and then make matters difficult for realizing it.[6] In part two of *Christian Discourses*, the first repelling act of "working against" the common view of the promise is that he inducts us into the discourse through terror. Before he speaks of the promise — that we suffer only once — he confronts us, by way of anticipation, with the reality that we cannot pass through unscathed without *passing into or by way of the terror* that leads to inward upbuilding (CD, 95-97). Worse, there is a double-edged sword in the inward journey for, ironically, as one awakens to consciousness of one's sin (the terror) and can thus receive forgiveness, the terror increases in due proportion to one's new-found consciousness. "[F]rom the worldly point of view," we are told, "Christian consolation is much more to despair over than the hardest earthly suffering and the greatest temporal misfortune" (CD, 97). At a minimum, Kierkegaard warns that consolation does not eradicate so much as intensify the possible terror we hope to escape.

Second, not only does the title of part two highlight strife and not merely suffering, the discourses on " . . . The Strife of Suffering" unfold in a pattern. Each of the eight discourses preach for "The Joy of It." And yet the first two discourses prepare us by placing the promise of eternal joy in between (a) the jolting reminder of terror that we must "work against" ourselves in how we appropriate the promise and (b) the rigorous induction, enacted in discourses III-V, into *the requirements* of inverse dialectics, all of which show that we

---

[4]On the distinction between simple belief (first immediacy) and faith (second immediacy), see *Fear and Trembling*, 82 and 98. I equate first order faith in God or, more specifically, Christian dogma with the first immediacy that has not appropriated an inward relation to the eternal.

[5]For *Self-Examination* and *Judge for Yourself!* provide the clearest reminders that we can start where we are.

[6]Walsh, *Living Christianly*, 10-11; she quotes Kierkegaard JP, 6: 6593 and PV, 9n.

win the power to let eternity hold back time *on pain of loss* and not, thus, by direct gain.[7] "Upbuilding," in other words, is a potentially misleading term for inward growth in that we rise up to spirit and the eternal by going down; that is, by becoming stripped of all we misguidedly hold dear until we are nothing in ourselves. So we are reminded of the requirements, expressed through inverse dialectics, that we must become poor in order for God's richness to become manifest (CD, 114-23), that we must grow weak in order that eternity grow strong in our lives (CD, 124-33), and that we are to lose all in which we place our hopes in order that Hope reign (CD, 134-43X), for only through loss do we gain the eternal promise.[8]

These two axes of repulsion are written into the discursive mode despite the fact that "States of Mind" preach for consolation and joy; and they work against the first order belief that wants to realize the *wishful hope* for a *direct* entry into eternal joy by *avoiding strife*. There is, then, no simple route of ascent to eternal joy that jumps over adversity and prevents hardship from occasioning a wounding of the soul. With repelling words and the power of inverse dialectics, Kierkegaard's discourses induct us into the need to pass — not immediately and directly through life to the afterlife — but from faith of the first order (belief in the afterlife) to faith of the second order (the activity whereby we avail ourselves of the eternal's influx into time so that eternity's power may hold down temporal suffering with its occasion for human corruption).

---

[7]Walsh offers the most sustained explication of inverse dialectics in *Living Christianly.* She emphasizes that, for Kierkegaard, "the positive is known and expressed through the negative," since "the positive and the negative, Christianly understood, are always the inverse of the natural, human, worldly, and pagan understandings of these terms" (8). Two aspects of inverse dialectics inform this essay: first, the middle discourses all operate according to an inverse dialectic whereby God grows strong when the person grows weak; and second, the nature and character of how we strive within suffering undergoes an inversion when we come to apprehend adversity as prosperity.

[8]There is, then, a parallelism between Kierkegaard's discursive style and the substantial aim of the text to build up. Stylistically, the discourse must enact or refract the need to gain eternal joy through the inward turn. It must repel all attempts to realize the wish for hope-filled consolation by beating an "impatien[t]" path "that wants to attain its end at once"; that is, directly without passage into terror (CD, 95). Existentially, hardship performs the role of repelling the direct ascent to eternal happiness.

If we take these cues[9] seriously, we can recognize, among manifold options, two vital concerns they signal to us at the outset. Ultimately, I believe they signal, as does the title, the most unspoken aspect of Kierkegaard's text, namely, that hidden within our ordinary hope for temporal suffering to end we find a profound desire to avoid the struggle and labor involved in inward growth. In a word, we confound strife with suffering. And the existential labor in meeting adversity well will entail the painful work of learning to differentiate these two dimensions of existence in the human soul and in action. Yet in order to apprehend this confusion, we must first examine another matter signaled in the opening text, namely, that time and eternity are inherently yoked together in human existence. Let us begin, then, by exploring our complaint that time wearies us, that to live in time is to suffer.

---

[9]These cues can be interpreted as musical and staging signals. Such cues comprise a well-known feature that runs throughout Kierkegaard's pseudonymous authorship; for example, we find that Johannes de Silentio, in the opening passages of *Fear and Trembling*, not only writes in the mode "dialectical lyrical" but begins with an "Exordium," modeled after the musical form of the "Prelude," in a manner parallel to the way an orchestra tunes up before a performance. The "Exordium" aims to attune and thereby prepare the soul to meet the existential-conceptual problems to follow in a firmed up tonality of spirit, and it is even arguable that these preliminary attempts to find a right attunement fail (FT, 9-14). See Edward F. Mooney, *Knights of Faith and Resignation: Reading Kierkegaard's 'Fear and Trembling'* (Albany, N.Y.: State University of New York Press, 1991) 14-15, 25-31. See also, Louis Mackey, *Kierkegaard: A Kind of Poet* (Philadelphia: University of Pennsylvania Press, 1971) and Ronald L. Hall, *Word and Spirit: A Kierkegaardian Critique of the Modern Age* (Bloomington, IN.: Indiana University Press, 1993) chaps. III and IV. Kierkegaard himself calls attention to the musicality of the authorship in volume 1 of *Either/Or* by having the poet (A) discuss "The Musical-Erotic" (EO, 1, 47-135) and "The Tragic in Ancient Drama" (EO, 1, 139-64). Although it falls beyond the scope of this paper to elaborate, my working assumption is that the musical and staging aspects of Kierkegaard's pseudonymous authorship rest upon a pedagogics of indirect communication which, while deriving its model from God's living relation to the individual, must be lived between human persons. Thus, I hold that Kierkegaard continues to employ such cues as staging directives in his veronymous writings with an aim at fortification of spirit in the reader.

Suffering "Only Once": A Strange Calculus

It is utterly crucial to consider what the discourses take for granted, namely, that *temporality is bound up with eternity for us*. To say that temporal suffering is yoked to eternity means (at least) two vital things. First, suffering is redoubled for us, as mortal beings.[10] In our temporal suffering, we do not merely suffer what occurs but we, who are conscious of ourselves as existing, can and do suffer over our suffering. Temporal passage is qualified one way or another for us, either in that we despair (suffer over our suffering) or by eternal joy (renounce despair). In other words, "sin is a human being's corruption" (CD, 113, 123, 133, 143, 149, 159). Second, the discourse presupposes that any attempt to consider temporal suffering in abstraction from how time is refracted to us by our inherent relation to eternity proves abstract (first immediacy is, in a word, an abstraction).

Kierkegaard does not spend time addressing all the ordinary ways we experience life's sufferings in abstraction from the question of eternity. Yet we do, in fact, often regard time-bound existence as a kind of suffering. Otherwise we would not wish to be relieved of time; otherwise we could not imagine perfect joy as something realizable only when we can drop the cloak of temporal existence. Existence, it seems, is a kind of suffering in the simple and unqualified sense that we must undergo.[11] We suffer peopled events for

---

[10]This, in fact, is the underlying premise of Anti-Climacus's consummate diagnoses as a distinguished pathologist of the intensities of despair into which we can plummet. In adversity we suffer not precisely "over something" (the adversity) but rather "over the self" (SUD, 19-20), though more accurately understood we despair "of the eternal" (SUD, 20-21, 60-74). In relation to the task to hold back temporality, it would be enlightening to map the religious qualifications of despair onto various facets of *Christian Discourses*.

[11]Here again, Climacus, in *Concluding Unscientific Postscript*, shows that living in the modality of immediacy leads us inevitably to misunderstand undergoing (as fortune or misfortune, as sheer happening). Without the existential pathos that qualifies how we live, we cannot truly understand suffering as undergoing or, better, that undergoing must be actively suffered even if the fact of suffering exceeds human control (443). In other words, we must suffer in the mode of dying away to immediacy, as a matter of inwardness, and ultimately, at least in potential, as ordeal. See Westphal's rendition of the active and passive dimensions of

which we do not wish and over which we wield no control to abate; we live in the first place, we know not initially why or to what end; and we must become, choose, grow, and decide. In all these ways and more, we suffer in the simple and unqualified sense that we undergo. With the passage of time, we begin to wonder that sheer undergoing—whether it brings adversity or no—seems to hold a power to work its weary and leave a mark upon the soul. Temporal undergoing, as we ordinarily reckon it, seems to be a burden in that we not only must live out but also fear that our finite powers will inevitably prove too feeble to bear the duration of our days.

Yet even if the viewpoint of first immediacy has some warrant, it would be all too easy to confound the sheer unqualified fact of temporal passage, in so far as it is a kind of suffering, with the qualified mode within which I can undergo time *despairingly*—"over the earthly *in toto*"—rather than *hopefully* (SUD, 60). It would be too easy not to apprehend that temporal suffering is dialectically yoked to the task of religious awakening. Yet Kierkegaard never ceased to remind us that *ordeal* lies at the heart of human undergoing because for us the problem of eternity (how) is yoked to that of time (what and that we undergo).[12] How I undergo, the quality of my passage, whether my soul comes out scathed, wounded, crushed or mortified, is not a mere matter of undergoing. There is, then, something analytically abstract in thinking of temporal suffering as if it were not linked to the problem of suffering in religious terms (for ultimate purpose, for the good, to win an eternal hope and joy, to find something enduring).

A very strange "mathematics" lies embedded in the first discourse on how we suffer "only once." The "only once" cannot be understood independent of the reality that existence is, for us, a task, a battle, a strife (and not a brute fact or a sheer datum). We decide the quality of our passage in freedom. "Only once" cannot thus be

---

suffering in *Becoming a Self*, 161.

[12]"Ordeal" is Kierkegaard's word for spiritual trial and thus denotes a form of adversity that turns one upon religious suffering in relation to God (FT, 341n2, cf. 343n14, JP, 2:1952-53, JP, 5:6076-77). And it is precisely this order of suffering to which "the natural man never submits willingly" (CD, 112). And yet we are called to become willing. On the fact that religious suffering is inward (before God) rather than outward (temporal), see Walsh, *Living Christianly*, 114-15.

realized for us, so long as we live in time, as if we just have to get through the duration of our days as quickly as possible so we can shed temporal life, with its strife and struggle and conflict, and then alone will we be able to rest in peace. Kierkegaard tells us that all of time, quantitatively understood as duration, is, by a most uncanny mystery, "a moment" from the standpoint of eternity. Yet herein lies the great temptation to misconstrue the ideal, as if one could turn all of temporality into the "only once" merely by believing that joy will be perfected *after* life. That temporality is or can be undergone "only once" may only be realized in the mode of my existing. For whether I experience my life as "only once," that is, as a moment when refracted by eternity, hinges upon whether I win free of despair and human corruption or whether I buckle beneath the weight of time.

Temporal undergoing, even though it is a kind of suffering, cannot, without qualification, *cause* us to break and thereby lay a mark upon the soul. However wearisome it may seem, time, in that we never experience it in unqualified or neutral terms, cannot be what makes life unbearable.[13] We could call the enigma of the "only once" the mystery of the one and the all, for we never notice time as burdensome until a single one time of hardship befalls us. And then suddenly we undergo all of time at once as adversarial. The strange mathematics of the yoke reveals that eternity "is not the opposite of a single moment in temporality . . . it is the opposite of the whole of temporality" (CD, 98). We enter a proportional mathematics. In proportion to the faith-endowed capacity to hold down temporality, suffering a specific hardship (what occurs) becomes bearable, we are to understand, because it frees me from the impatient standpoint that can only see the duration of my time on earth as one, long, unfolding, never-ending soon enough suffering. So too, inversely, does despairing over a single hardship by extension make one's whole life weigh down upon one, in proportion to the intensity of despair, as if it were a continuum of hardships amassed, one upon another, that proves crushingly unbearable (CD, 99).[14]

---

[13]In counseling us to be sure "to lose the lost temporal thing only temporally" (CD, 141) Kierkegaard admonishes us, "Do not shove [*skyde*] the blame [*Skyld*] onto temporality" (CD, 143).

[14]Note that bodily suffering remains a limit of finitude where the inward/outer distinction can lose some of its cleanliness. Nevertheless, I embrace Kierkegaard's

The "only once" contains within it this dialectical mystery that how I face one hardship—which confronts me in the present with the yoke between time and eternity—either alleviates the felt burden of all time or, through falling into the chasmic breach of despair, crushes me beneath the weight not simply of this one hardship but of all the times I have undergone and, by anticipation, believe I will have yet to undergo. You might say, this one suffering refracts previous sufferings as if their effects were a single, unbroken chain of suffering upon suffering across time so that this one final hardship works an effect "like the straw that broke the camel's back." And, though this is how we ordinarily talk, we rarely recognize such talk as despair.

Dialectically apprehended, the magnitude of time's power hinges upon either eternity's countervailing ability to annul inward suffering or, in falling away, the inverse loss of eternity's sway that lets suffering grow unbearable.[15] But this is a way of saying two things at once: first, inward suffering (over temporal suffering) can be annulled; and second, the annulling of inward suffering transforms how we undergo outer or worldly adversity (as crushing or an occasion for inward fortification). In effect, temporality (outer adversity) can only harbor the force requisite to crush us in direct proportion as we neglect to win a right relation to eternity. It might even be more precise to say that we are either happily safeguarded from or unhappily assailed by the inward effects of adversity depending upon whether we live in the protective and uplifting power of eternal joy or not. Yet this certainly means that we cannot merely overcome adversity, strive beyond it, or even reconcile ourselves to it simply by placing our hopes and expectations in a "time" after life that alleviates temporal suffering. In order to pass through unscathed, a living faith, actively realized in the present moment of adversity, will be required. For "seven times seventy" (CD, 98) years of suffering either become nothing "only once" (in that all time is redeemed by eternity) or each single time of adversity becomes "the false everything" (CD, 145) and then life becomes

---

stance that what makes existence essentially bearable or unbearable stems from the quality of one's existential pathos.

[15]Again inward suffering does not eliminate adversity outwardly (CD, 113). Cf. Walsh, *Living Christianly*, 119.

perdition because one lives perpetually in anguish.

For those who inhabit the yoke between time and eternity, it is an illusion to imagine that temporal suffering (and more focally adversity) constitutes the source of evil or even merely the source of wearisomeness in that we never have or know time in unqualified terms. In Kierkegaard's words, "there is a chasmic difference between suffering and sin" (CD, 102-103). Temporal suffering is not evil, in itself, even when it brings adversity or even when the whole of it seems adversarial, for only sin is "an eternal falling away from the eternal" (CD, 102). Time, when measured by eternity, must be apprehended as a qualified "passing through," one marked by ongoing renewal of joy in that the soul not only comes through unscathed but "purified" and "cleanse[d]" (CD, 102) or, conversely, one marked by a horrid sequential calculus of one suffering added upon another that enslaves and corrupts the soul. "Never begin," we are warned, "the terrible calculating that wants to count the moments and the times, something that no one who started ever finished!" (CD, 100). What, then, are we to conclude if not that simple and unqualified release from the sheer adversity of temporal existence holds no power, in and of itself, to qualify my passage *into* the afterlife as a passage *unto* joyousness anymore than Anti-Climacus (SUD, 21) can remove the sting of believing, falsely, that suicide provides a solution to despair rather than leading one unto a despairing death?

Strife and the Deceitful "Wish-Connection"

Reflection on adversity reveals that our battle over temporal suffering is *deeply personal*, structured at core by an inter-personal relation with God.[16] Adversity, I suggest, avails us the yoke that binds eternity to temporality. "Yoke" is not a Kiergaardian term, yet I want to emphasize the term because it denotes not merely a

---

[16]My reading takes the inter-personal relation between the individual and God to be the ultimate point of reference for the discourses of "States of Mind." Nevertheless, the focus on temporality and adversity takes the foreground such that the ultimate referent, namely, to come into relation to God is signaled largely indirectly and on occasion directly. On the conflict with God, see CD, 125; on God's assistance, CD, 129; and for references to governance, CD, 157.

stable dialectical structure but an activity. It can be understood in the middle voice. There is a yoking of time to eternity that qualifies human existence; nevertheless, there is a vast qualitative difference between taking up that yoke *actively as a requirement* and refusing to do so. Yoking is both a reality and an activity. By suggesting that adversity avails us the yoke, I underscore that adversity, in revealing that we abide the tension between time and eternity, proffers that which hides within the yoke, namely, the possibility of living on the most intimate terms with God. Reflection on adversity thus deepens our understanding of suffering by disclosing that we *are* engaged *in strife* with God, whether we like it or not (CD, 125). The task, then, cannot be to escape strife but rather to take it up willingly and in the right spirit.

It is important, in this light, to reflect upon Kierkegaard's view that hardship "procures" but cannot "give" or "take away" eternal hope (CD, 110). In the same way that temporal suffering cannot in itself, that is, outside its negative inward qualification by despair of the eternal, prove unbearable, Kierkegaardian dialectics show that hardship—the very thing we hate or resist most in life—lacks intrinsic causal power either to acquire or to take away eternal goods. He likens hardship rather to a most intensive "pressure" (CD, 111). In fact, he calls it *the* pressure, as in the superlative, the one without compare. By emphasizing adversity's power to procure rather than secure or destroy, Kierkegaard gives greater specification to his thesis that temporal suffering cannot be understood impersonally and abstractly. Hence, he insists, against all ordinary measures of pain and pleasure or worth and dignity that I use to determine to what I should or should not submit in life, that hardship, this tremendous pressure that bears down on us, whatever its power, cannot in and of itself *break us*.[17]

Nevertheless, while devoid of the power either to cause or alleviate sin, adversity *occasions* the fall into perdition because it catalyzes awakening and thereby brings the person before the need to choose in freedom his or her relation to the eternal. Kierkegaard held that hardship played a unique role in God's pedagogy (CD,

---

[17]Consistent with his emphasis on the power of human freedom (CD, 179), Kierkegaard reminds us that "[i]t is the person himself who *acquires* it, eternity's hope, which is planted in him, hidden in his innermost being" (CD, 110).

154-55) because it holds a special quality, a special power, a special virtue, no matter how inefficacious it may be with respect to my freedom (and we might add happily so). In the ancient sense, hardship's virtue lies in its power to *procure*.[18] In sharp contrast to the power of easy times to seduce us into sleepy complacency, Kierkegaard tells us that hardship holds the power to "tear off" the dreamy state of spiritual sleep (CD, 109) by depriving us of worldly secured hopes.[19] The difference between worldly and eternal goods cannot pass unnoticed here, for hardship is precisely the loss of something temporal (CD, 139). At issue, then, is not whether we will lose something but whether, in losing the temporal, we will lose it badly; that is to say, we let go of the eternal in ourselves (CD, 141). Thus, while it cannot acquire and give eternal hope, adversity's singular virtue rests in its negative power to repel (CD, 110), to strip down, to clear away space (CD, 111). Hardship procures, hardship "draw's forth" eternal hope (CD, 112) by repelling all that clutters up the space within which alone I can exercise the freedom consciously to choose to enter into a proper relation to eternity.

Amidst temporal suffering we are engaged in strife. It is strife over whether we will sink or rise, die away from the eternal or be "born again to the eternal with perhaps even greater pain" than first birth (CD, 112). Yet this strife is not impersonal. In so far as adversity is sent by governance, it reveals *deliberate intent* and *divine intelligence*. It does not take much pause, in the face of adversity, to wonder that specific things are sent to me which others do not have to bear and to stumble into offense at the apparent distributive

---

[18]The Latin etymology of procure means "to take care of." While hardship may lead us to become midwives to the seed of eternal hope planted in the soul, the ordinary connotations of procure in English — "to get possession of" something, "to get and make available for promiscuous sexual intercourse," and "to bring about" or "achieve" — do not well fit Kierkegaard's meaning. The power to acquire is precisely what Kierkegaard denies hardship.

[19]Times of ease have a power we typically exert, to our own disgrace, very little initiative contemplating. Yet we know that they hold the power to tempt and seduce us into altered states of elation that we confound with true rising unto the eternal. Though here, too, one must take care not to blame ease anymore than we can blame hardship for what only we can acquire in freedom, namely, loss of sobriety, weakening of earnestness, and general dissipation.

inequity of my existence set-up.[20] In awakening me to the inter-personal character of existence, adversity draws me deeper into the strife that unfolds between God and me, a strife initiated from the divine side. Adversity, then, can be understood as working a divine operation, surgical-like in character because it aims, in the game of indirect communication between God and person, to divest me of "everything provisional" (CD, 112) that stands in the way of the reception of eternal goods. But here, too, we can no longer think "eternal goods" impersonally, for to let eternal hope come to birth in me is to enter into the scope and sphere of God's grace and love.

It would not be far-fetched, then, to suggest that the *indirect*, that is, unspoken and hidden intent of divinely-sent adversity is precisely to take away, though directly God cannot take away what I must renounce in freedom. Yet more carefully stated, adversity cannot in and of itself deprive me of pride and steal from me false hopes and false measures. It is but the pressure whereby God encourages me to let go without thereby violating freedom. No more can temporal loss in itself guarantee that I cease to wish falsely than we can ever say, in truth, that adversity breaks us. Rather, the reality of the yoke is far more grave. It can only be said that when we stumble over adversity, our hidden intent is precisely to break off and refuse what often remains silent and unspoken, the possibility of holding intimate relations with God. Do human beings not break by shattering bonds of intimacy with self (e.g., by failing the task to care for the seed of eternal hope in oneself), with others, and with God? Is this not always the indirectly conveyed truth whenever we claim that it is

---

[20]"Existence set-up" is a term I develop in part four of "Loneliness and Lament: A Philosophy of Receptivity" (unpubl. ms.) in order to indicate that my circumstance in life—that into which I am born and which I must live out—is not merely a product of social, cultural, historical, and interpersonal forces but rather arrives through divine dispensation. So understood, God sets me up for the measure and order of ordeal I face in life. One cannot make sense out of offense if one does not awaken to the reality that God sets us up for the suffering we meet. Faith takes as its point of reference the difficulty of believing that God sends me, even by wounding, the fitting occasion for my winning through to a constructive appreciation of strife and thereby a constructive embodiment of compassion. I win such an understanding through a profound self-confrontation, occasioned by ordeal, with my unique psychic weaknesses and my specific erratic tendencies toward faithlessness and hopelessness.

something external — the adversity that was sent, the deeds of another, the world in general — which required or caused us to break?

When, in adversity, I cannot comprehend why I should suffer, I undergo temporal loss as if God took aim, by the arrow of adversity, to make me shatter and break. In counseling that adversity is prosperity, Kierkegaard's discourses on strife do not simply catalyze the realization that how we undergo suffering can be transformed from joylessness into joyfulness. They indirectly call us to believe that God, in sending us adversity and requiring the movement of renunciation, does not aim to shatter and enslave us so much as avail God's self to us in intimacy. The implication is that we confound adversity (the suffering that is sent) with strife (ill motivation to do us in); our inter-personal judgements and perceptions prove faulty for want of trusting faith (CD, 158).

We do stumble over the negative, though arguably because of the inter-personal relation that lies within it and not because adversity must be seen as unjust in itself (as if adversity could be divorced from eternity's dispensation). The negative, the loss, the stripping away, the repulsion that adversity works bring us to a halt. These clear a space between God and a human being, a space within which a conscious and free relation could arise. Yet we hold no place for the movement of repulsion, that is, the movement that inaugurates strife or awakening to strife, in our ordinary conceptions of love and intimacy. We must ask, then, why God initiates intimacy through a negative operation that aims at working loss rather than inducting us directly into gain? The presupposition of the discourse, as every reader of Kierkegaard's authorship knows well, is that "it is always the person himself who stands in his way" (CD, 109). Yet the matter I wish to underscore is this, that the difficulty we confront in facing repulsion is not simply that, thrust back upon ourselves, we must choose faith, hope, and love in freedom. The difficulty lies, rather, in that we begin asleep in untruth. We must see, in effect, the ugly truths about ourselves, that we do wish falsely, that we prize the petty over the glorious, and, worst of all, that we begrudge the consoling hope and merciful love that are proffered. Between my wish and renunciation lies the moment in which I must see my heartlessness, and to this most of us do not take kindly.

We stumble, then, because we lack a robust willingness for ultimate intimacy. We have not awakened, in point of fact, to the truth that stripping away is an ongoing prerequisite for the acquisition of our own heart and for deeper entry into intimacy. Should the discourses not, then, lead us to acknowledge that God must undertake the most treacherous of operations to come close to the domain where we have not distinguished in ourselves false hopes from true hope, the "false everything" of the world that is nothing from the "true everything" (CD, 145)? Something stands in the way of hope-filled intimacy: "the person," we are told (CD, 109). More specifically, the discourses name things that must be renounced — selfishness, attachment to worldly riches, prideful belief in one's desert, and want of power and strength in the world. Yet still more crystallized, we find underlying all these a common thread, namely, that the manner in which we hope is deceitful (CD, 122).

Let us, then, return to the peculiar mathematics of the one (time) and the many (all times). Earlier I noted that how we bear the one time of suffering (one hardship) decides our relation to all of time (duration). Yet the conversion of all time into the "atom of eternity" (CA, 88) depends, we are told, upon how we hope, wish, and expect in the face of the one time of hardship. Just as each time refracts our entire relation to temporality depending upon our relation to eternity, so too does Kierkegaard tell us that the one final hope — upon which we hang all our expectations when confronted with adversity — gathers all hopes unto itself. To be denied the "one and only wish" for which I would otherwise sacrifice all, is to lose not just this one hope but all earthly hopes (CD, 129). For by that strange divine mathematics, one final hope stands in relation to the whole of worldly striving as the possibility or impossibility of eternal gain. Thus, just as the one time of hardship avails us the eternal gift that transforms all temporality into "*the moment*" (CA, 82), so too does loss of the one final hope unleash the power of adversity to procure. For in denying us our one final wish, it draws us into a vigorous encounter with the immeasurable difference between hopes and Hope; that is the quantitative "one that I believe contains all" (earthly hopes and expectations) and the eternal hope that defies all calculus.[21]

---

[21]When he first introduces the notion of "the moment" in *The Concept of Anxiety: A Simple Psychologically Orienting Deliberation on the Dogmatic Issue of Hereditary Sin*

Horrific as it may sound, Kierkegaard reminds us that God assists the person to win spiritual goods precisely "by wounding him in the tenderest spot, by denying him his one and only wish, by taking his final hope away from him" (CD, 129). We are confronted with the shocking reality that the greatest assistance we could receive in the face of our deceitful forms of wishing for the ideals of joy and hope would be to suffer the greatest adversity, for we must awaken to the apprehension of how we confound the eternal with the one worldly thing upon which we hang our final wish. Here we stumble. The key impediment to eternal hope is that the soul may "cling to things of this earth" and thereby maintain "a deceitful wish-connection" (CD, 121, 122) with those earthly things that have been lost or taken away. We could infer that it was not false to wish for those things in themselves in a condition of naive existence, but when governance sees fit to preach for awakening by denying us them, then strife opens up concerning whether I will let go. Hence, we are warned that it would be supreme deceit to persist in the wish that what we lose temporally we shall get back in eternity *in the same form* as we lost or desired it temporally (CD, 139). When it is time to wake up from our childish ways of wishing to the incomparable difference between eternal hope and worldly hopes, then all such

---

(81-93), Kierkegaard takes great pains to distinguish between the "silent atomistic abstraction" (84**) whereby Greek philosophy treats the moment as a mere now-point in a sequential view of time and his own understanding of the moment as "not properly an atom of time but an atom of eternity" (88). Thus, he argues that the present cannot be known metaphysically but only through existential pathos. Despite the implications of Kierkegaard's understanding of the present for his notion of sin, his written texts, pseudonymous and veronymous, may still depend too greatly on the Augustinian heritage which renders the fall a spatio-temporal category rather than an strictly inward one. At a minimum, Heidegger's ecstatic theory of time (*Being and Time,* trans. John Macquarrie and Edward Robinson [New York: Harper and Row, 1962] sections 68-69) could help Kierkegaard to lay the temporal foundation for the distinction between the instant and the moment and the transformation of all temporality into "a moment," though there would be questions about Heidegger's prioritizing the future. Moreover, Kierkegaard did not, in conceptual terms, ponder the temporal ecstases of the moment in terms of the question raised by the Buddhist, Dōgen, concerning whether all times are concurrent and can be known to be so, not *sub specie aeterni,* but from within the eternal now. See *The Heart of Dōgen's Shōbōgenzō,* trans. Norman Wadell and Masao Abe (Albany: State University of New York Press, 2002) chap. 5, "Uji (Being-Time)."

persistence unleashes conflict with God in the mode of conscious or declared war rather than as the possibility of embracing faith, hope, and love. Strife becomes qualified in the negative direction of falling away from the eternal as open rebellion against divine love.

In the final analysis, the deceitful wish-connection denotes the attempt to deny eternity what is its own, namely, the eternal.[22] Each hope, when hoped for as if it must be the form deliverance would take, assumes the shape of deceitful striving because it transmutes the belief that "all things are possible for God" into something lesser, namely, the conditional dictate that we receive eternal joy in the precise worldly form we wished it. Two existentially corrupting effects arise from such deceit. First, the *conditional dictate* marks not merely confusion between a hope and Hope but it reflects a decisive act whereby we break with God, for in advancing this dictate we refuse *the requirement* of intimacy, namely, to enter into a relation to the eternal that is freely and unconditionally chosen.

Second, in binding God to dispense Hope in the form of our worldly wish, we do not let adversity procure care of the soul for us. Rather, we prevent ourselves from apprehending that, in the most vital sense, what we wish to gain through a person or event avails itself already. For God unflaggingly offers eternal joy to us within adversity and extends to us the prospect that this time of hardship can become "a moment" in the redemptive sense, and not simply a passing instant of pain, if only we would receive the yoke. How we typically wish reflects an ungodly want of confusing the absolute and the relative, and refusing the occasion to let them become distinguished in and for us. Our choice of the absolute can only become known to us on pain of renouncing the one wish that represents all for us, for in this manner we choose quality over quantity and we relinquish all measures for deciding what form the good will take (CD, 156).

It would not be off target to claim that an erratic movement constitutes the form of every deceitful wish-connection. Either we want to pull eternity down to time or we want to hold on to the

---

[22]Implicit in this claim is the understanding that the shadow of the eternal haunts the very wish-structure of human desire because human existence is yoked to the eternal. Either we reduce the eternal to all worldly hopes or we win the "true everything."

eternal by leaping over time. In the end, they are the same. The former refuses to give up a wish, while the latter wishes that the eternal be like unto its relative image. In each case, I believe the true evasion lies in refusing to face the middle term of adversity and win the jewel contained within it. For the former wants to redeem life's suffering without struggle for Hope and the latter wants Hope without struggling in life's stream. In each case, I cling to an image of perfected joy that frees me of the existential requirement to enter *willingly* and *in good faith* into the strife with God; that is, to lose something freely via renunciation and in faith. By deciding that I will only renounce the wish if God gives it back in the form I want it, I try to cheat eternity of its rightful claim to make the relative relative. And in attempting to win the absolute without awakening to joy from within temporal suffering, I cheat the absolute of its divine pedagogy; that is, of its attempt to draw me into an active and trusting intimacy.

What, then, are the lessons that Kierkegaard's strange mathematics of suffering reveals to us? What makes temporality bearable or unbearable, I have shown, is not that we suffer in the immediate sense of undergo. It is, rather, whether we suffer over our suffering in despair or truly undergo. Why, then, do we want time to cease? And if adversity can become prosperity and deliver us unto eternal joy and hope, then why do we wish to escape adversity? If we take seriously the indirect communication of the discourses, I believe we must conclude that what underlies every deceitful wish-connection is, finally, want of avoiding strife. We want to eliminate temporal suffering and adversity in order to evade the strife contained within them. By strife, I mean the need to battle with God to enter into a right relation to eternity; that is, by loss upon loss until I am nothing and God is made great in me. It is the jewel of strife that adversity turns me upon and that I wish to avoid at all costs, especially given the unusual nature of the strife, that I grow great by growing small.

This means, I believe, that we are not innocently asleep. At the very least, the catalyst to awaken leads us to discover that our sleepy passivity harbors pronounced resistance. At first we may think it is resistance to temporal suffering, and then we find it centers prejudicially on adversity, though upon closer examination still we discover that it is the very strife contained within suffering that we resist. And this resistance is, thus, sin, for it is tantamount to refusing the invitation to live on the most intimate terms with God. That the absolute must be absolute is not finally a mere structural relation of existence. It reflects, rather, that God cannot betray divine integrity in the manner in which we are admitted into intimacy. What must be removed is deeply personal, namely, our ungodly persistence in transgressing against God in how we seek intimacy without taking up the yoke of strife.

Is Strife Not, then, Love?

Kierkegaard walks us up to the prospect that adversity is prosperity, with his final discourse on strife, but then goes no further. He does not tell us directly whether strife will end when temporal suffering ends. It was his task to hold forth the Christian ideal — of perfect joy in the afterlife — and then makes matters hard by turning us upon inwardness. Clearly, as Walsh so deftly captures in her wonderful book, *Living Christianly*, Kierkegaard aims to fortify us on a diet of inverse dialectics. Thus he tells us that, while hardship performs the "painful operation" of procuring hope, there is no reason to assume that hardship will end once hope is born (CD, 113). He shows us first that adversity can become a *"matter of indifference"* (CD, 154) to us because the goal matters more than what leads to it. For the coup de grace he proclaims that we can even come to embrace adversity as the very best teacher who could have been dispensed to assist us in learning not to place absolute hopes in things relative (CD, 155-56). While I believe my reflections could be much enhanced by Walsh's analyses of the various forms of suffering found in the Christian writings, I have wanted to tease out a more unspoken dimension of Kierkegaard's thought, namely, the positive matter of strife signaled in the title of these discourses. Rather than emphasize strife as something I must suffer merely for the sake of the goal but which I thus persist in holding to be an impediment to perfect joy, I wish to highlight its most constructive significance in my concluding thought.

Strife can be understood as a term for religious suffering. Walsh notes that Climacus, in *Concluding Unscientific Postscript*, defines religious suffering in its general or immanent form as "the expression for the attempt of religious individuals to transform their inner existence in order to sustain an absolute relation to the absolute."[23] As a purely inward datum, religious suffering does not end when adversity abates. Thus, she further clarifies that "the persistence of suffering is essential for the maintenance of a pathetic or passional relation to the absolute *telos*."[24] Yet, as Walsh clarifies, Kierkegaard recognizes a specifically Christian mode of religious suffering that moves beyond Climacus in that one can transcend outer suffering through winning inward joy. Moreover, Christian living may entail choosing hardship, that is to say, innocent or redemptive suffering for the sake of the good. Although one suffers opposition from the world, one paradoxically gains greater inward joy through the ongoing conquest of despair or inward suffering.[25]

Bearing this in mind, it does not suffice, I submit, to treat inverse dialectics as the realization that adversity in the world can be the ongoing occasion to win prosperity through the inward defeat of suffering before God. We certainly can, as we wake up to the activity whereby we win eternal hope, come to appreciate the negative need to defeat despair and false hope as well as learn to embrace outer adversity in the world. Yet even these formulations fail to cast light fully on the core dimension of strife that we continue to evade. I have suggested that we want out of strife because we want the inward joy and hope of love without the labor of love. Yet even when we assume the labor of love in negative terms through willingness to be mocked in the world or for the sake of redemption, there remains the question of awakening to the constructive nature of strife as strife. Strife cannot merely be the necessary condition through which I renounce want of worldly acclaim but which will be discarded in the afterlife. Nor is it simply that whereby I suffer worldly opposition as God's servant before whom I always remain guilty and in need of purification. Strife is not simply the means to an end or the outer medium of inward religious or Christian suffering to be discarded after life. It is rather, essentially understood, the very "yoking" activity whereby we cultivate intimacy with God. So understood, strife, lived fully and well, entails love and love entails strife. While the discourses show us how to embrace adversity, they

[23]Walsh, *Living Christianly*, 114.
[24]Walsh, *Living Christianly*, 115.
[25]Walsh, *Living Christianly*, 117-22.

conclude on a note that leaves unspoken the precise and specific truth that the most essential transformation of adversity into prosperity would be that whereby I become capable of embracing strife in a welcoming spirit as the very game of love.

Permit me, in this light, one final reflection on time. That eternity is yoked to temporality not only promises that we can (and must) win hope within time (even as eternal hope is not of time) but it also refracts to us the *ongoing* nature of task. By virtue of time, we do not "hold temporality down" only once numerically but must realize the "only once" ongoingly—as willing only one thing! We cannot be lifted up to hope within suffering and then, like the momentum of habit or mechanism, just float along joyously. We can sink again in the face of new adversity and trial. As temporal, we are not spared the ongoing realization of the "only once" in and through strife. Yet we want the numerical once (which promises rest in the form of passivity) rather than the qualitative once (which must be actively sustained). Here we hit more sharply upon the contradiction that lies at heart of our wishing and willing. We imagine that the perfection of joy promised in afterlife will take this numerical shape. Yet on earth, it's as though everything is designed to drive home the implacable *requirement* not merely to prize quality over quantity but also to understand quality in verbal terms. We are to acquire a taste for the eternal activity of hoping over the finite want of a numerical one or a finalized "state of hopes fulfilled." By refracting the ongoing nature of the requirement to realize joy and hope anew, temporality serves the eternal not merely by fortifying us on willingness to suffer for the good so long as we live in time. It teaches, I submit, a transcendent lesson that active willingness to battle for spiritual goods may lie at the very heart of intimacy. But, rather than realize the paradox that eternal rest is found in creative motion, we persist in imagining that our sleep will be restored in the afterlife.

If strife, understood as an activity, transcends the temporal medium of its unfolding, then can we hope that strife will cease when time ends? What we forget, even up to the endpoint where we become willing to suffer all variety of unjust opposition from the world in the service of the good, is the constructive dimension of battling. I believe the last bastion of the deceitful wish-connection lies in the hope that one day, when time ends, strife will end. Suffering in time may end but that which we seek to avoid, namely, that love is an activity in which I must do battle, may never end if, indeed, it lies at the very center of divine operation. Truly, we do not know whether strife will end with death. And yet I have intimated with these reflections that there may be evidence within love to abolish from our minds all want of imagining the afterlife as if resting peacefully in love were antithetical to strife. The paradigm of love we come to know in life suggests, to the contrary, that strife is love and love is strife.

What we cannot imagine, when we look too far ahead in time and see only that we must renew hope ongoingly, is that the strenuous labor of giving birth to love is utterly funded. Love's labor, in effect, is graced. And that labor whereby God grants and we avail ourselves of grace is never-ending because it is active and must be realized actively. Strife, then, cannot be equated with sin or pain or punishment. Taking up the yoke; that is, willingness to strive to win love anew is intrinsic to love. Our unduly negative understanding of strife as a warring conflict in which someone loses and someone wins prevents us from understanding strife in constructive terms. Yet in the battle whereby God gains and I lose, the uncanny mathematics of divine love makes me a winner, too.

Strife, positively embraced, defines the nature of every relationship in so far as love is not mere sentiment. Strife is the activity whereby we win ever greater intimacy with others, just as we do with God. When we enter into engagement, we face each other as two spirits who will have to win a right understanding of each other. Possible misunderstandings will have to be cleared away, prejudices, faulty wishes and expectations renounced in order that we win the heart to bear witness to the other. Stripping away is an active precondition of loving reception of another, just as unveiling remains fundamental to intensities of revelation. There is never a direct path to intimacy, nor can the battle we fight be understood merely relationally rather than much more vibrantly as a holistic battle with another person's hiddenness to apprehend what cannot be communicated directly but which is, nevertheless, revealed actively albeit indirectly in the nature of his or her personal love.[26]

---

[26] I do not speak of hiddenness in reference to moral failing or the demonic but in the simple sense that, like God, our spirit manifests indirectly.

In this essential sense, adversity is not merely the "painful opera-tion" I must undergo in the world for the sake of a higher good. It is the very form that strife in the interest of love takes in this world. Yet who can say that the tension of hiddenness that runs across differ-ence does not define the whole nature of the cosmos or that strife in love will cease when its worldly form dies away? And, with respect to suffering in this world, why don't we ever wonder that the greater adversity delivered upon awakening may be a living mark of God's trusting faith in us and neither persecution nor punishment? In all this, I believe willingness for strife — to bear with another until a new order of intensity of love dawns — is the very annulment of sin in this world and may be the very nature of love in itself. For this reason we ought to take seriously that what adversity teaches us here on earth might shatter our dogmatic inheritance: the persistent need to cling to the belief that joy and love and hope will be perfected in the afterlife because *struggle and strife and conflict will cease*. Before you suffer for the good while holding onto the wish that sooner or later strife will cease when temporal suffering ends, think rather on how to hold on while letting go. Hold on, if you will, to the ideal belief that love will obtain perfectly only in the afterlife, but let go, I encourage you, of the image whereby you decide in advance, and thereby nurture a possible deceitful wish-connection, that your passage "through" time into the afterlife will take the shape of something other than what love revealed itself to be in the "atom of eternity," namely, strife.

5

The Joy of It
Christopher A. P. Nelson

Introduction

From beginning to end, Kierkegaard's is a philosophy of joy.[1] In fact, in response to the question as to why in the world anyone would want to become involved with Christianity in the first place — a question that has presumably occurred to many of Kierkegaard's readers as well as many who have only encountered him second

---

[1]Space simply will not permit the much-needed juxtaposition of the philosophy of Kierkegaard thusly conceived with the philosophies of those most often thought of in this regard (as philosophers of joy), namely, Epicurus, Spinoza, and Nietzsche. As a beginning in this regard, the interested reader may find the following of some assistance. On "joy" in the writings of Epicurus, see Philip Merlan, "Ἡδονή in Epicurus and Aristotle," in *Studies in Epicurus and Aristotle* (Wiesbaden: Harrassowitz, 1960) 1-37; Jeffrey S. Purinton, "Epicurus on the Telos," *Phronesis* 38/3 (1993): 281-320. On "joy" in the writings of Spinoza, see Arne Næss, *Freedom, Emotion and Self-Subsistence: The Structure of a Central Part of Spinoza's Ethics* (Oslo: Universitets Forlag, 1972) 95-112; Aryeh Leo Motzkin, "Spinoza and Luzzatto: Philosophy and Religion," *Journal of the History of Philosophy* 17 (1979): 43-51; Gilles Deleuze, *Expressionism in Philosophy*, trans. M. Joughin (New York: Zone Books, 1992). On "joy" in the writings of Nietzsche, see Michel Haar, "The Joyous Struggle of the Sublime," *Research in Phenomenology* 25 (1995): 68-89; Alex McIntyre, *The Sovereignty of Joy: Nietzsche's Vision of Grand Politics* (Toronto: University of Toronto Press, 1997); Mathias Risse, "Nietzsche's Trusting and Joyous Fatalism," *International Studies in Philosophy* 35/3 (2003): 147-62; Joan Stambaugh, "All Joy Wants Eternity," *Nietzsche-Studien* 33 (2004): 335-41; Babette E. Babich, "Nietzsche's 'Gay' Science," in *A Companion to Nietzsche*, ed. Keith Ansell-Pearson (Malden MA: Blackwell, 2006) 97-114. It is worth noting as well that an interrelated set of questions arise hereabouts regarding the suitability of the English "joy" in and about the writings of Epicurus, Spinoza, and Nietzsche, apropos the relationship between the Greek ηδονή and χαρά (in Epicurus), the Latin *laetitia* and *gaudium* (in Spinoza), and the German *Lust* and *Freude* (in Nietzsche). Happily, the English "joy" appears to serve well enough for the Danish *Glæde*.

hand — Kierkegaard's answer is simply, *the joy of it*.[2] The subsequent question seems innocent and appropriate enough: So what exactly is the distinctively Christian sort of joy,[3] this joy that is promised to the individual who elects a life that appears to consist entirely and increasingly in the intensification of suffering? Kierkegaard gives no direct answer to this question. The task of the present paper is the elucidation of the development and significance of this reticence — a reticence that is especially attenuated in three discourses in particular: the seventh discourse of "The Gospel of Sufferings" (UDVS, 321-41), the seventh discourse of "States of Mind in the Strife of Suffering" (CD, 150-59), and the third discourse of *The Lily in the Field and the Bird of the Air* (WA, 36-45). Before turning to these discourses however, it is well to begin, with Kierkegaard, on the morning of 19 May 1838.

Ante-Phenomenology: "An Indescribable Joy"

In one of the most famous entries in the whole of his journals — an entry dated (and timed) "10:30 A.M. May 19, 1838" — Kierkegaard writes the following:

> There is an *indescribable joy* [*ubeskrivelig Glæde*] that glows all through us just as inexplicably as the apostle's exclamation breaks forth for no apparent reason: "Rejoice, and again I say, Rejoice."[4] — Not a joy over this or that, but the soul's full outcry "with tongue and mouth and from the bottom of the heart": "I rejoice over my joy, of, in, by, at, on, through, and with my joy" — a heavenly refrain which, as it were, suddenly interrupts our other singing, a joy which cools and refreshes like a breath of air, a breeze from the

---

[2]On this point, see Jonathan Mason, "Jesus Is Offensive: Contemporaneity, Freedom, and Joy in Kierkegaard," *Dialogue* 39/1 (1996): 21-29.

[3]Following the insightful recognition of Robert C. Roberts, that joy "may come in a number of sorts, depending on the sphere-identity of the concerns and thoughts involved," it is necessary to speak already and specifically of the distinctively Christian sort of joy. See Roberts, "Existence, Emotion, and Virtue: Classical Themes in Kierkegaard," in *The Cambridge Companion to Kierkegaard*, ed. Alastair Hannay and Gordon D. Marino (New York: Cambridge University Press, 1998) 193. According to Kierkegaard's ultimate reckoning of the matter, however, every other sort of "joy" is really only an impoverished intimation of the distinctively Christian sort of joy.

[4]See Philippians 4:4; cf. JP, 2:2177, 2182.

trade winds which blow across the plains of the Mamre to the everlasting mansions. (JP, 5:5324)[5]

Walter Lowrie writes that this passage "reads like the record of a characteristic mystical experience of a definitely ecstatic sort."[6] In their edition of the *Journals and Papers of Søren Kierkegaard*, Howard and Edna Hong follow suit and make a point of including reference to this particular entry in their chronology of significant events in Kierkegaard's life.[7] As a result, it has become fairly commonplace in discussions of Kierkegaard to refer simply to the "indescribable joy" *experienced* by Kierkegaard on the morning of 19 May 1838.[8] Granting for a moment the hypothesis implicit in any such reference and the corresponding significance of this entry, the question remains: What becomes of this "indescribable joy" throughout Kierkegaard's subsequent and richly descriptive authorship?

The phrase itself — *ubeskrivelig Glæde* — or some variation thereof appears in a handful of places throughout the authorship.[9] Occasionally, and less frequently, the even more constrictive *uudsigelig Glæde* (unutterable joy) is employed.[10] One would think that this would be the end of the matter. The "joy" in question is indescribable, unutterable, unsayable, ineffable, etc., and any discursive endeavor thereabouts is immediately brought to a close. And then there are provocative passages in Kierkegaard's writings such as the following:

> If anyone says that Christian joy is unutterable — well, then that is what is to be discussed, and the theme becomes *the unutterable joy*. It is even a beautiful theme, but then there must be discussion of the unutterable, why it is unutterable, etc. On the other hand, one

---

[5]Translation slightly modified, following Walter Lowrie, *Kierkegaard* (New York: Oxford University Press, 1938) 170.

[6]Lowrie, *Kierkegaard*, 170.

[7]JP, 1:viii; 2:viii; 3:viii; 4:viii; 5:v, viii; 6:viii.

[8]Curiously, there is a relative dearth of attention in precisely this regard to the entry penned approximately one year later (May 17, 1839), in which Kierkegaard writes of the "indescribable joy" that he feels, "as a prose writer . . . in surrendering all objective thinking and really exhausting [himself] in wishes and hopes, in a secret whispering with the reader," apropos a certain "preface" that he was working on at the time (JP, 5:5387).

[9]See SLW, 321-22; UDVS, 319, 333; WL, 305, 341; CD, 286; WA, 37, 42.

[10]See CUP, 1:221; WA, 43; PC, 174-75.

does not discuss the unutterable by talking about something else which is so easy to utter that one can even say it by rote . . . That which really should be accentuated in religious joy is suffering and the idea that is the hinge of the category, namely, that the joy of poetry, art, and scholarship stands in an accidental relationship to suffering, because one person becomes a poet without suffering, another by suffering, a thinker without suffering (as a genius), another by suffering, but religious joy is in the danger. From here on it is easy to show why it is unutterable. (JP, 1:625)

Having thus thematized the indescribable and unutterable joy, Kierkegaard attempts to redirect attention from the tantalizing but obviously futile task of saying the unsayable to the arguably more manageable task of showing exactly *why* the unsayable is unsayable. This, Kierkegaard thinks, can be shown — indeed, he even suggests that it will be easy to show — and the subsequent showing will have everything to do with "suffering."[11] As borne out in the second authorship (1847–1851), and most clearly in "The Gospel of Sufferings" (1847) and "States of Mind in the Strife of Suffering" (1848), Kierkegaard never really departs from this thought. Before arriving at the second authorship, the reader of Kierkegaard's writings is treated to an earlier showing in this regard, albeit in a slightly different vein. Tucked away practically as an aside within Johannes Climacus's discussion and critique of the "explanation" of "the paradox" in the hands of positive speculation,[12] the reader will discover the following passage:

> To explain the unutterable joy — what does that mean? Does it mean to explain that it is this and that? In that case, the predicate "unutterable" becomes just a rhetorical predicate, a strong expression, and the like. The explaining jack-of-all-trades has everything

---

[11]The mere correlation of "joy" and "suffering" is by no means a thought unique to Kierkegaard. One finds it, for instance, in the writings of Martin Heidegger and of Henry Nelson Wieman. See Orville Clark, "Heidegger and the Mystery of Pain," *Man and World* 10 (1977): 330-50; and David Lee Miller, "Buddhism and Wieman on Suffering and Joy," in *Buddhism and American Thinkers*, ed. Kenneth P. Inada and Nolan P. Jacobson (Albany: SUNY Press, 1984) 90-110.

[12]*Concluding Unscientific Postscript*, pt. II, sect. II, chap. II, "Subjective Truth, Inwardness; Truth Is Subjectivity." That the theme of the unutterable joy would be taken up somewhere in the *Postscript* is signaled already in the journal entries subsequent to the entry quoted above (see JP, 5:5787-5792), which suggest that Kierkegaard had begun work upon this text at or around this time.

in readiness before the beginning of the performance, and now it begins. He dupes the listener; he calls the joy unutterable, and then a new surprise, a truly surprising surprise—he utters it. Suppose that the unutterable joy is based upon the contradiction that an existing human being is composed of the infinite and the finite, is situated in time, so that the joy of the eternal in him becomes unutterable because he is existing [*existerende*]; it becomes a supreme drawing of breath that cannot take shape, because the existing person is existing.[13] In that case, the explanation would be that it is unutterable; it cannot be anything else—no nonsense. If, however, a profound person first condemns someone or other who denies that there is an unutterable joy and then says: No, I assume that there is an unutterable joy, but I go further and utter it, then he is only making a fool of himself, and the only difference between him and the other whom he condemns is that the other is more honest and direct and says what the profound person is also saying, since they are both saying essentially the same thing. (CUP, 1:221)

As suggested in the above passages, the unutterable joy is unutterable, on the one hand, because it lies "in the danger" of the suffering that is somehow essential (nonaccidental) to Christian existence, and, on the other hand, because "the existing person is existing." Though she does not put it exactly this way, it is precisely at the coincidence of these two suggestions that Sylvia Walsh picks up the thread and proceeds with a remarkable dexterity to elucidate the "joy" problematic exclusively in terms of Kierkegaard's development of its inversely dialectical counterpart, "suffering."[14] In a very real sense, this is entirely appropriate and even mandated by the course of Kierkegaard's authorship. *Because* the joy is indescribable, unutterable, etc., one *can* only speak to the cause of its indescribability, whether in the manner of Johannes Climacus (adopting "existence" as the featured item of discourse), or in the manner of

---

[13]In this respect, and although it is perhaps a mistake to take any of the etymologies proposed in the *Cratylus* too seriously, the etymology Socrates proposes for "joy" [χαρα] is remarkably apropos: "Chara seems to have its name from the plenteous diffusion of the flow of the soul" (*Cratylus* 419c, trans. Harold N. Fowler). Indeed, and in proportion to the stock one chooses to place in the significance of word origins (and especially in those that tend to yield an onomatopoeic original), the likely etymology of the English "joy" is noteworthy inasmuch as it appears to originate in a guttural exhalation (the Indo-European *gau*).

[14]See Walsh, *Living Christianly: Kierkegaard's Dialectic of Christian Existence* (University Park: Pennsylvania State University Press, 2006) 113-48.

the Kierkegaard of the second authorship (adopting "suffering" as the featured item of discourse). Nevertheless, Kierkegaard's reticence vis-à-vis the unutterable joy is itself subject to a series of interesting and peculiar twists and turns, according to which he successively provides a new rationale for the joy's being unutterable (in "The Gospel of Sufferings"), suggests that he is actually more *unwilling* than *unable* to utter it (in "States of Mind in the Strife of Suffering"), and appears at last to utter it nonetheless (in *The Lily in the Field and the Bird of the Air*).

Breaking through Language: "The Gospel of Sufferings"

In what is arguably the inaugural work of the middle or second period of his authorship,[15] Kierkegaard presents, as he puts it, a collection of discourses "in various spirits." In the subtitle to the third part of the collection, a new spirit is explicitly introduced: the "Christian" (UDVS, 213). The title itself is indicative in precisely this regard: "The Gospel of Sufferings." A more accessible translation might read: "The Good News of Feeling Terrible," or even, "How Great It Is When Things Are Awful." In the "Preface" to this peculiar sounding "gospel," Kierkegaard alludes to the significance of the title by encouraging the reader (in a secretively whispering kind of way) to find the "trail" of "joy" that runs through suffering (UDVS, 215). As it turns out, the discovery of this trail has everything to do with what Kierkegaard finds distinctive about "Christian" existence.

In all seven discourses, Kierkegaard — operating according to what Walsh aptly diagnoses as the "inverse dialectic"[16] — painstakingly probes the nature of human suffering in a variety of lights, and each time discovers a source of joy therein.[17] Of course, presuming that his reader is sufficiently aware of what "suffering" is, Kierkegaard does not take the further step of actually stating what it is that he means by "joy," other than its somehow comprising the positive counterpart to the negativity of suffering. While it would seem that the alleged indescribability of joy would by itself

---

[15]*Upbuilding Discourses in Various Spirits.*

[16]Walsh, *Living Christianly*, 123.

[17]See esp. UDVS, 226 (GS I), 237 (GS II), 263 (GS III), 275 (GS IV), 300 (GS V), 319 (GS VI), 337 (GS VII).

command such reticence, a further consideration is brought into play. For, were the question to be put directly — "What is joy, or what is it to be joyful?" — and put directly by one who is actually among the intended target audience of the text — i.e., "a single sufferer" (UDVS, 215) — it would seem that there is in fact an answer that would make a great deal of sense, an answer, therefore, that is also presumably the desired response, namely, that "joy" is the elimination of suffering and "to be joyful" is the state of being in which suffering has been eliminated. And yet, it is precisely this answer that Kierkegaard is most reluctant to give. In fact, the more he writes of suffering, and the more inversely dialectical the matter becomes, the more it begins to sound like Kierkegaard is actually saying the exact opposite.

Of course, Kierkegaard does not say that "joy is suffering" anymore than he says "that it is this and that." But he appears to be heading in precisely that direction. Accordingly, as amply prepared as the reader may be to hear the word "suffering" when asking about the nature of joy — and Kierkegaard has already afforded a great deal of preparation in precisely this regard — it would seem that at some point a sensible mind would prevail and simply wonder: Has this man lost his mind? Even granting the ineffability of joy, is he not gesturing in exactly the wrong direction? Does he even know what the word — our word — *Glæde* (joy) means? Appropriately enough, it is against the presumed backdrop of these very questions that Kierkegaard composes the seventh and final discourse of "The Gospel of Sufferings."

Kierkegaard begins the discourse with an extended discussion of the difficulty inherent in being called to confess Christ in the midst of Christendom where all are (or rather claim to be) Christians (UDVS, 321-28). While such a difficulty is a far cry from the danger inherent in the original situation — where being called to confess Christ meant colliding unequivocally with the world — Kierkegaard proceeds to draw attention to a particularly powerful passage of scripture, "so that from the highest we might learn for the lesser" (UDVS, 325). The passage in question is Acts 5:41, according to which the apostles, after being flogged, were "joyful because they had been deemed worthy to be scorned for the sake of Christ's name" (UDVS, 328). This leads to the theme of the discourse: "the joy of it for everyone who suffers for a conviction: *that bold confidence is able in suffering to take power from the world and has the power to change scorn into honor, downfall into victory*" (UDVS, 328). The idea of such a "bold confidence" is then fleshed out according to a kind of minimalist thought experiment according to which a relatively naïve "youth" is horrified upon entering actuality and discovering two rather pronounced reversals of what he had imagined the world would be like: that there are people who are not only evil but openly so, and that the good sometimes suffer for the sake of truth (UDVS, 328-30). Bold confidence is thus characterized as a reversing of the reverseness: "the bold confidence to turn everything around the second time when it was turned around the first time," and thus "to transform shame into honor" (UDVS, 330). The discourse is then unfolded along two successive lines—a consideration of "the joy in the thought that bold confidence has this power of victory" (UDVS, 339),[18] and a consideration of "how the apostles understood themselves in this thought" (UDVS, 340)[19]—before drawing to a close in the call to "strive to win" and "hold fast" to this "joyous thought of bold confidence" (UDVS, 341).

Once again, however, Kierkegaard's discussion of "the joy of it" does not contain anything pertaining directly to the nature of joy itself, but this time, a new rationale for this reticence is introduced. The rationale is introduced gradually, as Kierkegaard refers to the apostle as one who "speaks in tongues," "breaks through language," and does not "have language and concepts in common" with the world when he speaks of being joyful because he was deemed worthy of being scorned (UDVS, 331-32). The crescendo culminates in the following passage:

> Nevertheless it is joyful, indescribably joyful, that bold confidence has the power to be victorious in this way and is able in this way, despite language and all people, to stamp the concepts, and let us not forget this—with the genuine mark of the divine. Thus to triumphant bold confidence what we simplemindedly and whiningly call loss is gain, what the world rebelliously calls shame is honor; thus what the world childishly calls downfall is victory; thus the language a whole race speaks in unanimous agreement is still turned upside down, and there is only one single human being

---

[18]See UDVS, 330-33.
[19]See UDVS, 333-39.

who speaks the human language correctly, he whom the whole race is unanimous in thrusting from itself. (UDVS, 333)

According to the world's reckoning, such a person is clearly "at the height of madness" (UDVS, 332), facing in exactly the wrong direction, and completely misusing language. According to Kierkegaard's reckoning, however, such a person has discovered an indescribable joy. While it may be nothing more than the other side of the problem, the joy is now deemed indescribable because the language in which it would be described is itself "turned upside down." In other words, and insofar as the words are still somehow appropriate, the upside-down way in which the world uses the very word "joy" is a contributing factor to the indescribability of true joy. What is required, therefore, is a radical shift in perspective, a reversing of the reverseness, according to which the whole of language (and a great deal else) is completely turned around.[20] This is precisely what Kierkegaard proposes in the next series of discourses with "joy of it" themes, namely, "States of Mind in the Strife of Suffering."

Turning Around: "Joyful Notes in the Strife of Suffering"

Recalling the juxtaposition attested in the title of part three of *Upbuilding Discourses in Various Spirits* ("The Gospel of Sufferings"), part two of *Christian Discourses* bears a comparably suggestive title that reads, in the original Danish, "*Stemninger i Lidelsers Strid.*" Howard and Edna Hong translate *Stemninger* as "States of Mind" (CD, 93). Walter Lowrie, however, opts to translate *Stemninger* as "Joyful Notes."[21] Either translation is acceptable and captures something of the spirit of the original. However, when one considers

---

[20]On this point, see Jonathan Mason, "Jesus Is Offensive," 26; Lee Barrett, "The Joy in the Cross: Kierkegaard's Appropriation of Lutheran Christology in 'The Gospel of Sufferings'," in *International Kierkegaard Commentary: Upbuilding Discourses in Various Spirits*, ed. Robert L. Perkins (Macon: Mercer University Press, 2005) 268; Walsh, *Living Christianly*, 122. Even when construed merely in terms of a shift in language, Kierkegaard calls such a transformation "more marvelous" and miraculous than if one were to "descend from the cross" (UDVS, 336-37).

[21]Søren Kierkegaard, *Christian Discourses* and *The Lilies of the Field and the Birds of the Air* and *Three Discourses at the Communion on Fridays*, trans. Walter Lowrie (New York: Oxford University Press, 1952) 97.

the following entry in Kierkegaard's journals, it appears that Lowrie's translation is actually preferable:

> No preface was written for "States of Mind [*Stemninger*] in the Strife of Suffering." If it were to be written, it would be of the following nature. That most valiant of nations in antiquity (the Lacedæmonians) prepared for battle with music — in the same way these are states of mind of triumphant joy that tune one [*stemme*] for the struggle, and far from discouraging [*forstemme*] a person in the struggle will definitely keep him well tuned [*velstemt*]. (JP, 2:2201)

With regard to this proposed preface, Lowrie writes the following: "It is just as well this preface was not used, for it contains little but a play on words, yet it helps us to understand how the title is to be understood and translated."[22] The epigraph eventually attached to "Joyful Notes" (in lieu of the proposed preface) supports this decision: "I will incline my ear to the proverb; I will set my dark saying to the music of the harp" (CD, 93).[23] The epigraph thus manages to convey much of what was to have been spelled out less succinctly in the preface. And yet, when Sylvia Walsh explains her preference for Lowrie's rendering of the title rather than that of the Hongs — because the latter "does not adequately express the more emotional than mental connotation of the term and its association with music through being derived from the Danish word *stemme*, which means 'voice', especially 'singing voice'"[24] — it begins to seem that there is something more than merely "a play on words" in the abandoned preface. Indeed, as read aloud, "*stemme . . . forstemme . . . velstemt*," it sounds almost musical.

As with "The Gospel of Sufferings," the peculiar juxtaposition attested in the title of "Joyful Notes in the Strife of Suffering" is borne out by the substance and titles of its constitutive discourses.

---

[22]Kierkegaard, *Christian Discourses*, trans. Lowrie, 96.

[23]Cf. Psalm 49:4. The reader may note with interest that the four parts that comprise *Christian Discourses* are thus tied together in an interesting way: Part one is adorned with a prayer (CD, 5) and an introduction (CD, 9-12); part two is adorned with an epigraph (CD, 93); part three is adorned with a motto (CD, 162); and part four is adorned with a preface (CD, 249). In other words, each of Kierkegaard's preferred prefatory devices is utilized exactly once. The entire work, of course, bears no such adornments, lacking even a subtitle.

[24]Walsh, *Living Christianly*, 179n8.

Each of the seven discourses share the same generic title, "The Joy of It," with each sub-title then identifying or intimating a particular reversal of ordinary prudential thinking: (I) "That One Suffers Once But Is Victorious Eternally," (II) "That Hardship Does Not Take Away But Procures Hope," (III) "That the Poorer You Become the Richer You Are Able to Make Others," (IV) "That the Weaker You Become the Stronger God Becomes in You," (V) "That What You Lose Temporally You Gain Eternally," (VI) "That When I 'Gain Everything' I Lose Nothing At All," and (VII) "That Adversity Is Prosperity." Once again, Kierkegaard refuses to say what "joy" is, often merely stipulating that it is to be found in the strife of such sufferings.[25]

Attuned to the allegedly joyful undertone of the text, however, a careful reader will begin to hear a series of markers—a musical refrain, as it were, that marks the trail of joy. This is the ritornello.[26] It is heard in the first discourse: "How wonderful, the way it turns around [hvor det vender sig om]" (CD, 105).[27] And in the second discourse: "the pressure continues but continually makes itself known inversely [omvendt] as hope" (CD, 113).[28] And in the third discourse: "Then he walks along the same path, but in the opposite direction [omvendt]" (CD, 114).[29] And in the fourth discourse: "But when this is the case, the relationship is in another sense, in the sense of truth, turned around [omvendt]" (CD, 129). And in the fifth discourse: "With regard to eternity, the difficulty is the reverse [omvendte]" (CD, 135).[30] And in the sixth discourse: "this is the reverse [omvendte] comparison in which everything is turned around [vendt om]" (CD, 144-45). Whether one chooses to speak in terms of "reversal," "inversion," "conversion," or even "repentance," this "turning-around" is the key to finding the trail of joy in "Joyful

---

[25]See esp. CD, 101 (SMSS I), 107 (SMSS II), 123 (SMSS III), 127 (SMSS IV), 138 (SMSS V), 144 (SMSS VI), 158 (SMSS VII).

[26]An expression of gratitude is due to Sharon O'Leary for assistance in hearing "Joyful Notes" in this manner.

[27]See also CD, 104 ("For you the task is the reverse [omvendte] . . . ").

[28]See also CD, 109 ("Or the reverse [omvendt] . . . ").

[29]See also CD, 116 ("Yet it is just the opposite [omvendt] . . . ").

[30]See also CD, 136 ("Words unto repentance [Omvendelse] . . . ").

Notes,"[31] as Kierkegaard proceeds to make clear in the seventh and final discourse in which the ritornello is developed and expanded into a major theme.

The title itself — as Kierkegaard will go on to explain — is pointedly revealing in this regard: *Det Glædelige I: At Modgang Er Medgang*. In contrast to the welcome simplicity of the Hongs' translation — "The Joy of It: That Adversity Is Prosperity" (CD, 150) — Lowrie laments the prospects of an adequately "musical" translation before settling upon "The Joy of It: That Misfortune Is Good Fortune."[32] If a more cumbersomely expository title is desired, an alternative is suggested in the journals: "the joy of it — that the more the world goes against us, the less we are delayed along the way in our pilgrimage to heaven" (JP, 2:2196). None of these titles, however, manages to capture or convey the sheer juxtaposition attained in the Danish, *at Modgang er Medgang*. As written or spoken, a single vowel is altered and the result is the clearest of oppositions. Relative to all of the other "Joy of It" sub-titles, "*At Modgang Er Medgang*" involves and invites what may be called the quickest turn. In fact, the turn is so quick, and in a sense so slight, that one may well wonder whether Kierkegaard is at last merely playing with words. This very thought provides the point of departure for the discourse:

> Adversity is prosperity. But do I hear someone say: This surely is only a jest and easy to understand, because if one just looks at everything turned around, it is quite correct: in a straightforward sense adversity is adversity, adversity turned around is prosperity. Such a statement is only a jest, just like guessing riddles, or when a jack-of-all-trades says, "Nothing is easier to do than this, provided one is in the habit of walking on one's head instead of on one's legs." Well, yes, but is it also so easy to do it? (CD, 150)

"*At Modgang Er Medgang*," "That Adversity Is Prosperity" — indeed, such a thing is easy to say provided that thought has adopted the habit of merely speaking this way: "here" is "there," "right" is "left," "up" is "down," "this" is "that," etc. "But when it is thought with a name," asks Kierkegaard — i.e., when it is a matter of my

---

[31]Indeed, as argued compellingly by Walsh throughout *Living Christianly*, this turning-around lies at the very heart of the "inverse dialectic" that animates the entirety of Kierkegaard's middle authorship.

[32]Kierkegaard, *Christian Discourses*, trans. Lowrie, 154.

actually seeing adversity (in the strife of actual suffering) and actually seeing it as prosperity and relating to it accordingly — "is this, then, so easy" (CD, 150)? Presumably, the answer is a resounding "no." And yet, it is just such an impossible turn that "eternity" requires of one, as Kierkegaard, adopting the voice of eternity, proceeds to explain:

> This is the task, because it is indeed my, eternity's, view of life to see everything turned around. You are to accustom yourself to looking at everything turned around. And you suffering one, if you want to be comforted in earnest, comforted so that even joy is victorious, you must let me, eternity, help you — but then you, too, must look at everything turned around. (CD, 151)

Kierkegaard thus leads into the theme of the discourse — "the joy of it: that adversity is prosperity" — with an introduction that could well have served as such for any of the "joy of it" discourses. For, all that is required in order to find the joy of it — which, although a seemingly easy task for thought and speech, proves to be a very difficult feat for an actually existing individual — is to look at everything turned around. Accordingly, before endeavoring to describe the subsequent view of the matter,[33] Kierkegaard devotes the first half of the discourse to an orientation (the development and expansion of the ritornello),[34] such that the reader "might have an eye for the turned-aroundness" (CD, 151). As summarily delineated in a passage from an earlier draft of the discourse, the procedure itself is relatively straightforward and practically syllogistic: prosperity is what leads a person to the true goal (CD, 151); the true goal is the goal of eternity (CD, 151-54); therefore, when (worldly) adversity leads a person to the true goal, it is really prosperity (CD, 154-55).[35] As tempting as it may be to hear and therefore append here a little "*quod erat demonstrandum*" — and thereby prepare the argument (and the second premise in particular) for analysis according to the logistics of discursive demonstration — the character and purpose of these preliminary pages as an orientation must be borne squarely in mind. Kierkegaard is not attempting to prove anything — he is attempting

---

[33]CD, 155-59.
[34]CD, 151-55.
[35]See CD, 377.

to encourage the one who is suffering to be willing to turn around, *quod erat faciendum*, in order to see "the joy of it: that adversity is prosperity." Nevertheless, the second (and demonstratively problematic) "premise" in the above "argument" retains and even gains significance in this light.

The goal that is set before human beings is the goal of eternity. How can this be shown? As far as discursive demonstration is concerned, the following remarks are all that Kierkegaard bothers to muster in this regard: "Now, there are many different things for which people strive, but essentially there are only two goals: one goal that a person desires, craves to reach, and the other that he should reach. The one goal is temporality's; the other is eternity's. They are opposite to each other" (CD, 152). "In other words, eternity presupposes that the natural man does not know at all what the goal is, that on the contrary he has the false conception. Temporality presupposes that everyone knows very well what the goal is" (CD, 153). To complicate matters further, both goals are (often enough) called by the same name: "joy."[36] This is the heart of the problem. The operative assumption is that temporality's goal, the worldly conception of "joy," is not merely impoverished, but backwards, upside-down, inside-out. From the vantage point of temporality, any argument that proceeds on the basis of this assumption is bound to be construed as ultimately and essentially begging the question. But to insist that the advantages to be gained from adopting eternity's view of the matter be made clear and comprehensible in advance — i.e., according to temporality's conception of the matter — is ultimately and essentially to betray "a dubious agreement with temporality's goal" (CD, 152). This is the whole point of the orientation: to encourage the individual (to find the courage) to abandon this agreement altogether, and with it virtually everything that the world

---

[36]In a journal entry from 1849 — titled, "The Conclusion" — Kierkegaard writes that the one who has felt the presence of God "should be full of hope, rich in comfort, *nothing but joy*" (JP, 2:2202; emphasis added). And again, in a journal entry from 1854 — titled, "Believing in God" — Kierkegaard writes that "to believe in God means essentially always to rejoice impartially in and over God, essentially to be *impartially joyous*" (JP, 2:2205; emphasis added). By contrast — although they appear to be saying the same thing — the goal of temporality, according to Kierkegaard's repeated reckonings, is to "enjoy life" (see, e.g., JP, 2:1935; 3:2332; 4:4799).

understands by the word "joy."

The second half of the discourse consists of Kierkegaard's elucidation of "the joy of it: that adversity is prosperity" from the "turned around" point of view. From this new vantage point, Kierkegaard sees that, since the goal of temporal prosperity is precisely what delays and prevents a person from reaching (or even beginning to reach for) the goal of eternity, the less temporal prosperity the better (CD, 155). In fact, the one who suffers temporal adversity is actually in a preferable position relative to the person who enjoys temporal prosperity, inasmuch as the former has that much less to renounce in order to reach the goal of eternity (CD, 156-57). Thus, adversity is prosperity, and Kierkegaard is seemingly positioned at last to speak to the peculiar character of "the joy of it" thusly discovered. The discourse, however, is instead brought to a rather abrupt conclusion: "That this is joyful need not be developed. The one who has faith that adversity is prosperity does not really need to have the discourse explain to him that this is joyful. And for the one who does not really believe it, it is more important not to waste a moment but to grasp the faith" (CD, 158).

In a very real sense, Kierkegaard's continued reluctance to speak directly about the nature of true joy is a dually informed reticence. On the one hand, of course, the joy in question is unutterable, indescribable, etc., and Kierkegaard is therefore simply unable to utter, describe, or otherwise say it.[37] On the other hand, however, his reluctance to speak of it appears (in this case) to be manifestly just that—a refusal, or unwillingness to speak of it, as per the succinctly stated rationale in the above conclusion (the one who can hear it does not need it to be said, and the one who cannot hear it should not have it said), according to which Kierkegaard is unwilling to utter, describe, or otherwise say it, even if he were able. Thus far in

---

[37]For the reader who remains willing to suffer the tacit adoption of temporality's presupposition, the following treatments of "joy" will be of some interest: Jean Paul Sartre, *The Emotions: Outline of a Theory*, trans. Bernard Frechtman (New York: Philosophical Library, 1948) 68-70; Carroll E. Izard, *Human Emotions* (New York: Plenum Press, 1977) 86, 239-76; Nel Noddings, *Caring: A Feminine Approach to Ethics and Moral Education* (Berkeley: University of California Press, 1984) 132-47; Susan Robbins, "The Practice of Joy in the Western Tradition," *Contemporary Philosophy* 22/3-4 (2000): 45-52.

the authorship the "joy" has remained faithfully unuttered for one or another (or both) of these reasons, but all of this appears to change dramatically in the third discourse of *The Lily in the Field and the Bird of the Air*.

Catching One's Breath:
"Look at the Birds . . . Look at the Grass . . . "

In order to understand Kierkegaard's enduring fascination with the directive to learn from the lily and the bird (Matthew 6:24-34),[38] his treatment of the matter in the second discourse of the posthumously published *Judge for Yourself!*, "Christ as the Prototype, or No One Can Serve Two Masters" (JFY, 145-209), is simply indispensable. The discourse is roughly divisible into halves, the first of which is concerned with an elucidation of Christ's life construed in terms of his having served only one master (JFY, 160-79), and the second of which is concerned with an elucidation of the gradual toning down of the requirement of serving only one master in the centuries since (JFY, 187-209). The obvious continuity between the halves of the discourse thusly conceived is interrupted, however, by an extended discussion of the directive to learn from the lily and the bird (JFY, 179-87). The interruption begins as follows:

> In order, however, that for us human beings the matter does not become all too earnest, deadly with anxiety, he draws our attention away from himself and directs it toward something else, almost as if it were encouragement, a diversion [*Adspredelse*]: "Consider the lilies of the field; look at the birds of the air." Consequently, he does not say: "No one can serve two masters . . . look at me"; no, he says, "No one can serve two masters . . . look at the lilies of the field; consider the birds of the air." (JFY, 179)

Given the textual surroundings of the subsequent "diversion" — a diversion that lasts several pages and thus constitutes a substantial portion of the discourse — the question cannot but arise: What exactly is the point of diverting attention from the ideality ("Christ as the Prototype") as manifest in the life of Jesus, only to return to this same ideality ("Christ as the Prototype") as forsaken in the centuries since by his so-called "followers?" What else indeed, but to afford

---

[38]See UDVS, 155-212; CD, 3-91; WA, 1-45.

the earnest follower a chance to catch his or her breath, as it were.[39]

---

[39]While the similarities may or may not end here, Kierkegaard is thinking with Aristotle on this point. As finite beings existentially situated vis-à-vis an ever intensifying and ultimately unbearable ideality, we require the occasional amusing diversion, or *Adspredelse*. See Aristotle, *Nicomachean Ethics* 1176b-77a. A helpful approach to this issue is afforded by Gary M. Gurtler, "The Activity of Happiness in Aristotle's Ethics," *The Review of Metaphysics* 56/4 (2003): 801-34. See also John Morreal, "The Philosopher as Teacher, Humor and Philosophy," *Metaphilosophy* 15/3-4 (1984): 305-17, although the reader who heads off in this direction ought to be forewarned that Morreal operates according to a curious understanding of what Aristotle means by "happiness" and the various criteria for an activity's counting as such — e.g., that the criterion of "continuation" may be sufficiently satisfied whenever "exertion" is lacking or "not required" (309), and that the criterion of involving "our highest faculty" may be sufficiently satisfied whenever any kind of "thinking" or "understanding" is in play (310). Kierkegaard, for his part, would find Morreal's account troubling both in itself and as a commentary upon Aristotle.

By using the word *Adspredelse* in this context, however, Kierkegaard touches upon a further and equally important question. In addition to "diversion" or "amusement," *Adspredelse* can be (and elsewhere in the authorship is) translated as "dissipation," "dispersion," or "scattering" (literally, a "spreading out"), as well as "relaxation," "absent-mindedness," "distraction," or "preoccupation." The connotations that attend the deployment of this word are thus typically negative, as it tends to mean "distraction" from the one thing needful (EUD, 339), the "scattering" of the self in busyness as opposed to the ideal of unity and wholeness (WL, 98-99; cf. WA, 42), the dark and darkening "diversions" consciously or unconsciously sought by the despairing self (SUD, 48), etc. Thus, and notwithstanding the precedent and admittedly daring identification of such a thing as a "godly diversion" [*gudelig Adspredelse*] (see UDVS, 183-87, 200; cf. UDVS, 335), the question basically amounts to this: When exactly (and for how long) is such a diversion actually necessary, and how exactly is one to know that the seeming need for diversion is not actually and essentially the commencement or continuance of a self-indulgent evasion of the task allotted to one? Such a question effectively recalls the incredibly long-winded, admittedly tedious, and appropriately titled "upbuilding diversion" [*opbyggeligt Divertissement*] buried deep within *Concluding Unscientific Postscript* (CUP, 1:464-99), in which Johannes Climacus discusses the difficulties associated with "bring[ing] such trifles as going out to the amusement park into connection with the thought of God" (CUP, 1:477). Like Aristotle, Johannes Climcaus recognizes the necessity of diversion for human beings (CUP, 1:489, 491, 495, 496). But in order to understand the latter's navigation of the double-danger occasioned by this concession, one simply must insist that the question (regarding when and for how long diversion is actually necessary) be posed by one in possession of what Kierkegaard (following Luther) calls "a sin-crushed conscience" (JP, 6:6686). If this much is granted, the requisite corrective need only be applied in one direction: "Humility. What kind of humility? The humility that entirely acknowledges its human lowliness with

As a momentary reprieve from the deadly anxiety of the matter, Kierkegaard even imagines Jesus "smiling" (JFY, 179) as he redirects attention to the lilies and the birds.[40] It is this recognition that provides the requisite context for engaging the discourse on "joy" published in 1849.

The discourse in question is titled (following Matthew 6:26, 30), "'Look at the Birds of the Air; They Sow Not and Reap Not and Gather Not into Barns' — *without Worries about Tomorrow.* 'Look at the Grass in the Field, *Which Today Is'*" (WA, 36). Having already devoted a fair share of discursive attention to "silence" and "obedience" in the first two discourses of *The Lily in the Field and the Bird of the Air*, respectively, Kierkegaard launches immediately into the explicit theme of the third discourse: "Do this and learn: *Joy*" (WA, 36). This is already enough to throw the attentive reader for a loop. For, relative to every precedent "joy of it" discourse, the typical prelude to the theme of the discourse is altogether nonexistent. At the outset, the theme is identified, with absolutely no build up. Moreover, and again in contrast to every precedent "joy of it" discourse, the explicit theme of the discourse appears to be precisely what Kierkegaard has hitherto refused to explicate. The set theme is not the joy of this or the joy of that — it is simply, and emphatically, "*joy.*"

Having thus set himself the task of saying something about "joy," the first thing that Kierkegaard proposes, remarkably enough,

---

humble bold confidence before God as the one who certainly knows this [i.e., the necessity of diversion] better than the person himself" (CUP, 1:492). If asked in any other spirit, the question (regarding when and for how long diversion is actually necessary) is essentially "a childish form of religiousness" according to which "the earnest moment is when it must ask permission from the parents" (CUP, 1:473). In other words, the diversion is only ever divinely sanctioned when it is afforded to the one prone to the temptation opposite the (ultimately self-defeating) tendency to indulge in ceaseless amusement (see UDVS, 184), namely, the temptation of "the monastic movement" (CUP, 1:491), "the way to the monastery" (CUP, 1:492) "in which there is no distraction [*Adspredelse*]" (CUP, 1:416-17). This is why the diversion takes the form of an *admonition*: look at the birds, look at the lily, look at the grass.

[40]On the appropriateness of thinking of Jesus as "joyful," see Benjamin Breckinridge Warfield, *The Person and Work of Christ*, ed. Samuel G. Craig (Philadelphia: The Presbyterian and Reformed Publishing Company, 1950) 122-27; and Elton Trueblood, *The Humor of Christ: A Bold Challenge to the Traditional Stereotype of a Somber, Gloomy Jesus* (San Francisco: Harper and Row, 1964).

is that "joy is communicable" (WA, 36).[41] Were the "inverse dialectic" brought to bear upon this insight, Kierkegaard may just as well have proclaimed, "the joy of it: that the unutterable is communicable."[42] In fact—and to allay the understandable suspicion that he might here be writing of a "joy" other than the "indescribable" or "unutterable"—Kierkegaard actually uses the phrase "indescribable joy" or "unutterable joy" (or some slight variation thereof) three times in this discourse (WA, 37, 42, 43). And yet, it is a scant few pages into the discourse that Kierkegaard actually proposes what sounds awfully like a definition:

> What is joy, or what is it to be joyful? It is truly to be present to oneself; but truly to be present to oneself is this *today*, this *to be* today, truly *to be today*. The more true it is that you are today, the more completely present you are to yourself today, the less the day of trouble, tomorrow, exists for you. Joy is the present time with the whole emphasis on: the present time. Therefore God is blessed, he who eternally says: Today, he who eternally and infinitely is present to himself in being today. And therefore the lily and the bird are joy, because by silence and unconditional obedience they are completely present to themselves in being today. (WA, 39)

Conspicuously absent from this definition is the word *existere*, as Kierkegaard consistently opts for the copula, *være*—also intimated in the Danish word for "presence" (*nærværelse*). This is no accident, and Kierkegaard's subsequent delineation of the principal obstacle to joy renders this an important point:

---

[41]Cf. EO, 1:169. That Kierkegaard's entire authorship may be conceived as a communication of joy is clearly suggested in his reflection upon "Governance's Part" in that authorship: "This, my God-relationship, is in many ways the happy love of my unhappy and troubled life. And even though this love story (if I dare to call it that) has the essential mark of the true love story, that only one can completely understand it, and to only one does a person have absolute joy [*absolut Glæde*] in telling it, to the beloved, therefore here the one by whom one is loved—it nevertheless is enjoyable [*glædeligt*] to speak of it to others also" (PV, 71).

[42]"[God] has only one joy: to communicate, and therefore the one most welcome is the one most in need" (JP, 2:1414). A dialogue forged on this point between Kierkegaard and Thomas Aquinas appears most inviting; see Charles Reutman, *The Thomistic Concept of Pleasure, as Compared with Hedonistic and Rigoristic Philosophies* (Washington DC: Catholic University of America Press, 1953); and Norman Kretzmann, "Aquinas on God's Joy, Love, and Liberality," *The Modern Schoolman* 72/2-3 (1995): 125-48.

The unconditional joy is simply joy over God, over whom and in whom you can always unconditionally rejoice. If you do not become unconditionally joyful in this relationship, then the fault lies unconditionally in you, in your ineptitude in casting all your sorrow upon him, in your unwillingness to do so, in your conceitedness, in your self-willfulness — in short, it lies in your not being like the lily and the bird. There is only one sorrow concerning which the lily and the bird cannot be your teacher and which we therefore will not discuss here: the sorrow of sin. (WA, 43)

The problem — at least that posed for the course of the present investigation — should be clear enough. Prior to the composition of *The Lily in the Field and the Bird of the Air*, Kierkegaard has consistently refused to describe or say what the nature of joy is in itself or as such. Indeed, notwithstanding his obvious fondness for the word, Kierkegaard is actually (or at least has hitherto been) doubly reticent in this regard. And yet here he is, writing directly and unreservedly about "joy" in the third discourse of *The Lily in the Field and the Bird of the Air*. As suggested already, and fully intimated in Kierkegaard's diagnosis of the obstacle(s) to achieving this joy, the solution to this problem lies in the recognition of the nature and significance of the diversion.

Having defined "joy" as the complete presence of the self to itself in the present, Kierkegaard identifies the sole obstacle to the actualization of this experience as the individual's "not being like the lily and the bird." But herein lies the all-important question: Can an *existing* human being, even if he or she is willing in this regard, *be* sufficiently like the lily and the bird to enjoy the immediacy of uninterrupted self-presence?[43] Indeed, what if the individual's ineptitude, unwillingness, conceitedness, and self-willfulness themselves (recognized as such) became a source of sorrow — the sorrow of sin — may one then, proceeding according to the general dictate of Matthew 6:25-34, "not worry" about it, and say to this sorrow, "yes, yes, tomorrow" (JFY, 181)? "Don't worry about being a sinner" — is that the ultimate lesson of the directive to learn from

---

[43]For a slightly different reading of the discourse, and a corresponding entertainment of this question, see George Pattison, "The Joy of Birdsong or Lyrical Dialectics," in *International Kierkegaard Commentary: Without Authority*, ed. Robert L. Perkins (Macon: Mercer University Press, 2007) 111-26.

the lily and the bird? Conceived as a diversion from the real task set before the existing individual, Kierkegaard's understanding of the lesson is the exact opposite. It is for this reason, and in this regard, that Kierkegaard preserves a marked lacuna in the discourse, a void untapped by either the lily or the bird: "the sorrow of sin." Viewed accordingly, Kierkegaard is (still) not describing or saying what joy is — he is defining what joy would be were one sufficiently like the lily and the bird.

As quickly as this recognition dispenses with the problem of reading what Kierkegaard appears to say about joy in light of his repeated insistences that he cannot and will not do so, does it not immediately raise an altogether more torturous problem? Indeed, if Kierkegaard is only able and willing to say what joy would be were one like the lily and the bird — and this is acknowledged to be impossible for an existing human being — is this not precisely the kind of dreadful joke that will leave the religiously inclined individual (who wishes that it were so) pulling out his hair? "Here is what true joy is, and you can never have it" — is that what Kierkegaard means to say? Once again, conceived as a diversion from the real task set before the existing individual — a task to which the individual is presently called to return — Kierkegaard's appropriation of the directive of attention to the lily and the bird points in exactly the opposite direction. For, if there is a sorrow with which neither the lily nor the bird is conversant, this would appear to suggest that there is a joy that is uniquely afforded to the human being as well. Or rather, insofar as the attribution of "sorrow" to the lily and the bird fails to encompass the depth and essential character of human sorrow, the same may be said of the "joy" similarly (i.e., metaphorically) attributed.

It seems at last, then, that Kierkegaard has only pretended to write about "joy" in order to remind his readers that he is not writing about joy. But this is not convoluted discourse for the sake of discursive convolution. The entire exercise — indeed, from its inception in the Gospel of Matthew down through its entertainment in the third discourse of *The Lily in the Field and the Bird of the Air* — is a diversion, an amusement, an enjoyable reprieve, a jest. But it is, as Kierkegaard would say, a jest in earnest. There is a point to the diversion, and it is this: to allow the one who is veritably suffocating in sin a moment to catch a breath — a refreshing breath of "the trade winds which blow across the plains of Mamre to the everlasting mansions" (JP, 5:5324), an intimation of "the supreme drawing of breath that cannot take shape because the existing person is existing" (CUP, 1:221), a momentous experience that can rightly be called "inspiration" (JFY, 182). But as willing as we all are to take the hint, indulge in this momentary reprieve as if it were the genuine article, and thus spare ourselves the horrifying earnestness of the imitation of Christ, the point of the *Adspredelse* remains: to return to the task, turn back around, and engage the obstacles (or obstacle) that lie(s) between the sinner and true joy.[44]

Conclusion

Having traced the development of Kierkegaard's careful and manifold treatment of the theme of the distinctively Christian sort of joy up through the writings that comprise the second or middle period of his authorship, and having inaugurated this endeavor with the claim that "from beginning to end, Kierkegaard's is a philosophy of joy," the present exercise is confronted with a single question that hangs thick in the air: Where is the joy in the *end*—i.e., in the exclamatory outburst of attack literature that comprises the final period of Kierkegaard's authorship? This is perhaps merely one more way of posing the generic question as to whether (and in what respect) the writings of the late period of the authorship comprise a significant continuation of or departure from the precedent authorship(s). When posed specifically in terms of the theme of the distinctively Christian sort of joy, however, the question actually affords a significant and telling response.

In the terms afforded by the preceding analysis, the problem

---

[44]Already in "What We Learn from the Lilies in the Field and from the Birds of the Air" (UDVS, 155-212), Kierkegaard displays his appreciation of and commitment to this thought: "But when the Gospel speaks authoritatively, it speaks with the earnestness of eternity; then there is no more time to dwell dreamily over the lily or longingly to follow the bird—a brief, an instructive reference to the lily and the bird, but then the eternal requirement of earnestness. And just as it holds true of diversion [*Adspredelse*] that it mitigatingly give the worried one something else to think about, so it also holds true of the rigorous words of earnestness that in earnestness and truth they give the worried one something different from his worry to think about" (UDVS, 204).

with Christendom is that it continues to use backwards language, it refuses to turn around, and it tries to turn what was intended as a momentary reprieve into an indefinite (indeed, life-long) vacation. Over and over again in the years leading up to the final period of the authorship (1850–1854), Kierkegaard writes journal entry after journal entry lamenting the fate of the word "joy" in the hands of Christendom.[45] If there is a question of Kierkegaard's having 'gone over the edge' in the late writings, it is this recognition that provides the push. The word "joy" — and along with it the dictum that Christianity is "sheer joy" and every passage in the New Testament in which the call to "rejoice" appears — has been so thoroughly appropriated by Christendom — a kind of "refined Epicureanism"[46] — that the quest of this unfathomably beatifying experience is "twice removed from actually beginning" (JP, 4:4729). As if the quest itself were not already difficult enough according to the recognition that basically "it is always the person himself who stands in his way" (CD, 110), the institution of Christendom has taken the name of the goal and used it to point people in exactly the wrong direction.

As a result, the use of the word "joy" in the late writings is more often than not characterized by a kind of palpable disdain as Kierkegaard speaks over and over again to the mock "joy" and the mock "rejoicing" that he discerns in Christendom.[47] But through it all — indeed, from the very beginning of this period of the authorship to the very end — one also finds the occasional, pointed remark pointing in the other direction, as Kierkegaard, in reflecting upon his task as an author and critic of Christendom, counts himself profoundly "joyful and grateful" (TM, 78, 210, 311) to have been used by God in this capacity, however much it means being misunderstood by the world, and however much he may happen to "dislike it" (TM, 68).[48] Thus, joy remains at the end what it was in the beginning, namely, the very sustenance of the authorship.

---

[45]See esp. JP, 2:1935, 2204; 3:2332; 4:4313, 4729, 4799; 6:6686.
[46]See JP, 1:372, 602, 1000; 2:1276, 1619; 3:2484, 2763, 3209, 3378, 3529, 3530, 3771; 4:3878, 4362, 4725, 4728, 4803, 5037; 6:6793, 6876.
[47]See TM, 42, 178-79, 185-86, 189-90, 231, 243, 249, 323.
[48]Cf. TM, 13, 46, 208, 290.

6

Kierkegaard's Christian Discourses *on Upbuilding, Mildness, and Polemic:* "A Temple-Cleansing Celebration — and Then the Quiet"

David J. Gouwens

An Author's Uncertainties

As is clear from Kierkegaard's journals, the final form of *Christian Discourses* was not decided until the last minute (JP, 5:6110-13, 6125; CD, 399-403).[1] The initial structure of the volume was to include three parts, but shortly before publication Kierkegaard decided to include in the volume, as part three, "Thoughts That Wound from Behind — for Upbuilding," with the subtitle of "Christian Addresses" (rather than "Christian Discourses" used for parts one, two, and four) (CD, 161). The genesis of part three, written in January-February 1848,[2] lay in the plan to include it as the first part of a "new book . . . entitled: **Thoughts That Cure Radically, Christian Healing**" (JP, 5:6110; CD, 399). "This will be the polemical element, something like 'The Cares of the Pagans' [CD, part one], but somewhat stronger than that, since Christian discourses should be given in an altogether milder tone" (JP, 5:6110; CD, 399). "Thoughts That Wound from Behind" was to have been followed, in this original plan, by *The Sickness unto Death* and "what eventually became" *Practice in Christianity*, dealing with "the doctrine of the Atonement."[3]

The journals indicate too how Kierkegaard struggled with

---

[1]Søren Kierkegaard, *Christian Discourses* and *The Crisis and a Crisis in the Life of an Actress*, ed. and trans. with introduction and notes, Howard V. Hong and Edna H. Hong (Princeton: Princeton University Press, 1997), "Historical Introduction," xiii.

[2]CD, "Historical Introduction," xii.

[3]CD, "Historical Introduction," xiii.

including "Thoughts That Wound from Behind" within *Christian Discourses*. In one entry, evidently having decided not to include this part, he writes that

> I almost went and upset the whole design of *Christian Discourses* and their original purpose by including in them "Thoughts That Wound from Behind for Upbuilding" simply because these discourses were lying there ready. A polemical piece like that belongs there least of all; it will itself be weakened by its surroundings and divert all attention away from the "Friday Discourses" [what became *Christian Discourses*, part four]. No, my intention is to be as gentle as possible, right after the powerful polemic in *Works of Love*. The Christian discourses are given in this way. (JP, 5:6111; CD, 399)

So too, Kierkegaard continues in more mundane spirit, "I may take a journey, and I would like to depart in peace. Finally, the book was getting too large; the smaller, the better I am read" (JP, 5:6111; CD, 399). In these two journal entries, the stress on the distinctive "gentleness" of *Christian Discourses* is clear, especially in contrast to the "powerful polemic" of *Works of Love*, and this despite the relatively polemical tone of "The Cares of the Pagans" (CD, part one).

Yet Kierkegaard did finally include "Thoughts That Wound from Behind," and in a lengthy journal entry rehearses the change in his decision, which he attributes to Governance that overruled his sagacity, his desire to arrange something himself (JP, 5:6112; CD, 400-401). The additional reasons signal, however, a change in tone and tactics for *Christian Discourses*. In contrast to his earlier judgment, Kierkegaard now concludes that, "Without the third part *Christian Discourses* is much too mild, for me truly not in character; they are mild enough as it is. And how in the world would I get a more felicitous juxtaposition than with the enormous thrust in the third part—and the hidden inwardness in the fourth, simply because it is the Communion on Friday" (JP, 5:6112; CD, 400). "Then too, without part three *Christian Discourses* is too repetitious" (JP, 5:6112; CD, 400). In yet another entry, he concludes that "The contrast between the third and fourth parts of *Christian Discourses* is as sharp as possible and very intense: first there is something like a temple-cleansing celebration—and then the quiet and most intimate of all worship services—the Communion service on Fridays" (JP, 5:6121; CD, 402).

Bishop Mynster and the Politics of 1848

Between his submitting the manuscript of *Christian Discourses* to the publisher on March 6, 1848, and its publication the following April 26, Kierkegaard dwells extensively in his journals upon how he felt that Governance had led him, but not forced him, to include this more polemical piece as part three of *Christian Discourses*, this despite his fears of how Bishop Mynster would receive the book (JP, 5:6112; CD, 400-401).

> But Mynster has touched me by retaining his friendship for me in spite of *Works of Love*. I would so much like to humor him once. I know he would like *Christian Discourses* if it did not have part three. But I cannot do it. I would also have liked to dedicate the fourth part to him ["Discourses at the Communion on Fridays"], but that cannot be done. Perhaps here again it is only a gloomy thought that he would get angry about part three. (JP, 5:6112; CD, 401)

To understand Kierkegaard's shifting sense of responsibility reflects not only his ambivalent relation with Bishop Mynster, but also the political turmoil in Denmark in 1848. On March 27, Kierkegaard writes in his journal, "Once again for a moment I have been concerned about my responsibility in letting *Christian Discourses*, especially part three, be published" (JP, 5:6125; CD, 402). He fears that there may be personal repercussions, even personal dangers, arising from its publication, given the shifting political situation in Denmark, and this despite the fact that the manuscript was sent to the publisher before the political crisis that quickly emerged around the demand for a constitutional monarchy and the Slesvig-Holsten crisis with Germany (JP, 5:6125; CD, 402; CD, 463n36). In any event, at the same moment he feared that perhaps "I will be the maltreated victim," he also acknowledged that "perhaps not a soul will read my *Christian Discourses*" (*Pap.* VIII1 A 617; CD, 403; cf. JP, 1:647; CD, 381-82).

In discussing *Christian Discourses* in his biography of Kierkegaard, Joakim Garff focuses upon the relation with Mynster and the Danish political situation, arguing that in these anxious ruminations about his new book "what Kierkegaard had in mind was a *biographical* reading of his *Christian Discourses*," concerned as he was with "the intimate connection between life and writings," and this "is what forced him to consider whether he was to write leniently or strictly."[4] Garff sees the center of Kierkegaard's concern particularly in the second discourse of part three of *Christian Discourses*, on Peter's abandoning his people; "in this negative definition of the national cause the discourse risked placing its author on the front line."[5] It is this, Garff argues, that led to Kierkegaard's developing self-image as one who "gradually wrote himself more and more into the role of martyr."[6]

That the immediate political and biographical considerations of 1848 played a significant role in Kierkegaard's decision on the final form of *Christian Discourses* is clear. Kierkegaard's relations with Mynster and his continuing evaluation of what the political situation called for are evident from the journals.

The Rhetoric of Christian Discourse

In addition, however, attention may be given to how the decision to include part three in *Christian Discourses* reflects Kierkegaard's developing understanding of "upbuilding," "mildness," and "polemic" as interrelated elements in the rhetoric of Christian discourse. The issue is not only the biographical question of Kierkegaard's conception of his public role as a religious writer; it is also the related question of the tactics of how one may rhetorically communicate Christian concepts within "Christendom," and in particular the extent to which the "polemical" may be employed in Christian discourse. If part three of *Christian Discourses* is "the overture to Kierkegaard's collision with the established order of Christendom,"[7] what is the significance of the fact that part three, borrowed from an initial plan for a future polemical book, is placed now in the context of "Christian discourses" that were initially envisioned as embodying the "gentle"? So too, when we recall that this most polemical part of *Christian Discourses* is also the only one to have in its title "For

---

[4]Joakim Garff, *Søren Kierkegaard: A Biography*, trans. Bruce H. Kirmmse (Princeton: Princeton University Press, 2005) 496.

[5]Garff, *Søren Kierkegaard*, 496.

[6]Garff, *Søren Kierkegaard*, 497.

[7]CD, "Historical Introduction," xiii.

Upbuilding" (CD, 161), the question arises: what is then the emerging relation in *Christian Discourses* among the categories of the "upbuilding," "mildness," and "polemic"?

The thesis of this paper is that in *Christian Discourses* Kierkegaard forges a union of these categories in this book that heightens their internal dialectical and rhetorical relations, in which the "polemical," hardly a new element in his writing, is raised to new prominence, is seen as in itself upbuilding, and is placed in a positive relation to "mildness." In its rhetorical and maieutic structure, Kierkegaard's *Christian Discourses* presents a careful dialectic in which the reader is "gently" invited to make the movements of self-reflection that will allow her or him to hear the force of the polemical attack, yet for the larger purposes of upbuilding and repentance. The procedure will be to consider Kierkegaard's developing views of the relations among "upbuilding," "mildness," and "polemic."

Upbuilding

First, it is well to consider the concepts of the *upbuilding* and of *Christian discourses*. The overall development of Kierkegaard's up-building literature, as the Hongs note in their "Historical Introduction" to *Christian Discourses*, is its progression through ethical-religious categories of immanence (*Eighteen Upbuilding Discourses*) to specifically Christian categories. In *Upbuilding Discourses in Various Spirits* (March 13, 1847), it is part three, "The Gospel of Sufferings," that first carries the designation "Christian Discourses,"[8] and this is indeed the first of Kierkegaard's works to carry the designation "Christian."[9] So too, *Works of Love* (September 29, 1847) carries the subtitle "Some Christian Deliberations in the Form of Discourses." The term "discourses," as well as the more specific "Christian discourses," indicate too that they are offered without the authority of sermonic address, and do not deal with doubt.[10] But it is at this point, as Sylvia Walsh argues, that the designation of "Christian discourses" points to the specific way of handling doubt, viz., by

---

[8]CD, "Historical Introduction," xii.
[9]Sylvia Walsh, *Living Christianly: Kierkegaard's Dialectic of Christian Existence* (University Park: The Pennsylvania State University Press, 2005) 35.
[10]CD, "Historical Introduction," xii.

appeal to the authority of Scripture rather than universal human reflection (as in "upbuilding discourses").[11] The rhetorical strategy in Christian discourses, in short, changes at this point to include appeals to a commonly held scriptural tradition that is presumed (at least in theory) to carry authority. The answer to doubt is not speculation, but scriptural authority. It is for this reason that the "Christian discourses" will, to a greater or lesser degree, make explicit use of scripture.

Nonetheless, it is at this point that Kierkegaard's own lack of authority caused him to hesitate in his use of the term "upbuilding" with regard to decisively Christian categories. Again, to cite Walsh, whereas Kierkegaard claims that the category of the "upbuilding" is his own, it is also the case that he hesitates "to educate people in the strictest Christian categories," he demurs, and so one year later, with the publication of *The Sickness unto Death* in 1849, employs the pseudonym Anti-Climacus to instruct in the decisively Christian categories, and it is *The Sickness unto Death* that carries the subtitle of "for Upbuilding and Awakening."[12]

This development indicates, however, that Kierkegaard's moving "Thoughts That Wound from Behind" from the projected new volume back into *Christian Discourses* signals a renewed exploration of the way in which, writing under his own name, and even as one writing without authority, Christian discourses (or "Christian Addresses," the subtitle of "Thoughts That Wound from Behind") may serve "for Upbuilding" (CD, 161) on the way to the decisively Christian. It is this that we must now explore more fully by looking at Kierkegaard's developing strategies of "mildness" and "polemic."

Mildness

Second, we turn to the "gentle" or "mild" quality of the *Christian Discourses* as Kierkegaard originally understood the plan of the volume. At the time that he decided against including "Thoughts That Wound from Behind," he wrote, "No, my intention is to be as gentle as possible, right after the powerful polemic in *Works of Love*. The Christian discourses are given in this way" (JP, 5:6111; CD, 399).

---

[11]Walsh, *Living Christianly*, 171n19.
[12]Walsh, *Living Christianly*, 21.

In point of fact, however, the original plan of *Christian Discourses*, even before the decision to add part three, includes a strong polemical element. If Kierkegaard says, "My intention is to be as gentle as possible," in contrast to *Works of Love*, this does not mean that the original plan lacked polemic. Indeed, Bruce H. Kirmmse is struck by a consistent polemical character in *Christian Discourses*, setting the tone for Kierkegaard's cultural critique.

> The structure of the *Discourses* could perhaps be called musical, with an opening shock which consists in the assertion that it is precisely the participants in Christian culture who are the "heathens" *par excellence*. This section is followed by a series of exhortations — "dark sayings," SK called them, citing Psalm 49, where the psalmist, like SK himself, sings in evil days of the empty pomposity of the great. This second section stresses the unavoidability of suffering to the Christian, while discounting its significance to the believer. Next come the "Thoughts Which Stab in the Back" (literal translation: "Thoughts Which Wound from Behind"), in which SK's troublemaking sallies against the established culture reach new heights of polemical daring. Finally, the communion discourses form an abrupt transition to a peaceable emphasis upon inwardness and conclude on a note so tranquil that SK even entertained the idea of dedicating them to Bishop Mynster — but decided against it lest he be seen as making gestures to the establishment in expectation of official favor . . . ![13]

Yet one may appreciate why Kierkegaard saw the direct attack of part three as distinctively different from the original plan for the book, in contrast not only to part four but also to parts one and two as more "gentle" in mood. This can be seen by looking more closely at the themes and the rhetorical strategies of parts one and two, which will allow us to turn to part three in relation to the communion discourses of part four.

The first part of *Christian Discourses*, "The Cares of the Pagans," is one that the Hongs rightly see as the second most polemical part of the book.[14] However, if the content is polemical, the rhetoric is relatively more guarded than in part three, much less a direct attack. Beginning with Matthew 6:24-34, the impossibility of serving two

---

[13]Bruce H. Kirmmse, *Kierkegaard in Golden Age Denmark* (Bloomington and Indianapolis: Indiana University Press, 1990) 340-41.
[14]CD, "Historical Introduction," xii-xiii.

masters and the importance of seeking "first God's kingdom and his righteousness," the conceit of the discourses is that the lily and the bird of the gospel lesson "make clear what paganism is, but thereby in turn in order to make clear what is required of the Christian. The lily and the bird are slipped in to prevent judging, because the lily and the bird judge no one—and you, you are certainly not to judge the pagan" (CD, 9-10). Of course, the reader knows that the discourses will press the question of whether there are Christians in Christendom, yet in the introduction Kierkegaard distances himself as author from condemnation, as if his discourses were a mockery "censuring us for our mediocre Christianity," and presents instead the assumption that such cares might not exist in Christendom. But then comes the final proviso: "Let us not forget . . . that the pagans who are found in Christendom have sunk the lowest" (CD, 12). Yet, as if retracting even this harsh judgment, the introduction concludes that "the upbuilding address is fighting in many ways for the eternal to be victorious in a person, but in the appropriate place and with the aid of the lily and the bird, it does not forget first and foremost to relax into a smile" (CD, 12).

In short, part one, "The Cares of the Pagans," in its conceit of describing the cares that presumably do not exist among Christians, avoids direct attack, and is deliberately couched within conventions that do not assault the reader, at the same time that they make clear to the discerning reader the pervasiveness of the "cares of the pagans" among putative Christians.

The "gentle" qualities of the original plan of the book are evident as well in part two, "States of Mind in the Strife of Suffering." Here the theme is not the "cares of the pagans," which are by implication the cares of those in Christendom, but the joy that is available to the Christian in the strife of suffering. This is not to deny the cultural critique implied by the "dark saying" of the motto to part two, from Psalm 49:5: "I will incline my ear to a proverb; I will set my dark saying to the music of the harp" (CD, 93). Neither is it to deny that this upbuilding is "terrifying" "at first," for "the upbuilding is not for the healthy but for the sick" (CD, 96). The upbuilding is now defined as "artesian-well drilling, in which one must dig many, many fathoms—then of course the jet spurts all the higher" (CD, 96). The confidence of the upbuilding is "triumphant" in that, as in the art of medicine, the upbuilding performs "the difficult task of turning poison into a remedy"; so too, "the terrifying is far more gloriously transformed into the upbuilding" (CD, 96-97).

Hence in transforming the terrifying into the upbuilding, the stress on the "moods" or "emotions" of Christian joy is paramount.[15] In a journal entry, Kierkegaard writes that if there were to be a preface for this part two,

> it would be of the following nature. That most valiant of nations in antiquity (the Lacedæmonians) prepared for battle with music — in the same way these are states of mind of triumphant joy that tune one [*stemme*] for the struggle, and far from discouraging [*forstemme*] a person in the struggle will definitely keep him well tuned [*velstemt*] (JP, 2: 2201; CD, 398).

Part two of *Christian Discourses* directly develops the themes of joy in suffering already sounded in the 1847 "The Gospel of Sufferings" in *Upbuilding Discourses in Various Spirits* (UDVS, 213-341). In *Christian Discourses*, as in "The Gospel of Sufferings," the central theme is the joy that is available to the Christian no matter the suffering she or he endures. The theme is thus the conquest of suffering through placing suffering within a broader context of Christian understanding. The juxtaposition of the musical images of the Psalmist's "dark sayings" with the Lacedæmonians' joyful martial music preparing for struggle points to Kierkegaard's self-conscious strategy of "inverted dialectic." In a journal entry on part two, discourses five and six, Kierkegaard labels as "Inverted Dialectic" the understanding that the loss of the temporal may occasion a gaining eternally. "Straightforwardly, to lose is to lose; inversely, to lose is to gain," "as the butterfly *gains* by *losing* its cocoon" (JP, 1:760; CD, 375). As Sylvia Walsh writes in her recent study of Kierkegaard's "inverse dialectic," in *Christian Discourses*, part two, inverted vision sees joy in the midst of sufferings in a variety of

---

[15]Kirmmse, *Kierkegaard in Golden Age Denmark*, 346, uses "Moods in the Struggle of Sufferings." The older Walter Lowrie translation of *Christian Discourses* (London: Oxford University Press, 1940) 97, uses "Joyful Notes" to translate *Stemninger*. I agree with Sylvia Walsh, *Living Christianly*, 179n8, that Lowrie's "Joyful Notes" is preferable to the Hongs' translation of the title as "States of Mind," for "Joyful Notes" better expresses "the more emotional than mental connotation of the term and its association with music through being derived from the Danish word *stemme*, which means 'voice,' especially 'singing voice.'"

circumstances, for example, "that suffering does not take away hope but recruits it; that the poorer Christians become, the richer they make others and themselves as well; that the weaker they become, the stronger they become; that to lose is to gain; and that misfortune is really good fortune."[16]

Another important aspect of the "gentleness" of part two is seen in how gradually Kierkegaard in "States of Mind in the Strife of Suffering" approaches the decisive Christian categories of suffering and the consciousness of sin. *Christian Discourses*, part two, is a step in a carefully modulated approach to the decisive Christian understandings of suffering, one that also approaches the consciousness of sin, in both of these themes looking back in particular to *Upbuilding Discourses in Various Spirits*, "The Gospel of Sufferings," but also looking ahead to more decisive definitions of both Christian suffering and sin in the later literature.[17] In an important journal entry Kierkegaard describes his understanding of the role of *Christian Discourses*, part two.

> "Instructions for States of Mind in the Strife of Suffering"
> These discourses are presented in such a way as to be continually tangential to the consciousness of sin and the suffering of sin—sin etc. are another matter: these discourses come to the subject of sin. Because the consolation lyrically rises as high as possible over all earthly need and misery, even the heaviest, the horror of sin, is continually shown. Thus another theme is cunningly concealed in these discourses: sin is the human being's corruption.
> In the ordinary sermon this is the confusion: need and adversity are preached together—with sin.
> Thus the category for these discourses is different from "The Gospel of Sufferings," which left the suffering indefinite. Here the distinction is made: the innocent suffering—in order then to approach sin. (JP, 5:6101; CD, 398-99; cf. UDVS, 392-93)

This places "States of Mind" as a stage in the dialectical development of Kierkegaard's gradual presentation of suffering. It in large part duplicates the general discussion in "The Gospel of Sufferings" that

---

[16]Walsh, *Living Christianly*, 123.

[17]My remarks here are informed in particular by Walsh's detailed and helpful discussion of the gradual unfolding of Kierkegaard's approach to the category of sin in his published literature, *Living Christianly*, 18-21, 35-50, as well as her discussion of the dialectic of suffering, 117-29.

"left the suffering indefinite," yet "States of Mind in the Strife of Suffering" focuses upon "innocent suffering" that is "continually tangential to the consciousness of sin."[18]

This journal entry thus illuminates the "gentleness" of *Christian Discourses*, part two, in making clear how gradually Kierkegaard approaches "the horror of sin." Key to this, in the journal entry, is Kierkegaard's identification of one of his central maieutic and rhetorical strategies, the theme that is "cunningly concealed." In a recent article on Kierkegaard's maieutic strategies in the 1847 works *Upbuilding Discourses in Various Spirits* and *Works of Love*, M. Jamie Ferreira helpfully notes the broader significance of this journal entry for understanding not only *Christian Discourses*, part two, but a repeated strategy of "cunningly concealing" a theme that, in her words, is "actually present in the discourse—it gives signs of itself."[19]

---

[18]This is not to suggest the "The Gospel of Sufferings" is unconcerned with the consciousness of sin. Walsh, *Living Christianly*, 35-36, notes that in "The Gospel of Sufferings" "Kierkegaard correlates the negative expression of guilt and sorrow specifically with the Christian consciousness of sin and introduces its dialectical relation to the consciousness of forgiveness in Christian existence." So too, "The Gospel of Sufferings" is deeply concerned with questions of innocent suffering, guilty suffering, and the suffering involved in following Christ. Kierkegaard's point in this journal entry, however, is that the more "indefinite" or generic treatment of suffering in "The Gospel of Sufferings" will now, in *Christian Discourses*, part two, be quietly pushed in the direction of the suffering associated with sin, and later, in *Christian Discourses*, part three, toward the specifically Christian form of voluntary suffering in the following of Christ. See Walsh, *Living Christianly*, 123-29. For recent discussions of the variety of sufferings treated in "The Gospel of Sufferings," see in particular Martin Andic, "The Secret of Sufferings," in *International Kierkegaard Commentary: Upbuilding Discourses in Various Spirits*, ed. Robert L. Perkins (Macon, GA: Mercer University Press, 2005) 199-228; David J. Kangas, "The Very Opposite of Beginning with Nothing: Guilt Consciousness in Kierkegaard's 'The Gospel of Sufferings' IV," IKC: UDVS, 287-313; Simon D. Podmore, "The Dark Night of Suffering and the Darkness of God: God-Forsakenness or Forsaking God in 'The Gospel of Sufferings,'" IKC: UDVS, 229-56, especially 253; Lee Barrett, "The Joy in the Cross: Kierkegaard's Appropriation of Lutheran Christology in 'The Gospel of Sufferings,'" IKC: UDVS, 257-85; and David R. Law, "Wrongness, Guilt, and Innocent Suffering in Kierkegaard's *Either/Or, Part II*, and *Upbuilding Discourses in Various Spirits*," IKC: UDVS, 315-48.

[19]M. Jamie Ferreira, "'The Next Thing': On the Maieutic Relations between the *Upbuilding Discourses in Various Spirits* and *Works of Love*," IKC: UDVS, 371-96. The quotation is in IKC: UDVS, 381. Ferreira employs the maieutic strategy of the "cunningly concealed" theme to explore relations between the 1847 works

How then is the theme of sin "cunningly concealed" in *Christian Discourses*, part two, yet gives signs of itself? As is clear from the journal entry, the answer is that in each of the discourses, the refrain is sounded that whatever "earthly need and misery" one encounters, there is nothing in the world to fear, for only "sin is the human being's corruption." The discourses in part two describe a "consolation lyrically" rising "as high as possible over all earthly need and misery." Yet "the heaviest, the horror of sin, is continually shown," for sin is close at hand (JP, 5:6101; CD, 398). Ominously, at the end of the seventh and final discourse, the reader is told that if one "refuses to have faith that adversity is prosperity," "This is perdition; only sin is a human being's corruption" (CD, 159). This concealed theme that nonetheless, as Ferreira notes, gives signs of itself, appears repeatedly in each of the discourses. It is sounded first in the initial discourse (CD, 101-102), and then serves as the concluding refrain at the end of discourses two through seven (CD, 113, 123, 133, 143, 149, 159). Hence, in the midst of this basically positive, albeit terrifying (CD, 96), upbuilding exercise in "joyful notes in the strife of suffering," Kierkegaard hints, but at this stage only hints, "gently," as it were, that for "the essentially Christian," "there is this infinite difference between evil and what is confusingly called evil," the infinite difference between the sufferings of temporality and that "sin, only sin, is the corruption" (CD, 103).[20]

Polemic

Third, moving from the "gentler" strategy of the "concealed theme" approach to sin in *Christian Discourses*, part two, we are now in position to consider again the placing of "Thoughts That Wound from Behind" as part three, and what this signifies for Kierkegaard's developing sense of the uses of *polemic*. The relative "gentleness" of part two, its fundamentally "joyful" mood, despite its ominous hints of the horror of sin as the only real corruption, is now disrupted by

---

Upbuilding Discourses in Various Spirits, part three, "The Gospel of Sufferings," and *Works of Love*. I wish to employ it, in the original context of the journal entry on the "cunningly concealed" theme, to illuminate the relations of *Christian Discourses*, parts two and three.

[20]Walsh, *Living Christianly*, 18-21.

the new part three, "Thoughts That Wound from Behind."[21] The polemical weight of the attack in part three names the consciousness of sin that was "cunningly concealed" yet gave signals of its presence in part two. In the first discourse of part three, "Watch Your Step When You Go to the House of the Lord," the reader is admonished that for whatever reason you do enter God's house, "you are coming to something still more terrible" (CD, 172).

> Here in God's house there is essentially discourse about a danger that the world does not know, a danger in comparison with which everything the world calls danger is child's play — the danger of sin. (CD, 172)[22]

The awareness of the danger of sin is heightened in part three of *Christian Discourses* in that these discourses outline also a suffering not yet explored: the voluntary suffering that results from following Christ.[23]

> The world can well comprehend that little consolation is found for those who suffer unavoidable loss. But that one should voluntarily expose oneself to loss and danger, this is madness in the eyes of the world — and it is altogether properly the essentially Christian. (CD, 179)

The Christian ideal of voluntary suffering indicates too the distance of established Christianity from Christian ideals, an ideal it could only think "madness."

In both of these themes, that of the consciousness of sin and the call to voluntary suffering, part three "wounds from behind," with undisguised cultural and political condemnation. As Kirmmse puts it, part three is an explicit attack upon "the decadent state of Christian culture — with its intellectualizing theorists, its well-spoken sermonizers, and its invocation of the name of Christianity to support the politics of liberal, of democratic-demagogic, and of

---

[21]Walsh, *Living Christianly*, 126.

[22]Here too Kierkegaard is duplicating earlier themes; see the explicit discussion of sin anticipated in the earlier "Christian Discourses" found in *Upbuilding Discourses in Various Spirits*, "The Gospel of Sufferings," 246. On this point, see also Walsh, *Living Christianly*, 34-35.

[23]Walsh, *Living Christianly*, 126-27.

snobbish conservative circles."[24]

In stressing what Kierkegaard calls "the enormous thrust" of part three (JP, 5:6112; CD, 400), we should not obscure, however, the presence of polemic in Kierkegaard's earlier Christian authorship. As we have seen, he understands *Works of Love* as embodying "powerful polemic" (JP, 5:6111; CD, 399), and initially hesitates to issue *Christian Discourses* in the same vein. Indeed, *Works of Love* was a deeply polemical work in exploring the inescapability of suffering that the loving person will experience, and how the way of Christian love leads to persecution in Christendom.[25] *Works of Love* sounds the theme of how Christian love is the way of persecution, and polemically criticizes how this is ignored in the preaching of the official church. The preaching in the established church "leaves out what later happens in the world to the essentially Christian" (WL, 191) in "foolish, ingratiating Sunday sermons" that ignore the demand of the "double danger" of Christian struggle, not only in the person's inner being, but in outward and worldly persecution (WL, 191-204). Hence, "Christianly the world's opposition stands in an *essential* relationship to the inwardness of Christianity" (WL, 194). In *Works of Love* too Kierkegaard urges, "If it is necessary, we should not hesitate either, under the highest responsibility, to preach **against** Christianity in *Christian* — yes, precisely in *Christian* sermons" (WL, 198).[26]

Hence, the elements of the polemical are in place in these earlier writings, and *Christian Discourses*, after Kierkegaard's initial hesitation, develops this polemic into a more forthright attack, stronger even than in *Works of Love*. Significant in Kierkegaard's incorporation of *Christian Discourses*, part three, into the book's overall design, therefore, is this heightened use of outright "attack." In the motto to part three Kierkegaard writes:

The essentially Christian needs no *defense*, is not served by any

---

[24]Kirmmse, *Kierkegaard in Golden Age Denmark*, 357.

[25]Kirmmse, *Kierkegaard in Golden Age Denmark*, 318-23.

[26]Again, it should be emphasized that *Works of Love*, published on September 29, 1847, in its discussion of Christian suffering continues themes sounded in *Upbuilding Discourses in Various Spirits*, part three, "The Gospel of Sufferings," published on March 13, 1847. On "The Gospel of Sufferings," see again Walsh, *Living Christianly*, 119-22.

defense — it is the *attacker*; to defend it is of all perversions the most indefensible, the most *inverted*, and the most dangerous — it is *unconsciously cunning treason*. Christianity is the attacker — in Christendom, of course, it attacks from behind. (CD, 162)

"The essentially Christian needs no *defense*" is a common theme sounded already in earlier works, including *Works of Love* (WL, 198-204), in connection with Christ and Christianity as offensive, but is now highlighted in a new way that will include new rhetorical strategies of attack.

In an 1847 journal entry, sketching out his plan for what would become "Thoughts That Wound from Behind," Kierkegaard explicitly states this strategy of attack as "satire." In considering such gospel texts as "What shall we have, we who have left all?," he comments upon "The satire for us in this question — we who have probably not left anything at all" (JP, 5:6096; CD, 378).

In this same journal entry Kierkegaard speaks of his strategy of satiric attack as the "stinger" (*Brod*). He observes that "in the following discourses the text is to be chosen in such a way that it appears to be a Gospel text, and is that also, but then comes the stinger" (JP, 5:6096; CD, 378). This is not the first instance of Kierkegaard's use of the concept of the "stinger" (*Brod*). M. Jamie Ferreira's recent work is again helpful. In addition to the strategy of the "cunningly concealed" theme that Kierkegaard applied to *Christian Discourses*, part two, Ferreira notes the importance of this second maieutic strategy, "the stinger." As Ferreira indicates, in another 1847 journal entry on *Upbuilding Discourses in Various Spirits*, "The Gospel of Sufferings," Kierkegaard reflects on the likelihood that "the wiseacres who know how to rattle off everything will charge my Christian discourses [i.e., "The Gospel of Sufferings"] with not containing the Atonement." He complains that "after five years of having the chance to learn," his readers do not yet appreciate "how maieutically I proceed," namely, "First the first and then the next." He goes on to explain that "I develop piece by piece in big books, always leaving behind in each book one stinger that is its connection with the next" (JP, 5:5991; UDVS, 391).[27] In this strategy, in Ferreira's words, there "is something that is left behind

---

[27]IKC: UDVS, 382.

that 'stings,' that burns, irritates, or even wounds, something that needs further attention, something that if left untreated may fester and become dangerous; figuratively it means a goad or stimulus, or something that rankles in one's mind."[28]

We will note later the sense in which the "stinger" in *Christian Discourses*, part three, looks ahead to later works. The point to understand now, however, is how Kierkegaard's use again of the concept of the rhetorical device of the "stinger" illuminates his maieutic strategy in part three, wherein he uses gospel texts in such a way that "it appears to be a Gospel text, and is that also, but then comes the stinger" (JP, 5:6096; CD, 378).[29] Here the rhetoric is that what "appears" to be gospel, "and is that also," includes a "stinger." The expectation of comfort a reader might expect is replaced not by a negation of gospel, for it "is that also," but by a gospel that includes judgment. The "stinger" is evident in the title as well as the content of each of the seven discourses of "Thoughts That Wound from Behind." As we have noted, the appeal of these "Christian Addresses," as with all of the *Christian Discourses*, is to the authority of scripture, yet with a direct polemical thrust. The use of the dash in the titles of part three and almost all of its discourses indicates the "stinger" in one form or another. In the overall title of part three, "Thoughts That Wound from Behind—for Upbuilding," the "stinger" comes first, the dash indicating the gospel that follows "for Upbuilding." In the titles for discourses two through six, the gospel text precedes the dash, ending with the "stinger": "'See, We Have Left Everything and Followed You; What Shall We Have?' (Matthew 19:27)—and What Shall We Have?"; "All Things Must Serve Us for Good—*When* We Love God"; "There Will Be the Resurrection of the Dead, of the Righteous—and of the Unrighteous"; "We Are Closer to Salvation Now—Than When We Became Believers"; "But It Is Blessed—to Suffer Mockery for a Good Cause."

The rhetorical strategy of the "stinger" is evident too, for example, in the content of the first discourse of part three, "Watch Your Step When You Go to the House of the Lord." The tone is one

---

[28]IKC: UDVS, 382.

[29]"Gospel" is used broadly in this context; the discourses of part three are all based upon biblical texts, but include only two texts from a gospel (Matthew); the other texts are from Ecclesiastes, Acts, and two epistles (Romans and First Timothy).

that begins with contemplating the security, stillness, and beauty of the house of worship, but then moves almost immediately to the danger of entering the house of the Lord, with the repeated admonition to "Take care" (CD, 163-75). Similarly, in the fourth discourse of part three, on the resurrection of the dead, the tone of the discourse begins with quietness and security but soon shifts to a mood of "assault." A person may quietly consider arguments for the immortality of the soul, the discourse begins. "He has obtained one or another book on the subject, has sat calmly and read it, or he has attended a lecture that undertook to demonstrate the immortality of the soul" (CD, 202). But the mood is false; it is one of security; one's mind is at ease. "But this discourse about immortality — yes, it aims to violate public or, more correctly here, private security; it intends to disturb peace of mind. It is like an assault, bold as an assault in broad daylight, as terrifying as an assault at night" (CD, 202). Instead of "demonstrating" immortality, it says, " 'Nothing is more certain than immortality. . . . Fear it, . . . tremble, because you are immortal' " (CD, 203).

Attack, however, is not an end in itself. The polemic, satire, and the "stinger" of part three, for all of their negativity, have in view a larger purpose. Just as in part two, where the "terrifying" may be "gloriously transformed into the upbuilding" (CD, 97) so too in part three the "thoughts that wound from behind" are discourses for "upbuilding" (CD, 161). Even the rigors of voluntary suffering are portrayed as sources of blessedness. As Sylvia Walsh rightly says of the discourses of part three, "Instead of mitigating the comfort and joy to be gained in Christian existence, these sobering reminders of the rigorous requirement and earnestness of Christianity enable one to discover the inverse source of joy and blessedness in the Christian life . . . in suffering mockery for a good cause."[30]

As we have seen, however, part three not only promises joy in the ideal of voluntary suffering in following Christ. It functions also as a profound call to repentance. For example, at the conclusion of the second discourse of part three, and after stating that God does not unconditionally require that all leave everything, Kierkegaard nonetheless sees this admission as the occasion for the true penance

[30]Walsh, *Living Christianly*, 127-28.

of "being genuinely honest toward God" (CD, 187). "According to my conception, therefore," Kierkegaard concludes, "the words by Peter we have chosen ["See, We Have Left Everything and Followed You"] are a theme for a call to repentance" (CD, 187). In similar fashion, as Kirmmse notes, the final discourse in part three, "He Was Believed in the World," is "muted in comparison to the others," it finds "an uneasy point of rest and balance," channeling the reader "away from overt criticism and into an intensification of the private, subjective God-relation of faith," preparing for the "Discourses at the Communion on Fridays," *Christian Discourses*, part four.[31]

"The contrast," Kierkegaard wrote in his journals, "between the third and fourth parts of *Christian Discourses* is as sharp as possible and very intense: first there is something like a temple-cleansing celebration—and then the quiet and most intimate of all worship services—the Communion service on Fridays" (JP, 5:6121; CD, 402). If part three is a call to repentance and self-examination, part four allows one to receive the assurance of the communion discourses, which stress the faithfulness of God. In this sense there is a profound shift of mood between the attack, the "stinger," of part three and the "quiet" and "intimacy" of the communion.

Yet it is not as if the "stinger" of part three is left behind; the communion discourses function, in very Lutheran fashion, to combine awareness of one's own sin with assurance of God's faithfulness. The reader is reminded again, in the first communion discourse, that "*sin is the corruption of the nations and of every human being*," which prompts even more a "heartfelt longing" for the supper (CD, 258, 261). Communion discourses were intended, it appears, not as sermons or "confessional discourses," but as discourses for the communion services that followed confession. Assuming confession, they address the moment a person "pauses" on the way to the communion table (CD, 270-71).[32]

The communion discourses, in calling the reader to "pause" on the way to the table, at the same time stress God's faithfulness. The

---

[31]Kirmmse, *Kierkegaard in Golden Age Denmark*, 357.

[32]Walsh, *Living Christianly*, 171-72n24, 172n25, provides a useful survey of recent literature on Kierkegaard's communion discourses, in *Christian Discourses* and beyond, including the function of communion discourses in the Friday worship services.

reader is invited to be aware of the "secret anxiety" of her or his own faithlessness (CD, 284), and even that "*fundamentally* we are faithless" (CD, 286), yet to "lay aside the burden" of that guilt in the knowledge that "If we are faithless, he still remains faithful" (CD, 287, 285). In the end, the reader is invited to the recognition that "*fundamentally* it is you [God] who are holding on to us" (CD, 286). It is in this way that *Christian Discourses*, despite all of its polemic, concludes nonetheless with a fundamentally positive affirmation, rooted in a conviction of God's ultimate faithfulness.[33] In the final discourse, Kierkegaard sums up the way in which the reader is invited to an utter reliance on God, for "at the Communion table you are able to do nothing at all" (CD, 299), for "if as a human being you are nothing before God, therefore entirely in need — at the Communion table as a sinner you are in relation to the Redeemer less than nothing — you feel all the more deeply the need of the blessing" (CD, 298).

Kierkegaard, as we have seen, complained of those who would rattle off the charge that his Christian discourses in "The Gospel of Sufferings" in 1847 would not contain the Atonement, to which he replied that people needed to remember how maieutically he proceeded, "First the first and then the next," and would leave a "stinger" in one book to develop in the next (JP, 5:5991; UDVS, 391). Near the end of *Christian Discourses*, part four, the "Atonement" is finally, explicitly treated, especially in the seventh and final discourse in its reflections upon the utter nothingness of persons before God, who as sinners rely entirely upon the forgiveness of sins: "the Atonement is accomplished — by the Redeemer" (CD, 298-99). Yet, as we have seen, Kierkegaard arrives at this point only by careful maieutic stages, exploring in "The Gospel of Sufferings" an "indefinite suffering," which is specified further in *Christian Discourses*, part two, as "suffering" that nonetheless "cunningly conceals" the theme of human sin. In part three Kierkegaard, in the context of attack, goes on to specify the Christian category of "dying to the world," "voluntary suffering," and also, in his use of the

[33]Kirmmse, *Kierkegaard in Golden Age Denmark*, 357, rightly notes the "echo of the underlying optimism that we glimpse in *Works of Love*, where SK talks of 'love's presence in the fundament of things' [*Kjerligheden i Grunden*] like 'the sprout in the seed.'"

"stinger," he gives a more explicit treatment of consciousness of sin. It is then that the theme of God's faithfulness in the face of human faithlessness, and the theme of Atonement, will be explored more fully in the communion discourses of part four.

There is also another sense in which part three presents a "stinger." The "stinger" in part three looks ahead not only to part four, the communion discourses of the present volume, but antici- pates later developments in the literature. Following *Christian Dis- courses*, in the writings of Anti-Climacus in 1849 and 1850 Kierke- gaard will develop ever more pointedly the specifically Christian categories of sin, despair, faith, and discipleship in following Christ as Pattern and Redeemer, all of which are themselves prelude to the polemical literature of Kierkegaard's last years. When we remember Kierkegaard's hesitancy to go beyond the "upbuilding" toward the definitively Christian categories in his own name, we can see how the "stinger" of *Christian Discourses*, part three, provides the impetus for a continuing thrust in the subsequent literature to develop "First the first and then the next" (JP, 5:5991; UDVS, 391).

Upbuilding, Mildness, and Polemic

Looking at *Christian Discourses* itself, however, Kierkegaard's use of "the stinger" and even outright "satire" profoundly alter the overall rhetorical shape of this one book from its original plan. They provide now the needed intensity that allows the volume to achieve an almost symphonic variation of mood. The images of musical modulation Kierkegaard uses to define part two—the psalmist's "dark saying to the music of the harp" (CD, 93) in counterpoint to the Lacedæmonians' triumphant battle music (JP, 2:2201; CD, 398) — suggest an overall rhetorical structure of the book. The moods of dis- course, like the movements of a symphony, are in this book extended to include rhetorical movement from the more muted polemic that includes strategies of "gentleness" of part one, to the still gentle yet increasingly "dark" and at the same time martial "triumphant joy" of part two, finding its climax within the "enormous thrust" of the satiric attack in the "stinger" of part three, only to be resolved in the relative quiet and intimacy of the "hidden inwardness" of the communion discourses of part four.

Rhetorically, then, the insertion of the polemical part three, the outright attack, represents an important creative breakthrough in Kierkegaard's rhetoric, for it opens a new space for polemic within his understanding of both the "upbuilding" of "Christian discourses" and, more important, a way of relating the literature of attack to the "gentle" requirements of Christian discourses after his discomfort with even the relatively mild "polemic" of *Works of Love*. From originally finding "Thoughts That Wound from Behind" too polemical for inclusion within the "gentle" and "mild" Christian discourses already planned for the book, he came rather to see part three as integral to the entire plan of the book, one that in its fierce attack is also a "celebration." The new model that he uses is a biblical one: Christ's throwing the moneychangers out of the temple.[34] "The contrast between the third and fourth parts of *Christian Discourses* is as sharp as possible and very intense: first there is something like a temple-cleansing celebration—and then the quiet and most intimate of all worship services—the Communion service on Fridays" (JP, 5:6121; CD, 402). The literature of attack now finds its own place within the larger maieutic and rhetorical purposes of Kierkegaard's "second literature," no longer as a breach with the gentleness of Christian discourses, but as a "temple-cleansing celebration," in itself a joyful exercise, required by the purposes of upbuilding on the way to the altar.

[34]Mark 11:15-19; Luke 19:45-48; Matthew 21:12-17; John 2:13-22.

7
Aristotle, Aquinas, and Kierkegaard on Prudence
Mark A. Tietjen

This paper examines the opposing conceptions of prudence held by Aristotle and Kierkegaard, with the intention of clarifying the extent to which one may appropriately read Kierkegaard in light of the virtue tradition. If some notion of prudence is appropriate within a Kierkegaardian ethic, it will have to be subordinate to the concept of Christian neighbor love. Therefore, I invoke Aquinas's conception of infused prudence as a virtue compatible with a Kierkegaardian ethic of neighbor love.

Introduction

According to Robert C. Roberts, "Kierkegaard is preeminently a 'virtue ethicist.' "[1] This claim, now more than a decade old, under-scores the recent swell of interest among commentators in placing Kierkegaard in more meaningful conversations with representatives of the virtue tradition, old and new.[2] In the following I wish both to continue and to challenge this line of inquiry by investigating the re-spective conceptions of prudence held by Aristotle, arguably the tra-dition's most important representative, and Kierkegaard. For

---

[1]Robert C. Roberts, "Kierkegaard, Wittgenstein, and a Method of 'Virtue Ethics,' " in *Kierkegaard in Post/Modernity*, ed. Martin J. Matuštík and Merold Westphal (Bloomington, IN: Indiana University Press, 1995) 148.

[2]These commentators include Roberts, David Gouwens, Edward Mooney, and John Davenport, among others. See also *Kierkegaard After MacIntyre: Essays on Freedom, Narrative, and Virtue*, ed. John J. Davenport and Anthony Rudd (Chicago: Open Court, 2001).

Aristotle, *phronesis*[3] is a central feature of the ethical life. It is the rudder of the ethical vessel, the virtue that correctly determines how one is to reach one's end, to achieve the good for a human life. By contrast, for Kierkegaard *Klogskab*,[4] or prudence, is something akin to a vice, the trait of one who wishes to "get ahead" in the world. The fact that many of his contemporaries view *Klogskab* as a virtue epitomizes what has gone wrong in Christendom. The distinct and opposing senses of these counterpart conceptions seem unmistakable upon first glance. More important for our consideration, however, is the possibility that the prudence Kierkegaard attacks resembles the prudence Aristotle prescribes. My aim is to draw into tension *Klogskab* and *phronesis* to clarify what avenues for further conversation avail the reader who wishes to make the most of virtue elements in the thought of Kierkegaard.

Toward this end I will first review the development of *Klogskab* in Kierkegaard's writings up to *Christian Discourses*, where it receives as much attention as in any other place in the authorship. We will discover that the prudence Kierkegaard critiques is *sui generis*, uniquely informed by the ills of Christendom. Next, I will examine Aristotle's conception of *phronesis* in Book VI of the *Nicomachean Ethics*, drawing attention both to the incongruities and apparent sympathies the reader finds when juxtaposing that concept with its Kierkegaardian counterpart. The third part of the paper will serve a more constructive end, as I will, with the aid of Aquinas, begin to envisage what a positive conception of prudence might be for Kierkegaard, and in doing so, move beyond some of the problematic implications that accompany Aristotelian *phronesis*. I will conclude by imagining how an ethic of Christian neighbor love like Kierkegaard's might accommodate a conception of prudence.

---

[3]*Phronesis* may also be translated wisdom and practical wisdom. As a terminological convention, I shall use the correlative term for each philosopher: *phronesis* when referring to Aristotle's concept, *prudentia* when referring to Aquinas's, and *Klogskab* when referring to Kierkegaard's. When speaking generally or comparatively, I will use prudence.

[4]*Klogskab* has also been translated sagacity, shrewdness, calculatedness, smartness or cleverness.

Kierkegaard's Klogskab

Kierkegaard writes most about *Klogskab* in *Christian Discourses* and other signed works composed around the same time (1847-48). In these writings he portrays it as a disposition that borders on a Christian vice, a trait that leads away from a life lived in Christian categories like faith, hope, and love. Kierkegaard understands the existential incongruity that *Klogskab* breeds within the context of Christendom, where Christian belief, action, and emotion are at stake. To assent to Christian belief (to be a member of the state church, etc.) is the "prudent" or "shrewd" or "sagacious" thing to do when living in Christendom — it is the way to gain (or keep) respect, one's office, and power. To risk in the many ways Christianity requires — both in terms of belief (e.g. unrelenting hope for the good or belief in Christ as the Son of God) and action (e.g. loving with neighbor love) — this is "too much," *Klogskab* reasons.[5] Thus, insofar as Kierkegaard's early works — both the signed, generically religious upbuilding discourses and the pseudonymous works — are not written with the perspective of Christianity in mind, *Klogskab* as a point of contention for Kierkegaard is more or less absent, or at least well beneath the surface.

Discussions of *Klogskab* in varying degrees of focus begin to emerge at the turning point of the authorship — with the publication of *Concluding Unscientific Postscript to Philosophical Fragments* and the "Corsair affair." In *Two Ages: the Age of Revolution and the Present Age* and *Upbuilding Discourses in Various Spirits*, which follow immediately after this period, we see the seedbed of *Klogskab* as a negative characteristic in relation to Christianity. However, in both places Kierkegaard seems ambivalent about it, employing it as potentially both a negative and positive trait. For example, at one point in *Two Ages* he correlates *Klogskab* with a lack of passion, too much reflection, "worldly wisdom," and "chatter." Toward the end of the book,

---

[5]There may be two senses in which Christian belief and action are "too much." First, Christian belief and action require great risk and self-denial, things that do not come easily to many of us. Second, to believe and act Christianly may be rather unpopular and result in the Christian's persecution. We will return to this 'double danger' below.

by contrast, he uses it in a discussion of Socrates, primarily a positive figure in the authorship (TA, 111). Prudence[6] has "seductive charm" that causes the "average man" to give in wholeheartedly, whereas Socrates, though prudent, does not order his life in full accordance with prudence—otherwise he would have escaped Athens (at least that would be worldly *Klogskab*). Thus, *Klogskab* is not unequivocally negative at this point.

The same holds true in "An Occasional Discourse" ("Purity of Heart"): "*Inwardly* a person uses *sagacity in a pernicious way* to prevent himself from stepping out into the decision . . . *to seek evasion*" (UDVS, 82). *Klogskab* can be used inwardly and outwardly, though in either case it breeds some form of deception, in the first case self-deception and in the second deception of others (which, in the end, can also be a form of self-deception). But just as *Klogskab* serves the evasion of ethical resolution and behavior, so too can it be employed against evasion.[7] "Only that sagacity is true that helps a person to make every sacrifice in order to will the good in truth" (UDVS, 94).

In *Works of Love, Practice in Christianity*, and *Christian Discourses*, Kierkegaard exclusively conceives of *Klogskab* as an entirely negative disposition. In the discourse "Love Hopes All Things" from the second series of *Works of Love*, *Klogskab* opposes the notion of Christian hope for the possibility of good in the future. As a bedfellow of despair, *Klogskab* believes that the reprobate's turning toward the good, an admittedly unlikely outcome, warrants disbelief in every case that such an outcome will obtain. Those who hope and love too often get deceived by wishful thinking, *Klogskab* reasons. While the father of the prodigal son "got lucky" when his son returned, generally speaking there is no good reason to hope or to believe[8] that the good will come about. As if to remind his reader what a Christian's beliefs entail, Kierkegaard exposes the radical nature of Christian

---

[6]In *Two Ages*, the Hongs translate *Klogskab* in several of the ways listed above, though in the discussion of Socrates at the end of the book they choose "prudence."

[7]One may be tempted to apply this more positive conception of *Klogskab* to Kierkegaard's own scheme of producing aesthetic writings early in his career. Below I will argue that a Thomistic view of prudence better describes this unusual authorial activity.

[8]The discourse that precedes "Love Hopes All Things," "Love Believes All Things—and Yet Is Never Deceived," complements these remarks about hope.

hope—namely, believing that even the greatest sinner, the furthest from God, may still turn to God. Not to hope for this unlikely possibility is, for Kierkegaard, a slight not against that reprobate neighbor but against God.[9] "[A]cting sagaciously is bearing false witness against the eternal with one's whole life, is simply stealing one's existence from God" (WL, 261). In closing oneself off to hoping and believing the best for one's neighbor, one closes oneself off to the possibility of the best for oneself, a genuine relation to God.

In *Practice in Christianity*, a work whose pseudonymity is invoked not because of a divergence in opinion but to disclaim Kierkegaard's own life as *the ideal* Christian life (JP, 6:6431), Anti-Climacus examines the multifaceted conception of Christian offense, or offense at the person of Jesus Christ. In one of the more memorable and humorous sections, Anti-Climacus considers several possible reactions to Christ by his contemporaries. Perhaps implying that *Klogskab* was not at all rare among his contemporaries, Anti-Climacus voices five of the ten responses from the mouths of "the sagacious and sensible person."[10] The absurdity of these comments serves as a kind of *reductio* of the commonplace view that *Klogskab* is among the highest virtues to attain. Speaking of Christ, the first offers,

> He who by many a statement betrays such a deep insight into the human heart, which I cannot deny him, he certainly must very well know what I with less than half of my sagacity can tell him in advance, that this is no way to get ahead in the world—unless, disdaining sagacity, one honestly aspires to become a fool or perhaps even go so far in honesty that one prefers to be put to death, but then one must indeed be really insane to want that. (PC, 42-43)

The theme of getting ahead in the world is central to the individual with *Klogskab*. Consider the queries of a second sagacious and sensible person: "What has he done about his future? Nothing. Does he have a permanent job? No. What are his prospects? None" (PC, 43). The one with *Klogskab* lives entirely in immanent categories and thus that which guides a successful life for this person involves immanent

---

[9]Note the similar sense of King David's confession after sleeping with Bathsheba: "Against you, you alone, have I sinned, and done what is evil in your sight" (Psalm 51:4a, NRSV).

[10]The other responses come from a clergyman, a philosopher, a "sagacious statesman," a "solid citizen, and a "scoffer" (see pages 40-53).

reasoning, immanent or worldly wisdom. Dying to the world, self-denial, and other Christian categories do not figure into this person's existence, are not appropriated in any personal sort of way.

The response of a third sagacious character expands the concept further. This one is impressed with Jesus' ethical insights. "Yes, if only one could deftly trick his wisdom out of him — for that extremely singular idea upon which he himself seems to place so much value, that he is God, I am happy to leave to him alone as his exclusive property — if only one could trick his wisdom out of him — without becoming his follower!" (PC, 44). Here Anti-Climacus summarizes the view of much liberal theology — glean the ethical wisdom of Christ, but leave behind the claims to divinity. Variations on this theme continue. For our purposes, we need only be reminded that unlike these fictional, non-Christian contemporaries of Christ, the majority (if not all) of Kierkegaard's readers in Christendom *did* in fact consider themselves followers of Christ; thus, this heavy dose of unmistakable irony and hyperbole aims to unsettle those sorts of readers. And, besides considering themselves followers of Christ, many of Kierkegaard's contemporaries presumably placed great value on the possession of *Klogskab*, a virtue of immanence. Thus, through his pseudonyms Kierkegaard creates an existential tension, a dialectical knot as Anti-Climacus describes it, with which the reader must struggle. In this ironic method of provocation Anti-Climacus mirrors Climacus's mission to make it difficult to be a Christian, though no more difficult than it really is (CUP, 1:186-87, 213, 607).

Part three of *Christian Discourses*, *"Thoughts That Wound from Behind,"* was originally to be published alongside both *The Sickness unto Death: A Christian Psychological Exposition for Upbuilding and Awakening* and *Practice in Christianity*. Thus, the critique of *Klogskab* in "Thoughts" is entirely consistent with what one finds in *Practice*. Explicit discussions of *Klogskab* occur to the fullest degree in discourses two and seven, though traces run throughout the pages of each discourse. In the second discourse, "'See, We Have Left Everything and Followed You; What Shall We Have?' (Matthew 19:27) — and What Shall We Have?," Kierkegaard sharply contrasts the biblical prescription of leaving all things behind with misconceptions of the gloriousness of Christianity. This scripture serves as "a mockery of those who say and think they are Christians, that is, follow Christ, and yet cling wholeheartedly to the things of this world" (CD, 176). The "gloriousness" of being a Christian runs counter to most things that can be described as praiseworthy in the world. The one who possesses much, the one who has much esteem in the eyes of others, and the one who has great power — each of these is glorious. From that perspective, the Christian view of what is glorious — giving up all things — seems absurd. Kierkegaard aims to drive as much space as possible between these conflicting conceptions. He advises the one who wishes to praise Christianity and speak of its gloriousness: "to the same degree that your life shows how much you have given up for its sake, to the same degree you praise Christianity" (CD, 177). The theme of a life expressing one's beliefs, of one possessing integrity, permeates "Thoughts." Kierkegaard contrasts the evasive tendencies of *Klogskab* with honesty before God that occurs when "your life expresses what you say" (CD, 167).

Kierkegaard's polemic against religious lip service in the previous statement accords with the general admonition of the first discourse, "Watch Your Step in the Lord's House." There he considers all of the predictable responses to the question "why do you go to church?" and relegates them all to secondary status. The bottom line, the fundamental reason to "step into the Lord's house," involves a basic confession of the penitent, a confession that makes any person — in Christendom or not — uncomfortable: "What is spoken about first and must be spoken about first is sin, that you are a sinner, that before God you are a sinner, that in fear and trembling before this thought you are to forget your earthly need. An odd way to comfort, is it not?" (CD, 172). Despite the harsh tone of this reminder, toward the end of the discourse Kierkegaard admits the upside of such confession, friendship with God. The individual with *Klogskab*, presumably willing to admit being a sinner, lacks the pathos that accompanies the confession, lacks the sin-consciousness Anti-Climacus describes in both *Practice in Christianity* and *The Sickness unto Death* (PC, 20; SUD, 79-82, 101). Accordingly, this person lacks a true God-relationship.

Upon presenting the initial incongruity between worldly and Christian perspectives of what is glorious and praiseworthy in the second discourse, Kierkegaard deepens the discussion by considering the implications of this incongruity, what it looks like in everyday life, and the result is a polemic against *Klogskab*. There are different ways that the one with *Klogskab* attempts to evade the demands of the prescription to leave everything and follow Christ. One involves an excuse that to give up all things is to tempt God, to put God on the spot for having to save the one who has given up everything. Kierkegaard argues, however, that the biblical account suggests the opposite — that giving up everything and, importantly, following Christ, pleases God. Kierkegaard does not deny the possibility that one can tempt God — *Klogskab* speaks a half truth. But the difference lies in whether one gives all things up *for Christ* or *for oneself*, that is, for self-serving reasons. Thus, to tempt God or to make a fool of God does not occur when one gives everything up for Christ, but oppositely — when one "cowardly and timorously" will not dare to venture exactly in this way.

Kierkegaard upsets conventional wisdom further when he asserts that "salvation is closer to him the more terrible the form in which his sin must appear to him. But there is no salvation for this cunning game of sagacity; the secret consists simply in maintaining the appearance that one has not, after all, denied Christ" (CD, 180). Kierkegaard's condemnation of *Klogskab* in this passage draws to mind the Aristotelian notion of character traits as developed over time through habit. *Klogskab* has freely made a habit of daily denying Christ in the subtlest ways, including buying into the worldly conception of what constitutes a glorious life. In paying lip service to the scripture under consideration (as one may do in a confession of sin), however, *Klogskab* appears committed to Christ. The following summary quotation portrays *Klogskab* as a disposition not unlike a view Socrates considers in the *Republic*,[11] that it is better to appear just than actually to be just.

> The sin of sagacity is to sin in such a way that one ingeniously knows how to avoid punishment, yes, knows how to give the appearance of the good. The sin of sagacity is ingeniously to avoid every decision and in that way to win the distinction of never having denied — this the world regards as something extraordinary. The world does not truly hate evil but loathes and hates what is unsagacious, that is, it loves evil. (CD, 181)

The disposition of *Klogskab* does not entail vicious or sinful action

---

[11]Plato, *Republic*, 360e-362c.

though it often leads to it. Insofar as the world is consumed with temporal goods, *Klogskab* seeks to enjoy these goods as the highest of goods, while at the same time appearing to acknowledge the eternal good, God (whom, after all, it is important to acknowledge!). Thus, *Klogskab* hedges its bet by relying heavily upon the category of probability[12] for its decision making, a category surmounted by the one who would leave "the certain" behind in obedience to Christ.

The themes of competing goods and competing conceptions of the highest good provide another foil for gaining clarity about the notion of *Klogskab*. At various points in part three, Kierkegaard refers to faith, love, blessedness (*Salighed*), and life itself, each as the highest good. In spite of this apparent contradiction — four "highest" goods — love of God is the preeminent good, while the others are ways of conceiving of that love. The following passage, set in the context of a distinction Kierkegaard makes between a guarded faith, characteristic of *Klogskab*, and genuine Christian faith, shows how two of these highest goods can be viewed as one. "A knowledge that God is love is still not a consciousness of it. Consciousness, personal consciousness, requires that in my knowledge I also have knowledge of myself and my relation to my knowledge. This is to believe, here to believe that God is love, and to believe that God is love is to love him" (CD, 194). Note the unity of the Christian virtues of faith and love compatible with the insights Kierkegaard draws in *Works of Love*, that love believes all things and hopes all things. Just as one cannot separate the operations of Christian love, one cannot divvy up a human's highest good — love of God, which *is* belief that God is love.

A more direct discussion of Christian faith occurs in the seventh discourse, "He Was Believed in the World" (CD, 234-46). To make clear the source of the personal inquiry, "do you believe?", Kierke-

---

[12]Probability as a guide to ethical and religious truth earns Kierkegaard's ire in many places in the authorship. The objective approach to religious truth Climacus reviews in *Postscript* is one that at best "approximates" a relation to God because an objective approach to God can do no better. Faith, conversely, is a total commitment that recognizes the "objective uncertainty" and holds fast in spite of that uncertainty. A true relation to God always involves a sort of risk that will not pass the test of the statistician. For Kierkegaard's critique of a probabilistic approach to God see "Becoming Sober" in *Judge for Yourself!* (93-143).

gaard considers a classical instantiation of shrewdness or cleverness. Odysseus, Kierkegaard notes, was unable to employ his crafty ways only when he lacked a sparring partner. Kierkegaard thus aims to place this question in the mind of reader and step away, thereby suggesting that one cannot get into a debate over the question with him or any other interlocutor, but only one's conscience. In its typical evasive way, *Klogskab* does all it can to postpone its response to the question "do you believe?" by attempting to engage in dialogue *about* the question instead. Kierkegaard hopes that if he, the interlocutor, steps away, the conversation will continue with one's self.

Klogskab also thinks up trivial questions about how many others have ever believed; it would prefer to run an opinion poll before moving forward. After all, *Klogskab* reasons, probabilities and other calculations must be taken into account. Anticipating these sorts of evasions, Kierkegaard responds to this maneuvering, "But faith is certainly not history. Faith's question, on the other hand, is to *you*: have you believed? . . . But if *I* have believed, then in the personal sense how many and how many also have believed is unimportant" (CD, 238). In wanting such matters to be settled first, *Klogskab* appears judicious and sincere but in fact operates deceitfully, precisely because it is "unwilling to venture out into the dangers and decisions where faith comes into existence" (CD, 245). Thus, while it seems that *Klogskab's* problem is epistemic, Kierkegaard wishes also to expose its defective will, its "existential" cowardice.

Giving up everything for Christ is a dangerous and risk-laden activity in the world, yet Kierkegaard reminds the reader that this is precisely what Christ requires in faith. The one with *Klogskab* prefers "the most comfortable way, which, however, does not lead to faith," but instead is "to begin to get busy about not being able to make historically definite what it is one is to believe" (CD, 245). In contrast to the busyness, the evasion, and the calculation, Kierkegaard finally offers a positive conception of faith toward the end of the discourse. Corroborating what Climacus says in *Concluding Unscientific Postscript*, Kierkegaard claims that objective (historical) knowledge is not what is lacking for the one without faith. Rather, it is "the inner transformation of the whole mind," which, unlike mere head knowledge of Christianity, is a rarity in the present age (CD, 246). Contrary to *Klogskab*, the one who believes has made this knowledge inward and possesses "honesty of heart" (CD, 246) "[R]esearching, ruminating, and pondering" over historical data in an effort to become comfortable with the idea of belief in Christ — this is "empty shadowboxing" (CD, 246). There is no amount of historical evidence that would or could bring the one with *Klogskab* to a point of belief — for Christian belief is a different sort of thing.

Let us review these remarks about *Klogskab* and then place the concept beside Aristotle's notion of prudence. *Klogskab* receives the most explication and analysis by Kierkegaard as a negative disposition that leads one away from a genuine Christian life. Its values and interests betray a divided mind and heart because on the one hand, *Klogskab* appears to take religious faith seriously, while in actuality it is unwilling to give up its "creature comforts," finite goods (including a way of reasoning) in exchange for a cross. *Klogskab* finds orthodox belief about Christ — his life and ministry, and his divinity — improbable and unpalatable, yet it recognizes the importance of affirming such belief, first because of the assumption that good citizens are religious folk, and second because, while improbable, the consequences of unbelief — eternal separation from God — should clearly be avoided. As we saw in *Practice in Christianity*, at times *Klogskab* even acknowledges a measure of truth in Christ's teachings. Still, Christian piety — loving one's neighbor and hoping for the neighbor's good — *Klogskab* finds utterly incomprehensible. Not only are loving and hoping as Christianity demands seemingly impossible tasks, but they are thankless tasks as well, since odds are against the unlovely or the reprobate turning toward God. *Klogskab*, therefore, is among the most defective dispositions in Christendom because at its root is the most serious self-deception, thinking one is a Christian when one is not. The primary commandment for the Christian is to love God and neighbor accordingly, but *Klogskab* is driven by love of the "dear self,"[13] an improper love of self incompatible with proper love for others and God.[14] In the final section we will ask whether *any* conception of prudence is compatible with Christian neighbor love. First, we turn to Aristotle.

Aristotle's Phronesis

[13]Iris Murdoch, *The Sovereignty of Good* (New York: Shocken Books, 1971) 52.
[14]In *Works of Love* Kierkegaard emphasizes the need for *proper* self-love in order to fulfill the command to love one's neighbor and God (WL, 17-43).

Despite the resemblance *Klogskab* and *phronesis* bear in our translation of each as prudence, a straightforward comparison of the two will not do. Two important questions remain: are there aspects of Aristotelian *phronesis* that, given his positive ethical views, Kierkegaard would consider vicious, along the lines of *Klogskab*? If the answer to this question is no or for the most part no, we might then ask whether Aristotle's *phronesis* is compatible with Kierkegaard's ethical views? A full answer to this question would involve a sketch of Kierkegaard's positive ethical views, a project that cannot be undertaken here. I will assume that central to Kierkegaard's ethics[15] is the notion of Christian neighbor love developed in *Works of Love*. We might then restate the second question as follows: is an Aristotelian conception of *phronesis* compatible with Kierkegaard's ethic of Christian neighbor love? In this section I will embark on an answer to both questions that will be fleshed out further in section three and the conclusion.

In book VI of the *Nicomachean Ethics* Aristotle defines *phronesis* as "a true disposition accompanied by rational prescription, relating to action in the sphere of what is good and bad for human beings."[16] It is a virtue or excellence of the rational part of the human soul, while traits like courage or temperance, moral virtues, are excellences of the other part of the human soul, that which has the capacity to "listen to reason."[17] Consequently, *phronesis* has a unique relationship to the moral virtues—it requires them, and they require *phronesis*.

> For φρόνησις [*phronesis*] apart from moral virtue (i.e. apart from rightness of aim) is not *phronesis* at all: it is the mere facility for taking steps cleverly in the abstract, a kind of cunning (δεινότης)

---

[15]Ethics means many things in Kierkegaard's writings; here I do not mean 'the ethical' of *Fear and Trembling* nor the ethical stage of existence of Judge William, for instance. Perhaps a better term would be the "ethical-religious," because in fact the ethics I am concerned with here—what I take to be the ethic Kierkegaard wishes finally to promote—is religiously grounded in the command of Christ.

[16]Aristotle, *Nicomachean Ethics*, ed. Sarah Broadie and Christopher Rowe (New York: Oxford University Press, 2001) 180 (VI. 5). Subsequent citations are to this translation.

[17]Aristotle, *Nicomachean Ethics*, 110. Broadie, "Philosophical Introduction," in *Ethics*, 17

[*deinotes*]. . . . And moral virtue (ἠθική ἀρετή) [*ethike arete*], apart from *phronesis*, is not really virtue or excellence (*arete*): it is, thus abstracted, at best a 'natural virtue' (φυσική ἀρετή) — i.e. a natural disposition which proper training will develop into an *arete*.[18]

This intimate connection further distinguishes *phronesis* from other intellectual virtues. Leaving to the side questions of the unity of the virtues, one can conceive both of geniuses who possess *sophia* (intellectual accomplishment) and master artisans who possess *techne* (technical expertise) who, neither of them, possess good character. But for Aristotle, the same is not possible for the one with *phronesis*. For unlike *sophia*, *phronesis* concerns itself with the sphere of human action, and unlike *techne*, its end is not beyond its activity. Like *sophia*, *phronesis* aims at truth, and like *techne*, it is a practical excellence. But the truth and the practice in question concern human action and the good toward which it aims. And while moral virtue determines that end, *phronesis* directs one toward that end through prescribing appropriate action. To sum up, *phronesis* is the characteristic of the person who thoughtfully acts in ways that constantly bear in mind what is best for one's life.

What about *phronesis* might accord with *Klogskab* and thereby earn Kierkegaard's rebuke? Four candidates in the conceptual family of *phronesis* stand out: calculation (or deliberation), cleverness, the mean, and the good. At the beginning of Book VI of the *Ethics*, Aristotle breaks down into further divisions the rational part of the soul, and we are told that *phronesis* corresponds to the calculative or deliberative part, while *sophia* is an excellence of the "scientific" part.[19] This distinction corresponds to the object with which reason interacts — the scientific ascertains necessary truths, while the calculative reflects "upon things that can be otherwise," for instance, human actions.[20] One of the faults of *Klogskab* we noted earlier involves a particular sort of calculated[21] approach to matters Johannes Climacus calls "essential truth," truths concerning ethical and religious matters (CUP, 1:197-99). Such calculatedness character-

---

[18]H. H. Joakim, *Aristotle. The Nicomachean Ethics: A Commentary*, ed. D.A. Rees (Oxford: Oxford University Press, 1966) 218.

[19]Aristotle, *Ethics*, 177 (VI. 1).

[20]Aristotle, *Ethics*, 177 (VI. 1).

[21]"Calculatedness" may be an appropriate translation of *Klogskab*.

izes the posture toward Christ taken by Anti-Climacus's fictional advisors in *Practice in Christianity*. *Klogskab's* calculation concerns how best to accomplish one's immanent goals—the acquisition of finite goods of one sort or another—while *appearing* to care for higher things such as a relation to God. That this is *not* the sort of calculation Aristotle intends can be seen in two ways. First, for Aristotle *phronesis* concerns "true" calculation, or calculation about the truth that constitutes the good for a human life and how one might move toward that end. This point can be seen more clearly given Rowe's decision to translate *phronesis* as wisdom; surely the wise person is wise in part because of a genuine love of and concern for truth and its acquisition, and an aversion toward the possibility of self-deception.

The second reason why the calculation that belongs to *phronesis* cannot be identified with that of *Klogskab* is that Aristotle has a different concept within his ethical system that accounts for the one whose calculation is not truthful but gives the appearance of such. Cleverness explains how, for example, one may perform just acts without being just. Cleverness "is of such a sort that, when it comes to the things that conduce to a proposed goal, it is able to carry these out and do so successfully. Now if the aim is a fine one, this ability is to be praised, but if the aim is a bad one, then it is unscrupulousness; which is why we say that both the wise and the unscrupulous are clever."[22] The determining factor for whether the clever person also possesses *phronesis* is whether that one possesses a true conception of the good and moral virtue. If the person lacks the good (understood both epistemologically and existentially), then it follows that cleverness cannot be a substitute for *phronesis*. Thus, while cleverness belongs to *phronesis*, the reverse does not hold true. Without moral virtue, the clever person is just clever. Cleverness *apart from phronesis* may be the closest counterpart to *Klogskab* in Aristotle's system of ethical concepts. In the end, though, the calculative and clever aspects of *phronesis* do not contradict Kierkegaard's views.

What about the mean? Aristotle employs the metaphor of hitting a target to illustrate the notion that the middle or intermediate

---

[22]Aristotle, *Ethics*, 187-88 (VI. 12).

should be what the prudent or wise person chooses — it is "as the correct prescription prescribes."[23] At times Kierkegaard seems to have something like this or the Delphic prescription in mind when he attacks mottos like "nothing too much." In *Judge for Yourself!*, Kierkegaard contrasts biblical and human conceptions of sobriety: "The purely human view is of the opposite opinion, that to be sober is specifically marked by exercising moderation in everything, by observing in everything this sober "to a certain degree" (JFY, 106). Here again there are two ways to mitigate the force of this potential incompatibility. First, what Kierkegaard disdains about such mottos pertains not to the range of virtues and vices (e.g. cowardice-courage-rashness) where the virtue comes between two vices; rather, it is the apparent lack of personal commitment to one's ethical or religious ideals that is implied in the phrase "nothing too much." Thus, Kierkegaard would presumably agree that one should "aim at the middle" and be moderate when it comes to alcohol consumption, for instance. However, he believes it not only unwise but sinful to love one's neighbor in moderate quantities. But this does not seem to be the intent of Aristotle's doctrine of the mean. For, secondly, another way Aristotle describes a virtue transcends the apparently mediocre: "Hence excellence, in terms of its essence, and the definition that states what it is for excellence to be, is intermediacy, *but in terms of what is best, and good practice, it is extremity*."[24] In summary, Kierkegaard's mockery of various mottos of mediocrity seems more like an attack against the faux ethical and religious commitments of *Klogskab* than attacks against the practice of the kind of virtues, including *phronesis*, of which Aristotle conceives. I do not mean to suggest that Kierkegaard endorses Aristotle's doctrine of the mean, nor Aristotle's catalog of virtues — in fact, he does not. (I am also not suggesting that Aristotle endorses Christian love or something like it.) Rather, I argue that the best way to conceive of Kierkegaard's rebuke of "mottos of mediocrity" is in light of the distinct notion of *Klogskab*. Thus, it is a rebuke of the one who is *merely* clever and lacks a true conception of and commitment to the good and, all the while, pretends to have that commitment (and is self-deceived about the

---

[23] Aristotle, *Ethics*, 176 (VI. 1).
[24] Aristotle, *Ethics*, 117 (II. 6, emphasis added).

conception). To state the point another way, there is nothing about Aristotelian *phronesis* that suggests it is a disposition *partly* committed to the good.

Before turning to the most formidable obstacle confronting a harmonization of Aristotelian and Kierkegaardian views of prudence, let us briefly note two apparent points of sympathy.[25] First, Aristotle breaks with the Socratic view that virtue is knowledge, a topic Anti-Climacus takes up in *The Sickness unto Death* as he aims to clarify the Christian doctrine of sin (SUD, 87-96). Obviously Aristotle's challenge to that view is not identical to the Christian challenge, but in admitting that one needs more than knowledge to become good, and that one does bad not simply out of ignorance, it is a step closer. Broadie notes the novelty of Aristotle's position vis-à-vis his contemporaries:

> Aristotle seems to have been the first to teach that abstract theoretical understanding does not confer practical wisdom, is not a precondition of that sort of wisdom, and is to be prized entirely for its own sake; and the first to see clearly that these are two quite different kinds of excellence. Whereas Plato used the terms '*phronēsis*' and '*sophia*' without distinction, Aristotle makes them names of different qualities, and brings out the differences to the point of being able to say that wisdom [*phronesis*] is "antithetical to [theoretical] intelligence."[26]

Like Kierkegaard, Aristotle argues that more than knowledge figures into one becoming wise, and therefore good. "In the soul, the things determining action and truth are three: perception, intelligence, and desire."[27] To become wise involves one getting each of these things correct. One must learn not just to think in the right

---

[25]Just as there are more obstacles standing between the harmonization of Aristotle's and Kierkegaard's ethics that do not pertain to prudence directly (e.g., Kierkegaard's egalitarianism versus Aristotle's elitism), there are, of course, more "points of sympathy" between Kierkegaard and Aristotle (and the classical virtue tradition) that do not pertain directly to prudence. Robert C. Roberts has highlighted these in several places. See, e.g., "The Virtue of Hope in *Eighteen Upbuilding Discourses*," in *International Kierkegaard Commentary: Eighteen Upbuilding Discourses*, vol. 5, ed. Robert L. Perkins (Macon GA: Mercer University Press, 2003) and "Kierkegaard, Wittgenstein, and a Method of 'Virtue Ethics.'"

[26]Broadie, "Philosophical Introduction," in *Ethics*, 47.

[27]Aristotle, *Ethics*, 177 (VI. 2).

way, but to feel, act, and desire in the right way, to *see* moral situations appropriately. One must also have a bit of moral luck—good parents, looks, and so forth.[28] Thus, while *phronesis* is an intellectual virtue, it is not, for Aristotle, an intellectualist conception. Of course Aristotle's correction to Plato does not admit the sort of passion so integral to Kierkegaard's ethics (or epistemology) nor does it admit the role God plays in an individual becoming a self. Still, the nonintellectualist aspect of *phronesis* should not go unnoticed, especially given the tendency to view Kierkegaard as much more aligned with Socrates.

Second, on the flipside, conceiving of prudence as a practical *intellectual* excellence takes seriously thoughtfulness and earnestness about living well. Good intentions or a good will are not the only requisite for a good life. Thus, the standard counterpart to the pathetic element in Kierkegaard's writing, the dialectical, comes to mind as mirroring to some degree the intellectual side of *phronesis*. In *The Book on Adler* one of Kierkegaard's primary criticisms of Magister Adler concerns his "deficient" and "confused" application of Christian concepts to his emotional religious experience (BA, 111). "In order to be able to express oneself Christianly, proficiency and schooling in the Christian conceptual definitions are also required in addition to the more universal heart language of deep emotion," (BA, 114). Thus, while Kierkegaard does not conceive of the importance of dialectic in the context of some notion of prudence, it is nevertheless essential to the ethical and religious life. For the objector who thinks the content of one's ethics is not the point but just appropriation of one ethical view or another—that Climacus's phrase "subjectivity is truth" means "truth is subjective"—Anti-Climacus warns one not to be so careless.

---

[28]M. F. Burnyeat emphasizes the nonrational role moral education can play in one's moral formation: "it follows not only that for a long time moral development must be a less than fully rational process but also, what is less often acknowledged, that a mature morality must in large part continue to be what it originally was, a matter of responses deriving from sources other than reflective reason. These being the fabric of moral character, in the fully developed man of virtue and practical wisdom they have become integrated with, indeed they are now infused and corrected by, his reasoned scheme of values" ("Aristotle on Learning to be Good," in *Essays on Aristotle's Ethics*, ed. Amélie Oksenberg Rorty (Berkeley CA: University of California Press, 1980) 80).

> Do not say that these are quibbling comments about words, anything but upbuilding. Believe me, it is very important for a person that his language be precise and true, because that means his thinking is that also. Furthermore, even though understanding and speaking correctly are not everything, since acting correctly is indeed also required, yet understanding in relation to acting is like the springboard from which the diver makes his leap — the clearer, the more precise, the more passionate (in the good sense) the understanding is, the more it rises (*lette*) to action, or the easier (*letter*) it is to rise to action for the one who is to act, just as it is easier for the bird to rise from the swinging branch whose pliancy is most closely related to and forms the easiest transition to flying. (PC, 158)

And just like Kierkegaard's clarification is never an end in itself, but a means toward evoking in self and others Christianly expressed lives, Aristotle understands the end of prudence as practice (*praxis*), an activity (*energia*).[29]

The topic of what constitutes the highest good for a human life represents the greatest divide in reconciling the ethical views of Aristotle and Kierkegaard. It is not so much that their respective conceptions contradict one another, though there is no small difference between an immanent highest good and a supernaturally transcendent highest good.[30] *Eudaimonia* (happiness or well-being) can be and has been harmonized with Christian conceptions like *evig Salighed* (eternal blessedness). Rather, it is the origination and determination of this good. How is this good gotten? How does one come to conceive of the good or properly understand what the good is,

---

[29]In fact, it is *eupraxia*, good practice. For an insightful discussion of the 'end' of prudence, see Gaëlle Fiasse, "Aristotle's φρόνησις: A True Grasp of Ends as Well as Means?", *Review of Metaphysics*. 55 (Dec 2001): 324-26.

[30]We might distinguish between two conceptions of transcendence, one naturalistic and one supernaturalistic. The former transcends any *particular* earthly good, and thus Aristotelian *eudaimonia* can be viewed in this light. In the case of the latter, however, transcendence comes from a good's origin in God or something like a Platonic Good. Given this qualification we can say that an Aristotelian end for a human life may be both naturally transcendent *and* immanent, just in that it is a good whose origin is not otherworldly or divine. Thus, it may be true that philosophical activity ultimately ends in theology as Aristotle believes, but the deity toward which metaphysics points us is not worthy of worship, personal, or, therefore, concerned with human lives and their direction.

and how does one actually acquire the good in one's life? For Aristotle, the answer concerns the process of acquiring the virtues, including *phronēsis*. *Phronēsis* offers a rational prescription, the marching orders for the human soul that accord with moral virtue. *Phronesis* has the charge of guiding an individual toward the good. This guiding activity of *phronēsis*, then, is very much a human project. That is not to say one can become prudent or wise without the help of others, but one does not need the help of God.[31] According to Broadie, "the subject cannot yet be said to operate well as a human individual as long as the orders have to come from outside."[32] This view reflects the Kantian notion of autonomy, that an individual cannot be a free moral agent unless the source of the duty or command is oneself. Kierkegaard mocks this notion of obligation, likening it to Sancho Panza spanking himself in *Don Quixote* (JP, 1:188). For Kierkegaard, the highest good concerns a loving relationship to God inseparable from love for one's neighbor, but unlike for Aristotle, this good has as its basis the command of Christ, and thus it is an order 'from outside.' Therefore, in the end it is God's activity that effects the realization of the good in a human's life. Edward Mooney captures the distinct sense of agency present in the Kierkegaardian view. Clarifying the sort of virtue thinker Kierkegaard is, he writes that the approach of someone like Aristotle "would typically set a goal we can achieve with effort and training. Yet some aims Kierkegaard will stress in his religious voice are aims we *cannot* achieve with effort and training. Attainment of these can only be welcomed as a gift from sources we cannot control."[33]

---

[31]Philip Quinn writes, "Noting that Aristotle does not place piety on his list of virtues, [Martha] Nussbaum conjectures that 'this probably indicates his interest in separating practical reason from religious authority, and in keeping reason, rather than such authorities, in control of the most important matters'," Martha Nussbaum, "Recoiling from Reason," *The New York Review of Books* 36 (7 Dec. 1989): 40; quoted in Philip Quinn, "The Primacy of God's Will in Christian Ethics," in *Christian Theism and Moral Philosophy*, ed. Michael Beaty, Carlton Fisher, and Mark Nelson (Macon GA: Mercer University Press, 1998) 280.

[32]Broadie, "Philosophical Introduction," in *Ethics*, 18.

[33]Edward Mooney, "The Perils of Polarity: Kierkegaard and MacIntyre in Search of Moral Truth," in *Kierkegaard after MacIntyre*, 250-51. Mooney here refers to Alasdair MacIntyre's notion of the Traditionalist position on the virtues in *Three Rival Versions of Moral Enquiry*. There MacIntyre includes within that group

The gravity of this disagreement can neither be overstated nor surmounted without violating the views of one or the other. As Philip Quinn warns, "incorporating parts of Aristotle's ethical legacy into Christian moral philosophy will inevitably involve radical transformation in order to enforce the required theoretical subordination."[34] To summarize, the greatest obstacle standing in the way of attempts to harmonize Aristotelian *phronesis* and Kierkegaard's love ethic concerns how one is to reach the highest good for a human life, in no way a minor detail of an ethical theory. No quantity or quality of human prudence or wisdom, for Kierkegaard, can transcend the "absolute difference" between humanity and the divine, can unite a human with God, can connect a human with the good for a human life (PF, 44-7; CUP, 1:217). It remains to be seen what place, if any, we can imagine for a conception of prudence that accords with an ethic of neighbor love.

Aquinas's Prudentia

If there is room for prudence within a Kierkegaardian ethic of Christian neighbor love,[35] then an obvious place to turn is to Aquinas, the great synthesizer of Athens and Jerusalem. In "Non-Aristotelian Prudence in the *Prima Secundae*," Robert Miner offers a reading of Aquinas's *prudentia* that facilitates this inquiry. Miner rejects the predominant views of Aquinas's conception of *prudentia*: (1) that it is an Aristotelian conception, and (2) that it is *not* an Aristotelian conception *because* Aquinas misreads Aristotle.[36] Conversely, he argues that Aquinas does, in fact, understand *phronesis*, but that he conceives of *prudentia* in a way strongly informed by Christian theology, thereby subordinating *prudentia* to *caritas*, Christian love.

Aquinas agrees with Aristotle in conceiving of prudence as an intellectual virtue and as requiring and required by the moral vir-

---

Aristotle, Augustine, and Aquinas.

[34]Philip L. Quinn, "The Primacy of God's Will in Christian Ethics," 262.

[35]It should be clear that from this point forward, my interests are imaginative and constructive, and thus when I speak of a 'Kierkegaardian ethic,' I simply mean an ethic compatible with the ethic of neighbor love present in *Works of Love*.

[36]Robert Miner, "Non-Aristotelian Prudence in the *Prima* Secundae," *The Thomist* 64 (2000): 401-402.

tues.[37] However, he by no means agrees with its centrality (or the other Aristotelian virtues) within the moral life. "That Thomas in fact regards the fourfold classification of the cardinal virtues as not merely different from, but somehow superior to, the Aristotelian division is evident from the ascending character of the ordering of the questions on the division of virtue."[38] In fact, the authorities Aquinas cites in defense of this ordering include Ambrose, Augustine, and Gregory. Beyond this, however, Miner points out how Aquinas, again relying upon Augustine's authority, transcends the "strict limits" of Aristotle's distinction between prudence and art "by subsuming it within a theology of creation and providence."[39] Thus, unlike Aristotle, Aquinas admits space for conceiving of living well as an art in a way that may illuminate one's conception of God's creative activity and the individual's participation in the divine art.

Aquinas moves further away from Aristotle's conception of the virtues and prudence by adopting Plotinus's fourfold categorization of them: political or social virtues, purgative (or perfecting) virtues, virtues of the purified soul (or perfected virtues), and exemplary virtues.[40] The first of the four categories represents Aristotle's view of virtue, whereas the latter represents the virtues as embodied by God.

> But since it behooves man to do his utmost to strive onward even to Divine things, as even the Philosopher declares in *Ethic.* x. 7, and as Scripture often admonishes us — for instance: *Be ye . . . perfect, as your heavenly Father is perfect* (Matth. 5:48), we must needs place some virtues between the social or human virtues, and the exemplar virtues which are Divine. Now these virtues differ by reason of a difference of movement and term: so that some are virtues of men who are on their way and tending towards the Divine similitude; and these are called *perfecting* virtues. **Thus prudence, by contemplating the things of God, counts as nothing all things of the world, and directs all the thoughts of the soul to God alone** . . . Besides these there are the virtues of those who have already attained to the Divine similitude: these are called the *perfect virtues.* — **Thus prudence sees nought else but the things of God** . . . Such as the virtues attributed to the Blessed, or, in this life, to

---

[37]Miner, "Non-Aristotelian Prudence," 407-408.
[38]Miner, "Non-Aristotelian Prudence," 408-409.
[39]Miner, "Non-Aristotelian Prudence," 411.
[40]Miner, "Non-Aristotelian Prudence," 411-12.

some who are at the summit of perfection.[41]

Here Aquinas extends the conception of *prudentia* to incorporate one's relation to God, and based upon that relation, one's relation to the world. Interestingly, we may note in the purgative or perfecting form something analogous to the first movement of faith in *Fear and Trembling*, infinite resignation, where one learns to count "as nothing all things of the world." And, in the description of perfected prudence we may also catch a glimpse of the common citizen de silentio describes as a knight of faith early in the same book. This person "has made and at every moment is making the movement of infinity" (FT, 40). That is, this person remains in the finite world, but having given it up, has received it back as a gift of God, and thus paradoxically, "sees nought else but the things of God."

The "final word" on prudence, however, is drawn not from Neo-platonism but from Christian scripture.[42] "For thus charity is the mother and the root of all the virtues, inasmuch as it is the form of them all."[43] Miner adds that "all" extends not just to the theological virtues but the cardinal virtues as well, including prudence.[44] Once again, the theological aspect of Aquinas's view seems to move *prudentia* further away from *phronesis*. But how does one acquire the virtues? Is the acquisition of love, a theological virtue, different than the acquisition of *prudentia*, a cardinal virtue? Here Aquinas agrees with Aristotle that social virtues come through habituation. Does this claim not return us to problems stated above, the Aristotelian view that human wisdom can, by its own efforts, achieve the highest good for a human?

Offering a new schema of the virtues, Aquinas conceives of a third class in addition to the social virtues (those acquired through habituation) and theological virtues (those infused by God) — infused versions of the cardinal virtues.[45] The reason for this third category follows from the idea that the three theological virtues (faith, hope,

---

[41]Thomas Aquinas, *Summa Theologiae*, tr. Fathers of the English Dominican Province (New York: Benziger Bros., 1947) 850 (I-II, q. 61, a. 5); emphasis added.

[42]Miner, "Non-Aristotelian Prudence," 414.

[43]Aquinas, *Summa*, 853 (I-II, q. 62, a. 4). (See also, Miner, "Non-Aristotelian Prudence," 414).

[44]Miner, "Non-Aristotelian Prudence," 414.

[45]Miner, "Non-Aristotelian Prudence," 416.

and love), infused by God alone, direct one to a supernatural end, and therefore they require a transformation of natural virtues in accordance with that new, supernatural end. Thus, we can imagine a prudent Aristotelian who aims toward some immanently-conceived good for a human life. Supposing this person comes to know God, the theological virtues are then infused, bringing about a "renewing of the mind"[46] that requires the further transformation of the natural virtues the person already possesses. This transformation occurs through the gracious activity of God, and so it is proper to speak of this person as having wisdom or prudence, yet to conceive of it in a new way because its end is a loving relationship to God, an end only God can provide. Aquinas notes that the specific difference between the infused and acquired forms involves the object and end of each. The end of the person who possesses *phronesis* is immanent, and thus immanent calculation determines an object rooted in human reason as a means to its end. For the person with infused prudence, the object is determined by "the divine rule."[47] The end of this person's life and activity, loving union with God, is transcendent, and the reasoning of the prudent or wise person, the calculation, is transcendent, of a new kind. Not only is this notion of infused prudence distinct from *phronesis*, but prudence is gathered under a new conceptual economy and subordinated to love. Thus, in Aquinas, where love presides over and guides all other virtues, we have one way to conceive how prudence may fit within a Kierkegaardian ethic of Christian neighbor love.[48]

Conclusion: Infused Prudence and Neighbor Love

In the end, *phronesis* will not accord with an ethic of Christian neighbor love where the highest good involves a loving relationship to God that enables (and requires) a loving relationship to one's neighbor. Both the concept of neighbor love and the ability to love

---

[46]Rom. 12:2. See also *Christian Discourses*, 246.

[47]Miner, "Non-Aristotelian Prudence," 419.

[48]I have not the space to consider the degree to which Kierkegaard would agree with Aquinas's ethical views, especially his adaptation of Aristotle in certain places; for this reason I will not speculate on whether Kierkegaard would allow a place for infused prudence in an ethic of neighbor love.

in this way are gifts of God, unattainable through human wisdom or striving.[49] What room is there for infused *prudentia* within a Kierke-gaardian ethic of love?

Consider an individual who, in trying to obey the command to love the neighbor, endures the 'double danger' Kierkegaard speaks of in *Works of Love* (WL, 76, 80-82, 194-204). Sylvia Walsh explains the double danger: "Christian strivers face not only the internal difficulty of coming to believe in Christ and undergoing an inward transformation of their attitudes and actions vis-à-vis the world, they also potentially face opposition from the world as a consequence of venturing to express Christian love in their relations to others."[50] The person with *Klogskab* would likely flee these dangers at the first sight of them. Perhaps because of the second danger—the risk of losing one's reputation before one's contemporaries—this person will not venture to commit to the rigorousness of Christian love in the first place. Or perhaps the reality of the first danger—ongoing self-denial—overwhelms this individual who, nevertheless, pays lip service to its importance in the Christian life.

The one with infused prudence will respond differently to the double danger. Perhaps a budding, young philosopher is called by God to sell every possession and to give up a tenure-track position and a promising future of scholarship and success to live with and serve the poor in downtown Los Angeles. The rigid requirement of absolute self-denial and the concurrent risk of scorn by one's colleagues seem almost inevitable in such a scenario. This is the furthest thing from prudence, *Klogskab* thinks, yet such reasoning reflects immanent calculation since *Klogskab* neither understands nor is committed to the supernatural end of a loving relationship to God. Thus, action that appears foolish to the world may be wise or prudent precisely because it is the appropriate response to God, and therefore the proper means toward the proper end.

Kierkegaard himself offers an excellent example of how Christian love and infused prudence might mingle. In *On My Work as an Author* he recounts the aims of his authorial production and remarks

---

[49]Metaphysical priority does not entail epistemological priority, and so it is possible that one might love in this way without first knowing Christ's command.

[50]Sylvia Walsh, *Living Christianly: Kierkegaard's Dialectic of Christian Existence* (University Park: Pennsylvania State University Press, 2005) 101-102.

that they are his own "work of love" (OMWA, 10n). And yet, his methods are at times very crafty. Consider, for instance, the aesthetic writings, where he offers "earnest money" he knows will entice his aesthetic audience, in order to 'deceive them into the truth' and guide them back to true conceptions of the Christian life (PV, 44, 53-5). It might be tempting merely to call such activity clever, and that would not be an incorrect description. But it seems prudent or wise as well. For in this authorial activity we find calculation about the means to an end that coheres with the ultimate end of his life, a loving relationship to God, and thus it is not immanent calculation, but transformed calculation, or calculation according to a super-natural end.[51] In fact, at the end of *The Point of View for My Work as an Author*, Kierkegaard invokes the guidance of Governance, the hand of God that he believes has guided the authorship from its beginning (though he himself does not admit to having always understood this) (PV, 71-90). Thus, by his own recounting Kierkegaard seems to embody infused prudence in the service of a work of love that is guided by God because his activity is guided by a proper conception of the highest good for a human.

Whether Kierkegaard himself would agree with this interpretation of his "report to history" and whether he would agree with the inclusion of infused prudence within an ethic of love is doubtful, and at any rate, questions we cannot answer. Still, it seems plausible for there to be a place within an ethic of neighbor love for a virtue or trait that truthfully calculates how one might love one's neighbors — aim toward one's true end — when it does not come easily or when that love will be misunderstood.

---

[51]It seems prudent, e.g., to convey a message in a way that accounts for the uniqueness of the situation including the characteristics of the intended audience.

8

The Opposition between Objective Knowledge and Subjective Appropriation in Kierkegaard and Climacus

Thomas C. Anderson

It is well known that from *Either/Or* to his attacks on Christendom Kierkegaard criticized those — whether aesthetes, speculative philosophers, or Christians in Christendom — who placed such importance on attaining knowledge, understanding, and demonstration of truths that they minimized or even neglected willing, living, and appropriating those truths. He is especially upset with people who in his day have turned Christianity into a set of doctrines to be known rather than a life to be lived in faithful imitation of Christ. At times, Kierkegaard and his pseudonyms even suggest, not just a sharp difference between knowing and appropriating truth, but an *opposition* between them. That is, they appear to say that the more one seeks or attains true and certain knowledge of something, the less can he or she appropriate and live that knowledge.

In this article I will focus on the relation between knowledge or the search for true knowledge and the appropriation or living of that knowledge. I will begin by examining Kierkegaard's view of that relation in his *Christian Discourses*. Next I will compare what he says with the more precise and technical discussion of the relation between objective knowledge and truth and subjective truth set out by Johannes Climacus, the pseudonymous author of *Concluding Unscientific Postscript to "Philosophical Fragments."* I make this comparison because I believe Climacus's more philosophically rigorous treatment of the issue can aid in understanding Kierkegaard's own position. Indeed, a great many commentators apparently take the opinions presented by the pseudonymous author to be Kierkegaard's.[1] I

---

[1]I say this because in their discussions of Kierkegaard's views many authors continually cite *Philosophical Fragments* and *Concluding Unscientific Postscript* to sup-

will try to show, however, that while the two authors do agree about many of the ways that objective knowledge and subjective appropriation are inversely related, they also differ significantly. Since the *Discourses*, unlike the *Postscript*, is written in Kierkegaard's own name, it is reasonable to conclude that it, rather than the work of the pseudonymous Climacus, presents his own view. In order to verify this further, I will conclude this paper by briefly surveying the relation between knowledge and appropriation that Kierkegaard sets out in four religious works written after the *Discourses*, works also written in his own name or that of Anti-Climacus[2]. I will argue that in these later works he repeats the views he presented in *Christian Discourses*, thereby supporting my contention that Kierkegaard's own position, while similar in many respects, does differ in some important ways from that presented in *Concluding Unscientific Postscript*.

Christian Discourses's View of Knowledge and Appropriation.

In these discourses, Kierkegaard discusses the opposition between knowledge and appropriation when talking about truths pertaining to God's existence and personal immortality. Although both inquiries take place in a context in which he is contrasting the search for knowledge with the appropriation which comes from Christian faith, I propose to investigate those passages in order to raise the *general* question about Kierkegaard's view of the relation

port their interpretations of his position, apparently making little or no distinction between Kierkegaard and Climacus. See, e.g., Louis Pojman, *The Logic of Subjectivity* (University AL: University of Alabama Press, 1984); Niels Thulstrup, "Commentator's Introduction" to the volume of *Philosophical Fragments* translated by David Swenson; Mark C. Taylor, *Kierkegaard's Pseudonymous Authorship* (Princeton NJ: Princeton University Press, 1975); Arnold Come, *Kierkegaard as Humanist* (Montreal: McGill-Queens, 1995); George Price, *The Narrow Pass* (London: Hutchinson & Co, 1963); Reider Thomte, *Kierkegaard's Philosophy of Religion* (New York: Greenwood Press, 1969); Jeremy Walker, *Kierkegaard, the Descent into God* (Montreal: McGill-Queens, 1985).

[2]Both *The Sickness unto Death* and *Practice in Christianity* are written by the pseudonymous Anti-Climacus. They can be taken to express Kierkegaard's own views because he tells his readers that he used that pseudonym, not because he disagreed with the content of these works, but because he did not want to imply that he himself lived Christianity at the ideal level presented in them (SUD, xx-xxii).

between knowledge and appropriation. This is legitimate, I believe, because the choice to believe is for him only one of many ways to appropriate and live a truth. Kierkegaard mentions many passions besides faith which turn one's knowledge toward one's self and involve appropriation, namely, interest, earnestness, concern, decision, and will.[3]

In the third essay of part three, entitled "All Things Must Serve Us for Good — When We Love God" (Romans 8:28), Kierkegaard talks about the individual who, in order to overcome doubts and become certain about the truth of that Biblical statement, attempts to demonstrate it (To demonstrate would be to prove conclusively and thus to know for certain that the Biblical statement is true, or is "eternally certain" [CD, 189]) . He comments ironically that even if such a person could "become so thoroughly familiar with God, so to speak, and . . . demonstrate that he is love and what follows from that, . . . [nevertheless] from the demonstration nothing follows *for me*" (CD, 191). That is, it does not follow from the demonstration that God is love that I in fact love God nor that I act according to the demonstrated truth. Knowledge about God is not the same as knowledge of my self and of my relation to my knowledge of God; he writes, "A knowledge that God is love is still not a consciousness of it. Consciousness, personal consciousness, requires that in my knowledge I also have knowledge of myself and my relation to my knowledge" (CD, 194). Similarly, a little later in that essay,[4] Kierkegaard imagines a thinker with exceptional mental gifts who has pondered the nature of God, specifically that He is love, and has clearly expounded his demonstrated conclusions in an "excellent book that is the pride of the whole human race." What this thinker "understood about God was surely . . . true and profound," he states, yet when adversity strikes him, the thinker doubts whether it really is for his good. He doubts, Kierkegaard says, because "the thinker had not understood himself, . . . he had lived under the delusion that when it had been demonstrated that God is love it followed as a matter of course that you and I believe it" (CD, 198). What he must do, Kierkegaard advises, is "turn around" his thought; turn away

---

[3]See CD, 88, 150-51, 189, 192-98; WL, 230-31; PC, 158, 186-90; JFY, 119.
[4]CD, 197-99.

from a quest for knowledge about God and passionately turn inward so that he personally chooses to accept the truth that God is love and that all things are, therefore, for his good and lives accordingly. And, then, Kierkegaard adds the general remark, "every demonstration" that God is love only "leads you away" (CD, 199) from the decision to believe and live accordingly. That suggests that he believes that a search for knowledge, even if it achieves "true and profound" understanding and the certainty of demonstration, inevitably leads one away from the decision to appropriate personally and live that knowledge. But before drawing that conclusion, let us examine another essay in the *Discourses*, one dealing with the question of immortality.

    In the fourth essay of part three, "There Will Be the Resurrection of the Dead, of the Righteous—and of the Unrighteous," Kierkegaard talks about those who seek to demonstrate the immortality of the soul so that they can be "secure in the intellectual sense" and put their mind at ease before they accept it.[5] He complains that a search for a demonstration of immortality, no matter how scholarly, keeps the issue of immortality at a distance from the one searching because that individual does not become anxious or afraid about *his or her own* immortality, nor whether he or she is "living in such a way as my immortality requires" (CD, 205), namely, living righteously. "Immortality has been turned into a question," Kierkegaard laments, "what is a task for action has been turned into a question for thought." This is simply an evasion, he claims, "because people have wanted to *demonstrate* it . . . then it has been left standing open, whether one will accept it" (CD, 206). In fact, since the most one can find are several reasons to support "the probability that you are immortal" (CD, 206); to insist on demonstrating it for certain will mean that one forever avoids the choice to accept and live it. (Besides, Kierkegaard adds, if I could be completely sure of it, that would mean that I would not welcome my immortality and my eternal salvation as a gift from God.) Once again, Kierkegaard posits an opposition between searching for or attaining demonstrative knowledge and living or appropriating that knowledge. He apparently denies the possibility that immortality or God's existence could

---

[5]CD, 202-205.

be *both* a "question for thought" (his phrase), that is, something whose truth one might attempt to demonstrate rationally *and also* something to be appropriated and lived.

In order to understand his position, let us note the way that Kierkegaard in these discourses characterizes the search for knowledge or demonstration and contrasts it with the decision to appropriate.[6] He repeatedly describes the pursuit of knowledge as detached, impersonal, and uninterested in the inquirer's own personal choices or life. He also often characterizes that search as calm, secure, at rest, and not in earnest; in other words, as lacking in passion. He contrasts this with the anxious concerns of earnest individuals who in fear and trembling wonder about their personal relation to the knowledge in question and whether or how they should decide to live what they know. Of course, Kierkegaard admits that individuals can also be passionately committed to the search for truth.[7] Even so, the passionate search for knowledge focuses such seekers in the wrong direction, he says, for they devote their efforts to trying to understand or demonstrate some truth rather than reflecting on their personal relation to that truth and their choice to live it or not.[8] But does this mean that Kierkegaard believes that the intellectual pursuit of truth is *necessarily* impersonal, *necessarily* indifferent to the seekers' relation to that truth? Does he think that one cannot ever both passionately seek knowledge and also earnestly strive to appropriate and live that knowledge? As we shall see, Kierkegaard does indeed think that in some fundamental ways knowledge and the pursuit of truth are opposed to the appropriation and living of that truth. Before pursuing this, however, I want to turn to Johannes Climacus's discussion of the distinction between knowing the truth and being the truth. As I stated earlier, I believe that comparing *Concluding Unscientific Postscript*'s view of that relationship with that of the *Christian Discourses* will enable us to grasp Kierkegaard's own position with more clarity and precision.

---

[6]CD, 88-90, 189-90, 202-204.
[7]CD, 212-13; PC, 158; FSE, 26-27.
[8]CD, 189-90, 198-99, 202-205, 245-46.

The Opposition between Objective and Subjective Truth in <u>Concluding Unscientific Postscript.</u>

Climacus's[9] stress on the difference between an objective and a subjective approach to truth and between objective and subjective truth is well known. From the very beginning of the *Postscript*, he describes the objective path as focused on attaining knowledge of truth but not on the subjective truth which is the subject's appropriation and living of truth. An objective inquirer, he writes, no matter how zealously he pursues objective truth is "disinterested" in the individual subject and in his "relation to the known truth." The search for knowledge can then be a way to evade personal choice.[10] On the other hand the subjective inquirer is "infinitely, passionately interested in his relation to this truth" (CUP, 1:29). An especially clear passage is the following: "to objective reflection, truth becomes something objective, an object, and the point is to disregard the subject. To subjective reflection, truth becomes appropriation, inwardness, subjectivity, and the point is to immerse oneself, existing, in subjectivity" (CUP, 1:192). So far the position appears to be the same as Kierkegaard's in his *Discourses*. In addition, and this is especially important for our investigation, Climacus also repeatedly insists that these are the *only* two possibilities for an inquiring subject—either to be infinitely interested in one's personal relation to the truth or to be a disinterested seeker of objective truth. He writes, "Objectively the question is *only* [my emphasis] about categories of thought; subjectively about inwardness" (CUP, 1:203). And he stresses that no mediation or combination of objectivity and subjectivity is possible for an existing subject.[11]

But why does Climacus contend that it is impossible to combine objective knowledge and subjective appropriation? Why must the

---

[9]I refer to Climacus as the author of the material in the *Postscript* in order to leave open the question whether the positions he enunciates are held by Kierkegaard. The Dane himself asks the reader who quotes passages from his pseudonymous works to cite "the pseudonymous author's name, not mine" (CUP, 1:627). Also, as we will see later, Climacus himself takes no stand on some of the positions he discusses.

[10]CUP, 1: 115-16, 574-78 and in general all of part one.

[11]CUP, 1:129-30, 192-93, 196-99, 204-13.

objective pursuit of knowledge be *only* about categories of thought? Why could not an individual earnestly seek true knowledge about God or the soul's immortality (two items that Climacus, like Kierkegaard, discusses) and also be passionately interested in subjectively incorporating such knowledge in his or her life?[12]

Part of the answer lies in the way Climacus describes the nature of knowledge. Knowledge or thought inevitably abstracts from and thereby "annuls" or "cancels" the real. By its very nature thought leaves out the particular, concrete features of actual existents.[13] "The particular cannot be thought," Climacus writes, "only the universal" (CUP, 1:326). Furthermore, thought grasps its object as eternal, that is, it prescinds from its changing temporal existence. To take his example, when I think man or humanity, I consider the general intelligible content of these notions and leave aside (annul) the particular, temporal features of actual concrete human beings. Accordingly, Climacus says that actual concrete individuals are not included as such in thought's realm of abstraction. That is one reason that there is a fundamental "qualitative" and "essential" difference (CUP, 1:339-40) between the realm of knowledge and that of actual concrete existents. No wonder, then, that he considers a combination of these two realms problematic. No wonder, too, that like *Christian Discourses*, the *Concluding Unscientific Postscript* maintains that to know something, even to demonstrate and be certain of its truth, does not of itself mean that one makes that truth part of his or her concrete existence.

However, this is not the end of the story, for Climacus adds that although thought may be abstract by nature, it can be brought down to earth, so to speak, and think the concrete existent. Even though "thought is in an alien medium" (CUP, 1:332) when it thinks con-

---

[12]I agree with C. Stephen Evans, *Kierkegaard's Fragments and Postscript* (Atlantic Highlands NJ: Humanities Press, 1983), who states, "There is a tendency in Climacus to dichotomize the objective and the subjective" (112), and with Pojman, *The Logic of Subjectivity*, "there is a disjunctive relationship between objective and subjective inquiry, an exclusive (as opposed to inclusive) disjunctive relationship," (36), and with his general criticism that Kierkegaard makes too many sweeping either/ors (48). However, I would add that many of the sweeping either/ors are made by Climacus, not by Kierkegaard
[13]CUP, 1:302, 307-309, 314-17, 332, 339-40.

crete existents, it can be made to do so if something external is added to it, namely passion, in the form of interest or seriousness or earnestness. That is precisely what the subjective thinker does, for he or she "understands the abstract concept [human being] to be a concrete human being, to be this individual existing human being" (CUP, 1:352), namely, himself or herself.[14] Of course, in order to appropriate what we know, we must be reflectively interested in ourselves, in our personal relation to what is known, and earnestly desire to inform our lives with our knowledge. Only a passionate self-interest will ultimately culminate in the choice or decision actually to appropriate and subjectively *be* the truth known. Yet, if this is so, if knowledge, even though essentially different from concrete existence, can with the aid of passion become concrete and, also with the aid of passion, be appropriated by particular individuals, why does Climacus say (above) that objectivity and subjectivity cannot be combined? Why must truths grasped by objective thought be impersonal and disinterested?

Part of the answer, I believe, rests on the conception of passion and of passion's relation to knowledge, even to concrete knowledge, presented in *Concluding Unscientific Postscript*. Passion is absolutely central to subjectivity. In fact, Climacus writes, "passion *is* subjectivity" (CUP, 1:131), "subjectivity *is* essentially passion" (CUP, 1:33) and "passion is the highest pitch of subjectivity" (CUP, 1:199). However, Climacus also puts forward the view that the more one's knowledge approaches certainty[15] about the truth of something, the less

---

[14]See also, CUP, 1:121-23, 308, 339-40, 342, 350-51. Climacus (and SK) limits concrete knowledge to knowledge of one's own self, a position I have criticized in "The Extent of Kierkegaard's Skepticism," in *Man and World* 27, 1994, 271-89.

[15]I appreciate the suggestion of a reader that for clarity's sake I distinguish verbally between objective "certainty" and subjective or psychological "certitude." The problem is that to do so introduces into Kierkegaard's Danish a precision and distinction that is not there since the word for certainty and for certitude is the same in Danish (*vished*). (The Hongs sometimes translate *vished* as certainty and sometimes as certitude.) Marilyn Piety first made me aware of that fact in her dissertation, *Kierkegaard on Knowledge,* 22, written in 1994 and available at UMI Dissertation Services, Ann Arbor, MI. Let me add that I have benefitted greatly from that work not only because of her thorough discussion of the kinds of knowledge in Kierkegaard but also because of her excellent knowledge of the Danish of Kierkegaard's time. I thank Robert Perkins for recommending Piety's work.

passionately can he or she will that known truth and hence appropriate and become it. "Certainty and passion do not hitch up as a team" (CUP, 1:29) he writes; "inwardness" which "in an existing subject is passion" (CUP 1:199) "has an inverse relation to it [viz. objective truth]" (CUP, 1:202).[16]

Climacus's remarks about the passion of faith clearly make this point. Take the following well known definition of (subjective)[17] truth: "An objective uncertainty [*uvished*] held fast through appropriation with the most passionate inwardness is the truth, the highest truth there is for an existing person" (CUP, 1:203). This is the highest subjective truth for an existing person, Climacus explains, because "objectively he has only uncertainty, but this is precisely what intensifies the infinite passion of inwardness" (CUP, 1:203). To illustrate he refers briefly to an individual who attempts to prove that God is by studying nature. Such a person finds some evidence for a cause with "omnipotence and wisdom" but he or she also finds much (presumably evil of various kinds) that argues against such a cause. "The *summa summarum* of this," Climacus concludes, "is an objective uncertainty" (CUP, 1:204). Since the individual's attempts to demonstrate that God is result in uncertainty, if he or she affirms God's reality it is not because he/she is intellectually certain of it but because he or she *wills* to do so; wills, in other words, to believe in it. Such a choice, which involves a passionate appropriation of an objective uncertainty, is, he says, the "highest truth there is for an existing person" (CUP, 1:203); that is, it is the highest truth one can appropriate and exist in. It is "highest" because it requires more passion,

---

[16]For a good discussion of inwardness and its connection to will and passion see David Gouwens, *Kierkegaard as Religious Thinker* (Cambridge: Cambridge University Press, 1996), 96-102.

[17]The entire section (CUP, 1, pt. II, sect. II, chap. II) focuses on "subjective" truth, "essential" truth, on being "in" the truth, not on truth carte blanche. Climacus himself points that out in a footnote (CUP, 1:199*). Not all commentators seem to recognize this focus. Some who do are Alastair Hannay, *Kierkegaard: The Arguments of the Philosophers* (London: Routledge & Kegan Paul, 1982) 130-35; Reider Thomte, *Kierkegaard's Philosophy of Religion*, 116; Merold Westphal, *Becoming a Self* (West Lafayette: Purdue University Press, 1996) 116-19; Robert Perkins, "Kierkegaard, a kind of epistemologist" in *History of European Ideas* 12, #1 (1990) 13. I found Westphal's discussion of this portion of *Concluding Unscientific Postscript* particularly helpful.

more will, to choose to believe in and live something known to be uncertain than to choose to appropriate something known to be highly probable, certain or almost certain. And, to repeat, the more passion, the more subjectivity, according to Climacus, for the more I passionately embrace something, the more I live and become it.[18] That is the reason he says, "For the existing person passion is existence at its very highest" (CUP, 1:197).

In fact, the affirmation of God just mentioned is not the highest subjective truth Climacus discusses, for he immediately points out that even more passion is necessary to believe in something that is not just objectively uncertain but in its objective content is absurd, even self-contradictory, namely, the existence of the God-man. Since knowledge of such an object is repellant to the understanding, to profess its reality requires even more passion, more will, more faith.[19] The point is clear. The degree of passion necessary to affirm and subjectively appropriate some truth about an object of knowledge is directly proportional to the degree of uncertainty involved in knowing that truth about that object. The more uncertainty, the more passion.

Now suppose something is known to be neither absurd nor simply uncertain but to be probable, or quite probable, or very highly probable. It follows from what Climacus says about the different degrees of passion necessary for the two kinds of faith mentioned above, that the amount of passion necessary to affirm the reality of a known object will *decrease* precisely to the extent that

---

[18]Another way to put this is that the more passionately I embrace some truth, the more that truth is upbuilding for me. In his article, "Kierkegaard, a kind of epistemologist," Robert L. Perkins argues that "Kierkegaard's concepts of truth, inwardness or subjectivity are mirror images of the concept of upbuilding," 7. See also 13-14. I completely agree. The truth one passionately appropriates is the truth that builds up his or her subjectivity.

[19]CUP, 1:204-14. I should add that Climacus repeatedly states that he takes no position about the truth or falsity of this fundamental belief of Christianity (CUP, 1:204). In general he refuses to take a stand about *any* of the truths of Christianity. See, CUP, 1:204, 213-16, 222-26, 271-73, 587, 617-19. However, in a very provocative article, "The Reality of the World in Kierkegaard's *Postscript*" in *International Kierkegaard Commentary: Concluding Unscientific Postscript to 'Philosophical Fragments'*, ed. Robert L. Perkins (Macon GA: Mercer University Press, 1997) M. G. Piety argues that Climacus is in fact a Christian (174-76)!

one's knowledge of that object's reality increases in probability. Therefore, if one knew for certain the truth about an object, no passion at all would be needed to accept that truth — and Climacus does say just that about mathematical truths.[20] But to hold that the more one's knowledge of something approximates objective certainty, the less passion is needed to affirm the truth about that object, means that the more a subject's knowledge approaches certainty, the less can he or she inwardly appropriate and live that knowledge, for, to repeat, "inwardness . . . is passion" (CUP, 1:199) and "passion is subjectivity" (CUP, 1:131). And that is exactly what Climacus states, "the more objective reliability the less inwardness (since inwardness is subjectivity), the less objective reliability the deeper is the possible inwardness" (CUP, 1:209) and, therefore, the possible subjectivity. This is another reason why Climacus proposes an inverse relation between objective knowledge and subjective appropriation. Although knowledge can be made concrete by passion so that it can know the individual existent, to the degree that knowledge approaches objective certainty, it cannot be, or can less and less be, inwardly, passionately, subjectively appropriated.

Yet this cannot be the whole story. Surely, the pseudonymous author of *Concluding Unscientific Postscript* (and its editor) are aware that thinkers throughout history, as diverse as Augustine, Anselm, Aquinas, Spinoza, and Leibniz, thought that they could rationally demonstrate the existence of God and the immortality of the soul and also appropriate that knowledge and form their lives with it. Furthermore, Climacus himself devotes large sections of the *Postscript* to making many truth claims about the self (and about God), which "truths," even if not demonstratively certain, are at the very least highly probable. And he wants his readers both to know and appropriate them.[21] Among the proposed truths about the self

---

[20]CUP, 1:204.

[21]See his whole discussion in CUP, 1, pt. II, chap. I, "Becoming Subjective" and chap. II, sect. 4. Some seem to think that because Climacus takes no stand about the truth of Christianity vis a vis Religiousness A and uses the term hypothesis, that he takes no stand about the truth of anything. On the contrary *Concluding Unscientific Postscript* makes many truth claims about the nature of subjectivity, about knowledge and about passion — to name just three items. Moreover, Climacus never says that the whole of the *Postscript* is an hypothesis, it is Christianity that is his hypothesis or "imaginary construction." CUP, 1:206, 213-14, 369, 587, 617. He says

are the following: (1) An existing individual should recognize that his or her most important task is to become a subject; (2) This demands passionate self-interest and reflection on the self, and (3) repeated choices to appropriate and thus become the subject he or she should be, and (4) knowing and unifying into a concrete harmony his or her human faculties of imagination, feeling, passion, and thought.[22] In addition, (5) an existing individual needs to establish an absolute relation to the absolute in order to attain eternal salvation, and (6) repeated failures to do so and to become one's ideal self will result in guilt. Now insofar as these assertions purport to be true, that is to correspond to actual characteristics of a subject,[23] they, like all knowledge claims about empirical objects, can not be demonstratively certain. It is just possible that some of Climacus's truth claims are inaccurate and that he misreads some attributes of the subject. Nevertheless, it seems clear that the probability of their truth is extremely high and that does not prevent a subject passionately appropriating them. Indeed that is what Climacus desires.

Furthermore, and very important, the above truth claims about the subject can legitimately be called "objective truths" about the subject. Although many have overlooked it, sometimes Climacus uses the term objective to refer not to disinterested knowledge or knowledge of objects other than the self but to "what" one knows or says. When he writes "objectively the emphasis is on *what* is said" (CUP, 1: 202), the term objective refers to the content of knowledge or of a statement. Now knowledge or statements with content (such as some characteristics of subjectivity) can claim to be true, that is, claim to correspond to the reality of the object[24] known — in this case, the subject. Climacus calls the statement "the earth is round" an "objective truth" meaning that what is said corresponds to the way the object, the earth, is.[25] In the same way, the above statements about features of the subject claim to be objective truths, that is,

---

the same thing in *Philosophical Fragments*, 22, 87, 107, 109.

[22]CUP, 1:343-49.

[23]Climacus accepts the correspondence theory of truth: CUP, 1:189.

[24]The term object here simply refers to whatever is known, whether features of nature or of subjectivity.

[25]CUP, 1:195.

"*what*" they say claims to correspond to real features of the subject.[26] (And, by the way, this is the case even if the individual who knows them never chooses to appropriate them.) Likewise, the person who attempts to demonstrate that God is attempts to prove that "*what*" is said, "God is," corresponds to reality and so is objectively true. Yet nothing prevents such "objective" truths about the self or about God from being passionately appropriated by an individual. (I will return to this point shortly.)

Finally, I want to mention Climacus's discussion of Religiousness A, his term for all religions other than Christianity in the strict sense. As I have shown at length in an earlier article, the *Postscript* presents *two* forms of this kind of religiousness.[27] One, inspired by Plato, claims that humans by their own powers of self-reflection (called recollection)[28] can come to realize that they are essentially eternal (immortal) and can "find" or "discover" that God is within them. Such truths about God and the self are objective in the way mentioned above, that is, they claim to correspond to what is real. The other form of Religiousness A is exemplified by Socrates who ignores the truths found by recollection and instead stresses the need for the existing individual to risk and venture to believe in immortality and in God. Now it is significant that when Climacus chooses to contrast Religiousness A with Christianity, the Religiousness A that he most often refers to is the Platonic form.[29] That is because he

---

[26]Of course knowledge and truths about the characteristics of the subject could in one sense be called subjective knowledge and truths. However, and this is very important, they are not what Climacus designates as subjective knowledge and truth in the strict sense for by that he means knowledge and truth *appropriated* and *lived* by the subject. Truths about the nature of the subject are objectively true, that is, they correspond to the nature of the subject, even if they are not appropriated.

[27]For a discussion of the two kinds of Religiousness A, see my article, "Is the Religion of *Eighteen Upbuilding Discourses* Religiousness A?" in *International Kierkegaard Commentary: Eighteen Upbuilding Discourses,* ed. Robert L. Perkins (Macon GA: Mercer University Press, 2003) esp. sect. 2.

[28]Climacus admits taking the term recollection from Plato, even though he does not agree that the soul preexists its bodily existence. Throughout both his *Philosophical Fragments* (PF, 9-19, 25, 31, 62, 87) and *Concluding Unscientific Postscript* (CUP, 1: 205-209, 226-27, 270-73, 424, 556-61) Climacus frequently uses recollection to mean an inner deepening of one's self awareness.

[29]The most extensive discussion of the contrast between the two is in the last 200 pages of *Concluding Unscientific Postscript,* esp. 555-86.

believes that Platonic Religiousness A's position about the possibility of "taking oneself out of existence into the eternal by recollection" is "the only consistent position outside Christianity" (CUP 1:226). Furthermore, he repeatedly states that he makes no judgment about whether Christianity or the Platonic form of Religiousness A is true. That is to say, he refuses to decide whether human beings by using their own powers of self-reflection can come to know the eternity/immortality of the subject and discover God's presence within themselves or whether Christianity is correct in insisting that humans know these truths only through divine revelation.[30] But note that Climacus's indecision indicates that he thinks that the Platonic form of Religiousness A *may be true!*[31] Yet, even if it is, he says the proper response to truths about the self and about God gained by deep self-reflection is for the individual to renounce the world and establish an absolute relation to the absolute (eternal salvation/God) in his or her life.[32] In other words, even if objective truths about the self and God can be known by natural human powers, such truths are meant to be inwardly, passionately, appropriated by the subject.

Thus, to put it gently, there seems to be an incompatibility between some of the positions Climacus presents about the relation of objective knowledge and truth and subjective truth and appropriation. In some places he maintains that objective knowledge, especially as it approaches certainty, is the opposite of subjective passion and cannot be combined with it — and so cannot be or can hardly be appropriated. In others he encourages his readers passionately, subjectively to appropriate knowledge of the self and God which he considers objectively true (though not necessarily certain), that is, to be knowledge that corresponds to the reality of the self and God.

In my opinion the incompatibility occurs because *Concluding Un-*

---

[30]CUP 1:204-206*; 270-72; 560-61, 573 note; 581-82 .

[31]Climacus does call himself a humorist. However, it is important to recognize that he sometimes describes a humorist as one who accepts recollection (the Platonic form of Religiousness A) and so sees the incongruity in anyone spending a great deal of time attempting to attain the immortality and the God he or she already possesses. (See CUP, 1:270*-72 and 581-82.) Note the following passage where Climacus explicitly links humor and recollection: "Humor is always a revocation of existence into the eternal by recollection backwards" (CUP 1,602).

[32]CUP, 1:387-90.

scientific Postscript gives at least *three* different meanings to the terms objective knowledge and truth. As we have seen, many times objective knowledge or truth means: (1) Knowledge that focuses on objects rather than subjects[33] or, (2) Knowledge or truth that is indifferent to the subject and the subject's relation to that knowledge.[34] But, as we just pointed out (3) Sometimes objective knowledge and truth refer to *what* is known, the object of knowledge, and to the degree of certainty one has about the truth of statements about that object. By definition objective knowledge and truth which disregard the subject or are indifferent to subjective appropriation are incompatible with subjective passion and appropriation However, objective knowledge and truth whose correspondence with reality approaches certainty or a high degree of probability is not. Climacus's blanket statements about the inverse relation between objective knowledge/truth and subjective truth/appropriation apparently overlook the significant difference between his third meaning of objective knowledge/truth and the first two.

I would also suggest that Climacus occasionally fails to keep in mind the difference between two closely related passions. There is the passion involved in the choice to believe, where to believe means to affirm something to be true, whether or not it can be understood. On the other hand, there is the passion involved in the choice to believe, where to believe means to appropriate and live that truth. Because he does not always distinguish them, Climacus seems to suggest that if it takes little or no passion to affirm a known truth (because it can be demonstrated or almost demonstrated), then little or no passion can be brought to bear in appropriating that truth.

In any case, whatever the reasons for Climacus's apparently incompatible statements about the relation of objectivity and subjectivity, this paper is primarily devoted to determining Kierkegaard's views. Let us return, then, to his *Christian Discourses* and see how the *Postscript*'s analysis of the relation between objective knowledge and subjective passion (and appropriation) can assist our understanding of the Dane's position and reveal its differences with the views set forth in Climacus's work.

---

[33]See CUP, 1:21-22, 129-30, 192, 196
[34]CUP, 1:129-131, 193, 200-203.

Applying Climacus's Analysis to the Christian Discourses

Even though in these discourses, Kierkegaard does not engage in a technical examination of the nature of knowledge, it is quite apparent that he agrees with the pseudonymous author of the *Postscript* that knowledge by its very nature is qualitatively different from concrete reality. Passages cited above support that interpretation. Recall his repeated description of the search for knowledge as impersonal and indifferent to the subject's relation to that knowledge. Recall, too, his insistence that even if one attained profound insights into a truth, even to the point of attaining demonstrative certitude about it, that does not necessarily mean that one accepts or lives that truth. Also, just as Climacus distinguished between abstract and concrete thought, Kierkegaard distinguishes between what he calls "thought in general" and "thought with a name" (CD, 150), that is, thought about one's own personal self. Also like Climacus, he maintains that something must be added to thought, namely, passion, if one is to apply thought to one's self and appropriate/live a known truth.[35] Kierkegaard also believes that because knowledge is by nature impersonal, the intellectual pursuit of truth or certainty, even if, and perhaps, especially if, engaged in passionately, leads the thinker away from the concrete appropriation of that truth.[36]

Does this mean that Kierkegaard also agrees with Climacus's statements that objective knowledge and subjective appropriation are inversely related and cannot be combined; that the more one approaches true and certain knowledge, the less he or she can passionately choose to appropriate that knowledge? To answer, that question let us investigate the various kinds of opposition between the pursuit of knowledge and its appropriation that Kierkegaard discusses in his *Discourses*.

For one thing, like Climacus, Kierkegaard repeatedly interprets the search for knowledge as a means of evading choice.[37] He criticizes those doubters who postpone their decisions about God until they have demonstrated that God exists. They may consider

---

[35]See texts cited in n. 3.
[36]See texts cited in n. 8.
[37]CD, 88-90, 189-94, 202-207, 240, 244-46.

their extensive deliberations to be a mark of their earnestness and think that the longer they strive to prove God's existence, the more serious they are about it. On the contrary, Kierkegaard says, the longer they deliberate, no matter how scholarly and learned their reasoning becomes, the more they "calmly postpone the question whether [they] should choose God now" (CD, 88). And the longer they are unwilling to choose God *now*, the more indecisive they become, the more they demonstrate their lack of earnestness. As a result they distance themselves further from God.

One reason that people use the search for knowledge to evade choice is that people *naturally*, spontaneously, are dominated by their lower, sensate, rather than their spiritual, side according to Kierkegaard.[38] Such "natural men" (CD, 112, 153, 180, 287) are instinctively self-centered and believe that attaining the goods of this world (he mentions health, honor, privilege, wealth, power, security, pleasure, success, erotic love) will result in their happiness and fulfillment.[39] They prefer the temporal realm to the eternal. Needless to say, a "natural" human being is offended by the Christian demands to renounce the world and one's natural, self-centered self. More to our point, Kierkegaard describes "natural" human beings as prizing shrewdness, deliberation, proof, demonstration, understanding, reasons, sagacity, the probable and the certain and, as a consequence, as being unwilling to risk the venture of believing.[40]

Add to this that humans are not just "natural men" but sinners: "to be a human being is to be a sinful human being," Kierkegaard writes (CD, 274). Sin is the reason for the innate selfishness of human beings and for their preferring this world over God and eternity and for their rejecting Christian teachings about self-denial and death to the world. Sin also accounts for the human being's preference for the reasonable, the probable and the certain and, accordingly, for considering the notions of a God-man, self-sacrificing love, sin and

---

[38]Ultimately, however, it is the spirit which consents to be dominated (SUD, 82).

[39]CD, 62-64, 108-109, 146-49, 152-55, 171-72, 227. John Elrod, *Kierkegaard and Christendom* (Princeton NJ: Princeton University Press, 1981) chap. 3, has a good discussion of the social side of the natural self.

[40]CD, 88-90, 179-82, 189-91, 197-99, 202-206, 211-13, 240, 245-46.

its forgiveness to be impossible and even foolish.[41]

Kierkegaard considers such preferences to be the sin of disobedi-ence for we are commanded by God to believe, right now, *at this very moment*.[42] The person who seeks reasons and knowledge and so "is calmly postponing the question whether he should choose God now" is guilty of impiety and "insubordination because in this way God is thrust down from the throne, from being the master" (CD, 89). It is the sin of pride for individuals to make their choice of God dependent on their knowledge, for that gives their intellectual powers priority over God. In his discussion of immortality,[43] Kierkegaard puts it this way: "With immortality . . . the immortality of every individual, God is the lord and ruler and the single individual relates himself to him" as the source of immortality. But, "by becoming an object of demonstrations immortality is hurled from the throne . . . God is abolished and the human race is God" (CD, 213) because, to repeat, human intellectual powers take precedence over God's command to believe this very moment in one's immortality and live accordingly.

There is more. What compounds the issue in Kierkegaard's eyes and makes the search for knowledge, reasons, and demonstrations especially disobedient is that such a search is in fact *unnecessary* for attaining the most important truths. In a number of places in *Christian Discourses* Kierkegaard expresses his belief that if persons earnestly turn inward and recognize their total powerlessness and sinfulness and humbly admit their absolute need for God, the all-loving Creator will reveal to them the truths they need to know and live for their eternal salvation. In the following passage he offers a powerful analogy:

> Truly, no more than God allows a species of fish to come into existence in a particular lake unless the plant that is its nourishment is also growing there, no more will God allow the truly concerned person to be ignorant of what he is to believe. That is, the need brings its nourishment with it. . . . The need brings the nourishment with it, not *by itself* . . . but by virtue of a divine determination that

[41]CD 97, 107, 170-74, 180-81, 213, 264-65. Also see texts cited in the previous footnote.
[42]CD, 86-89. See also, 98-99, 189-91.
[43]CD, 205-206, 211-13.

joins the two. (CD, 244-45)

And in another place he writes, "If only it is altogether definite before God that this person feels the need to believe, he will very definitely find out what he is to believe" (CD, 246).[44] Since knowledge, at least of those truths about the self, the world, and God necessary for eternal salvation, can be gained from God by taking a subjective path of self-discovery, there is simply no need to become involved in an objective search for human understanding, reasons and demonstrations of such matters. If one persists in the latter, it is no wonder that Kierkegaard considers it to be a willful refusal to turn inward and become subjective and seriously face one's sinfulness and absolute need for a Savior. (Let me add, that it may be, as some commentators suggest,[45] that Climacus's famous statement "subjectivity is truth" is his way of saying something similar, namely, that a certain kind of passionate subjective approach is a necessary and sufficient condition, with God's help, for attaining objective truth. However, Climacus's statement is made within Religiousness A, for it is said in reference to Socratic, not Christian, faith.[46] In Platonic Religiousness A, as I pointed out above, truths about one's self and God are known subjectively, but not by means of God's revelation, rather through a deep reflection on one's self.)

In conclusion, then, in his *Christian Discourses* Kierkegaard does indicate that in many ways he agrees with *Concluding Unscientific Postscript* that the search for knowledge is inversely related, even opposed, to personal appropriation. Kierkegaard agrees that knowledge is by nature abstract and impersonal and thus that a zealous pursuit of intellectual truth can lead the thinker away from personal appropriation of that truth. Kierkegaard also agrees with Climacus that knowledge can be made concrete only if something external, passion, is added to it and that passion enables one to take a subjective path to attain truths about God and the self. For both authors, an objective route to such truths is unnecessary if not impossible.

---

[44]See also, CD, 88, 123, 132, 246.

[45]Pojman, *The Logic of Subjectivity*, chap. 3; Evans, *Kierkegaard's Fragments and Postscript*, chap. 8, and, if I understand him correctly, Hannay, *Kierkegaard: The Arguments of the Philosophers*, 46-47, 137-39.

[46]CUP, 1:198-210. In fact, the Christian position according to Climacus is that "subjectivity is untruth" (CUP, 1:207) due to sin.

However, Kierkegaard adds to all this his Christian belief in sin, something Climacus accurately describes but says he does not believe.[47] Insofar as the search for knowledge is undertaken by sinful human beings, Kierkegaard considers it to be a path we use to evade our divine obligation to accept Christianity personally and live it now.[48] The pursuits of reasons, understanding, and demonstrations are sinful distractions from the real path to truth which is reflection on ourselves and our total need for God.

Furthermore, the Kierkegaard of the second authorship seems to be extremely skeptical about the ability of human beings by their natural powers to attain any truth about the self or God. That would, of course, rule out the path of recollection or deep reflection on one's self that Climacus left open in the *Postscript* as a possible way to truth. In his *Discourses*, Kierkegaard does have a few scattered statements about some characteristics of the self, for example, that it is both temporal and eternal, both sensate and spiritual, but he never says that these features can be known by human reason.[49] In fact, he never explains how he knows that the self has such features. Likewise, in the *Christian Discourses* Kierkegaard never refers to a natural human knowledge of God or immortality, a knowledge obtained by human powers alone.[50] Rather, he so emphasizes the terrible effects of sin on human beings that it seems reasonable to conclude that he thinks sin makes it impossible for humans to arrive at a knowledge

---

[47]See texts cited in n. 19.

[48]It is interesting to speculate on what Kierkegaard would say about a real person who was not a Christian and engaged in the lengthy philosophizing of *Philosophical Fragments* and *Concluding Unscientific Postscript*. I suspect Kierkegaard would consider that person sinful because, although he or she accurately describes Christianity, he or she refuses to take a stand on whether it is true. It would appear that through his or her intellectual pursuits such a person evades the divine command to believe *at this very moment*.

[49]CD 4, 71, 77, 89-90, 137, 141, 182.

[50]I agree with James Collins, *The Mind of Kierkegaard* (Chicago: Henry Regnery Co., 1967) 266, that "Kierkegaard took unnecessary scandal at every sort of philosophical treatment of immortality and God's existence. To handle these matters philosophically meant to reduce the content of faith to the level of natural reason and philosophical criteria." I would simply add that I believe it is Kierkegaard's view of sin that is at the root of his suspicion of reason and philosophy. Evans makes much the same point as Collins in his *Passionate Reason* (Bloomington: Indiana University Press, 1992) 90-95.

of God and of the soul and its immortality through their natural power of self-reflection or recollection.[51] Such truths can be known but only through divine revelation and faith. That brings me to a final difference between Kierkegaard and the author of *Concluding Unscientific Postscript*. The former does not agree that truths known with certainty cannot be appropriated. Even though Kierkegaard shares Climacus's view that it is not possible to demonstrate objectively the immortality of the soul or God's reality, he is *certain* that the soul is immortal and that God is. That is because he posits a type of certainty hardly mentioned in *Concluding Unscientific Postscript*,[52] one that is compatible with appropriation. I am referring to certainty about the truths of Christian faith, such truths as, Jesus is the God-man who atoned for human sins and offers eternal salvation. To be sure, certainty about those truths is not attained by human reason or rational demonstration but through the grace of the Spirit; "only God can give him this certitude [*vished*]" (CD, 194), Kierkegaard writes. Nevertheless, since God commands me to believe in the God-man, in sin and Christ's atonement, and in personal immortality, I can be certain that they are true. I know that they *must* correspond to the way reality is. And such certainties should be inwardly appropriated and lived, Kierkegaard insists—by taking Jesus as the pattern for my life. Granted, the certainty/certitude[53] of those truths is a divine gift. Granted that they are mysteries insofar as I am

----

[51]Some commentators maintain that Kierkegaard himself accepts the Platonic form of Religiousness A's view on recollection, i.e. that there is a natural human ability to attain through self reflection knowledge of God and of the subject's eternity. (See Come, *Kierkegaard as Humanist*; Evans, *Kierkegaard's Fragments and Postscript*, chap. 8; Pojman, *The Logic of Subjectivity*, chap. 3). However, the evidence that he accepts recollection comes from only a few remarks in his *Eighteen Upbuilding Discourses*, (309, 312-19) and a few entries in *Soren Kierkegaard's Journals and Papers:* (JP, 1:649, p. 268-73; 2:2274, p. 528; 3:3085, p. 404 and 3606, p. 662). And there are other journal entries that maintain that sin renders "man's cognition defective," JP, III:3245, p. 496-97 and also 3247, p. 498-99.

[52]In a few places (CUP, 1:55, 491, 506, 515) Climacus speaks of faith as certain but he never pursues the point.

[53]I remind the reader that the Danish word for certainty and certitude are the same—*vished*. In each of the following passages Kierkegaard speaks either of the certainty [*vished*] of Christian truths or refers to them as certain [*vis*]: CD, 157-58, 194, 197, 285. On 199 he says faith is "blessedly sure [*forvisse*]." Also see footnote 15 above.

unable to understand them *fully* or even understand how they are possible.[54] Nevertheless, their certainty is not just a psychological, purely subjective blind conviction. Faith has some cognitive content. There is a "what" that the Christian asserts is true of reality.[55] Just as I know that "the earth is round" is an objective truth, so through God's gift of faith I know that it is objectively true that the first century Jew, Jesus of Nazareth, was God incarnate—not Socrates, not Caesar, not Napoleon. And I know that this truth is certain, meaning that it *must* correspond to what is real, since God commands me to believe it. Similarly, I know that it is objectively true that Christ (not John) atoned for our sins and that he offers us immortality (not extinction) and eternal salvation (not temporal bliss). Again, the contents of these truths, even though far from fully knowable, are objectively certain. These truths *must* correspond to the real because God commands me to believe them—and they should be subjectively appropriated.

Climacus makes few references to the certainty that accompanies Christian faith, the certainty that what Christianity proclaims is true because God commands us to believe it. He never discusses such certainty nor its basis in God's commands. Perhaps that is not surprising since he says he is not a Christian believer. The only certainty that Kierkegaard's pseudonymous author treats at some length is the certainty gained by rational deduction.

The Relation between Knowledge and Appropriation in Religious Works after Christian Discourses

Since some Kierkegaard scholars assume that the positions set forth in *Concluding Unscientific Postscript* are Kierkegaard's, I will conclude this paper with a brief survey of the relation between

---

[54]*Merriam-Webster's Online Dictionary* defines a mystery as "a religious truth that one can know only by revelation and cannot fully understand." See <www.M-W.com/dictionary/mystery>. Mysteries cannot be totally unknowable else I would never "know" what mysteries I should believe as a Christian and not a Jew or a Muslim.

[55]Even Climacus states that it is the 'what' that is believed that decides whether someone is a Christian or not" (CUP, 1: 609). He also claims "one can know what Christianity is without being a Christian" (CUP, 1:372) and calls it chicanery "to say that Christianity is empty of content" (CUP, 1: 380).

knowledge and appropriation that Kierkegaard sets forth in the major religious works he wrote after the 1848 publication of *Christian Discourses*. A review of *The Sickness unto Death* (1849), *Practice in Christianity* (1850), *For Self-Examination* (1851) and *Judge for Yourself!* (written in 1851-52, published posthumously) will further support my contention that, although there are many similarities between them, Kierkegaard and Climacus differ in important ways about the relation between knowledge and appropriation.[56]

All of the four above mentioned works follow the *Discourses* in speaking of knowledge as by nature distinct from, or other than, actuality or being or concrete existence. Accordingly, all stress that understanding, thinking, or knowing something, no matter how correct or truthful, does not mean doing or living or being it.[57] *Judge for Yourself!* even uses the language of the *Concluding Unscientific Postscript* in stating that there is a "difference of essence," an "infinite" distance, between understanding something and doing it (JFY, 115-16). Like *Christian Discourses* (and the *Postscript*), these later works explain that difference by describing thought as abstracting from actuality and thereby "nullifying" it (SUD, 98) and thinking it *sub specie aeterno modo* (SUD, 97). Thought cannot on its own think concrete temporal individuals but only the abstract, timeless, universal concept.[58] *The Sickness unto Death* even speaks of the "*impotence* of the concept in relation to actuality" (SUD, 119) and each of the works expresses the view that passion (will, choice, earnestness, decision, and conscience are mentioned) must be added to thought to enable it to think the concrete and to enable the individual to appropriate and become what he or she knows.[59] *Practice in Christianity, For Self-*

---

[56]There are some very good studies of various aspects of Kierkegaard's second authorship: Gouwens, *Kierkegaard as religious thinker*; Bruce Kirmmse, *Kierkegaard in Golden Age Denmark* (Bloomington: Indiana University Press, 1990); Elrod, *Kierkegaard and Christendom*; Walker, *Kierkegaard, the Descent into God*; Sylvia Walsh, *Living Christianly* (University Park, PA: Pennsylvania State University Press, 2005). While they all discuss the relation between knowledge and the appropriation which comes from Christian faith, no one has investigated the relation between knowledge and appropriation *in general* in Kierkegaard's later religious works, nor has his position been compared to the views presented in the *Postscript*.

[57]SUD, 93-98, 116-20; PC, 64, 86-87, 190, 205-206; FSE, 39; JFY, 115-17.

[58]SUD, 119-212; PC, 186-90; JFY, 116-20.

[59]SUD, 90-94, 119-21; PC, 158, 190; FSE, 34-40; JFY, 110, 119.

Examination, and *Judge for Yourself!* also adopt the *Postscript*'s language about the contrast between an objective and a subjective approach to truth. The objective impartially and impersonally focuses on the knowledge, comprehension, and understanding of an object and thus "forgets" (PC, 233) or "loses" (JFY, 105) one's self. The subjective turns within the individual and asks about his or her relation to what is known, that is, does he or she act and live and become what he or she claims to know.[60]

In addition, in these later works Kierkegaard refers frequently to the "natural man" or "merely human" who uses the pursuit of knowledge (understanding, probability, proof, reasons, speculation) to divert him or her self from, and avoid, decisions. (As in the *Christian Discourses*, he continues to label such avoidance disobedience and sinfulness, for we are commanded to believe in God's word *now*, not to deliberate about it and analyze it.) Like the *Discourses*, the natural human being is described as selfish and self-centered and focused on his or her lower sensate nature. Because of this, he or she is intent on seeking earthly, temporal, finite goods and on using his or her intellectual powers to calculate the most prudent, sagacious, sensible, probable and reasonable path to worldly success and happiness.[61] Also, like the *Discourses*, Kierkegaard suggests that human beings have these characteristics because they are deeply rooted in sin. *For Self-Examination* explicitly attributes to "hereditary sin" the human's "congenital genius" to avoid the personal, the subjective, by making "God's Word into something impersonal, objective, a doctrine" (FSE, 39-40). Clearly, then, these later works continue to present Kierkegaard's view that for natural, sinful human beings the pursuit of knowledge is in opposition to the choice to appropriate,

Finally, in these works Kierkegaard reiterates the position of *Christian Discourses* that one can obtain knowledge of the truths necessary for salvation, not by objectively pursuing them intellectually, but subjectively, by a deepening self-knowledge that eventually comes to the recognition of one's total powerlessness (because of sin) and complete need for God. *For Self-Examination*

---

[60]PC, 233-35; FSE, 36-39; JFY, 105.
[61]SUD, 43-45, 80-82, 89-96, 121-22; PC, 37-39, 42-43, 60-63, 90, 110-19, 182-83, 227-34; FSE, 34-43; JFY, 98-106, 112-20, 175-77.

makes the same analogy with food that the *Discourses* did. Because the apostles needed the comfort of Christ's Ascension in order to endure suffering and rejection, "therefore it is certain [*vis*]" Kierkegaard states! "So it always is with need in a human being," he explains, "out of the eater comes something to eat; where there is need, it itself produces, as it were, that which it needs" (FSE, 69).[62] (Of course, as *Christian Discourses* explained, the "food" is not literally from the eater but from God.) Commenting on the Biblical passage which states that it is "the sick who need the physician," *Judge for Yourself!* says that God will reveal to sincere penitents who admit their sickness and their inability to cure themselves, and, thus, their need for a physician, the Divine Remedy. God will reveal the true nature of the illness, namely, sin, and its medicine, forgiveness and new life, offered through faith in the Divine Physician and his Atonement.[63]

In a similar vein, the pseudonymous author of *The Sickness unto Death*, Anti-Climacus, refers to himself as a "physician . . . at the sickbed" (SUD, 5). His whole purpose in writing that work is to assist people in becoming aware of the illness that is despair, that despair is sin, and that its cure is faith in Christ. Anti-Climacus has no doubt that God will reveal the true nature of their illness and its medicine to those who sincerely ask, for after all, he points out, infinite love entered the world precisely to save each and every human being.[64] *Practice in Christianity* makes much the same point. Through "consciousness of sin," the contrite individual will recognize his or her need for Christ and will be enabled "to enter into Christianity" (PC, 68).

Thus, we see in the four religious works written after the *Christian Discourses* that Kierkegaard repeats his view that the path to truth, particularly truths necessary for salvation, is a subjective one. It is unnecessary to engage in an objective pursuit of

---

[62]Similarly, he states that when suffering and sin have driven you to despair and there is no hope, then, because "you needed it . . . you receive *the hope* that is against hope, the Spirit's gift!" (FSE, 83). Similar statements can be found in PC, 68 and JFY, 201.

[63]JFY, 151-53, 190-91. Even the knowledge that one's sickness, despair, is sin must be divinely revealed, SUD, 95-96.

[64]SUD, 85, 113, 125-28.

knowledge, reasons, or proofs and, in fact, to do so may well be a sinful way to evade the inner route.

I should add that Kierkegaard also gives little indication in these works that he thinks the subjective path through our natural human powers of self-reflection or recollection (which Climacus hypothesized might possibly be true) can attain truths about God or the spiritual self. He does refer to many things that he knows to be true about the self and God and wants his readers both to understand and earnestly appropriate. For example, he describes the human self as both sensate and spiritual, temporal and eternal, as possessing knowledge, imagination, and will, and so forth. Nevertheless, he continues to stress the sinful state of human nature and to insist, therefore, that a purely human understanding or point of view is fundamentally in error about, and opposed to, the real truth about human reality and God.[65] Sinful humans just do not have the power to successfully navigate the subjective route to truth on their own. Truths about the self and about God necessary for salvation must be revealed by God and He will do so to those who admit their sinfulness and powerlessness.

The one slight exception is in *The Sickness unto Death* (SUD, 116). There Anti-Climacus states that the highest "human understanding and thought" can go is to reach a "depth" of self-understanding and of "ethical qualifications" which results in the despair of "sin" (or, more accurately, of guilt). However, he adds "rarely does anyone come so far." Among the "ethical qualifications" he has in mind are apparently the following. Individuals should recognize their freedom and its limitations and their need to choose to become selves. They should recognize the eternal dimension of their selves, their obligations to be selves in the fullest sense and their failures to fulfill these obligations. Perhaps some rare individuals can come this far through their natural powers. Even then, however, Anti-Climacus insists that their natural understanding of the self and its guilt does *not* involve an awareness of sin before God nor even of the self as spirit.[66]

As in *Christian Discourses*, Kierkegaard refers to such truths about

[65]See texts cited in n. 61.
[66]SUD., 26-27, 45-46, 80-81, 89.

the self and God as certain. They are grasped through "the certitude [*vished*] of faith" (PC, 27, 250), he says. In *For Self-Examination* he writes that because those who imitate Christ "need the Ascension in order to endure the life they were living. . . . Therefore it is certain [*vis*]" (69). Similarly, *Judge for Yourself!* states that the imitation of Christ that comes from belief in him masters all doubt. "The proof" about Christ "does not precede [faith] but follows in and with the imitation that follows Christ" (191). In other words, by faithfully following Christ one can through faith know for certain some truths about Him, such as he is God and man, forgives sin, and promises eternal life. These truths are part of the content (the "what") that the Christian believes. *The Sickness unto Death* goes even further and exhorts one to look at Christ "and know for certain [*forvis*] what it is to be a human being" (SUD, 128). Since God commands us to imitate Christ, and we can imitate him only in his humanity, we know for certain what the ideal human being is. In general, we can be certain of all the truths that make up the content of Christianity because God commands us to believe them. Granted many are mysteries which cannot be *fully* understood or comprehended. Nevertheless, I do know that Jesus of Nazareth (not someone else) is God and man even though I do not understand how one individual can be such an absurd combination. Nor do I understand how Christ's death (not Socrates') atoned for the sins of all human beings. But because God commands me to believe these things I know that they *must* be true, that they *must* correspond to reality. I know for certain that Christ is God and man and that he died for our sins. And, again, there is no opposition between knowing through faith that these divinely revealed truths are certain and appropriating them in our lives.

I will conclude with a brief summary. There are numerous similarities between Kierkegaard and his pseudonymous author, Climacus, on the relation between objective knowledge and subjective appropriation. They share the view that knowledge is in itself abstract and impersonal and that passion or interest is necessary for it to become concrete and appropriated. They also agree on the need to undertake a subjective not objective path to truth. Yet they also have important differences, rooted in the fact that Kierkegaard accepts the Christian doctrine of sin and Climacus does not. Thus, the former considers the search for objective understanding and reasons, knowledge, and rational proof, to be, not just misdirected, but *sinful* attempts to evade the choice to believe and sinful avoidance of the subjective path. Kierkegaard is also very skeptical that the particular subjective approach Climacus opined might be true, the path of natural self-reflection or recollection, can be used by sinful human beings to attain truth—although, he admits, there may be rare exceptions. Finally, Kierkegaard emphasizes the certainty that comes through faith and, therefore, sees no opposition or inverse relation between knowing particular truths to be certain and appropriating those same truths. We know that truths revealed by God are certain because He commands us to believe them and they are also meant to be lived by all, especially by Christians in Christendom.

9

The Sickbed Preacher:
Kierkegaard on Adversity and the Awakening of Faith
Ronald F. Marshall

Even though Kierkegaard wrote extensively on topics in psychology, literature and philosophy, he said his whole authorship was "religious from first to last."[1] By this he meant he was concerned in his books with the matter of "becoming a Christian" (PV 6, 23). In this essay I want to show how Kierkegaard, in his book *Christian Discourses*, believed illness helps in this matter of becoming a Christian — the overall theme of his authorship. I will do this first by defining illness in his book, *Christian Discourses*. Next I will show what this sickness teaches us about ourselves, especially through endangerment and nothingness. Third I will explain how and why he thinks illness does a better job at preaching than pastors in the pulpit do, by exploring the failure of preaching in his time. I will do this by stressing artistic distance, heterogeneity and earnestness in preaching. Then I will show how illness awakens faith in Christ. In this section I will study the place of reversals, Christ's crucifixion, and

---

[1]Even though this is Kierkegaard's avowal, it nevertheless remains hotly contested among the scholars. On this dispute see Ronald Goetz, "A Secularized Kierkegaard," *The Christian Century* 111 (March 9, 1994) 259-260. Goetz argues that a nonreligious view of Kierkegaard does much damage to his authorship, reducing it to a "stylistic exercise in ironic indeterminism" (259). It also turns Kierkegaard himself into "a mere aesthetic, who plays with language in order to luxuriate in its potential for ambiguity" (260). But even as a religious author, Kierkegaard remains a "perplexing" one, situated somewhere between "C. S. Lewis and Heidegger" (John D. Caputo, *How to Read Kierkegaard* [London: Granta, 2007] 5, 89). On Kierkegaard's religious strategy, see George Pattison, *Kierkegaard and the Crisis of Faith* (London: SPCK, 1997): "Kierkegaard . . . begins by presenting in some detail the 'aesthetic' attitude which he regards as the typical attitude of modern bourgeois society in order to expose its inner contradictions and so lure the reader on to a confrontation with Christianity as an alternative stance towards life that is worth taking seriously" (5).

gracious unsureness in this awakening. And finally I will make a judgment on the sickbed preacher itself, showing that what Kierkegaard says about the positive role of sickness in Christianity is confirmed by a series of compelling contemporary cases.

Defining Illness in Christian Discourses

In this section I want to define what Kierkegaard meant by illness in *Christian Discourses*. In part three, "Thoughts That Wound from Behind — For Upbuilding," he praises illness, calling it our best preacher. The "sickbed and the nighttime hour," he writes, "preach more powerfully than all the orators" (CD, 164). His reason for this was that in illness we have "the terrors implicit in the power of circumstance" thrust upon us.[2] The power in illness to press these terrors on us is important because it produces the "ups and downs and ordeals and spiritual trials" which move us "in earnest for awakening" (CD, 165). Illness engulfs us in these ordeals through the preacher of repentance that is "deep within every person's heart" (CD, 192). From this we see that it is illness that helps us repent. This is highly significant because without repentance there can be no awakening, and without awakening, no one can become a Christian.

For Kierkegaard the illness that drives us to repentance is simple physical sickness. This definition is quite different from the one he gives in his book, *Sickness unto Death*. There sickness is spiritual.[3] It has nothing to do with "earthly and temporal suffering: need, illness, misery, hardship, adversities, torments, mental sufferings, cares, grief" (SUD, 8). Indeed, "no earthly, physical sickness is the sickness unto death, for death is indeed the end of sickness, but death is not the end" (SUD, 17). This makes sickness unto death quite unlike ordinary physical illness. For indeed, not being spiritually sick or in

---

[2]I believe that this celebration of sickness contributes to the "very dark . . . mood" in *Christian Discourses* [Bruce Kirmmse, *Kierkegaard in Golden Age Denmark* (Bloomington IN: Indiana University Press, 1990) 358]. I for one think that it is this mood that makes *Christian Discourses* one of Kierkegaard's "greatest works." Søren Kierkegaard, *Christian Discourses, Etc.*, trans. Walter Lowrie (1940; repr.: Princeton NJ: Princeton University Press, 1971) xvi.

[3]Kierkegaard also treats this spiritual sickness before the publication of *The Sickness unto Death*. In 1844 he writes about "soul rot" which comes from "the monotony of self-concern" (EUD, 207).

despair "is not similar to not being sick, for not being sick cannot be the same as being sick, whereas not being in despair can be the very same as being in despair. It is not with despair as with sickness, where feeling indisposed is the sickness" (SUD, 24-25). Sickness unto death is therefore more complex than simple physical illness. That is because it is a "sickness of the spirit" (SUD, 22). And the human spirit, unlike the body, is "a relation that relates itself to itself," and is grounded "transparently in the power that established it" (SUD, 13, 14, and 49, 79). These relations make the spirit more complex than the body and so also spiritual sickness more complex than physical illness.

Illness in *Christian Discourses*, therefore, is simpler than this Sickness unto death. It is more straightforward. It cannot be disguised under its opposites, such as physical ailments like cancer or pneumonia, or being in bed due to a broken bone or the like. Physical illness is not the Sickness unto death, but it is the contributions of such illness to the matter of becoming a Christian that I want to explicate in this essay.[4]

Learning from Sickness

These physical ailments are important for Christianity because they have the potential to lead a person to faith in Christ.[5] In this

---

[4]This does not mean that this more complex Sickness unto death cannot also help one in becoming a Christian. "Only he whose being has been so shaken," Kierkegaard writes, "that he has become spirit by understanding that everything is possible, only he has anything to do with God" (SUD, 40). Unfortunately "the majority of people" are "too sensate to have the courage to venture out and to endure being spirit" (SUD, 43). They chafe at the proposition that "the self must be broken in order to become itself" (SUD, 65). So while physical illness might well push one in the right direction—one who also suffers from this Sickness unto death—that nudge alone will not keep one from retreating "again to the illusory sanctuary of their self-deception." Michael Watts, *Kierkegaard* (Oxford: Oneworld, 2003) 181.

[5]This is so even if medical science one day succeeds in making us immortal. This is because such immortality is not "absolute. [It] cannot come with a guarantee . . . against accident or suicide. Even immortal life cannot be insured against new zoonotic viral epidemics or even against infectious diseases presently defying our best efforts at cure. All that can be reasonably expected of immortality is the permanent suspension of degenerative diseases that would otherwise accompany

section I will try to show how this is so. Illness can do this for Kierkegaard because it both endangers us and reduces us to nothing. St. Paul experienced just this. After suffering his unrelenting "thorn in the flesh," he says of himself, "I am nothing" (2 Corinthians 12:7-11). Kierkegaard seems to have something like this in mind when he says that sickness can "grip a person" and "hurl him into the power of circumstances" (CD, 165). This hurling is what endangers us. He elaborates this point in a journal entry the year right after *Christian Discourses* was published:

> Do you believe . . . that if you were thoroughly healthy you would easily or more easily achieve perfection? Just the opposite: then you would yield easily to your passions, to pride if not to others, to an intensified self-esteem and the like. In that way sufferings, even though a burden, are a beneficial burden, like braces used in the orthopedic institute.
>
> To be thoroughly healthy physically and mentally and then to lead a truly spiritual life—that no man can do. The sense of spontaneous well being immediately runs away with him . . . . This is why sufferings are a help. If a person suffers every day, if he is so infirm that the thought of death is simply right at hand, then he may be somewhat successful in being continually conscious of needing God.
>
> Physical health, the immediate sense of well being, is a far greater danger than riches, power, and esteem.
>
> Of course it has a deceptive appearance, as if it would still be a help to be physically, spontaneously strong. But if one is that, it is almost a superhuman task actually to live qua spirit . . . . Physical suffering, the infirm body, is a beneficial memento. (JP, 4:4637)[6]

---

aging and senescence." Stanley Shostak, *Becoming Immortal: Combining Cloning and Stem-Cell Therapy* (Albany NY: State University of New York Press, 2002) 42.

[6]"Some warn against seeing in Kierkegaard's *Journals* a clear interpretive tool for his published writings since they are "littered with so much incoherent material . . . [and] contain so many reading notes." Robert L. Perkins, "Introduction" in *International Kierkegaard Commentary: Fear and Trembling* and *Repetition*, ed. Robert L. Perkins (Macon GA: Mercer University Press, 1993) 7 n.3. I, however, agree with Alexander Dru that Kierkegaard's *Journals* provide helpful "clarification." *The Soul of Kierkegaard: Selections from His Journals*, trans. and ed. Alexander Dru (1959; repr.: Minoola NY: Dover, 2003) 7. For the publication history of the *Journals*, see Niels Jørgen Cappelørn, Joakim Garff and Johnny Kondrup, *Written Images: Søren Kierkegaard's Journals, Notebooks, Booklets, Sheets, Scraps, and Slips of Paper*, trans. Bruce H. Kirmmse (Princeton NJ: Princeton University Press, 2003).

This entry says the opposite of what we normally think, namely, that uninterrupted health, wealth and happiness are clear, unqualified benefits. Against this popular view, Kierkegaard dares to say that health and well being are very dangerous. This is because such blessedness intensifies our self-esteem which pulls us away from God.[7] So sickness is not a simple trauma, but actually a beneficial burden. It is so because it helps us realize our need for God. Without such a burden it would be quite unlikely for one ever to develop a need for God. This insight into physical illness is what gives it a silver lining for Kierkegaard. This benefit is often missed or defied by those burdened down by illness. What they long for is more than a silver lining. They would much prefer the security and comfort that only health can bring. Kierkegaard therefore rightly concludes that there is "danger in this security" (CD, 163). For the security that good health brings leads to pride.[8] Good health and prosperity leave us in our selfishness and sin. Nothing in health and prosperity can rouse us from these.

But with sickness, the tables are turned. Sickness can be a cup of icy cold water thrown in our face. Kierkegaard does not distinguish between types of physical ailments, indexing them for their potential in spiritual renewal. He just lumps them altogether. He simply says that physical sickness can be arresting. It can teach us that we suffer because we sin.[9] We desperately need this realization because "most

---

[7]On this thought see the chilling passage, Hosea 13:4-6, "I am the Lord your God, . . . It was I who knew you in the wilderness, . . . but when they had fed to the full, . . . and their heart was lifted up; therefore they forgot me."

[8]On this judgment against self-esteem, see Martin Luther, "The Sermon on the Mount" (1532), *Luther's Works*, 55 volumes, ed. Jaroslav Pelikan and Helmut Lehmann (St. Louis and Philadelphia: Concordia and Fortress, 1955–1986) 21:67, "Any self-esteem [*eigen ehre*] . . . is really a slander of [God's] honor and praise." See also Gerhard O. Forde, *On Being a Theologian of the Cross: Reflections on Luther's Heidelberg Disputation, 1518* (Grand Rapids MI: Eerdmans, 1997): "Self-esteem [is] the current circumlocution for pride" (27). This is especially a problem for marriage. For my critique of self-esteem in marriage, see "Kierkegaard's Cure for Divorce," *Søren Kierkegaard Newsletter* 44 (September 2002): 6-10.

[9]Kierkegaard does not pull back from this highly contestable assertion. No doubt that is in large part due to his devotion to the Bible. On this see John 5:14: "Sin no more, that nothing worse befall you." Note that this is not incompatible with John 9:3 which says, "It is not that this man sinned, or his parents, but that the

Christians are spiritless mollycoddlers" who are incapable of knowing how sinful they are.[10] Sickness is therefore especially valuable. It
drives us to repent—which is the labor required of those who are
"burdened" by the guilt of their sin (CD, 264). But normally we do
not want to be "disturbed by hearing about or thinking about
terrible things." We would rather settle "into meaninglessness"
(UDVS, 107). We would rather settle quickly for the ease of health.
Sickness, on the other hand, charges ahead boldly, making us question ourselves. It strikes out against us. It attacks us in our complacency. And this is good, for by so doing we are drawn into a new life
with God. So the truth is that salvation

> corresponds to being in danger; the one who is not in danger can-
> not be saved. . . . Just as the shipwrecked person who saved himself
> by means of a plank and now, tossed by the waves and hovering
> over the abyss between life and death, strains his eyes for land, so
> indeed should a person be concerned about his salvation. (CD, 220)

Being shipwrecked is an apt image. This is what illness does to

---

works of God might be made manifest in him." The first addresses personal culpability; the second divine mercy. Luke 13:2-3 is less complex: "Do you think that
these Galileans were worse sinners than all the other Galileans, because they suffered thus? I tell you, No; but unless you repent you will likewise perish." Against
this view of suffering being caused by sin, see Fredrik Lindström, *Suffering and Sin*:
Interpretations of Illness in the Individual Complaint Psalms, trans. Michael McLamb
(Stockholm: Almquist & Wiksell, 1994). Lindström argues that "sickness can give
rise to sin, rather than the other way around" (323) because any neat correlation
which says sin causes sickness clouds over the telling "irrationality" in how sickness
actually arises (464). Even so Martin Luther incorporated this contentious correlation between sin and suffering into the way he visited the sick: "When Dr. Luther
came to visit a sick man, he spoke to him in a very friendly manner . . . [asking]
whether during this illness he had been patient towards God. And after he had
discovered how the sick man had borne himself while sick, and that he wished to
bear his affliction patiently, because God had sent it upon him out of his fatherly
goodness and mercy, and that . . . by his sins he had deserved such visitation, and
that he was willing to die if it is pleased God to take him—then he began to praise
this Christian disposition as the work of the Holy Ghost." *Minister's Prayer Book: An
Order of Prayers and Readings*, ed. John W. Doberstein (1959; Philadelphia: Fortress,
1986) 367. For a historical study against this correlation between sin and suffering,
see Peter Lewis Allen, *The Wages of Sin: Sex and Disease, Past and Present* (Chicago:
University of Chicago Press, 2000): "[This correlation] reveals a failure of two qualities I believe are essential to civilized life, namely, charity and compassion" (159).
   [10]John D. Caputo, *How to Read Kierkegaard*, 108.

us. It is very dangerous and damaging to us. In a more abstract and later version, he says this is as appalling and "ethically dubious" as a "vivisection." For when the crisis hits, one is forced by circumstances to be "a man of will who no longer wills his own will but with the passion of his crushed will—radically changed—wills another's will," that is, God's will (JP. 6:6966).

Endangerment. To be saved we need to realize that we are endangered by the terrors of sin—and these dangers are the "*conditio sine qua non* for all Christianity" (JP, 1:452). Now there are dangers aplenty in the world, but what is even more terrible is the danger of sin, which makes all the other ones look like "child's play." It is just this danger of sin that illness presses upon us. So instead of "having sympathy for your earthly misery and busily remedying it, an even heavier weight is laid upon you—you are made a sinner" (CD, 172-73). But the sin that truly terrifies us is neither the garden variety infraction nor some moral peccadilloe. In a late journal entry Kierkegaard explains the seriousness of sin:

> What the world regards as sin and makes an uproar about is either stealing and anything related to the security of property and possessions, or it is sins of the flesh, indeed, precisely that which Christianity regards as most pardonable. A man who tricks and swindles day in and day out but otherwise is an extremely cultivated gentleman[11] belonging to the society of the cultivated—if he has the bad luck to get drunk once—heaven help him, it is an irreparable loss, and he himself condemns it so severely that he perhaps, as they say, never forgives himself, while it probably never occurs to him that he should need to be forgiven for all the tricks and frauds and dishonesty, for all the spiritually revolting passions[12]

---

[11]In Martin Luther's "Large Catechism" (1529) in *The Book of Concord: The Confessions of the Evangelical Lutheran Church* (1580), trans. and ed. Theodore G. Tappert (1580; Philadelphia: Fortress, 1959) he argues that "gentlemen swindlers or big operators . . . are the greatest thieves. . . . Far from being picklocks and sneak-thieves who loot a cash box, they sit in office chairs and are called great lords and honorable, good citizens, and yet with a great show of legality they rob and steal" (396).

[12]See the distinction between minor and major sins in *The Book of Concord*: "The major ones [are] . . . carnal security, contempt of God, hate of God, and similar faults that we are born with, . . . [which make up] the inner uncleanness of human nature" (102). This hatred of God is easily concealed. For an exposure of it, see Martin Luther, "The Sermon on the Mount" (1532), *Luther's Works* 21:190, "A lover of money and property inevitably becomes an enemy of God. . . . [These false

which make their home within him and are his life. (JP, 4:4049)

These severe sins, these spiritually revolting passions, help us "find the terrifying and thus take the time . . . to understand . . . the most somber view of life" (CD, 97). What is so sobering about these sins is that they are worse than we imagine. So if we refuse to repent of them, the consequences are great. Those sins will damn us to hell forever, no matter how much we try to cover them up.[13]

Nothingness. Since sickness opens up this salutary realization for us, it is God's gift.[14] For indeed, "no healthy person has ever been or can ever be saved by Christ" (CD, 53). Sickness fashions a somber view of life which brings salvation. It creates penitents. And it is God who helps with this by sending "hard sufferings, by taking away his dearest possession, by wounding him in the tenderest spot, by denying him his one and only wish, by taking his final hope away

---

Christians] make a great show of serving Him, . . . but fundamentally all they are is genuine demonic saints, who hate God cordially and persecute Him, His Word, and His work. For hating the Word of God is really hating God."

[13]So Martin Luther in his beloved "Small Catechism" (1529) says that "we sin daily and deserve nothing but punishment," that our lives here are but a "world of sorrow," and that "the old Adam in us . . . should be drowned by daily sorrow and repentance and put to death" (*The Book of Concord*, 347-49). So *Christian Discourses* are rightly called Christian because they attack "smug churchianity . . . by the presentation of Christianity's severe demands." George E. Arbaugh and George B. Arbaugh, *Kierkegaard's Authorship: A Guide to the Writings of Kierkegaard* (Rock Island IL: Augustana College, 1967) 275.

[14]Others think that while God has good reasons for making us suffer, we cannot figure them out, and so we must reject all such explanations while maintaining our trust in God's goodness. On this see Marilyn McCord Adams, *Horrendous Evils and the Goodness of God* (Ithaca NY: Cornell University Press, 1999) 156, 180. She knows God is good even though he lets us suffer so because in heaven "concrete ills are balanced off" (168). Kierkegaard would think we know more than this because of what the Bible teaches us about why we suffer so. But on her account, the Bible is far too "short on explanations of why God permits evils" to be of much help (137). Against such a judgment, Kierkegaard, of course, objects. For him the explanations in the Bible are long and they have to do with punishment and edification. And so he writes that "eternity disperses the crowd by giving each person separately an infinite weight by making him heavy—as the single individual. There the same thing that is the highest blessedness is the highest earnestness; there the same thing that is the most blissful comfort is also the most dreadful responsibility" (UDVS, 134).

from him" (CD, 129).[15] All this reduces us to nothing[16]—which is what we need if we are going to be saved from our sins. When we are reduced to nothing, we realize our desperate need for God.[17] "Woe to the presumptuous who would dare to love God without needing him! . . . . You are not to presume to love God for God's sake. You are humbly to understand that your own welfare eternally depends on this need" (CD, 188).[18] It depends on God because in matters of our salvation, "God does everything, and that . . . is sheer grace" (CD, 85).[19]

---

[15]So true Christian belief definitely includes "vulnerability" before God, who ought not therefore be thought of as "a very large bird, an elderly uncle, a fluffy marshmallow, or any other objective entity that can be imagined to exist on a cloud somewhere." Rick Anthony Furtak, *Wisdom in Love: Kierkegaard and the Ancient Quest for Emotional Integrity* (Notre Dame IN: University of Notre Dame, 2005) 111.

[16]On this reduction to nothingness, see Leonard M. Hummel, *Clothed in Nothingness: Consolation for Suffering* (Minneapolis: Fortress, 2003). He argues that this reduction is necessary because it shows how God's help cannot be "stored up" in ourselves (143). That help rather comes only "in the history of address and response" (147). This is reminiscent of the manna from heaven in Exodus 16:20-21 that would rot or melt if stored up. See also Martin Luther, "Commentary on Psalm 38" (1525), *Luther's Works* 14:163, "It is God's nature to make something out of nothing. . . . Therefore God accepts only the forsaken, cures only the sick, gives sight only to the blind, restores only the dead, sanctifies only the sinners, gives wisdom only to the unwise. In short he has mercy only on those who are wretched. . . . Therefore no proud saint, no wise or righteous person, can become God's material, and God's purpose cannot be fulfilled in him." Matt Frawley argues that this nothingness is "the basic ontological position" of Kierkegaard's anthropology, and that the struggle to accept it "is the essential, existential struggle raging within the inner being of every individual." "The Doctrine of *Creatio Ex Nihilo* in the Thought of Søren Kierkegaard," *Kierkegaardiana* 23 (2004): 7-25, 8, 20.

[17]See Gordon Marino, *Kierkegaard in the Present Age* (Milwaukee WI: Marquette University Press, 2001): "It is . . . infinitely better to understand feelingly how badly you need God than it is to be psychologically well adjusted relative to a community that Kierkegaard literally saw as a madhouse" (105).

[18]Ever since the time of the church in Laodicea, Christians have suffered from presumptuousness. On this see Revelation 3:17, "You say, I am rich, I have prospered, and I need nothing; not knowing that you are wretched, pitiable, poor, blind, and naked."

[19]"Kierkegaard has always insisted that when it comes to salvation collaboration from the person's side is out of the question." Gregor Malantschuk, *Kierkegaard's Concept of Existence*, ed. and trans. Howard V. Hong and Edna H. Hong (Milwaukee WI: Marquette University Press, 2003) 215.

So when God, out of love for us, makes us "into something in relation to himself" so that we may have a "reciprocal relationship with him" (CD, 127), he did not intend that transformation to make us independent, self-initiating and selfish. That is because there is "only one obstacle for God, a person's selfishness, which comes between him and God like the earth's shadow when it causes the eclipse of the moon" (CD, 129).[20] So we are to take the personal power given to us by God and give it up. Yes indeed, the very "independence . . . that love gave" us (CD, 129), we are to set aside. The "Christian gives up his self-will" (CD, 91) — that is the proper use of our power and will before God. We are "always" to sacrifice our will to God (CD, 84). And this obedience glorifies God, for one can become and be a Christian "only as or in the capacity of a lowly person" (CD, 53). Indeed, in glorifying God through our lowliness, the "worshiper has lost himself, and [as a result] he has won God" (CD, 132).[21] "Thus a human being is great and at his highest when he

---

[20]Parallels between Kierkegaard and Ludwig Wittgenstein (1889-1951) are illuminating. On this see Stanley Cavell's judgment that they both share in the image of "the philosopher as a physician of the soul." *Themes Out of School* (Chicago: University of Chicago Press, 1988) 218. We can see this trait in Wittgenstein when he says that Christianity is "only for the one who needs infinite help, that is only for the one who suffers infinite distress. . . . Someone to whom it is given in such distress to open his heart instead of contracting it, absorbs the remedy into his heart. . . . If someone feels himself lost, that is the ultimate distress." Ludwig Wittgenstein, *Culture and Value*, rev. ed., trans. Peter Winch (1994; Oxford: Blackwell, 1998) 52e. Note also: "Is being alone with oneself — or with God, not like being alone with a wild animal? It can attack you any moment. — But isn't that precisely why you shouldn't run away?! Isn't that, so to speak, what's glorious?! Doesn't it mean: grow fond of this wild animal! — And yet one must ask: Lead us not into temptation!" *Ludwig Wittgenstein: Public and Private Occasions*, ed. James C. Klagge and Alfred Nordmann (New York: Rowman & Littlefield, 2003) 247. Wittgenstein may well have learned this view of Christianity from reading Kierkegaard. Note his admiration for Kierkegaard: "Kierkegaard was by far the most profound thinker of the last century. Kierkegaard was a saint. . . . Mind you I don't believe what Kierkegaard believed, but of this I am certain, that we are not here in order to have a good time." *Recollections of Wittgenstein*, ed. Rush Rhees (Oxford: Oxford University Press, 1984) 87-88.

[21]Paul Sponheim misses this salutary loss of self in the *Christian Discourses* due to his overly exuberant — and therefore undialectic — celebration of God making us "something in relation to himself" (CD, 127). "Relational Transcendence in Divine Agency," in *International Kierkegaard Commentary: Practice in Christianity*, ed. Robert

corresponds to God by being nothing at all himself" (EUD, 311). Illness brings this nothingness and lowliness upon us. And that is glorious because it is the condition which makes our salvation possible.[22] Illness does this by increasing our dependence on God. When we are sick, we lose control. We are laid low. We cannot regain our health on our schedule. We must wait for it to return, if it is to return, at all. At this moment, when we realize our helplessness, we start looking to God for healing. This is the principle benefit hidden in illness.

The Failure of Preaching

Kierkegaard was struck by this overwhelming experience of being sick. And so he called the sickbed *the best preacher* (CD, 164). In this section I want to examine the last part of that line—the preaching part. Why does he tie sickness in with preaching? This no doubt was largely due to the general failure of preaching in Kierkegaard's day.[23] Without much coming from the church's pulpits, illness

---

L. Perkins (Macon GA: Mercer University Press, 2004) 52. Note the same mistake in Daphne Hampson, *Christian Contradictions: The Structures of Lutheran and Catholic Thought* (Cambridge, UK: Cambridge University Press, 2001) 261. I do, however, agree with her that "Kierkegaard's way of conceptualizing the self is profoundly Lutheran" (281).

[22]Kierkegaard also thought that death, like illness, can help us draw near to God. When the thought of our death strikes us, earnestness then "grasps the present this very day, disdains no task as too insignificant, rejects no time as too short, works with all its might even though it is willing to smile at itself if this effort is said to be merit before God, in weakness is willing to understand that a human being is nothing at all and that one who works with all one's might gains only the proper opportunity to wonder at God" (TDIO, 83).

[23]This failure was not unique but shared in the maladies of generations before and after. On this see Martin Luther, "Sermon on the Mount" (1532), *Luther's Works* 21:56-57: "Preachers no longer rebuke the people or show them their misery and incapacity or press for repentance. . . . They permit them to go along as if they were . . . all right. Thus they [destroy] . . . the true doctrine of faith." Kierkegaard agrees: "The clerical company that speculates in human numbers has . . . led [people] to think that they are Christians by duping them into something under the name of Christianity, something that appeals to them. Millions have then been very gratified to be, in addition, Christians in such a cheap and appealing way, in one half hour and with the turn of a hand to have the whole matter of eternity arranged in order then rightly to be able to enjoy this life" (TM, 170-71). And Kai Munk (1898–1944),

looked good by comparison. Since preaching was failing, illness could then step into the breach and proclaim Christianity as it should be proclaimed.[24]

being influenced by Kierkegaard, gives memorable formulation to this same misgiving: "Do not trust too much in the preachers. . . . They are brought up as humanists. They have forgotten — or never learned — what Christianity is. They have imbibed lo-o-o-ve with the bottle milk in the cradle. . . . They preach peace at any price for the uplift of the devil, who rejoices to see evil develop in peace. . . . Do not trust the preachers until they wake up and remember that they are servants of the whole gospel, and of the Prince of Peace who came not to bring peace but a sword; of Him who forgave Peter and permitted Judas to hang himself; of Him who was meek and humble of heart and yet drove the sacrilegists from the temple courts." *Four Sermons*, trans. John M. Jensen (Blair NE: Lutheran House Publishing, 1944) 27.

[24]The link between Christianity and sickness may even be tighter than this accidental correlation. See Matthew 9:13, Mark 2:17 and Luke 5:32 where Jesus says he has come for the sick only. On this tighter connection Kierkegaard says: "If this were the case, then the Gospel . . . would exclude the happy people. . . . [those who] are healthy and do not need healing. . . . [But] the Gospel does not want to be an escape, a comfort and solace for a few troubled people" (CD, 263). This Gospel is for all — but with the requirement "that the invited person labor and be burdened in the more profound sense. . . . [This burden does not] pertain to externals, not to your fortunes, past or future. . . . [Rather it pertains to] sin and the consciousness of sin. The one who bears this burden — alas, yes, he is burdened, extremely burdened, but . . . in the very way the Gospel's invitation requires it" (CD, 264). Noting these biblical ideas in *Christians Discourses* is justified since the book is saturated with over 160 biblical references and allusions. L. Joseph Rosas III, *Scripture in the Thought of Søren Kierkegaard* (Nashville TN: Broadman & Holman, 1994) 179-83. But Jolita Pons cautions restraint, insisting that Kierkegaard's biblical allusions are more uncertain and delicate, being "blended" with his own ideas, on a Scriptural surface that is anything but "hard." Jolita Pons, *Stealing a Gift: Kierkegaard's Pseudonyms and the Bible* (New York: Fordham University Press, 2004) 141-47. She thinks the Bible floats throughout Kierkegaard's writings like his image of Napoleon's ghost unexplainably emerging in "an empty space" in the graveyard (CI, 19). She further says that Kierkegaard's Biblical references are playful and without authority (xiv, xix, 120-22, 140, 180). But this mild view belittles Kierkegaard's point that the Bible is "an extremely dangerous book" that wants to give us sinners a good "licking" (FSE, 31, 35)! The truth is that for Kierkegaard the Bible is quite pushy — something altogether unlike an ethereal, graveyard apparition! For Kierkegaard "all of scripture has a shingle hanging out saying, 'Follow Me!'" Timothy Polk, *The Biblical Kierkegaard: Reading By the Rule of Faith* (Macon GA: Mercer University Press, 1997) 32.

Preachers in his time, Kierkegaard says, were "becoming more and more fastidious in craving the trumpery of eloquence."[25] He goes on to say that they "do not want to hear in earnest anything about the terror; they want to play at it, much as soldiers in peace-

[25]They should have known better since 1 Corinthians 2:1-5 speaks against such eloquence. Kierkegaard also speaks against eloquence because it anesthetizes us with its glorious but "protracted deliberation" (EUD, 113).

time, or rather nonsoldiers, play war; they demand everything artistic in the beauty of the surrounding" (CD, 165) — "in the magnificent house of God" (CD, 164). They want to keep all the tough issues at bay, and even, if possible, completely out of sight.[26] Unlike this pleasing, false preaching, illness is anything but. It rather is inexorably upsetting. It pushes all the hard issues. It makes us think about the terrifying things we would just as soon ignore. Illness grabs us and makes us pay attention.

Artistic Distance. In the same year *Christian Discourses* was published, Kierkegaard explains further in a journal entry this craving for the "trumpery of eloquence." Sermons, he writes, should be tough enough to expose the hypocrisy and corruption of our Christian lives, but on this score the celebrated Bishop Mynster, for one, is "without a compass" (JP, 6:6150). This is because Mynster wants — like most other preachers —

> to protect himself and remain aloof. — It would be impossible, yes, most impossible of all, for Mynster to preach in the public square. And yet preaching in churches has practically become paganism and theatricality,[27] and Luther was right in declaring that preaching should really not be done in churches.
> In paganism the theater was worship — in Christendom the

---

[26]In Kierkegaard's time his critics ridiculed him with cartoons (COR, 109-37). Guy & Rodd's cartoon, *Brevity* (August 30, 2005) returns the favor, blasting preachers who sugar-coat what frightens the sick — for this pandering "aborts" their spirits (JP, 4:4942)! See cartoon on p. 231.

[27]The church still suffers from theatricality. On this see Kennon L. Callahan, *Dynamic Worship* (New York: HarperCollins, 1994): "People are not helped by music that is mournful and . . . focuses solely on the experience of the cross. . . . The kingdom is not like a solemn, serious ceremony. Have fun, enjoy life . . . " (76, 22). Or see Rick Warren, *The Purpose Driven Church* (Grand Rapids MI: Zondervan, 1995): "[People] like bright, happy, cheerful music with a strong beat. Their ears are accustomed to music with a strong bass line and rhythm. . . . Within a year of deciding [to use this sort of music in our worship services, our church] *exploded* with growth" (285). Finally, see Walt Kallestad, *Entertainment Evangelism* (Nashville: Abingdon, 1996): "The three foundational principles Martin Luther believed were essential to making the Gospel relevant [were] . . . simplicity, . . . heartfelt relevancy . . . and entertainment. . . . [So at our worship we] may have a stage band, a comedian, clowns, drama, mini-concerts, and other forms of entertainment" (10, 12). It must be noted in passing, however, that Martin Luther expressly admonishes in his "Large Catechism" (1529) that worship must be free of all "entertainment" — *contra* Kallestad (*The Book of Concord,* 378).

churches have generally become the theater. How? In this way: it is pleasant, even enjoyable, to commune with the highest once a week by way of the imagination.[28] No more than that. And that actually has become the norm for sermons in Denmark. Hence the artistic distance — even in the most bungled sermons.

In a late journal entry he expands upon this corrupting, artistic distance. Preaching, he writes,

certainly . . . should not be done inside of churches. It is extremely damaging for Christianity and represents a changing (a modifying) of Christianity by placing it at an artistic distance from actuality instead of letting it be heard right in the middle of actuality — and precisely for the sake of conflict (collision), for all this talk about quiet and quiet places and quiet hours as the proper element for the essentially Christian is upside down.

Therefore preaching should not be done in churches but on the street, right in the middle of life, the actuality of the ordinary, weekday life. (JP, 6:6957)

The point about preaching in the streets is to make sermons tough, confrontational and disruptive.[29] This is because the "essentially Christian . . . is the *attacker*" (CD, 162). So instead of telling sweet little stories, sermons should go on the attack. But this "militant piety" (PV, 130), if you will, was missing from the pulpits in Kierkegaard's day, and so he rightly lamented:

Ah, there is so much in the ordinary course of life that will lull a person to sleep, teach him to say "peace and no danger." Therefore we go to God's house to be awakened from sleep and to be pulled out of the spell. But when in turn there is at times so much in God's

---

[28]Imagination is also taking over much of American preaching today. On this see Walter Brueggemann, *Texts Under Negotiation: The Bible and Postmodern Imagination* (Minneapolis: Fortress, 1993): "Preaching . . . is not for instruction (doctrinal or moral) or even for advocacy, but it is for one more reenactment of the drama of the text . . . [where] the listener is invited . . . to imagine the lines just beyond those voiced in the script. . . . Most, however, depends upon the freedom and courage with which the director [preacher] plays the script" (68-69). See also his *Cadences of Home: Preaching Among Exiles* (Louisville: Westminster John Knox, 1997): "The work of preaching is an act of imagination [which] . . . requires a break with . . . doctrinal . . . preaching . . . [thereby allowing] a good bit of room for maneuverability and idiosyncrasy" (32, 33).

[29]I explore this interest of Kierkegaard's further in my "Walking With Kierkegaard," *Lutheran Forum* 35 (Winter 2001): 51-52.

house that will lull us to sleep! Even that which in itself is awakening—thoughts, reflection, ideas—can completely lose meaning through the force of habit and monotony, just as a spring can lose the tension by which alone it really is what it is. (CD, 165)

Heterogeneity. This requisite tension is primarily found in the idea that Christianity is heterogeneous to society (JFY, 191). Christians are therefore to strike a "polemical stance against the great human society" (JP 4:4175). Indeed followers of Christ must die to the world since their faith in Christ requires them to stand in opposition to the world. They must die to "finitude (to its pleasures, its preoccupations, its projects, its diversions), must go through this death to life, . . . and realize how empty is that with which busyness fills up life, how trivial is that which is the lust of the eye and the craving of the carnal heart" (CD, 172).[30] This tension—this heterogeneity—cannot be expressed in the sermon in some blasé way. Reading a well-written essay from the pulpit cannot carry the load of Christian proclamation. The form must be wilder. Martin Luther thought sermons should be more like barroom yelling fits, filled with shouting and raving[31]—warning the sinner and trumpeting God's excessive mercy.[32]

---

[30]Here we have an allusion to 1 John 2:15-16, "Do not love the world or the things of the world . . . the lust of the flesh and the lust of the eyes and the pride of life."

[31]Martin Luther, *Lectures on Genesis* (1545), *Luther's Works*, 8:260. On Kierkegaard's assessment of Luther, see Craig Hinkson, "Will the *Real* Martin Luther Please Stand Up! Kierkegaard's View of Luther versus the Evolving Perceptions of the Tradition," in *International Kierkegaard Commentary: For Self-Examination* and *Judge for Yourself!*, ed. Robert L. Perkins (Macon GA: Mercer University Press, 2002) 37-76 and Herman Deuser, "Kierkegaard and Luther: Kierkegaard's 'One Thesis,'" in *The Gift of Grace: The Future of Lutheran Theology*, ed. Niels Henrik Gregersen et al. (Minneapolis: Fortress, 2005) 205-12. Kierkegaard thought Luther was the truest Christian figure, second only to Jesus Christ himself (JP, 3:2898). He said Luther was "extraordinary" (JP 2:2046) and "masterful" (JP, 3:2422, 3:2465). But he also thought Luther could be too soft on sinners (JP, 3:2556, 3:2682). I have tried to show how radically Lutheran Kierkegaard was in my "Kierkegaard's Music Box," *Lutheran Forum* 39 (Fall 2005) 37-41. So I cannot agree with Viggo Mortensen that "Kierkegaard's understanding of Christianity, at least as it comes out in his last stage, comes in conflict with Luther—a conflict that borders on incompatibility" (quoted in Gregor Malantschuk, *Kierkegaard's Concept of Existence*, 296).

[32]This image is most likely a gloss on the word "urgency" in 2 Timothy 4:2.

Kierkegaard's version of this was a woman in labor. He says the voice of the preacher — or the "apostolic" voice — should be

> concerned, ardent, burning, inflamed, everywhere and always stirred by the forces of the new life, calling, shouting, beckoning, explosive in its outbursts, brief, disjointed, harrowing, itself violently shaken as much by fear and trembling as by longing and blessed expectancy, everywhere witnessing to the powerful unrest of the spirit and the profound impatience of the heart . . . . If apostolic speech is always as impatient as that of a woman in labor, then two considerations in particular are likely to stir it up even more — on the one hand, the idea that the night has lasted long enough and the point is to use the day; on the other hand, the idea that the time is coming when one can no longer work, that the days are numbered, the end is near, that the end of all things is approaching. (EUD, 69)

Such explosive sermons are well suited for the heterogeneity of Christianity. They can create collision and conflict in a way that a well-written essay, delivered with rhetorical poise, cannot. Without this exuberant form, the heterogeneous content of true Christian preaching is either blunted or lost. This is a catastrophe because a muffled warning protects no one, and an ambiguous declaration inspires no one.[33]

Earnestness. Without such harrowing and violently shaken sermons, the church wilts. It needs ardent, burning, inflamed sermons.[34] Without them, the church will mistake

> the artistic for the Christian, human upbringing for Christian character, human cleverness for Christian recklessness, human superiority for Christian worth, the charming magnificence of appearance for the plain everyday dress of truth, a secular, not to say pagan, Sunday-Christianity for New Testament Monday-Christianity; it mistakes artistic seriousness in playing Christianity for the real earnestness of Christianity, the idyllic enjoyment of quiet hours for New Testament painful decision; it mistakes enjoyment for

---

[33]A possible Biblical line inspiring these thoughts is "if the bugle gives an indistinct sound, who will get ready for battle?" (1 Cor. 14:8). Martin J. Heinecken (1902–1998), author of *The Moment Before God: An Interpretation of Kierkegaard* (Philadelphia: Muhlenberg, 1956), said this verse was his lifelong motto.

[34]"What our age needs is *pathos* . . . (just as scurvy needs green vegetables). . . . That is why there has to be a man who is able to short-suit reflectively all reflections" (JP, 3:3129).

suffering, winning the world for renunciation of the world, heightening life's enjoyment for painfully dying to the world. (JP, 1:825)

So attacks must be launched from the pulpits of the church.[35] Martin Luther also promoted militant preaching. He argued that sermons should "jab the soul," by taking away "every ground of trust" and ascribing redemption "solely to the blood of Christ."[36] They must suppress and cast out "the salvation, peace, life, and grace of the flesh."[37] By so doing they never are "discourses on paltry things, such as temporal riches, honor, might, and pleasures. For all these are nothing but sow dung and filth, dropped into the straw by swine."[38] So true, militant sermons are clearly not for gaining

> favor from men and from the world. For the world finds nothing more irritating and intolerable than hearing its wisdom, righteousness, religion, and power condemned. To denounce these mighty and glorious gifts of the world is not to curry the world's favor but to go out looking for, and quickly to find, hatred and misfortune, as it is called.[39]

So Kierkegaard had it right, that "God intends Christianity to remain embattled to the end, oriented not to victory in time but to [triumph in] eternity" (JP, 4:4856). If sermons are to remain faithful to the New Testament, they must have this orientation.[40] Without it we

---

[35]Once the preached word sinks in—with all of its shouting, yelling, and explosive outbursts—then there can be meditative silence—after the dust settles: "Ah, but a woman who looks at herself in the mirror of the Word becomes silent! And if she becomes silent, this perhaps is the strongest indication that she is not a forgetful reader or hearer" (FSE, 50-51).

[36]Martin Luther, "Commentary on Psalm 45" (1532), *Luther's Works* 12:225.

[37]Martin Luther, "Commentary on Psalm 2" (1519), *Luther's Works* 14:335.

[38]Martin Luther, *Sermons on John's Gospel* (1531), *Luther's Works* 23:402.

[39]Martin Luther, *Lectures on Galatians* (1535), *Luther's Works* 26:58.

[40]John Updike's character, the Rev. Fritz Kruppenbach, expresses this well in his harangue on death, misery, and Christian preaching: "If [God] wants to end misery He'll declare the Kingdom now. . . . How big do you think your little friends look among the billions that God sees? In Bombay now they die in the streets every minute. . . . I say you don't know what your role is or you'd be home locked in prayer. *There* is your role: to make yourself an exemplar of faith. *There* is where comfort comes from: faith, not what little finagling a body can do here and there; stirring the bucket. In running back and forth you run from the duty given you by God, to make your faith powerful, so when the call comes you can go out and tell

are quickly back to "craving the trumpery of eloquence" (CD, 165). Seeing the sickbed, then, as the best preacher, as Kierkegaard does, makes good sense. For illness does not suffer from eloquence and artistic distance. It clearly trades in earnestness and heterogeneity. It attacks us and upsets us. Or as Kierkegaard says of the apostolic voice itself (EUD, 69), illness shouts out and is explosive. It violently shakes us. Illness, in fact, does exactly what a sermon is supposed to do, but which rarely, if ever, is heard from the church's modern, well-adjusted pulpits.

Awakening Faith

No one becomes a Christian naturally. Being a Christian goes against everything in us. So in order to be one, we must be radically transformed, that is, born again and made into a new creation, so we can actually believe in Jesus Christ. In this section I want to show how illness does not have to lead to despair and unmitigated ruin, but can actually awaken faith in us. Having faith in Christ is not as easy and simple "as pulling on one's socks" (PC, 35). For belief to

---

them, 'Yes, he is dead, but you will see him again in Heaven. Yes, you suffer, but you must love your pain, because it is *Christ's* pain.' When on Sunday morning then, when we go before their faces, we must walk up not worn out with misery but full of Christ, *hot* . . . with Christ, on *fire: burn* them with the force of our belief. That is why they come; why else would they pay us? Anything else we can do or say anyone else can do and say. They have doctors and lawyers for that. It's all in the Book—a thief with faith is worth all the Pharisees. Make no mistake. There is nothing but Christ for us. All the rest, all this decency and busyness, is nothing. It is Devil's work." *Rabbit, Run* (1960; New York: Knopf, 1994) 170-71. See also Updike's study on Kierkegaard entitled "The Fork," in *Kierkegaard*, ed. Josiah Thompson (New York: Doubleday, 1972) 164-82. Unfortunately this fine essay — originally published in 1966—ends in failure, quoting Kierkegaard saying we will all be saved (JP 6:6934)—supposing it to mean there will be no eternal damnation for anyone (182). Updike's failure is that he misses Kierkegaard's twist: "The N.T. clearly rests on the assumption that there is an eternal damnation and—perhaps not one in a million is saved. We who are brought up in Christianity live on the assumption that all of us surely will be saved. . . . O, but the N. T. is a terrifying book; for it takes into account this kind of a collision with true Christianity" (JP, 6:6843, p. 484). Updike also errs in attributing to Kierkegaard the saying, "It is a fearful thing to fall into the hands of the living God" (175). That actually is Kierkegaard *quoting* Hebrews 10:31—a felicitous mistake on Updike's part, especially for those of us who see Kierkegaard as an advocate of Holy Scriptures!

happen, God "grabs" us to make us his (JP, 4:4532). He barges in through closed doors to wake us up (JP 5:5313). The Christian faith comes to a person only after much tribulation and soul-searching.[41]

So even though it is true[42] that the Sacrament of Baptism can draw a little infant into Christianity, Kierkegaard still insisted that we must all the more "vigorously see to it that rebirth becomes a decisive determinant" as the baptized child grows in years (JP, 1:537). Baptism, as Mark 10:39 says, must also become a matter of suffering. The sickbed preacher works for just that rebirth, which brings about the awakening of faith. For many baptized children, the suffering caused from "out-living" (JP, 2:1215) is needed *before* the lights go and they come to "count it worthy to suffer dishonor for the name" of Jesus Christ (Acts 5:41).

Reversals. Illness and physical suffering, therefore, are what miraculously turn us around. In this reversal, faith is awakened. "When in adversity it seems impossible to move . . . a foot—then eternity makes adversity into prosperity, ... so lightly does he walk. Eternity provides feet to walk on." With these new feet, faith makes the sufferer buoyant. For indeed,

> when eternity comforts, it makes one joyful; its comfort truly is joy, is the true joy. It is with the human grounds of comfort as it is when the sick person, who has already had many physicians, has a new one who thinks of something new that temporarily produces a little change, but soon it is the same old story again. No, when eternity is brought in to the sick person, it not only cures him completely but makes him healthier than the healthy (CD, 159).

---

[41]The Bible verses informing this paragraph are, *seriatim*, Romans 11:24; John 3:5; 2 Corinthians 5:17; John 6:44, 20:19; Acts 14:22, 26:28. These verses explain why it is so that "the way to Christianity is long and difficult if one is going to take it seriously and not be satisfied with being a Christian in name only." Gregor Malantschuk, *Kierkegaard's Concept of Existence*, 256.

[42]David Law misses this dialectic, erroneously supposing that Kierkegaard rejected infant baptism. "Kierkegaard on Baptism," *Theology* 91 (March 1988): 114-22, 120. See JP, 1:494 where Kierkegaard actually affirms infant baptism. It is true that at the end he questions infant baptism because it does not produce an "actual personality" which is needed for grasping the promises of Christianity (TM, 244). But that personality, he also held, can actually come from the "rebirth" which is to follow upon baptism (JP, 1:537). If that correlation holds, then infant baptism is not a problem.

This enhanced health comes from the awakening of faith in Jesus
Christ. This faith sees life differently from that of an unbeliever. To
unbelievers, "adversity is and remains adversity" (CD, 158). But not
for Christians. They have a bizarre view of the world. It is marked
with unexpected reversals.[43] For Christians, adversity is prosperity,
and visa-versa. And what the world thinks of as sobering is actually
intoxicating, and visa-versa (JFY, 106). And furthermore, "precisely
what worldliness regards as health is, Christianly, sickness, just as,
inversely, Christian health is regarded by worldliness as sickness"
(TM, 158).[44]

Christ's Crucifixion. These reversals do not create instability but
spiritual fortitude instead. One might think they would make us un-
stable because "from the worldly point of view Christian consolation
is much more to despair over than the hardest earthly suffering and
the greatest temporal misfortune" (CD, 97). One would have to "look
closely" for the consolation because of "the magnitude of the terror
in the inwardness of guilt-consciousness" which overshadows everything else (CD, 96). But even so, the upbuilding that follows upon
these terrors is so sure,

> so reliable in itself. One must not be afraid of the terrifying, as if it
> hindered the upbuilding, must not timorously keep it away in the
> hope of making the upbuilding more pleasant, because the up-
> building itself leaves with the terrifying. But, on the other hand, the
> upbuilding is precisely in the terrifying. So triumphant is the up-
> building that whatever at first glance could seem to be its enemy is
> made a presupposition, a servant, a friend. If the art of medicine
> successfully performs the difficult task of turning poison into
> remedy, in the upbuilding the terrifying is far more gloriously

---

[43]On these reversals see Sylvia Walsh, *Living Christianly: Kierkegaard's Dialectic
of Christian Existence* (University Park PA: Pennsylvania State University Press,
2005): "True Christians . . . live without the ordinary human anxieties over wealth
and station in life because their understanding of poverty, riches, lowliness, and
highness are the opposite of the merely human, pagan, or natural understanding of
them. One is able essentially to conquer temporal losses and misfortunes by
inverting one's understanding of them" (48). These reversals, Walsh points out,
Kierkegaard "identifies as . . . 'the dialectic of inversion'" (7).

[44]On these reversals see Martin Luther, *Lectures on Galatians* (1519), *Luther's
Works* 27:403: "One who is really a Christian is uplifted in adversity, because he
trusts in God; he is downcast in prosperity, because he fears God."

transformed into the upbuilding (CD, 96-97).

The reason the upbuilding is so certainly there *in the terrifying moments* is because of Christ's presence. "*There* begins the upbuilding, the Christian upbuilding, which is named after him, our Lord and Savior, for he also suffered" (CD, 97). Christ is the only true rest for the terrified sinner because in Christ

> there is forgiveness [which is built] on the one and only ground that can support a penitent, that atonement has been made . . . . That is what the exhausted laborer, the fatigued traveler, desires; and the sailor who is tossed about on the sea seeks . . . ; and the weary old man longs for . . . ; and the sick one who lies restless on his bed and does not find an alleviating position craves . . . ; and the doubter who does not find a foothold in the ocean of thoughts craves (CD, 265).

The Savior Jesus Christ does not disappoint. So Kierkegaard says "I will seek my refuge with him, the Crucified One. I will beseech him to save me from evil and to save me from myself" (CD, 280). Indeed Jesus is "not only your spiritual guide; he is also your Savior" (CD, 266). And we need this Savior because we hide "from the truth as Adam hid among the trees." There is in our "innermost being a secret anxiety about and wariness of the truth." So we run from the truth which is our need to practice self-denial and we resist having it made "so clear that every excuse, every evasion, every extenuation, every refuge in the false but favorable opinion of others is cut off" (CD, 170).

Christ saves us on the cross by winning "God's love" for us there (JP, 3:2442). This is needed because "God is love, but not love to sinners. This he is first in Christ: i.e., the Atonement" (JP, 2:1329). "By his holy suffering and death, . . . Christ has made full satisfaction for your sin" (JP, 3:2442). This is the comfort of redemption, that Christ, "the substitute, . . . puts himself completely in your place and in mine!" (WA, 123). This redemption happens between God and Christ, so that "Christianity is the divine combat of divine passion with itself, so that in a sense we human beings disappear like ants" (JP, 1:532)![45] Because this redemption is found nowhere else, we "can

---

[45]These five statements from Kierkegaard contrast with the judgment that there is no objective theory of atonement in the *Philosophical Fragments*. John D. Glenn, Jr.,

be saved only by the blood of Christ" (JP, 2:2300).[46] So we are to pray:

> Great are you, O God . . . . When under the arch of heaven I stand surrounded by the wonder of creation, I rapturously and adoringly praise your greatness, you who lightly hold the stars in the infinite and concern yourself fatherly with the sparrow . . . . You are indeed great, Creator and Sustainer of the world; but when you, O God, forgave the sin of the world and reconciled yourself with the fallen human race, then you were even greater in your incomprehensible compassion! (CD, 289).

This reality of redemption awakens our faith in the Savior Jesus Christ—the One who both suffers and comforts, and comforts because he suffers. Our adversity ought not repel us for it did not repel Christ. Adversity rather is to awaken faith in Christ in us.

Gracious Unsureness. So redemption unexpectedly begins its work in our very unbelief. In our uncertainty we are kept awake that we

---

"Kierkegaard and Anselm" in *International Kierkegaard Commentary: Philosophical Fragments* and *Johannes Climacus*, ed. Robert L. Perkins (Macon GA: Mercer University Press, 1994) 242. While that may be true for the *Philosophical Fragments*, it is not necessarily so for his entire authorship. Closer to the truth is the view that in the entire authorship, Kierkegaard proposed "some sort of unified theory of the atonement which retains the objective and subjective elements of both." J. Preston Cole, "Kierkegaard's Doctrine of the Atonement," *Religion in Life* 33 (Autumn 1964): 592-601, 600. On Anselm's objective view of the atonement, see Paul Tillich, *A History of Christian Thought: From Its Judaic and Hellenistic Origins to Existentialism*, ed. Carl E. Braaten (1967; New York: Touchstone, 1972): "Behind its legalistic, quantitative thinking there is a profound idea, namely, that sin has produced a tension in God himself. This tension is felt. Anselm's theory became so popular because everyone felt that it is not simple for God to forgive sins. . . . The church has never dogmatized Anselm's theory, . . . but it is obvious that it liked Anselm's most, probably because it has the deepest psychological roots. This is the feeling that a price must be paid for our guilt, and since we cannot pay it, God must do it" (166). Against traditional atonement theory, see S. Mark Heim, *Saved From Sacrifice: A Theology of the Cross* (Grand Rapids MI: Eerdmans, 2006): "[Such theory is] a consistent fault line in the whole foundation [of Christianity] that runs from distorted views of God to spiritual guilt fixation to sacrificial bloodshed to anti-Semitic persecution to arrogant ignorance of world mythology" (27).

[46]On this see Gregor Malantschuk, *The Controversial Kierkegaard*, trans. Howard V. Hong and Edna H. Hong (1976; Waterloo ON: Wilfrid Laurier University Press, 1980): "Christianity alone is able to give a solution to all the existential problems" (74).

might "seek after certitude" (CD, 194). For disbelief is not "spiritless ignorance; disbelief wants to deny God and is therefore in a way involved with God" (CD, 67). The trauma and turmoil that sickness brings actually holds us close to God — instead of pushing us away as we would expect.[47] So "God's greatness in showing mercy is first an occasion *for offense* and then is *for faith*" (CD, 291). Even so, the offense lingers in the heart of faith — and so Kierkegaard encourages us to pray:

> Save me, O God, from ever becoming completely sure; keep me unsure until the end so that then, if I receive eternal blessedness, I might be completely sure that I have it by grace! It is empty shadowboxing to give assurances that one believes that it is by grace — and then to be completely sure. The true, the essential expressions of its being by grace is the very fear and trembling of unsureness. There lies faith — as far, just as far, from despair and from sureness . . . . Eternal God, therefore, ... save me from deceiving any other person, because this deception lies all too close when one treats one's relationship with God as if it were a direct relationship with other human beings, so that one gets into comparisons and human sureness. If someone, regarded by many as extraordinarily noble and upright, were to continue in fear and trembling to work out his salvation, the others would become furious with him. In other words, they would want to have his sureness as an excuse for their own peace of mind, and they would want their own peace of mind to be his sureness. But, my God and Father, the question of my salvation indeed pertains to no other person, but only to me — and to you . . . . Should there not be, ought there not be, and must there not be fear and trembling until the end? Was this not the fault of the foolish bridesmaids, that they became sure and went to sleep — the sensible ones, however, stayed awake. But what is it to stay awake? It is unsureness in fear and trembling. And what is faith but an empty delusion if it is not awake? And if faith is not awake, what else is it but that pernicious sureness? (CD, 211-12)[48]

---

[47]On this see Martin Luther, *Lectures on Isaiah* (1528), *Luther's Works* 16:232: "The more a . . . man falls outwardly and is wounded in his conscience, the more he lets go of himself and is driven to Christ [*agitatur ad Christum*]."

[48]Kierkegaard is not saying, mind you, that we are to doubt, for instance, doctrine and the Bible and the divinity of Christ Jesus. No, "the doctrine . . . does not have to be reformed. . . . If anything has to be done — then it is penance on the part of all of us. . . . The doctrine . . . [is] very good. But the lives, our lives — believe me, they are mediocre. . . . Our lives are only slightly touched by the doctrine" (JP,

In this magnificent prayer we see that just as illness upsets us with its unsureness, it awakens faith in us by fighting against all pernicious sureness. Illness plays the role of the five maidens that were ready for the bridegroom, Christ Jesus, because they remained uncertain—they remained awake (Matthew 25:1-13). So the very thing that frightens us, miraculously becomes our friend. And so the fear and trembling of illness draws us to God. It does not defeat faith in God as it is usually supposed to do. This insight is Kierkegaard's great service to the promulgation of Christian faith.

Judging the Sickbed Preacher

But is Kierkegaard right about all of this? Can illness really awaken faith in Christ Jesus? Or does it not rather shut down Christianity altogether? Does not illness prove that Christianity's promises fail? Does not illness instead show that in Christ there is no health and victory, but only loss and shame? In this section I want to test Kierkegaard's claim that the sickbed is our best preacher. Does this claim have any compelling confirmations? William James notes in his famed Gifford Lectures the venerable place sickness has in Christianity. There it is viewed "as a visitation; something sent by God for our good, either as chastisement, as warning, or as opportunity for exercising virtue.... According to this view, disease should . . . be submissively accepted, and it might under certain circumstances even be blasphemous to wish it away."[49]

6:6727). So what we are to be unsure about is that we are living up to Christian teachings as we should. Now it is also true that Kierkegaard cares that the "comprehensive view of the whole of Christianity" is properly presented (JP, 3:2550). That would be the same concern as is in Acts 20:27 about preaching the "whole counsel of God." But what he cares about most is the practice and exercise of those holy Words. On this same point see Martin Luther, "Sermons on 2 Peter" (1523), *Luther's Works* 30:159, "Your faith is [to be] well exercised [*trieben*] and applied [*üben*]." A wonderful summarization of this Kierkegaardian point is: "The Christian ideal has not been tried and found wanting. It has been found difficult; and left untried." G. K. Chesterton, *What's Wrong with the World* (1910; New York: Sheed & Ward, 1956) 29.

[49]William James, *The Varieties of Religious Experience* (1902; New York: Penguin, 1982) 113n1. See also David G. Schoessow, "Sin, Sickness, and Salvation from Nazareth to Lake Wobegone," *Logia* 10 (Eastertide 2001): 5-12: "The sick and dying

Many, however, disagree.[50] When Rabbi Harold S. Kushner's son, Aaron, was stricken with progeria, or early aging disease, he did not see any visitation from God. It was offensive to suppose that misfortunes come from God. Aaron had nothing good to gain from being sick with progeria. God was not punishing or blessing him with this illness. Illnesses, Kushner concludes, are only "the painful consequences of being human" — nothing more, nothing less.[51]

On this view, Kierkegaard, in celebrating the sickbed preacher, appears to be peddling a "jaundiced view of life." Indeed "this strange man [appears to think] so poorly of our life in the temporal world[52] that he could characterize this life as a mere 'test' or 'examination.' "[53] And so Kierkegaard's Christianity looks "so extreme that no one could practice it."[54] Sickness is that hard on us. The famed comedian, Richard Pryor, would agree. Stricken with multiple sclerosis in 1986, it was no blessing for him in his illness. It "robbed him of his trademark physicality," leaving him "immobilized and imprisoned."[55] Many of the survivors of Hurricane Katrina in New

---

play an important role in our world, reminding the healthy not to lose sight of those matters that are of ultimate importance (Job; Hosea 6:1-3; John 9:1-3; 11:4)" (5).

[50]This disagreement may be rooted in sin. On such a pervasive and devastating view of sin, see Martin Luther, "A Short Order of Confession" (1529), *Luther's Works* 53:117: "Miserable person that I am, I confess and lament to you before God that I am a sinful and weak creature. I do not keep God's commandments; I do not really believe the gospel; I do nothing good; I cannot bear ill."

[51]Harold S. Kushner, *When Bad Things Happen to Good People* (New York: Schocken, 1981) 44, 76.

[52]On this negativity see Martin Luther, *Lectures on Genesis* (1545), *Luther's Works* 8:114: "This life is horribly wretched, difficult, and troubled because of the various tribulations and vexations of all the devils and the whole world. . . . Therefore this life is not a life. No, it is a mortification and vexation of life." Luther could also rejoice in life — but only because of his faith in Christ Jesus. Therefore his negativity actually goes together with his joy.

[53]Charles Hartshorne, *Insights and Oversights of Great Thinkers: An Evaluation of Western Philosophy* (Albany NY: State University of New York Press, 1983) 216.

[54]Paul Ricoeur, "Two Encounters with Kierkegaard," in *Kierkegaard's Truth*, ed. John H. Smith (New Haven CT: Yale University Press, 1981) 329.

[55]Lynell George, "I Was Being Richard Pryor," *The Seattle Times*, 11 December 2005. Note also the flippant approach of Miriam Engelberg, *Cancer Made Me a Shallower Person: A Memoir in Comics* (New York: Harper, 2006): "Maybe nobility and courage aren't the only approaches to life with an illness; maybe the path of shallowness deserves more attention!" (xiii).

Orleans feel the same way. Their misery "goes beyond 9/11, . . . the Oklahoma City bombing . . . . and Hurricanes Andrew, Hugo and Ivan." New Orleans is experiencing "a near epidemic of depression, ... of an intensity rarely seen in this country." And so the suicide rate has tripled. Because many have lost everything, they just want to die.[56] This sadness and despair, however, does not take away all silver linings. But to say even that, sounds criminal to some.[57]

Nevertheless, these contrary cases stand tall. Take forest fires, for instance. They create much suffering and loss. But they are not all bad. These fires in fact are "essential for the survival and reproduction of many species," and so fire is "not evil [but] often good. . . . Without it, our world would be a much poorer, less diverse, less interesting place. It is time for Smokey Bear to retire."[58] Another case is Pearl Harbor. At anniversary proceedings, Admiral Michael Mullen, the Navy's most senior sailor said "December 7, 1941, was not just a day of infamy. In many ways it was a day of discovery. . . . It changed us, it hurt us, it made us stronger."[59] The movie star,

---

[56]Susan Saulny, "Suicide Rate Soars in Devastated New Orleans," *Seattle Post-Intelligencer*, 21 June 2006.

[57]On this see the famous case of the Chamberlains who were accused of killing their daughter simply because they were "overcalm" regarding her death due to their belief in "Divine Purpose." John Bryson, *Evil Angels: The Case of Lindy Chamberlain* (New York: Summit Books, 1985) 162. A similar obtuseness is in Kierkegaard's praise for the sickbed preacher. But for some this makes him paradoxically attractive. On this see Dorothee Soelle, *The Window of Vulnerability*, trans. Linda M. Maloney (Minneapolis: Fortress, 1990): "Kierkegaard seduced me into religion. I devoured him. Today I could say that I fell in love with Søren. . . . I submerged myself in Kierkegaard. . . . Anxiety, according to Kierkegaard . . . drives us to conversion. . . . Those who cannot get free of it . . . are hanging on God's hooks" (117, 118, 121). See also Antje Jackelen, "Why is Søren So Popular?" *Dialog* 45 (Spring 2006): 101-105. She says Kierkegaard is so popular because what he says makes life "more difficult" and thereby more meaningful (105).

[58]Seth R. Reice, *The Silver Lining: The Benefits of Natural Disasters* (Princeton NJ: Princeton University Press, 2001) 99. See also Randolph M. Nesse and George C. Williams, *Why We Get Sick: The New Science of Darwinian Medicine* (New York: Vintage, 1996): "We would never argue that any disease is good, even though we will offer many examples in which pathology is associated with some unappreciated benefits" (11-12).

[59]Audrey McAvoy, "Pearl Harbor Made Us Stronger," *Seattle Post-Intelligencer*, 8 December 2005. President Clinton says something similar to this in his celebration of the Kansas State motto, *Ad astra per aspera*, "To the stars through difficulties." Bill

Michael J. Fox, says something similar about being inflicted with Parkinson's disease in the height of his career. "Despite appearances," he writes, "this disease has unquestionably directed me toward what is . . . good." So if his disease could miraculously be healed, he would unhesitatingly refuse taking back his previous good health. This is because he needed the disease to rescue him from his destructive "fun-house self."[60] Nothing else could have done it for him. NPR correspondent John Hockenberry says the same. The car crash that left him a paraplegic provided the "leap" he needed to help him truly appreciate people and give up the illusion that we control our lives. So he writes, I am "grateful to have been a [cripple] for the past nineteen years; I may miss walking, running, or tree climbing from time to time, but I do not miss being a spectator."[61]

These reports on the benefits of illness and calamity reinforce Kierkegaard's praise of the sickbed preacher. They show that Kierkegaard has tapped into a rich vein of human well being. They show that Kierkegaard is not unjustifiably extreme[62] in his claims. His

---

Clinton, *My Life* (New York: Knopf, 2004) 741.

[60]Michael J. Fox, *Lucky Man: A Memoir* (New York: Hyperion, 2002) 5-6, 135. The famed creative writer, Reynolds Price, says the same about his paralyzing spinal cancer in *A Whole New Life: An Illness and a Healing* (1982; New York: Plume, 1995). "I know," he writes, "that this new life is better for me, and for most of my friends." He says this, having "tested that word *better* for the stench of sentimentality, narcissism, blind optimism, or lunacy." His paraplegia made his life better by making him more patient and watchful. And secondly it forced "the slow migration of a sleepless and welcome sexuality from the center of my life to the cooler edge [which] contributed hugely to the increased speed and volume of my work, not to speak of the gradual resolution of hungers that—however precious to mind and body—had seemed past feeding" (189-90). When he retells this story in *Letters to a Godchild Concerning Faith* (New York: Scribner, 2006) he no longer says he *knows* that his new life is better, but only that such a view is but one of a few "fragmentary guesses" on why he suffered so (62).

[61]John Hockenberry, *Moving Violations: War Zones, Wheelchairs, and Declarations of Independence* (New York: Hyperion, 1995) 96, 101, 351. On this matter of control, Hockenberry writes: "Loss of control is a dark fear, particularly in America. Why we should so fear losing control in a world that we have no control over anymore is one of the central questions of American culture" (101).

[62]On this option see Tolly Burkan, *Extreme Spirituality: Radical Approaches to Awakening* (San Francisco: Council Oak Books, 2001): "The skin all over my body began to tingle, and the hair on the back of my neck stood up. I could barely catch

hope in the sickbed preacher is inspired by the truth that suffering builds character through endurance, as Romans 5 says.[63] This Kierke-gaard calls "the best learning" ever taught (EUD, 95). And that is so even if it might mean that fewer people will want to be Christian and the church, as it stands, will have to be relieved of some of its many "battalions" (PV, 126). For the church

> in the next several decades is going to be a smaller, leaner, tougher company . . . . The way for the church now is to accept the shrink-age, to penetrate the meaning and the threat of the prevailing secularity, and to tighten its mind around the task given to the critical cadre.[64]

So rather than belittling Kierkegaard's sickbed preacher, we should take on a deeper appreciation of illness, and its darkness, considering

> how tremendous the spiritual change that it brings, how astonishing, when the lights of health go down, the undiscovered countries that are then disclosed, what wastes and deserts of the soul a slight attack of influenza brings to view, what precipices and lawns sprinkled with bright flowers a little rise of temperature reveals, [and] what ancient and obdurate oaks are uprooted in us

----

my breath. The experience was not unlike an orgasm. I was in bliss! . . . More than any other challenge described in this book, pushing a needle through my hand has to stand out as the most difficult victory I've achieved. As a result, the lessons gleaned from this are more vital and valuable" (34). The rest of the book is about firewalking, skydiving, smelling foul odors, sweating and walking on broken glass. Against this extremism see Martin Luther, "Sermons on 1 Peter" (1522), *Luther's Works* 30:110: "We should not [suffer] of our own accord. . . . If God inflicts [it] on you, then it is better."

[63]This benefit, which "human flabbiness might wish [would come] without dangerous suffering" (EUD, 329), Jacob Bøggild dismisses as self-contradictory. "Revocated Trials" in *The New Kierkegaard*, ed. Elsebet Jegstrup (Bloomington: Indiana University Press, 2004) 118, 125. But the possibility of interfering with the upbuilding (EUD, 346) does not "nullify" the benefit as Bøggild alleges. All it does it separate the paths between the person who "fights the good fight of danger and terror; [and the one who] becomes sagacious and spiritlessly rejoices over the security of life" (EUD, 346). This echoes 2 Corinthians 2:16 which says that the same Savior can both have the odor of life and the odor of death.

[64]This admonition is from the Lutheran doyen, Joseph A. Sittler (1904–1987) in his *Grace Notes and Other Fragments*, ed. Robert M. Herhold and Linda M. Delloff (Philadelphia: Fortress, 1981) 99.

by the act of sickness.[65]

This intensification of the importance of illness for Christianity will also help us see more clearly what Kierkegaard was about. Indeed his "originality and uniqueness" in describing Christian life is found "chiefly in his conception and use of inverse dialectic" whereby, for instance, adversity is prosperity and sickness is health.[66] Studying his praise of illness reveals this deep inversion in his Christian thought. So what might appear to be an embarrassing idea at the beginning, proves in the end to be nothing but profound.

A Crumpled Amen

When Kierkegaard tells us that the sickbed is our best preacher, this claim entirely hinges on his inverse dialectic. Seeing the truth in that inversion enables us to experience illness as anything but the defeat of Christianity. When we are sick, we will have balance enough, as a result of this inverse dialectic, to fight the temptation to cry out to God, "Why me?" "This isn't fair!" "Please end it now it!" In the place of this defiance and impatience, illness will teach us to pray to God with a resolved heart. Under the tutelage of our sickness, we will pray differently. We will pray for help to endure the pain and fear brought on by our illness, so we might learn what God is teaching us. For this insight we are indebted to Kierkegaard, who

> ... crawled
> To the monastery of his chaste thoughts
> To offer up his crumpled amen.[67]

---

[65]Virginia Woolf, *On Being Ill* (1930; Ashfield MA: Paris Press, 2002) 3.

[66]Sylvia Walsh, *Living Christianly: Kierkegaard's Dialectic of Christian Existence*, 162. I have pursued this view of Kierkegaard in my parish, First Lutheran Church of West Seattle (Seattle WA), since the beginning of our annual Kierkegaard celebrations in 1980. On this see Paul Sponheim, "America," *Bibliotheca Kierkegaardiana* 15, ed. Niels and Marie Thulstrup (Copenhagen: C. A. Reitzels, 1987) 36, and my "Søren Kierkegaard Comes to Seattle," *Lutheran Forum* 19 (Summer 1985): 15-16; and "Kierkegaard's Sesquicentennial," *Lutheran Forum* 40 (Summer 2006): 17-19.

[67]*Poems of R. S. Thomas* (Fayetteville: University of Arkansas Press, 1985) 49. These last lines from the poem, "Kierkegaard," were originally published by Thomas in 1966 in a collection called *Pietà*. I think this poem measures up to what Robert Bly calls a great poem, namely, one that "helps us get rid of self-pity, and re-

Crumpled no doubt, difficult and chaste indeed, painful to say the least, but an amen all the same. And so we rejoice in our sickness because we finally see that it has value for us. In the face of suffering and sickness, then, "Christianity is collectively the great reassurance and the great protest, turned polemically against all human abjectness."[68] For in the face of illness we have learned from Christianity to say our crumpled, uncertain amen. Now we see how grateful we should be for the gains we can receive when we are sick. When we are ill we have a chance to "pierce the superficial optimism which claims that with . . . better health, a longer life, and more personal liberty, human beings can be made happy."[69] But even so we still would hope for a less painful way. We wish that faith could be awakened in us, in some easier, more pleasant setting. We cannot help but want this. But that—lamentably—will never be. "Fantasies about alternative pain-free paths . . . are countered with talk of Jesus' divine authority, with its affirmation of the ultimate reliability of this suffering path to joy."[70] For indeed the message of Christianity in the New Testament and elaborated by Kierkegaard is this, and only this, that salvation comes through trauma, pain and suffering. And it is for that reason alone that the sickbed remains our best preacher.

---

places self-pity with awe at the complicated misery of all living things." *The Rag and Bone Shop of the Heart*, ed. Robert Bly et al. (New York: HarperPerennial, 1992) 198.

[68]Johannes Sløk, *Kierkegaard's Universe: A New Guide to the Genius*, trans. Kenneth Tindall (Copenhagen: The Danish Cultural Institute, 1994) 119.

[69]Diogenes Allen, *Three Outsiders: Pascal, Kierkegaard, Simone Weil* (Cambridge, MA: Cowley, 1983) 13. Kierkegaard, it would seem, is naturally drawn to such piercing, since he saw in Christianity "the subversion of the values of wealth and status." Steven Shakespeare, "Stirring the Waters of Language: Kierkegaard on the Dangers of Doing Theology," *The Heythrop Journal* 37 (October 1996): 421-36, 435.

[70]Lee Barrett, "The Joy in the Cross: Kierkegaard's Appropriation of Lutheran Christology in 'The Gospel of Sufferings,'" in *International Kierkegaard Commentary: Upbuilding Discourses in Various Spirits*, ed. Robert L. Perkins (Macon GA: Mercer University Press, 2005) 283.

10

Christ's Efficacious Love and Human Responsibility:
The Lutheran Dialectic
of "Discourses at the Communion on Fridays"

Lee C. Barrett

Kierkegaard's seven discourses intended for the communion service on Fridays that constitute part four of *Christian Discourses* all exhibit a striking tension. On the one hand, many evince a strong exhortatory force, emphatically urging the reader/auditor to engage in some arduous course of action. More specifically, the reader/auditor is encouraged to actively cultivate a set of dispositions, virtues, and habits appropriate for the reception of communion. For example, in the second discourse's exposition of Christ's invitation to come to him and rest, Kierkegaard emphasizes the theme that the invitation "contains a requirement; it requires that the invited person labor and be burdened in the most profound sense" (CD, 264). Even many of the introductory prayers to the discourses, although directly addressed to God, contain tacit exhortations to the communicants to become active and prepare themselves for the sacred meal. On the other hand, in all of the discourses Kierkegaard also insists, often in the strongest possible terms, that humans, through their own agency, can accomplish nothing in regard to the Eucharistic encounter with Christ. At times this warning reaches a crescendo in the reminder that reconciliation with God, including the communicant's own preparation to receive it, depends entirely upon God and not at all on the individual's own efforts. For example, in the last discourse Kierkegaard maintains, "At the Communion table you are able to do nothing at all, not even this, that you hold fast the thought of your unworthiness and in this make yourself receptive to the blessing" (CD, 299). Ostensibly, these two themes do not fit together well. The one emphasizes human agency, and suggests some sort of human cooperation with God, while the second emphasizes divine agency, and tends to reject any suggestion of human cooperation.

I shall argue that this tension concerning the relation of divine and human agencies in the process of reconciliation with God is not an idiosyncratic quirk in Kierkegaard's discourses. The tension in his pages reflects a complex dialectic of divine grace and human responsibility in the historic Lutheran tradition. I will also contend that, unlike the doctrinal tradition of his Lutheran heritage, Kierkegaard relied upon a careful sorting out of the rhetorical purposes of these two theological motifs to give them meaning and to render them compatible, eschewing the tradition's tendency to resolve the tension in various metaphysical theories concerning the interaction of divine and human agencies. Instead of adopting a "synergistic" theory of the human will's cooperation with God's gracious action, or a "monergistic" theory of the sole agency of God, Kierkegaard clarifies the differences between contexts in which it is appropriate to use the language of human responsibility, and the contexts in which it is appropriate to employ the language of efficacious grace.

The Tension of Human Agency and God's Gracious Action in Historic Lutheranism

In order to grasp the import of this tension, Kierkegaard's discourses for communion on Fridays must be considered in the context of certain theological controversies that kept reappearing in the history of the Lutheran doctrinal tradition. Most relevant is the "synergistic" dispute of the sixteenth and early seventeenth centuries, a dispute that was never entirely resolved in spite of the efforts of the authors of the *Formula of Concord* to produce a unifying statement.[1] The controversy involved the relationship of God's action to human agency in the genesis and development of faith in the converted individual. In the mid-sixteenth century, certain followers of the enormously influential Lutheran theologian Philip Melanchthon proposed the view that, although salvation is due to the grace of God alone and not to any meritorious human works, nevertheless the human will must cooperate with God's grace in the development of repentance and faith. Victorin Strigel, a student of Melanchthon and one of the more vociferous of these "synergists,"

---

[1]For an account of this, see F. Bente, *Historical Introduction to "The Book of Concord"* (Saint Louis: Concordia Publishing House, 1965) 195-228.

argued that even in its unconverted state the human will retained enough power and freedom to accept or reject God's gracious initiative. Melanchthon's own elusive talk about the will's capacity to respond to the gospel after it had been moved by the Holy Spirit may not have implied Strigel's more extreme position,[2] but it did suggest that the will can respond positively to the coaxings of grace, adapting itself to the activity of God's grace. These "Philippists" like Strigel sought to avoid giving the impression that God forcibly converts individuals against their wills or without working through their volitional faculties. Against this view, Flacius Illyricus and the more conservative "Gnesio-Lutherans" argued that sinfulness has actually become the very substance of the fallen human will, rendering it utterly incapable of anything but resistance to God's gracious action. According to them, in conversion the thoroughly sinful old creaturely will must be destroyed and replaced by God with a new holy will. The creaturely human will can contribute absolutely nothing to the inception and development of faith. To many moderate Lutherans, this contention seemed to imply a Calvinist-like view of predestination, in which God's grace irresistibly transforms those whom God has chosen for salvation, and is simply not extended to those whom God has chosen for perdition. Such an extreme divine determinism in the matter of salvation seemed to place the responsibility for damnation on God, thereby restricting the universality of God's love, a theme dear to most Lutherans.

The *Formula of Concord* of 1577–1578 attempted to do justice to some of the concerns of both the synergists and the Gnesio-Lutherans.[3] Along with the Gnesio-Lutherans, this confessional document affirmed the will's total incapacity to contribute anything positive to salvation. As Luther had maintained, the will is in bondage to sin prior to its conversion and can do nothing by its own powers to heal itself. Salvation is due entirely to the operation of the Holy Spirit, which must give the convert the basic power to accept the grace of God. Consequently, a person can do nothing to prepare

---

[2]See Philip Melanchthon, *Melanchthon on Christian Doctrine: Loci Communes 1555*, trans. Clyde Manschreck (Grand Rapids MI: Baker, 1982).
[3]*The Book of Concord: The Confessions of the Evangelical Lutheran Church*, ed. Robert Kolb and Timothy Wingert (Minneapolis: Fortress Press, 2000) 487-94, 517-20, 531-62, 640-56.

for grace, or initiate anything in regard to conversion. The will does not even cooperate with God's activity. On this score *The Formula of Concord* was solidly in the "monergist" camp, insisting that only God's activity is efficacious for salvation. However, along with the synergists it affirmed that God acts by drawing and enticing the will rather than by forcing it or entirely recreating it. Against the suspicion of Calvinism it also maintained that God desires the salvation of all people and wills the damnation of no one. If an individual is not transformed by grace, the spiritual tragedy is not attributable to the predestining will of God but is entirely the individual's own fault. When an individual's will resists God's action, grace is not conveyed. Although the nonresistance of the will to grace cannot be regarded as an efficacious cause of salvation, the will's resistance to grace should be regarded as the cause of damnation. The origin of the rejection of grace is not to be sought in any defect in God's action but in the perversity of the individual's will. Whoever is saved must praise God for this felicitous gift and take no credit at all for it, while whoever is damned must blame only oneself. This position forced the authors of *The Formula* to maintain that although the human will cannot cooperate with God's grace, it can resist or block "the Holy Spirit's ordinary path."[4] Accordingly, the *Formula* laments "what a grievous sin it is to impede and resist the workings of the Holy Spirit."[5] Of course, if it is possible to resist the Holy Spirit, it would seem that it must also be possible to refrain from resisting the Holy Spirit, a fact that appeared to open the door to syngerism. To prevent this conclusion, *The Formula* distinguished nonresistance to grace from cooperation with grace. Nonresistance to grace was not regarded as an act of the will or even as a choice. For many, however, it continued to be difficult to see how the refusal to resist grace could not be regarded as some sort of choice. This subtle distinction of passive nonresistance and active cooperation failed to satisfy all parties and guaranteed that the synergist controversy would recur regularly in different guises in the history of Lutheranism.

Kierkegaard would have been familiar with this controversy

---

[4]*The Book of Concord*, 518.
[5]*The Book of Concord*, 558.

from his theological readings in preparation for his examinations. He used the standard textbooks on the nature and history of Lutheran doctrine by K. G. Bretschneider and Karl Hase, both of which devote considerable attention to this issue.[6] Kierkegaard would also have become acquainted with the synergist dispute through the lectures on doctrine by C. H. Clausen and H. L. Martensen.[7] Like most of his fellow Danes, Kierkegaard would have been immersed through formal and informal channels in the confessional teachings of the Lutheran church.[8] Most importantly for our purposes, Kierkegaard studied and even expressed appreciation for *The Formula of Concord*, even though it had not been officially adopted as a confessional standard by the Danish church (JP, 3:2459, 3656). The traces of the synergist/monergist controversy, including condemnations of contrary opinions, are unmistakable in its pages.

Echoes of this controversy can be heard in Kierkegaard's Friday communion discourses. All of the addresses touch upon the theme of salvation by grace alone, thus suggesting the exclusive efficacy of God's agency, and the theme of the cultivation of repentance, thus suggesting some role for responsible human agency. These two themes, the conflict of which had triggered the synergist controversy, coexist in an apparent dialectical tension in Kierkegaard's pages. In order to explore the purposes of the two poles of this tension and Kierkegaard's unique way of rendering them compatible, we shall first trace the theme of human agency and responsibility in the discourses, identifying a thematic development from one discourse to the next. In differing ways, each of the discourses exhorts the individual to engage in some project of spiritual self-development and encourages the individual to assume responsibility for growth in the Christian life.

---

[6]K. G. Bretscheider, *Handbuch der Dogmatik*, vol. II (Leipzig, 1838) 521-69; Karl Hase, *Hutterus Redvivus* (Leipzig, 1839) 211, 222-29, 277-81.

[7]For an overview of Martensen and Clausen, see Bruce Kirmmse, *Kierkegaard in Golden Age Denmark* (Bloomington: Indiana University Press, 1990) 169-96, 238-42.

[8]See Niels Thulstrup, *Kierkegaard and the Church in Denmark*, ed. Niels and Marie Thulstrup (Copenhagen: C. A. Reitzels Forlag, 1984) 70-71.

The "Synergist" Pole of Responsible Agency

The call to action, ostensibly suggesting sympathy with synergism, is most dramatic and salient in the **first** discourse. Most basically, it voices an imperative to grasp, cultivate, and utilize the longing to "renew fellowship with our Savior and Redeemer" (CD, 251). The nurturing of this heartfelt longing is foundational for Kierkegaard's basic purpose in these essays: to prepare individuals most aptly to participate in the communion service. The centrality of "longing" for Kierkegaard's project is evident in his observation that Luke 22:15, the passage upon which the discourse is based and in which Jesus expresses his own longing to eat the Passover meal with his disciples, is the introduction to the institution of the Lord's Supper. As such, it points to the most fundamental disposition, modeled by Jesus himself, that is necessary for a spiritually fruitful participation in the Eucharist. Kierkegaard does make it clear that this mysterious longing for fellowship with Christ is by no means self-generated; the individual does not decide by a Promethean exertion of will power to long for companionship with Christ. The presence of the longing in the individual's heart is a sheer gift of the Holy Spirit. But, however much its origins may reside beyond the sphere of human volition, the longing's presence in the individual's soul invites an intentional response. In fact, Kierkegaard repeats emphatically that such a response is "a requirement." He admonishes, "Truly, although God gives everything, he also requires everything, that the person himself shall do everything to use rightly what God gives" (CD, 254). The succession of verbs in the opening prayer underscores this imperative; we must "grasp hold of the longing," "surrender ourselves (to the longing)," "keep close to you (Christ)," "hold it (the longing) fast," and "sanctify it," so that the longing "might become the strong but also well-tested, heart-felt longing that is required of those who worthily want to partake of the holy meal of Communion" (CD, 251). Ominously, Kierkegaard warns against "wasting" the gift and points to "the terrible responsibility" of misusing it. In eternity accusing recollections of failing to heed God's communications will plague the irresponsible individual (CD, 253). The longing for reconciliation can be ignored, resisted, and even allowed to die unused (CD, 254).

Having alarmed the reader with the dire consequences of not responding to the longing adequately, Kierkegaard proceeds to illustrate how, by "resolution," the God-given longing can be used and increased. For example, an individual can deliberately concentrate upon the vanity of all temporal phenomena, recalling the susceptibility of all things to corruption. Similarly, an individual can dwell upon the uncertainty of all hopes and projects, the vulnerability of all life to sudden accidents, the obscurity of the meaning and significance of events, the inevitability of death, and the ultimate isolation of all persons. Edification can be found in the realization that all interpersonal relationships are subject to misunderstanding and betrayal. The longing for Christ can be even further augmented by considering the sinful corruption of humanity, the proliferation of atrocities in human history, and the damning reality that even oneself would have consented to the crucifixion of Christ. Kierkegaard concludes these somber musings with the observation that the more a person intently entertains these thoughts, the more the longing for fellowship with Christ increases (CD, 260). Through these self-initiated strategies the longing for Christ can and should become a progressively strengthened disposition. As Kierkegaard explains, " . . . the longing for fellowship with your Savior and Redeemer should increase every time you remember him" (CD, 261). In a manner that would have pleased Strigel and the synergists, this active remembering is presented as the product of the individual's intentional effort and is the individual's own responsibility.

The **second** discourse strikes an almost equally strong imperative note. Although it is couched as an exposition of Jesus' invitation to all who are burdened and heavy laden to come to him, the discourse quickly concentrates on the theme that this invitation contains a stringent requirement. Significantly, the discourse ends with that same "requirement" motif, reminding the reader/auditor that the invitation "requires that the invited person labor and be burdened in the more profound sense" (CD, 264). Harkening back to the "longing" theme of the first discourse, here Kierkegaard identifies this "laboring" with the longing for God, a painful and arduous longing that must be born silently and patiently in a creaturely world that cannot satisfy it. Correspondingly, the "heavy burden" in the passage is identified with the consciousness of sin. The "requirement" implicit in the invitation is therefore both the cultivation of patience and of repentance. Repentance is such an absolutely essential requirement that only a genuine penitent can even begin to understand the rest promised in the invitation. Repentance is a necessary prerequisite for resting in the promised forgiveness of sins. As Kierkegaard insists, the sighs of repentance should be diligently cultivated by the earnest individual. Patience and repentance are presented as virtues that the individual can nurture through repeated practice.

In the **third** discourse, Kierkegaard continues the dominantly imperative thrust, insisting that individuals should seize the offer of grace this very day. Of course, he makes it clear that God is the agent who gives the "time of grace," and in fact gives it constantly every day. But although God is the source of grace, the initiator of reconciliation, it is incumbent upon individuals to "pay attention to this phrase (the time of grace),"and to "be gripped by it" (CD, 268). The precious offer of grace should be received "in holy resolution." It demands a "profound change and a decision" (CD, 268). Continuing the focus on human volition, Kierkegaard observes that those present at the communion service have "resolved this day to seek reconciliation with you" (CD, 269). Similarly, he observes that because this communion service is not being held on a holy day, those present must have made a deliberate decision to come to the altar (CD, 270); their attendance is at least partially the fruit of their own volition. All this talk of previous responsible decisions sets the stage for an exhortation to realize that the Christ encountered at the altar will continue in fellowship with the individual, if the individual follows him. Kierkegaard explains that "where he is, there is the Communion table — and when you follow him, he accompanies you" (CD, 273). Christ's continuing fellowship seems to be contingent upon the individual's activity of "following." As with a literal altar, we are expected to bring an offering pleasing to God, in this case the spiritual offering of being reconciled with our enemies.

Kierkegaard's emphasis of the need for an appropriate human response continues with his suggestion that the individual's whole life should be presented as an offering. The imperative mood is reinforced by his admonition that "the task is to remain at the Communion table when you leave the Communion table" (CD, 274). Kierkegaard concludes by confessing his exhortatory intent, admitting that everything he has said was designed to concentrate attention on the communion table, so that the recollection of communion and the awareness of fellowship with Christ would become a permanent disposition. Here the longing and repentance elaborated in the first discourses can blossom through the appropriate participation in communion into a sense of being in the presence of Christ. It is the individual's responsibility to nurture this episodic sense of fellowship into a permanent consciousness of being in Christ's presence. This sense of ongoing fellowship with Christ is presented as yet another spiritually vital disposition that can be cultivated by the individual. This third discourse seems to suggest not only the *Formula of Concord's* theme of nonresistance to grace, but the stronger synergist position of active cooperation with grace.

Paradoxically, a shift occurs in the **fourth** discourse that seems to downplay human agency and responsibility, for the main theme is that individuals must not trust in their own moral and religious capabilities. However, this suspicion of one's own unaided abilities is treated as an attitude that can be nurtured by the individual. To foster this lack of trust in the self, Kierkegaard exhorts the reader/ auditor to actively remember Jesus' agony and suffering. The individual must recall that Christ's agony was caused by his heinous betrayal by the entire human race, including the individual's own self. Kierkegaard dwells on the alarming thought that if the addressee of the discourse had been present at Jesus' trial, the addressee would have acquiesced to the mob's clamoring for crucifixion. Therefore, every individual has betrayed Christ and made his sacrifice for the forgiveness of sins necessary. Kierkegaard encourages the reader/ auditor to vividly imagine him or herself as being present at the crucifixion as an accomplice (CD, 278). Speaking in the first person in order to dramatize his point, Kierkegaard exemplifies the appropriate resolution, saying "From this moment I will no longer believe in myself; I will not let myself be deceived as if I were better because I was not tried as were those contemporaries" (CD, 280). It is significant that the subject of these actions is "I." These resolutions are inward intentional activities that all persons can and should engage in. Kierkegaard's concluding exclamation that blessed is the one who is prepared for communion reveals that the purpose of the discourse has been to encourage individuals to actively prepare themselves for the reception of the sacrament. As the synergists had vehemently maintained, the cultivation of self-suspicion is a vital component of that preparation for which the individual can assume responsibility.

In the **fifth** discourse, attention to responsible human agency is recessive but nevertheless present. Although the main focus is on the faithfulness of Christ rather than on the fidelity of the believer, trust in Christ's faithfulness is presented as a virtue that can be developed through individual effort. Significantly, the discourse begins with attention to the ominous warning in II Timothy 2:12-13 that if we deny Christ he will deny us. Although the discourse is addressed to those who presumably have not denied Christ, an assumption based on their attendance at a nonobligatory communion service, the discourse nevertheless partially functions as a warning to avoid the denial of Christ, as well as unfaithfulness. Kierkegaard cautions that we must not "subtract the rigorousness from the leniency," and "not subtract from the Gospel the Law that is in it," because it is spiritually beneficial to recollect the warning (CD, 283). Although initially the monitory words seem to be addressed only to a certain class of persons, those who deny Christ, as Kierkegaard continues it becomes clear that they apply more broadly to the sinful aspect of all believers. The "terrifying thought," the possibility of being denied by Christ, does pertain to all Christians without exception (CD, 283). As the discourse develops, the feared denial of Christ is identified with spurning Christ's faithfulness and taking it in vain. To deny Christ is to rebel and harden oneself against Christ's faithfulness (CD, 285). Continuing this theme, the discourse concludes with an admonition about the dangers of enclosing oneself in one's own anxiety and guilt. In the light of the previous exposition, these words function as a warning against despairing of the possibility of forgiveness and doubting the reliability of Christ's forgiveness. Such despair is a vice that the individual should strive to avoid and trust is a virtue that should be cultivated. This exhortation to trust Christ complements the previous discourse's encouragement of mistrust of one's own moral and religious capabilities. Once again in a seemingly synergist fashion the individual is admonished to engage in the active cultivation of the religious dispositions appropriate to communion.

The **sixth** discourse, while concentrating on the power of God's forgiveness, also contains an implicit call to religious self-development. The opening prayer introduces the crucial theme of the need to be grateful and to praise God for the incomprehensible compassion exhibited in the forgiveness of sins. First Kierkegaard reminds the audience that they should condemn themselves with a heart overflowing with unfeigned repentance. After having accentuated the extent of human guilt and the virulence with which the heart should condemn itself, Kierkegaard encourages an appreciation of the stunning magnitude of God's mercy. The depth of human depravity is stressed in order to highlight the height of God's mercy. Whereas God's awesome creativity revealed in nature requires a response of astonishment and adoration, the vastness of God's mercy should be received by faith. Kierkegaard concludes, "Let us not deceive ourselves, let us not lie to ourselves, and let us not, which amounts to the same thing, deprecate God's greatness by wanting to make ourselves out to be better than we are, less guilty, or by naming our guilt with more frivolous names . . . " (CD, 295). This emphatic admonition, replete with the repetition of "let us," leads to the further imperative to accept the offered comfort of the forgiveness of sins, and to avoid the despairing conclusion that one's sins are unforgivable. Here the imperative, in this case a dialectic one, involves the cultivation of a sense of guilt in order to increase the sense of gratitude

The **seventh** discourse exhibits the least amount of attention to human agency, focusing instead on the constancy and reliability of God's activity of blessing. Nevertheless, even in this most theocentric context an imperative intrudes. Kierkegaard warns that one must not "bear the terrible responsibility" of spurning God's blessing and forcing Christ's departure (CD, 296). Here, at the very least, the resistibility of grace, as affirmed by *The Formula of Concord*, seems to be implied. Moreover, it is incumbent upon us humans not only to serve God but also to implore God's blessing of that intended service. Conversely, we should refrain from beseeching God to bless our self-aggrandizing projects aimed at worldly success. Here the ongoing Christian life that issues from communion with Christ involves the cultivation of dispositions of commitment and reliance on God's blessing.

We have seen that all of these discourses, to varying degrees, involve an encouragement to cultivate some set of dispositions appropriate for participation in communion. Moreover, a progressive movement in the development of these dispositions is evident from one discourse to the next. In the first discourse we must cultivate, and certainly not resist, the longing for reconciliation that the Holy Spirit awakens in us. In the second discourse we must accept the arduous task of laboring in a world that can never satisfy our longings and nurture anguished remorse over our sinfulness. In the third discourse we must develop the longing and repentance of the first two discourses into a settled, enduring willingness to grasp the offered grace of God and to offer one's life daily to God. The next three discourses qualify this movement from longing through repentance to the acceptance of grace, dealing with problematic issues that arise along the way. In the fourth discourse, we must foster a mistrust of our own capacities as a necessary component of our repentance. In the fifth discourse we must complement this mistrust of ourselves with a trust in the power of God's mercy. In the sixth discourse we must further develop this trust in the power of God's mercy to the point where it can overcome our most extreme tendencies toward self-condemnation. In the seventh discourse we must add to our on-going commitment to serve God (a theme introduced in the third essay) a willingness to recognize that all our efforts to serve God stand in need of God's continuing blessing, and to be confident that God's blessing is available. In all of these instances, Kierkegaard's rhetorical efforts to motivate the individual's passionate efforts imply that the recommended virtues are dispositions that can be cultivated through the individual's own efforts. In light of this, these exhortatory purposes would seem to indicate that Kierkegaard's natural theological allies would be the synergists of the sixteenth century.

The "Monergist" Pole of Efficacious Divine Agency

The call to the active cultivation of the virtues requisite for communion is just one dimension of these discourses. A countervailing theme is evident in each of them, a theme that downplays the power of human agency. In different ways each of the discourses draws attention to the activity of God that precedes, supports, supplements, overwhelms, and sometimes utterly displaces all human exertions. In some of the discourses the efficacy of human action is merely qualified, while in others it is relegated to a subordinate status by the potency of Christ's reconciling work, while in some it is virtually negated by the concentration on the power of God. As will become evident, the succession of discourses exhibits an increasing tendency to maximize the power of God and to minimize the contributions of human agency to the process of redemption. We shall now examine the progressive escalation and elaboration of this apparent "monergist" motif from discourse to discourse.

In the **first** discourse, as we have seen, the imperative note is the strongest, overshadowing attention to God's activity. Nevertheless, even here reliance upon human agency is strictly qualified. In spite of the pervasive and insistent imperative to cultivate the longing for fellowship with Christ, the discourse repeatedly reminds the hearer/auditor that the very presence of the longing in the soul is not due at all to the individual's own spiritual exertions. The prayer introducing the discourse begins with the reminder that one cannot give oneself the longing for communion with Christ; such a mysterious yearning is entirely the gift of the Spirit. Similarly, the expository section commences with the caveat that "The wind blows where it will; you are aware of its sloughing, but no one knows whence it comes or wither it goes. So also with longing . . . " (CD, 253). At the very end of the discourse, after encouraging the reader/hearer to cultivate the longing by meditating upon life's vanities and sin, Kierkegaard observes that sin has the "peculiar power" to impede the proper development of the longing and the concomitant renunciation of the worldly vanities. This remark, relatively undeveloped, introduces the possibility that the quest for religious earnestness is not entirely within the individual's power. At the very least, the human cultivation of Christian virtues requires the prior act of God in freely instilling the basic longing for communion, and requires the continuing help of God to combat sin's perduring impediment to growth. Here divine agency is treated both as an absolute precondition and as a necessary aid for human agency. Of course, these qualifications by themselves hardly signify a full-blown monergism, but they do at least introduce a trajectory that points away from Strigel's valorization of the human will's capacity to contribute significantly to the workings of grace.

Although the **second** discourse emphasizes the requirement implicit in the invitation to come to Christ, another motif is discernible. Half way through the discourse the focus shifts to Christ's promise "I will give you rest for your soul" (CD, 265). At this point

Kierkegaard concentrates on the reliability of the promised rest from agonized self-condemnation, a reliability based exclusively on the fact that atonement has been made by Christ. The reliability of this promise is exclusively a function of the identity and work of Jesus Christ the inviter. Accordingly, Kierkegaard's concluding imagery accentuates not the spiritual exertions of the penitent but rather the open and welcoming arms of Jesus. One can expect rest, mercy, and compassion in the midst of sorrow, temptation, and moral failure because Christ's reconciling act possesses extraordinary power. Here the reader/auditor is reminded that the very availability of restful reconciliation cannot in any way be construed as the individual's own accomplishment. Very slowly and subtly in the succession of discourses themes associated with the monergists are being introduced and emphasized.

Although the **third** discourse stresses the imperative to hear, know, and follow Jesus, as the exposition develops the attention shifts away from the communicant's knowing of Jesus to the fact that Jesus knows the communicant. As this theme of Jesus' knowledge of his sheep intensifies, preconditions for being known by Jesus drop out of the picture (CD, 273). The power of Jesus' knowledge of his sheep is foregrounded while the activity of the sheep recedes into the background. Increasingly the efficacious agency is ascribed only to Christ, as is evident in Kierkegaard's claim that "in the spiritual sense the Communion table is there only if you are known there by him" (CD, 273). The rhetorical focus falls on Jesus' direct and thorough knowing of individuals, not as members of a crowd or any sort of collectivity, but as specific persons. The specificity and intensity of Jesus' knowing is the exclusive source of the comfort for the Good Shepherd's sheep. Here, in a manner that any monergist would applaud, the initial imperative to hear and know is gradually displaced by the potency of God's action through Christ.

In the **fourth** discourse the rhetoric of divine agency gains the ascendancy. Although the discourse encourages the active recognition of one's own moral incapacity as a requisite for communion, the incapacity is emphasized so much that the possibility of cultivating any spiritually healthy disposition is thrown into question. This incapacity motif is so central that it dominates the opening prayer (CD, 275). Not only can we not achieve moral rectitude through our own efforts, but we cannot even maintain by our own power our own repentance. The opening prayer insists that God must be active in recalling our sin, our complicity in Jesus' betrayal and death. Although we are exhorted to remember our guilt, the prayer quickly adds that we will only fail to do this without God's active intervention. By the end of the prayer, God is thanked for reminding us of our sin, a recollection for which we can take no credit. Kierkegaard exclaims, "Not even in this dare we trust in our own strength" (CD, 275). Although active verbs suggesting holding fast to Christ are used, the sinfulness of the individual is accentuated to the point that by the end of the essay the individual is portrayed as so passive that the "Crucified One" can be said to move a person irresistibly (by his sacrifice). According to Kierkegaard, Christ "performs love's miracle, so that, without doing anything — by suffering he moves everyone who has a heart" (CD, 280). The propelling force in the discourse shifts from the individual who should cling to Christ, to Christ who irresistibly moves the individual. This transition from attention to human agency to a concentration on divine agency is appropriate in this context, given the fact that the individual had been issued the paradoxical exhortation to actively cultivate a sense of inability to cultivate spiritual health.

Although the **fifth** discourse does exhort the communicant to remain faithful to Christ, its main purpose is to underscore the faithfulness of Christ to the communicant. In the light of Christ's faithfulness to us in spite of our manifest unfaithfulness, our proper response should be to rejoice and be silent. Here we can do nothing but receive the gift of God's continuing benevolence. The increasing emphasis of divine agency is evident in Kierkegaard's discussion of Christ's faithfulness to us even in the midst of episodes that appear to be tests of our character. Even when we talk about God testing us, we must remember that it is God who is sustaining us through the test. To illustrate this, Kierkegaard employs the example of a child who thinks that it is walking alone although the mother is holding on to it from behind (see also JFY, 185). According to Kierkegaard, when God seems to test us with one hand, God is actually holding us up, supporting us through the test, with the other. We do not weather spiritual trials through our own intrinsic strength. Kierkegaard observes, "Thus we truly do not presume to ask that you, our Teacher and Savior, should apply a test to our faithfulness to you, because we very well know that in the moment of the ordeal you yourself must hold on to us, we know very well that *fundamentally* we are faithless and that at every moment and *fundamentally* it is you who are holding on to us" (CD, 286). We are not just slightly impaired in our ability to be faithful but rather are fundamentally faithless. This severe critique is not proffered to exacerbate our feelings of guilt, but to enable us lay aside the oppressive burden of culpability and responsibility. The discourse suggests that we cannot even repent properly by our own powers, for no one truly knows the extent or nature of one's own hidden faults. Our faltering self-examination and superficial repentance cannot be trusted and cannot serve as the basis for our spiritual rest. We are not justified by the strength and authenticity of our own remorse, but only by Christ's constant and reliable loving character. Only Christ's agency should be trusted, not our own. In an manner that Illyricus would have approved, here the individual's ability to cultivate the dispositions necessary for communion is minimized in order to make room for trust in the potency of God's mercy.

In the **sixth** discourse the agency of God receives even more attention. Although Kierkegaard admits that the individual should indeed feel guilty, the magnitude of that guilt is mentioned only in order to emphasize the infinitely greater power of God. God's agency is more potent than anything that the individual can possibly do. More specifically, God's forgiveness is greater than our own ability to excite tormenting feelings of guilt. Here the attainment of a high degree of guilt-consciousness is not treated as a meritorious achievement, but rather as a spiritual problem that must be overcome by reliance upon God's love. In this context Kierkegaard describes divine and human potencies as related by an inverse dialectic.[9] He observes, "God and the human being resemble each other only inversely" (CD, 292).We draw closer to God, not by lifting up our hearts, but by casting them down. Most significantly, a heart that condemns itself is not as deep as God's mercy is high. The discourse's conclusion is that the power of God's love is more potent than the power of the individual's despair, anxiety, and self-condem-

---

[9]For a broader account of other instances of this inverse dialectic in Kierkegaard, see Sylvia Walsh, *Living Christianly: Kierkegaard's Dialectic of Christian Existence* (University Park: Pennsylvania State University Press, 2005).

nation. All the discourse's rhetorical strategies combine to shift the reader/auditor's focus away from confidence in the efficacy of human repentance to utter reliance upon God's gracious acts.

The emphasis of God's loving activity reaches its culmination in the **seventh** discourse. The intensive focus on divine agency is signaled by the opening prayer for God's blessing. The importance of this theme of "blessing" is evident in the fact that it points to the conclusion of the communion service and the subsequent Christian life that should flow from the service. Kierkegaard describes this blessing as being bestowed through the departure of Christ, in this case a metaphor for the ending of the communion service. The blessing, then, is the ultimate purpose of the Eucharistic rite. Accordingly, in this discourse the need for God's active blessing in all things takes center stage. "Blessing" here suggests God's active acceptance and support of human activity, without which human activity would have no significance and no efficacy. Kierkegaard emphatically maintains that without God's act of blessing the communion service would be nothing at all. The discourse's concentration on God's act of blessing is extended beyond the communion service itself to embrace all activities constitutive of the Christian life. For Kierkegaard the good news is that Christ never parts from us without blessing us; in fact, he remains with us as the continuing blessing. The need for God's blessing of our lives and our endeavors is so critical that Kierkegaard insists that we are able to do nothing unless God blesses it. God must bless all our intentions and actions in order for them to possess any worth or power. Even our most seemingly genuine efforts to serve God are entirely futile without God's blessing. In fact, the more a faithful person intends a godly undertaking, the more that person must realize that the undertaking is pointless unless God blesses it. God must even bless the individual's praying so that it might be right praying.

As the discourse progresses it becomes clearer that God's blessing is not merely a bit of divine assistance supplementing an already potent human initiative. Kierkegaard claims that "the more you become involved with God, the more it will become clear how little you are capable of doing" (CD, 298). The greater the requirement, the more clear it should become that the individual is capable of nothing. In the same vein he continues, "If you become involved with him (God) with all your mind and with all your strength, then it will be entirely clear that you yourself are capable of doing nothing at all, and it will be all the more clear that you are entirely in need of the blessing" (CD, 298). Especially at the communion table penitents must realize that they are utterly incapable of contributing anything to their spiritual health. Before God we are nothing and are entirely and abjectly in need, particularly in regard to redemption. Kierkegaard reminds that someone else has saved the individual; human agency had nothing to do with it. Kierkegaard even asserts, "If at the Communion table you want to be capable of the least little thing yourself, even to merely step forward yourself, you confuse everything . . . "(CD, 299). He sternly warns, "You cannot be Christ's coworker in connection with the reconciliation, not in the remotest way" (CD, 299). At this point the rhetoric points most blatantly in a monergist direction. The individual cannot even cultivate or hold fast to the thought of the individual's own unworthiness. Kierkegaard concludes, "Alas, no, you are capable of nothing, not even of holding your soul by yourself at the peak of consciousness that you stand totally in need of grace and the blessing" (CD, 300). Most significantly, the series of discourses ends as a confession of extreme incapacity. The preparation for grace and the implications of synergism with which the series began seems to be entirely beyond the individual's own powers. Appropriately, the final discourse concludes with no hint of human agency but with a vision of Christ who "stretches out his arms at the Communion table" (CD, 300).

As we have seen, all of these discourses involve a shift away from a focus on human agency to a focus on divine agency. Moreover, progression is evident in the succession of discourses in which divine agency receives increasing emphasis. In the first discourse divine agency serves simply as a necessary precondition for responsible human agency; God's prior activity of stirring up a longing that no one can awaken through one's own efforts is required as the basis for the subsequent cultivation of Christian virtues. In the second discourse the requirement to cultivate patience and penitence in oneself is eventually upstaged by the power of God's promise that maintains these virtues; God's action becomes more important than human efforts. In the third discourse the true repentance that one should nurture in oneself is found to be rooted in the prior reality of being known by Jesus, shifting attention even more to God's initiative. In the fourth discourse human agency is severely qualified by the claim that the individual cannot even hold fast to Christ or repent by herself. In the fifth discourse the ostensibly purely human act of remaining faithful in the midst of trials and tests is seen as the fruit of the reality that one is being upheld by God. In the sixth discourse the individual's efforts to contribute to salvation through the potency of the individual's own guilt-consciousness are shown to be inadequate as God's forgiveness proves to be stronger than guilt; it is God's forgiveness and not the power of one's own repentance that saves a person. In the seventh discourse this dynamic of shifting attention from human to divine agency reaches its culmination. Here the individual can do nothing at all to assist in the salvation process or prepare for it; one cannot even maintain the consciousness of sin and neediness by oneself. By the end of the series human agency can take credit for absolutely nothing.

Conclusion: Beyond the Synergism/Monergism Impasse

Taken as a whole, the discourses first exhort the reader/auditor to do everything possible to prepare for communion with Christ, and then remind the reader/auditor that she can do nothing at all to prepare for communion and must take credit for nothing. Ostensibly it seems that the exhortation that Kierkegaard offers with his right hand is then retracted by the confession of incapacity in his left. Considered in the light of the history of Lutheran theology, it seems that he begins the discourses sounding like a synergist, suggesting a cooperation of the human will with God's grace, and ends them sounding like a monergist, suggesting that all the relevant agency is God's. This apparent contradiction or at least serious tension has puzzled Kierkegaard commentators. Some have attempted to situate him in classic theological theories of the interaction of divine and human agency, identifying him a standard "Arminian"[10] or even as

---

[10]See, e.g., Timothy Jackson, "Arminian Edification: Kierkegaard on Grace and Free Will," in *The Cambridge Companion to Kierkegaard*, ed. Alastair Hannay and Gordon Marino (Cambridge: Cambridge University Press, 1998) 235-56.

a proponent of some view of the will's cooperation with grace.[11] Against these views, I am arguing that Kierkegaard does not develop or even suggest any metaphysics of divine and human agency at all. Instead, he employs language about human action and about God's action differently in different contexts in order to pursue two different purposes. For one purpose he must emphasize human responsibility; for the other purpose he must exclusively stress God's efficacious activity.

The differentiation of Kierkegaard's rhetorical purposes is explicitly articulated by him in the crucial fifth discourse. Reflecting on the mysterious wording of II Timothy 2:12-13, "If we deny (Christ), he also will deny us; if we are faithless, he still remains faithful; he cannot deny himself," Kierkegaard asks if there is a contradiction between maintaining that Christ will deny us if we deny him, and also claiming that Christ will be faithful to us even if we are faithless to him. The first clause seems to ascribe a crucial role in redemption to human agency, at least to the human act of denying or not denying Christ. It would seem that human activity can either frustrate or promote God's redemptive purpose. However, the second clause seems to ascribe all saving power to God quite independently of any human action. In fact, God's faithfulness can triumph over the hostile human response of infidelity. Distinguishing "denying Christ" and being "unfaithful to Christ," Kierkegaard resolves the dilemma by proposing that the two clauses are directed to different audiences, the first to those who "deny" and spurn God's offer of fellowship, and the second to those who positively respond to that offer but fail to be faithful. However, this distinction of two classes of persons is immediately and severely qualified. Kierkegaard admits that both the warning about denying Christ and the comfort concerning God's faithfulness to the unfaithful are addressed to the same audience, to those who have not overtly denied Christ, in other words, to those who are coming for communion. Kierkegaard reminds the communicants that "it is beneficial that the rigorous words are brought to recollection" (CD, 283). The words of warning and the words of comfort should be "heard simultane-

---

[11]See Arnold Come, *Kierkegaard as Theologian: Recovering My Self* (Montreal and Kingston: McGill-Queen's University Press, 1997) 286-88.

ously, just as they inseparably belong together so that we at no time separate what God has joined together in Christ, neither add anything nor subtract anything, do not subtract from the Gospel the Law that is in it" (CD, 283). The audience for both the "rigor" and the "leniency" is the very people who have come to receive communion.

Kierkegaard clarifies the apparent tension between "rigor" and "leniency" by explaining that the two assertions in II Timothy serve different purposes. The purpose of the first clause is to promote fear and trembling, to motivate the individual to take seriously the possibility of perdition and appreciate the need for salvation. The purpose of the second clause is to awaken trust and confidence so that the individual can "take comfort in the Gospel's gentle word" (CD, 283). Of course the comfort will only be appreciated if the fear and trembling have been awakened. The elicitation of fear and trembling requires a concentration on human responsibility and therefore on human agency, while the evocation of trust and confidence requires a focus on God's unconditionally reliable and triumphant compassion, and therefore on divine agency.

Kierkegaard's seeming flip-flop between the language of human responsibility and the language of divine sovereign action is a function of these different purposes. When it is time to awaken passionate self-concern and urge individuals to take their religious lives with utter seriousness, Kierkegaard uses the language of human responsibility typical of the synergists. Should we struggle to prepare ourselves for communion with Christ? Should we cultivate the yearning for God, the pain of repentance, and the desire to serve God? Kierkegaard answers with a resounding affirmative. However, when it is time to encourage confidence in reconciliation and hope for salvation, Kierkegaard employs the language of exclusive divine agency typical of the monergists. Should we trust in our own powers and spiritual achievements? Should we take credit for preparing ourselves for fellowship with Christ or for cooperating with God's redemptive program? Here Kierkegaard answers with a resounding negative.

By striking both these notes, Kierkegaard was reflecting the basic pastoral intentions of *The Formula of Concord*. It too had wanted to encourage individuals to struggle and aspire to embrace the Christian life, a synergist concern, while also wanting to nurture resilient trust in the reliable power of God's compassion rather than in the unreliable potency of the individual's own faith, a monergist concern. However, Kierkegaard differs from *The Formula* and the orthodox Lutheran theologians who exposited it in one crucial regard: he refuses to speculate about the metaphysics of the interaction of divine and human agencies. He develops no systematic theory of divine/human agency and generally avoids language that would suggest any such theory. He does not speculate about such issues as the difference between consenting to God's grace and merely not resisting God's grace, a theoretic distinction that had been so critical for the theologians of *The Formula of Concord*. He does not worry about explaining how God's will motivates human volition, whether it urges, compels, elicits, or overrides. He does not develop a schema to relate divine and human agencies as primary and secondary modes of causality, nor does he systematically contrast them as competing potencies. Rather than developing a metaphysics of agency, Kierkegaard clarifies the meaning of doctrinal concepts by exhibiting their use in the Christian life. Put simply, he clarifies the meaning of "human responsibility" language by showing how, when used in the proper context for the proper purpose, it fosters the earnestness that the Christian life requires. He then clarifies the meaning of "efficacious grace" language by showing how, when used in the proper context for the proper purpose, it can foster confidence and trust in God's mercy. One must work out one's salvation with fear and trembling, and, in the process, take no credit for salvation and trust only in God, not in the intensity of one's *angst*. The integration of the "responsibility" theme and the "trust in God's grace alone" theme occurs not through the auspices of a theory of divine human/ agency, but through the practical wisdom of discerning when to emphasize the need for earnestness and when to emphasize comfort and confidence. The seeming theoretic conundrum about divine and human agencies is dissolved by resituating the issue in the rhythms of the Christian life.

11

Kierkegaard's Understanding of the Eucharist in Christian Discourses, Part Four

David R. Law

Kierkegaard never wrote a systematic theology of the sacraments. His comments on baptism and the Eucharist tend to be made during discussions of other issues. This does not mean, however, that Kierkegaard does not take a stand on questions of sacramental theology. It is possible on the basis of the scattered remarks in his works and in his journal entries to arrive at a relatively clear view of his understanding of baptism.[1] Similarly, it is possible on the basis of Kierkegaard's comments to arrive at some understanding of how he viewed the Eucharist.[2]

---

[1]For a discussion of Kierkegaard's understanding of baptism, see Vernard Eller, *Kierkegaard and Radical Discipleship: A New Perspective* (Princeton NJ: Princeton University Press, 1968) 309-19; W. von Kloeden, "Die Taufe", in Niels Thulstrup and Marie Mikulová Thulstrup, eds., *Theological Concepts in Kierkegaard*, Bibliotheca Kierkegaardiana 5 (Copenhagen: C. A. Reitzels Boghandel A/S, 1980) 228-40; David Law, "Kierkegaard on Baptism", in *Theology* 91/740 (March 1988): 114-22.

[2]Kierkegaard employs a variety of terms to describe the Eucharist: *Nadver* (CD, 251, 252, 253, 261), *det hellige Nadvere* (CD, 252), *Nadverens hellige Maaltid* (CD, 251), *Maaltid* (CD, 261), *det hellige Maaltid* (CD, 255, 283), *Naade-Maaltid* (CD, 296). He also employs such circumlocutions as *Herrens Bord* (CD, 251) and *Herrens Alter* (CD, 270). The phrase Kierkegaard most frequently uses to describe the Eucharist, however, is *at gaae til Alters* (CD, 253, 261, 269, 271,273, 274, 276, 287, 298). Unfortunately, Hong and Hong have been inconsistent in translating Kierkegaard's terms, especially the phrase *at gaae til Alters*, which they have translated in a variety of ways: "receive Holy Communion" (CD, 253, 271, 273, 287, 298), "went (up) to the Lord's table" (CD, 261, 273, 276), "going to Holy Communion" (CD, 269), "going to Communion" (CD, 274), "go to the altar" (CD, 273, 287). This emphasis on *receiving* Communion, which is not prominent in *Christian Discourses*, part four, rather than following Kierkegaard's emphasis on the believer's *going* to the altar, hampers the interpreter of Kierkegaard's understanding of the Eucharist. Terms such as "going to the altar" and "receiving Communion" are not synonymous but express important distinctions in the divine drama that is the Eucharist. Much of Kierkegaard's discussion is concerned with the thoughts and preparations of the

That Kierkegaard was well acquainted with the Eucharistic liturgy is indicated by a number of factors. Niels-Jørgen Cappelørn has shown in a detailed study that Kierkegaard followed the general custom of receiving communion two or three times a year.[3] We know from the *Auktionsprotokol over Søren Kierkegaards Bogsamling* that Kierkegaard owned a copy of the 1830 edition of *Forordnet Alter-Bog for Danmark*, the altar book prescribed for use in the worship of the Danish Church.[4] We also know from the *Auktionsprotokol* that Kierkegaard seems to have made considerable use of the altar book, for his copy contains numerous notes in Kierkegaard's own handwriting.[5] Kierkegaard himself regularly attended the communion service, especially on Fridays, and on three occasions preached at the Friday communion service.[6] Although in the last years of his

---

believer as he or she *approaches* the altar. He says relatively little about the action of *receiving* the body and blood of the Lord Jesus Christ. Hong and Hong's translation obscures this important distinction. The situation is further complicated by the variety of different ways in which Hong and Hong translate *Alter*. Their preferred translation is "Communion table," but this would more accurately render *Nadverbord* than *Alter*. This choice of translation presumably reflects the terminology of Hong and Hong's own denomination, but it is misleading when used to translate *Alter*, the most natural translation of which is surely "altar", a translation which Hong and Hong themselves adopt in CD, 267 and 274. In this paper we shall translate *at gaae til Alters* and its variants as "to go to the altar" and shall render *Alter* as "altar". As a general umbrella term to denote the sacred meal in which the Christian believer participates at the Lord's table, we shall employ the term "Eucharist", which has become a terminus technicus in liturgics for the Lord's Supper, for which reason we shall employ it here.

[3]Niels Jørgen Cappelørn, "Die ursprüngliche Unterbrechung: Søren Kierkegaard beim Abendmahl im Freitagsgottesdienst der Kopenhagener Frauen Kirche", trans. Krista-Maria Deuser, in Niels Jørgen Cappelørn and Hermann Deuser, eds., *Kierkegaard Studies Yearbook 1996* (Berlin, New York: Walter de Gruyter, 1996) 315-88; esp. 343-55. "Søren Kierkegaard at Friday Communion in the Church of Our Lady," translated by K. Brian Söderquist, in Robert L. Perkins, ed., *International Kierkegaard Commentary: Without Authority* 255-94; 258-64.

[4]H. P. Rohde, ed., *Auktionsprotokol over Søren Kierkegaards Bogsamling* (Copenhagen: The Royal Library, 1967) ASKB 381. *Forordnet Alter-Bog for Danmark* (Copenhagen: Gyldendalske Boghandlings Forlag, 1830). Pp. 252-55 contain the Eucharistic liturgy.

[5]For a study of Kierkegaard's use of the altar book, see Skat Arildsen, "Kierkegaard og *Forordnet Alter-Bog for Danmark*," in *Kierkegaardiana*, vol. XI (1980), 120-31.

[6]There is some dispute concerning whether Kierkegaard preached during the communion service itself or at the confessionary that preceded the service. For a

life Kierkegaard ceased attending the communion service because of his increasing disillusionment with the state church, the Eucharist always remained important to Kierkegaard. Thulstrup points out that confession, absolution, and the Eucharist were the only ecclesial actions which Kierkegaard continued throughout his life to regard as holy actions, and which were spared his otherwise merciless critique of the church.[7] Similarly, Skjoldager emphasizes that the Eucharist was of enormous and central importance for Kierkegaard. It was a "resting point for his faith," for it "proclaimed to him God's love, which [God] directs at all human beings without exception."[8]

It is of course true that despite his attachment to the communion service Kierkegaard nowhere provides a full Eucharistic theology.[9] It was not his concern to construct any sort of theology in the conventional sense, nor was he narrowly denominational in his thinking. Kierkegaard's focus was first and foremost on the single individual and his or her relationship with God, and theological issues entered his discussion only in so far as they were relevant to this more fundamental question.

This focus on the individual human being's relationship with God does not mean, however, that Kierkegaard lacked his own theological perspective. On the contrary, his theology is implicit in the way he unfolds the nature of the individual's God-relationship. Furthermore, Kierkegaard was not living in a theological vacuum and he took a stand on a variety of different theological issues of

discussion of this issue see Cappelørn, "Die ursprüngliche Unterbrechung," 315-17.

[7]Niels Thulstrup, *Kierkegaard og kirken in Danmark* (Copenhagen: C. A. Reitzels Forlag A/S, 1985) 37.

[8]Emanuel Skjoldager, *Den egentlige Kierkegaard: Søren Kierkegaards syn på kirken og de kirkelige handlinger* (Copenhagen: C. A. Reitzels Forlag A/S, 1982) 115.

[9]Studies of Kierkegaard's view of the Eucharist can be found in Eller, *Kierkegaard and Radical Discipleship*, 325-28; Anna Paulsen, "Communion", in Thulstrup and Thulstrup, eds., *Theological Concepts in Kierkegaard*, 254-57; Michael Plekon, "Kierkegaard and the Eucharist", *Studia Liturgica*, 22 (1992): 214-36; Skjoldager, *Den egentlige Kierkegaard*, 99-116. For the historical background and the shape of the Eucharistic liturgy in use in Kierkegaard's day, see Thulstrup, *Kierkegaard og kirken i Danmark*, 36-46, 84-85, 198-202. Cappelørn, , "Die ursprüngliche Unterbrechung," 315-88; "Søren Kierkegaard til altergang om fredagen i Vor Frue Kirke," in *Dansk Teologisk Tidsskrift* 63 (2000): 1-35; "Kierkegaard at Friday Communion in the Church of Our Lady," 255-93.

concern to the more conventional theologian. This is arguably the case with the Eucharist. Although Kierkegaard never set himself the task of developing a fully elaborated Eucharistic theology, he nevertheless takes a stand on certain issues of Eucharistic theology. This stand is implicit in his comments about the Eucharist, which appear at various points in his writings.

One of Kierkegaard's more sustained treatments of the Eucharist appears in part four of *Christian Discourses*, "Discourses at the Communion on Fridays." It is of course true that these discourses are concerned with reflecting on what it means for the individual to come into Christ's presence at the altar and are not concerned with developing a coherent theory of the Eucharist. We thus find in *Christian Discourses* no overt discussion of the traditional issues that have troubled theologians concerning the Eucharist, namely, in what sense are the bread and wine the body and blood of Christ, how do the elements become Christ's body and blood, in what sense is Christ present in the elements, are the validity and efficacy of the Eucharist dependent or independent of the worthiness of the minister and/or recipient of the Eucharist? The fact that Kierkegaard does not deal overtly with such questions, however, does not mean that he does not have a view on these matters. His understanding of the Eucharist and the theological issues it raises is arguably implicit in his reflections on how the believer should prepare himself or herself to receive communion. It is my intention in this essay to attempt to bring to the surface some of Kierkegaard's implicit theological assumptions by treating him as if he were a liturgical theologian concerned to address the traditional problems of Eucharistic theology. This essay will thus be organized around the themes that have long occupied theologians of the Eucharist, such as the nature of Christ's Eucharistic presence and the efficacy of the Eucharist.

Treating Kierkegaard as if he were concerned to resolve sacramental controversies is, of course, to a certain extent an artificial exercise, for Kierkegaard was neither a liturgist nor a systematic theologian. Nevertheless, viewing Kierkegaard's meditations on the Eucharist in *Christian Discourses*, part four, in the light of the questions asked by the sacramental theologian, may be an interesting way of shedding light on the distinctiveness of Kierkegaard's thinking concerning the Eucharist.

The Eucharist and Christian Discourses, Part Four

Christian Discourses as a whole is an exercise in Christian dialectic, and is concerned to explore the tension between promise and responsibility that constitutes Christian existence. This dialectic of promise and responsibility determines the four-part structure of the book. Parts one and three express the Christian ideal and show how far short of this ideal contemporary Christians have fallen. There is a sharpening of this ideal as the book progresses. Part one, entitled "The Cares of the Pagans," draws a contrast between the concerns and troubles of the pagans and the joy of the Christian. If Denmark were indeed a Christian country, Kierkegaard claims, then the cares of the pagans should be absent. The fact that such cares are all too evident indicates that, despite its claims to be Christian, Denmark is in reality a pagan country (CD, 11). Indeed, Kierkegaard complains that the Danes are worse than pagans: "Those in the pagan countries have not as yet been lifted up to Christianity; the pagans in Christendom have sunk below paganism. The former belong to the fallen race; the latter, after having been lifted up, have fallen once again and have fallen even lower" (CD, 12). Part three, which originally bore the subtitle "Christian Attack" (CD, 377), is even more polemical and marks the first stage in Kierkegaard's conflict with the established Church.[10] Parts two and four are concerned with the divine grace offered to human beings despite their failure to live up to the Christian ideal. This divine grace is God's forgiveness of sin. But this forgiveness, too, contains a dialectical element, for the gracious gift of God's forgiveness should spur human beings on to strive to realize the Christian ideal. Parts two and four constitute the counterparts to the condemnations of parts one and three. Part two is grace's answer to part one, while part four is the reply to part three. This means that parts one and two, and parts three and four can be treated respectively as two

---

[10]At this point Kierkegaard still hoped for an admission from Mynster that the Danish Church had grievously distorted Christianity (CD, 384-87, 405-406; JP, 1:376). Because of the polemical nature of part three, Kierkegaard removed the dedication to Bishop Mynster which he had originally intended to append to part four (CD, 384).

dialectical unities. This is a point Kierkegaard makes in a comment in his journals in which he describes part three as "a temple-cleansing celebration," which is then followed by "the quiet and most intimate of all worship services — the Communion service on Fridays" (JP, 6:6121; CD, 402).

As we shall see, one of the themes running through part four is the individual's worthy preparation for receiving communion. Part three can be regarded as setting the scene for this preparation. The discourses of part three are concerned with educating the reader into adopting the correct attitude when entering church. We should not seek comfort and security, but should enter God's house "to be awakened from sleep and to be pulled out of the spell" (CD, 165).

Like the other three parts of *Christian Discourses*, part four comprises seven discourses. Despite their theme being the communion, it is striking that only one of the discourses takes as its text a verse from the words of institution, namely the fourth discourse. The first three discourses take as their texts Lk. 22.15, Mt. 11.28, and Jn. 10.27 respectively, while the last three discourses are meditations on 2 Tim. 2.12-13, 1 Jn. 3.20, and Lk. 24.51. Of these six discourses only Lk. 22.15 has some connection with the Eucharistic liturgy, for it expresses Christ's desire to eat the Passover with his disciples before his suffering. The text, however, does not belong to Christ's words of institution of the Eucharist (CD, 251).

The only discourse which overtly deals with a passage taken from the words of institution is the fourth discourse, which takes as its text 1 Cor. 11.23, the verse which forms the opening line of the prayer with which the priest consecrates the bread and wine: "The Lord Jesus, on the night on which he was betrayed." The positioning of this discourse and its use of 1 Cor. 11.23 is significant. As the fourth of seven discourses, the discourse is situated at the *center* of part four of *Christian Discourses*. The centrality of this discourse is further indicated by the fact that it is the only one of the discourses to take as its text a verse from the Eucharistic liturgy. Kierkegaard meditates not on the Eucharist itself, however, but on the *betrayal* of Jesus, which forms the center, indeed the pivot on which not only the discourse but the whole of part four turns.

The reason for the centrality of this discourse in part four of *Christian Discourses* is that 1 Cor. 11.23 describes not a past but an *ongoing event*. As Kierkegaard puts it, Christ's "innocent sacrifice is not past even though the cup of suffering is empty, is not a bygone event although it is past, is not an event finished and done with although it was eighteen hundred years ago" (CD, 278). This is because it was not just a few individuals or even a whole generation who killed Christ, but *the entire human race*. Since we are all human beings, we who are living today are also "accomplices in a present event" (CD, 278). The significance of pronouncing 1 Cor. 11.23 at the beginning of the Eucharistic service is that this verse draws the congregation into the universal human act of betrayal of the Lord Jesus. The proclamation of the words "On the night on which he was betrayed" makes present the event to the congregation, and makes them accomplices in Judas's betrayal of Christ as well as in the other disciples' abandonment of Jesus. No one in the congregation, Kierkegaard warns, should forget the Apostle Peter, who is the "pitiful prototype" of all human beings' denial of Christ (CD, 278). Every one of the disciples betrayed Christ, and if anyone of us living today had been present at Christ's arrest, condemnation, and crucifixion we too would have betrayed him (CD, 279).

The central idea in part four of *Christian Discourses*, then, is the believer's becoming contemporaneous with Christ. But contemporaneity with Christ is not a comfortable event, for the first stage in becoming contemporaneous with him is to be drawn into the disciples' failure and thereby to be made radically conscious of human beings' sin. Christ does not leave us imprisoned in sin, however, and a second major theme of part four is the relationship the believer sustains to Christ the Redeemer at the Friday communion service. It is in exploring the nature of the believer's relationship to Christ in the context of the Friday service that Kierkegaard gives us some hints of his understanding of the purpose and efficacy of the Eucharist, and the manner in which Christ is present in the Eucharistic service.

The Purpose of the Eucharist
The Eucharist as Fellowship

A theme that runs through part four of *Christian Discourses* is the *fellowship* or *communion* (*Samfund*) with Christ which is affirmed in the Eucharistic service. In the first discourse Kierkegaard speaks of "the longing for fellowship with God through your Redeemer" as the means by which the individual prepares him or herself to receive the gift of divine grace (CD, 258, cf. 260). In the fourth discourse Kierkegaard states that believers approach the altar in order to renew their fellowship with Christ (CD, 276). Similarly, in the fifth discourse Kierkegaard writes that the Eucharistic service renews fellowship between the believer and the Savior (CD, 287). Finally, in the seventh discourse Kierkegaard writes that, "you go up to the altar in order to meet him, for whom you long more every time you are parted from him" (CD, 298).

Although Kierkegaard focuses primarily on the individual's communion with Christ at the altar, he is nevertheless conscious of the communal dimension of the Eucharistic service. It is in the way he develops his notion of communal fellowship that we can see one of the original features of his understanding of the Eucharist. This originality becomes apparent when we compare Kierkegaard's notion of fellowship with the conception of communal fellowship advanced by Paul in 1 Cor. 10.16-17: "The cup of blessing that we bless, is it not a *koinonia* [sharing, fellowship] in the blood of Christ? The bread that we break, is it not a *koinonia* in the body of Christ? Because there is one bread, we who are many are one body, for we all partake of the one bread" (I Cor. 10.16-17). In this passage Paul makes a clear connection between believers' participation in the Eucharist and their being members of the body of Christ. For Kierkegaard, however, the communal dimension of the Eucharist stems from the fact that *all* human beings have betrayed Christ. We live in a community of betrayers of Christ and for this very reason are in need of Christ's forgiveness not only as individuals but as a community.

The Eucharist as Meal
of Love, Forgiveness, and Reconciliation

The Eucharist is a meal of love and reconciliation (CD, 280), for at the altar the believer receives forgiveness of sins. To receive forgiveness of sins, the individual must first become aware of and acknowledge his or her sin. For Kierkegaard Christ both reveals sin and redeems human beings from sin. Christ's betrayal by human beings is itself a revelation of the sin of human beings and their need for a redeemer. In the fourth discourse Kierkegaard states that our betrayal of Christ is the most painful blow that we human beings can inflict upon love, "because for love there is nothing as blessed as faithfulness" (CD, 279). In seeing this love betrayed, "I have understood something about myself, that I also am a human being, and to be a human being is to be a sinful human being" (CD, 279).

Human beings' mistreatment of Christ makes clear their need for a redeemer. Kierkegaard writes: "The one whom the human race crucified was the Redeemer; as someone belonging to the human race, I, for this very reason feel the need for a redeemer — never has the need for a redeemer been clearer than when the human race crucified the Redeemer" (CD, 279).

Christ thus both reveals human beings' need for a redeemer and simultaneously is the redeemer. He offers human beings refuge from the guilt-consciousness they have incurred through their betrayal of their Lord. Christ himself addresses the human need for redemption by instituting the meal of reconciliation on the very night on which he was betrayed. This is not a meal offered to a select few, but to all. Because all human beings have betrayed Christ "all need to take part in the meal of reconciliation" (CD, 281).

The notion of forgiveness is also prominent in the sixth discourse, which takes 1 John 3.20 as its text: "even if our hearts condemn us, God is greater than our hearts." Those who are present at communion on Friday "are gathered here today to receive the forgiveness of sins and to appropriate anew reconciliation with [God] in Christ" (CD, 289). The sacrament is "the sign of God's greatness in showing mercy" (CD, 291). But this sign "is only *for faith*," for "God's greatness in showing mercy is a *mystery*, which must be believed" (CD, 291). For this reason God's mercy is a *revelation*, for it is not manifest to everyone, but only to those who have faith. God's greatness in showing mercy is thus, Kierkegaard writes, "first an occasion *for offense* and then is *for faith*" (CD, 291).

In short, the communion service is dialectical. It reveals and confirms the harsh reality of human sin while at the same time offering forgiveness of sins and reconciliation with God through his Son Jesus Christ.

The Eucharist as the Believer's Pledge of Faithfulness

In the fifth discourse Kierkegaard takes as his text 2 Tim. 2.12-13: "If we deny [him], he also will deny us; if we are faithless, he still remains faithful; he cannot deny himself" (CD, 282). Kierkegaard takes this as the basis for a meditation on the faithfulness of Christ and the faithlessness of human beings. Although human beings may be faithless, Christ is always faithful.

> This is why up there at the altar he stretches out his arms, he opens his arms to all; you see it on him—he does not deny himself. He does not deny himself, and neither does he deny you what you ask of him when you now renew your pledge of faithfulness to him. He is the same; he was and he remains faithful to you (CD, 288).

But why, Kierkegaard asks, do the members of the congregation not go straight to the altar? Why do they first make confession before renewing their pledge of faithfulness? The confession preceding the Eucharist, Kierkegaard notes, is prescribed by sacred tradition, but even if this were not the case, the devout listener would nevertheless "feel the need to go along this path to the altar" (CD, 287). The confession aims at unburdening the believer before he approaches the altar. Kierkegaard writes: "The confession does not want to burden you with the guilt of faithlessness; on the contrary, it wants to help you, through confession, to lay aside the burden. The confession does not want to make you confess; on the contrary it wants to unburden you through a confession; in the confessional there is no one who accuses you if you do not accuse yourself" (CD, 287). This public confession, however, is *individually* made. Only God knows what the individual has confessed.

The purpose of the Eucharist is to give believers the opportunity to renew their pledge of faithfulness (CD, 287), an act which first requires them to confess their sins, so that unburdened of their guilt of faithlessness they can approach the altar to receive Christ's blessing.

The Eucharist as Thanksgiving

Also present in Kierkegaard's understanding of the Eucharist is the notion of *thanksgiving*, though it is not prominent. In the fourth discourse the theme of thanksgiving appears in the opening prayer, in which Kierkegaard gives thanks to Christ for reminding us of his suffering and for giving us the opportunity to renew our fellowship with him at the Eucharistic service (CD, 275). In the fifth discourse Kierkegaard speaks of giving thanks for Christ's faithfulness (CD, 284), while the prayer which opens the sixth discourse gives thanks for God's forgiveness of sin and reconciliation with the human race through Christ (CD, 289). Also in the sixth discourse Kierkegaard speaks of giving thanks for God's mercy (CD, 295, cf. 291).

Christ's Presence in the Eucharist

Kierkegaard says little about the elements of bread and wine and how they mediate Christ's presence, but focuses rather on the *altar*. "Bread and wine" are mentioned on only three occasions in *Christian Discourses* (CD, 273, 300 (twice)), but the term "altar" appears frequently. The image Kierkegaard presents of the Eucharist is that of Christ the host inviting believers to his meal of reconciliation.[11] There is little discussion of the bread and wine that comprise the meal and no speculation on the sense in which the elements can be said to be Christ's body and blood. Despite this lack of attention to the Eucharistic elements, however, Kierkegaard does speak in various ways of Christ's presence in the Eucharist.

The Eucharist as Remembrance

A theme that appears in several of the discourses is that of *remembrance* (*Ihukommelse*). This is a term that appears in the Eucharistic liturgy when the priest consecrates the bread and the wine and repeats Jesus' words "Do this in remembrance of me" (1 Cor. 11.24). Kierkegaard takes up the notion of remembrance and meditates on its significance in several of the discourses.

In the first discourse Kierkegaard describes Christ as present in the Eucharist through God's gift of longing to the believer. Kierkegaard contrasts a person's longing for a deceased loved one with the believer's longing for Christ. In the case of a deceased loved one, the mourner may be able temporarily to still his longing by visiting the grave of the dead person. When the longing has been somewhat satisfied by such a visit, then life again exercises its power over the mourner and she or he recognizes that his or her path is separated from that of the deceased loved one. As Kierkegaard puts it in his address to the reader, "You understand that longing should not

---

[11]This image is certainly influenced by Thorvaldsen's statue in the Church of Our Lady of Christ welcoming with outstretched arms the believer as he or she approaches the altar. Kierkegaard gave the second discourse as a sermon in this church and it is surely no accident that he took as his text the verse inscribed beneath Thorvaldsen's statue, Mt. 11.28.

increase with the years so that you more and more become a co-tenant of the grave" (CD, 261).

Whereas the bereaved person's longing may be stilled by visiting the beloved's grave, the believer's longing is *increased* when the believer brings Christ to mind. In Christ's case, "the longing for fellowship with your Savior and Redeemer should increase every time you remember him" (CD, 261). This is the case for two reasons. Firstly, Christ "is not one who is dead and departed but one who is living" (CD, 261). Secondly, Christ lives in the believer. Alluding to Gal. 2:20 Kierkegaard writes of Christ that "he is to be and become your life, so that you do not live to yourself, no longer live yourself, but Christ lives in you" (CD, 261). Christ is present, then, in the longing of the believer, a longing that increases through bringing Christ to remembrance and allowing Christ to live in the believer.

In the fourth discourse, which as we noted earlier is the only discourse which takes as its text a passage from the words of institution, Kierkegaard links the notion of remembrance with Christ's suffering. He opens the discourse with a quotation from the hymn *Mind, O Jesu, tidt mit Hjerte*: "Remind, O Jesus, oft my heart / Of your pangs, torment, and need, / Remind me of your soul's pain" (CD, 275). In the prayer that immediately follows these verses Kierkegaard bewails the fact that human beings do not have the strength "to summon deeply enough or constantly to hold fast to [Christ's] memory," for they "prefer to dwell on the joyful than on the sorrowful" (CD, 275). Because of human beings' weakness, we need Christ's help to recollect his suffering and death: "we pray to you, you who are the one we want to remember, we pray to you that you yourself will remind us of it" (CD, 275). Kierkegaard points out how strange this act of remembrance is and how ill-suited human language is to describe human beings' relationship with Christ. He asks: "Is this also a remembrance when the one who is to be recollected must himself remind the one recollecting!" (CD, 275). Believers gather at the communion on Fridays to share in the Lord's Supper and to recall his suffering and death. The believer should pray not to see Christ in his glory, but "first and foremost prays that the terror might stand vividly before him" (CD, 276). For this the believer needs Christ's help, which Christ provides by recalling to the believer's mind his suffering and death in the communion meal which he has instituted.

The notion of the Eucharist as a service of remembrance appears also in the sixth discourse, which Kierkegaard concludes with the words, "The supper of remembrance is once again prepared; may you then beforehand be brought to mind and thanked for your greatness in showing mercy" (CD, 295). The Eucharist is the service at which we recall God's great mercy in forgiving our sins.

It is not only Christ himself, but also the blessing that Christ bestows at the Eucharist that believers remember. It is the memory of this blessing that believers take with them into their daily lives when they leave the church service. Kierkegaard ends the third discourse with the prayer that "the blessing of this day, recollected again and again, may still be a vivid recollection for you, so that the remembrance of the blessing may be a blessing" (CD, 274). Similarly, he concludes the fourth discourse with the exhortation to the believer to celebrate the Eucharist "in remembrance of him and for blessing to yourself!" (CD, 281). The prayer with which Kierkegaard opens the final discourse beseeches Christ to "bless also those who are assembled here today, bless their taking part in this holy meal in your remembrance" (CD, 296). Without Christ's blessing the Lord's Supper "would not exist at all, since it is indeed the meal of the blessing!" (CD, 296).

Christ's Voice

In the third discourse Kierkegaard describes Christ's Eucharistic presence in terms of his *voice*. He takes as his text Jn. 10.27: "My sheep hear my voice, and I know them, and they follow me" (CD, 269). Kierkegaard's discussion is organized around the three elements of the verse, namely "they hear his voice," "he knows them," and "they follow him." Kierkegaard applies each of these three phrases to the believer's experience when he or she approaches the altar.

Both the sermon and altar, Kierkegaard claims, are concerned with the word. But a sermon only bears witness to Christ, it is not Christ himself. The sermon, Kierkegaard writes, "proclaim[s] his word and his teaching, but a sermon is still not *his* voice" (CD, 271). At the altar, however, Christ himself is present and it is *his* voice that the believer is called upon to hear: "At the altar there is no speaking about him; there he himself is present in person; there it is he who is speaking" (CD, 271). In contrast to the sermon, then, where we hear

Christ's word and teaching but not his voice, at the altar it is Christ's voice itself that speaks. Christ is "present in person" (CD, 271) and addresses the human being, so much so that, if the human being is deaf to Christ's voice, then the altar is in the spiritual sense absent for the communicant. Even if the liturgy were perfect, even if the communicant resolved to live his life according to every word he had heard at the altar, if the individual does not hear Christ's voice at the altar, then the individual is not truly at the altar. As Kierkegaard puts it, "In the physical sense, one can point to the altar and say, 'There it is'; but, in the spiritual sense, it is actually *there* only if you hear *his* voice *there*" (CD, 271).

Kierkegaard leaves unexplained, however, how Christ is "present in person," nor does he explain how Christ's voice is heard at the altar. One possible solution to this problem would be to regard the priest presiding at the Eucharist as an "icon" of Christ who represents Christ to the congregation and speaks Christ's words on Christ's behalf. There is, however, no hint of such a theology of priesthood in the third discourse or for that matter anywhere else in *Christian Discourses*. In view of Kierkegaard's critical attitude towards the clergy, it is perhaps hardly surprising that he did not adopt this solution to the question of Christ's personal presence in the Eucharist.

Similar questions arise with Kierkegaard's application to the Eucharist of the second element of Jn. 10.27, "he knows them." Kierkegaard takes this phrase to mean that the altar is present to the believer only if he or she is known there by Christ: "One can point physically to the altar and say, 'See, there it is,' but in the spiritual sense the altar is *there* only if you are *known there* by him" (CD, 273). If Christ does not know the individual when he comes to the altar, if Christ speaks to the individual the terrifying words, "I do not know you, I never knew you" (CD, 272), then the individual's receiving bread and wine is in vain (CD, 273). Christ knows only those who hear his voice.

Christ's knowledge of those who come to the altar stems from his omnipresence. Although Kierkegaard does not employ such terms as omnipresence or ubiquity, these concepts seem to be implied by his description of Christ as "humankind's eternal sun" whose "acquaintance with humankind also penetrates to everyone everywhere like rays of light" (CD, 272). Even if the believer fled to "the uttermost parts of the world" or "hid in the bottomless pit," Christ knows the believer. It is this that allows Christ to know everyone at the altar as an *individual*. Regardless of how many people may be gathered at the altar, "indeed, even if all were assembled at the altar, there is no crowd at the altar. He is himself personally present, and he knows those who are his own" (CD, 272). Precisely Christ's knowledge of the believer is blessedness for the believer (CD, 272).

The hearing of Christ's voice and being known by Christ evoke a response from the believer. The believer hears Christ's voice and *follows him*. Following Christ means that the believer allows the communion with Christ experienced at the altar to continue when the communion service is over and the believer has left the church. The follower of Christ returns to his or her daily tasks after the communion service and thus in the physical sense has left the altar. In the spiritual sense, however, "it is as if the altar followed you, for where he is, there is the altar—and when you follow him, he accompanies you" (CD, 273). In the physical sense, of course, the altar remains where it always is, namely standing in the church. But Christ's presence and his communion with the believer are not dependent upon the communion service. Indeed, we should reverse the relation and say not that Christ is where the altar is, but that the altar is where Christ is. As Kierkegaard puts it, "The altar, to be sure, remains standing there, and you go to the altar, but yet it is the altar only if *he* is present *there*—therefore, where he is, there is the altar" (CD, 273). Where God is, there is the altar, even when no altar is physically visible. If this were not the case, then the believer "would have to remain at the altar, take up residence there, never budge from the spot, but such superstition is not Christianity" (CD, 274). The task facing the follower, then, is to remain in communion with Christ outside the church in the daily tasks of everyday life. Kierkegaard writes: "It is not as if everything were settled by someone's going up to the altar on rare occasions; no, the task is to remain at the altar when you leave the altar" (CD, 274). Consequently, "The event is not finished" when the believer leaves church, but "is just begun," and God will complete the good work in the believer on the Day of our Lord Jesus Christ (CD, 274).

Christ's Blessing

Christ is present in the communion service in his *blessing*. Kierkegaard takes as the text for the seventh and final discourse Lk. 24.51, Christ's blessing of the disciples before he ascended to his Father in heaven: "And it happened, as he blessed them, he was parted from them" (CD, 296). In the prayer with which he opens the discourse Kierkegaard comments that the Lord's Supper would not exist at all without Christ's blessing, "since it is indeed the meal of the blessing" (CD, 296). Just as Christ did not leave his disciples at the ascension without his blessing, so too does he not leave believers without a blessing when they encounter him in the communion service. It is this blessing that the believer takes with him or her when she or he returns home from the communion service

What, then, is the nature of Christ's blessing in the Eucharist? In answering this question Kierkegaard picks up on themes already touched upon in the other discourses in order to unfold the nature of Christ's blessing.

The communicant "goes to the altar in order to meet [Christ], for whom you long more every time you are parted from him" (CD, 298). This encounter with Christ means having a consciousness of oneself as nothing before God and therefore entirely in need of the blessing bestowed in the communion service (CD, 298). At the altar the human being is capable of nothing at all, for "at the altar as a sinner you are in relation to the Redeemer less than nothing" (CD, 298). The human being is capable of less than nothing, because she or he is in the debt of sin and thus separated from God. The individual can therefore do nothing, not even holding fast to the thought of unworthiness in order to make himself or herself receptive to the blessing. As Kierkegaard puts it, the human being is "capable of nothing, not even of holding your soul by yourself at the peak of consciousness that you stand totally in need of grace and the blessing" (CD, 300). Consequently, the more the human being is aware that she or he is capable of nothing, "all the more clear is the need for the blessing, or that it is everything" (CD, 298). The obstacles to a relationship with God seem insuperable. Sin posits such a radical breach between humanity and God that human beings are utterly helpless to overcome it.

But at the altar "declaration is made of satisfaction for guilt and sin" (CD, 298, cf. 299). It is Christ who achieves everything, for he makes satisfaction and accomplishes atonement for sinful human beings. Christ pays the debt and accomplishes reconciliation by suffering and dying on our behalf. If the human being wishes to be capable of something at the altar, then reconciliation and satisfaction are made impossible. The blessing that the believer receives from Christ is thus Christ himself and the atonement he has wrought in his person for sinful humanity. As Kierkegaard puts it: "But at the altar Christ is the blessing. The divine work of reconciliation is Christ's work, and in it a human being can do only less than nothing—therefore the blessing is everything, but if the work is Christ's, then Christ is indeed the blessing" (CD, 299). Because of their sin, however, human beings are of themselves incapable of receiving Christ's blessing. Consequently, Christ must not only give his blessing, but also give human beings the condition to receive it. As Kierkegaard puts it, when the human being receives Christ's blessing "it must encompassingly support you as it is communicated to you" (CD, 300).

How, then, is Christ's blessing communicated at the Eucharist? Kierkegaard emphasizes that it is *not* the priest who communicates Christ's blessing. Only Christ is capable of communicating the blessing and of giving the communicant the support he needs in order to receive and accept that blessing. Kierkegaard writes: "Only he who is personally present is able to do that, he who not only communicates but is the blessing at the altar. He himself is present; he blesses the bread when it is broken; it is his blessing in the cup that is handed to you" (CD, 300). Kierkegaard continues: "Only he who instituted this supper, only he can prepare it—because at the altar he is the blessing" (CD, 300).

It is through his blessing that Christ himself is present in the Eucharist. Kierkegaard writes: "He himself is present; he blesses the bread when it is broken; it is his blessing in the cup that is handed to you. But it is not only the gifts that are blessed—no, the supper itself is the blessing. You partake not only of the bread and wine as blessed, but when you partake of the bread and the wine you partake of the blessing, and this is really the supper" (CD, 300).

The Efficacy of the Eucharist

The question of the regularity and validity of the Eucharist and its administration does not seem to have concerned Kierkegaard in *Christian Discourses*. Indeed, it is striking how little mention is made of the role of the priest in administering the sacraments. Kierkegaard's focus is wholly on the role of Christ and the part played by the priest in administering the Eucharist is present only implicitly. Thus when Kierkegaard mentions the role of the priest in the communion service, he does so in order to make clear that it is *not* the priest who communicates the Eucharistic blessing to the communicant, but Christ himself (CD, 300). Kierkegaard either simply accepts the regularity and validity of the communion on Fridays or he does not consider the issue to be of importance. If the former is the case, then Kierkegaard would seem implicitly to accept the doctrine of *ex opere operato*, i.e., that God's grace operates in the sacraments independently of the worthiness of the human agent responsible for administering them. Alternatively, Kierkegaard may simply not consider the issue of the worthiness of the priest in administering the sacraments to be a significant issue. This seems more likely to be the case, for as we have seen Kierkegaard does not situate the presence of Christ in the elements themselves, but in the relationship between Christ and believer symbolized and expressed in the Eucharistic service. Consequently, the problem of the regularity and validity of the sacraments that has concerned the church at various points in its history is for Kierkegaard simply not an issue.

Although Kierkegaard may not have been concerned with the question of the regularity and validity of the sacraments, there are hints of a version of the doctrine of the *efficacy* of the Eucharist in part four of *Christian Discourses*. The doctrine of efficacy makes the effectiveness of the grace mediated by the sacraments dependent upon the worthiness of the individual receiving the Eucharist. This does not mean that grace is dependent on human achievement in some way. God's grace is freely offered to human beings and cannot be conditioned, modified, or impaired by the human beings to whom it is offered. Each individual, however, is capable of imposing obstacles to the effectiveness of God's grace. Thus the individual can reject God's offer and turn away from God's gift of fellowship. This does not make God's grace as such dependent on human agency, however. It is not the gift of grace itself, but only the acceptance or rejection of that gift which is dependent on human agency. God is continually stretching forth his hand in fellowship to human beings, he is constantly offering us his grace, but each individual human being can choose not to accept this offer. In short, the individual's disposition towards the gift she or he is offered determines the efficacy of divine grace in his or her life. Hints of a version of the efficacy of the Eucharist appear in Kierkegaard's warning that no one should dare to come to the Holy Supper unless well prepared (CD, 255) and in his discussion of the preparations the believer must make in order to approach the altar *worthily*. In *Christian Discourses* Kierkegaard's understanding of the worthiness of the communicant is discussed in terms of *longing* and *sin-consciousness*.

Longing

In the first discourse the doctrine of efficacy appears in Kierkegaard's discussion of the "well-tested, heart-felt longing that is required of those who worthily want to partake of the holy meal of Communion" (CD, 251). The springboard for Kierkegaard's discussion is Lk. 22.15, which Kierkegaard understands to be "the introductory words to the institution of the Lord's Supper" (CD, 252). Luke's account of Jesus' heartfelt longing to eat the Passover meal with his disciples is not merely a description of a now distant historical event, but belongs inwardly and in an exemplary way to the Eucharist. For Kierkegaard these words express the disposition each individual should adopt on approaching the Lord's table. They express "the true devout introduction or entrance" of the communicant, namely "to come with heartfelt longing" (CD, 252). Everyone who approaches the Lord's table should do so with heartfelt longing, just as Christ himself longed to eat the Passover with his friends. Anything else would be "the most terrible contrast to the sacred account of how the instituter longed with all his heart for this meal" (CD, 252). For these reasons Kierkegaard makes "the heartfelt longing for the holy meal of the Lord's Supper" the subject of the first discourse. He wishes "to try to express what was stirring within you when you felt the longing to go to the altar" (CD, 253).

The individual's longing for the Eucharist is "the longing for God and the eternal, the longing for our Savior and Redeemer" (CD, 253).

It is, Kierkegaard tells us, impossible to comprehend this longing, for it too is God's gift and in this longing God gives himself. The human being, however, is called upon not to understand but to *use* this longing (CD, 253). We might say that the longing is itself a sacrament which mediates God's presence by preparing the individual to receive Christ at the altar. It is the work of the Spirit in the human being. It is possible, however, to ignore or resist the call expressed by this longing, but if the individual accepts with gratitude this longing as a gift of God, then it will become a blessing to him or her (CD, 254). Despite the inexplicability of the longing for the Lord's table, the person who feels this longing knows what is required, namely, to "do everything to use rightly what God gives" (CD, 254).

The human being cooperates with this gift of longing "by earnest thoughts . . . so that I may tear myself completely away from what still might hold me back" (CD, 254). Kierkegaard provides a list of the earnest thoughts by means of which the individual cooperates with the gift of longing, namely the vanity of the earthly and the temporal, the uncertainty of existence, the certainty of death, and the loneliness of the human being in the world. Cultivating these earnest thoughts intensifies the longing the individual feels for the fellowship with God offered in the Eucharist. Kierkegaard writes: "The more you surrendered to these thoughts, the more the longing for the eternal conquered in you, the longing for fellowship with God through your Redeemer, and you said: I long with all my heart for this supper. Oh, there is indeed only one friend, one trustworthy friend in heaven and on earth, our Lord Jesus Christ" (CD, 257-58).

Consciousness of Sin

The individual prepares for the Eucharist by cultivating his or her awareness of sin. In the first discourse Kierkegaard cites the contemplation of sin as one of the earnest thoughts by means of which the individual cooperates with divine grace. The person who longs for the Eucharist will reflect on what Christianity has revealed, namely, how deep humankind has sunk in sin. He or she will remind himself or herself of human beings' inhumanity to each other and above all "will recall the experience of the Holy One when he walked here upon earth", his innocent suffering at the hands of sinners and his being mocked by the crowd (CD, 259). The more the person surrendered to these thoughts "the more the longing for fellowship with him, the Holy One, conquered in you, and you said to yourself: I long with all my heart for this supper; I long for fellowship with him, away from this evil world where sin prevails!" (CD, 260). This longing is also prompted by the individual's need for the forgiveness of sins. According to Kierkegaard, "sin has a peculiar power to hold back; it has an outstanding account to settle, a debt it wants paid by the sinner before it lets him go" (CD, 260). The individual's awareness that Christ has paid the debt for his sin intensifies the individual's longing for fellowship with Christ still further. The consciousness of sin "is why I long in an all the more heartfelt way to renew my fellowship with him, who has atoned for my sin also, has atoned for my every slightest actual sin, but also for the one that may lurk most deeply in my soul without my being aware of it and that possibly would yet burst out if I am led into the most terrible decision" (CD, 260).

Kierkegaard's "Eucharistic Theology" in Christian Discourses, Part Four

When we attempt to ascertain what understanding of the Eucharist underlies part four of *Christian Discourses*, we discover an eclectic mix of ideas that makes it impossible to place Kierkegaard in any single theological camp. Hirsch is probably right in his claim that Kierkegaard may have derived impulses for his understanding of the Eucharist from Schleiermacher,[12] for Kierkegaard's discussion of the Eucharist as a service at which the believer renews his fellowship with Christ is strongly reminiscent of Schleiermacher's treatment of the Lord's Supper in *The Christian Faith*.[13] There are also hints of a Zwinglian conception in Kierkegaard's thinking in his frequent description of Holy Communion as a service of *remembrance* of

---

[12]Commenting on the penultimate paragraph of *Christian Discourses* (CD, 300), Hirsch writes: "With these sentences Kierkegaard appropriates Schleiermacher's neo-Protestant conception of the Eucharist, according to which Christ's presence is not in the elements, but what is decisive is Christ's presence in the rite as such." Emanuel Hirsch and Hayo Gerdes, eds., *Sören Kierkegaard, Gesammelte Werke*, vol. 20, *Christliche Reden*, trans. Emanuel Hirsch (Gütersloher: Gütersloher Verlagshaus/Gerd Mohn, 1981) 343n337.

[13]F. D. E. Schleiermacher, *The Christian Faith*, ed. by H. R. Mackintosh and J. S. Stewart (Edinburgh: T&T Clark, 1989) §§139-42.

Christ's atonement of sins accomplished at Calvary long ago. This emphasis on remembrance, however, is coupled with an un-Zwinglian emphasis on Christ's living presence in the Eucharist.

Kierkegaard can also write as if Christ were physically present at the communion service. Thus in the final paragraph of the seventh discourse and thus the whole work he states: "See, therefore he stretches out his arms at the altar; he bows his head toward you — blessing! In this way he is present at the altar" (CD, 300). This seems to be a particularly vivid way of expressing the Lutheran doctrine of the real presence, a doctrine articulated in the emphasis in the *Alter-Bog* that the Eucharistic elements of bread and wine are the *true* body and the *true* blood of Christ.[14] For Kierkegaard Christ is really present at the Eucharist.

This emphasis on the real presence of Christ seems also to be indicated in the second discourse, on Mt. 11.28, where Christ is present as he who invites the believer to the communion meal. In this sense Christ is the "host" of the meal. A similar idea is present in the conclusion of the fourth discourse where Kierkegaard urges the reader to approach the altar in the knowledge that Christ "is waiting there at his holy table" (CD, 281). Kierkegaard seems to share Luther's view that the Eucharist is not a memorial of Christ's atoning sacrifice, as Zwingli would have us believe, but is a celebration of his real presence among believers. Unlike Luther, however, Kierkegaard does not seem to situate Christ's presence in the bread and wine, but in Christ's *voice*. This is vividly illustrated on the sole occasion that Kierkegaard quotes the words of consecration said over the elements: "And it must be his voice you hear when he says: This is my body" (CD, 271). The emphasis is on Christ's *voice*, even when speaking of Christ's body. We might say that Kierkegaard replaces Luther's doctrine of the real presence with a notion of the "acoustic" presence of Christ in the elements, a presence which resonates in the subjectivity of the communicant.

Kierkegaard seems to subordinate the Eucharistic elements to what he believes to be more central features of the Lord's Supper. In the third discourse he refers to the futility of the communicant's

---

[14]At the consecration of the elements the priest pronounces over the bread and wine the words: "Dette er Jesu sande Legem. Dette er Jesu sande Blod."

receiving bread and wine if Christ does not *know* the believer when he approaches the altar (CD, 273). He then unfolds this point not by meditating on Christ's presence in the elements, but by arguing that "in the spiritual sense the altar is *there* only if you are *known there* by him" (CD, 273). In the final discourse Kierkegaard makes another rare reference to the Eucharistic elements, when he comments that Christ "himself is present; he blesses the bread when it is broken; it is his blessing in the cup that is handed to you" (CD, 300). It is the blessing of Christ, who is himself the blessing offered to the believer, which is offered in the bread and wine. But this divine blessing, which is itself Christ's presence, is present not only in the Eucharistic elements, but in the entire divine drama of the Lord's Supper. As Kierkegaard puts it,

> But it is not only the gifts that are blessed — no, the supper itself is the blessing. You partake not only of the bread and wine as blessed, but when you partake of the bread and the wine you partake of the blessing, and this is really the supper (*Maaltid*). Only he who instituted this supper (*Maaltid*), only he can prepare it — because at the altar he is the blessing. (CD, 300).

Christ is present in the Eucharist, then, in his knowing the believer who hears his voice. His presence is situated in the blessing which Christ bestows on the believer, a blessing which is identical with his own self.

There also seem to be echoes of the Lutheran doctrine of ubiquitarianism in Kierkegaard's reflections on the nature of the Eucharist. We saw that in the third discourse Kierkegaard develops a notion of Christ's omnipresence and omniscience at the altar, so that Christ knows all those who hear his voice. Christ knows the believer wherever the believer might be, whether in "the uttermost parts of the world" or "hid in the bottomless pit" (CD, 272). Furthermore, Kierkegaard argues in the third discourse that wherever Christ is present, so too is the altar. Conversely, wherever the altar is present, i.e., in so far as the believer hears Christ's voice and is known by Christ, so too is Christ present. The believer who is in communion with Christ will find Christ not only at the altar in the communion service, but will remain always in communion with Christ even when the service is over and the believer has left the church. The believer can thus be said to be always at the altar. We can therefore speak of the notion of Eucharistic omnipresence or ubiquity in

Kierkegaard's thought.

Kierkegaard's "ubiquitarianism" differs in some important respects from that of Luther, however. Whereas Luther's ubiquitarianism is based on his conception of the hypostatic union, so that wherever Christ is he must be present in both divine and human natures, for Kierkegaard Christ's ubiquity is a spiritual presence which finds expression in his knowledge of the believer. Kierkegaard's emphasis is on the believer becoming contemporaneous with Christ, and the parallels with Luther arise from their common emphasis on Christ's real presence to the believer in the communion service.[15]

A distinctive feature of Kierkegaard's understanding of the Eucharist is his claim that what is crucial at the altar is that God looks at Christ and not at the sinful human being (CD, 299). We have the interesting notion of the Eucharist as a means of diverting God's attention away from human beings to Christ, so that God sees only the holy, sinless God-man and not the sinners who deserve his judgment and condemnation. This appears to be an alternative version of the idea Kierkegaard develops elsewhere in his writings that Christ's love hides the multitude of sins of which we human beings are guilty,[16] and his notion of the altar as the hiding place for the sinner (WA, 186-87).

Kierkegaard's understanding of the Eucharist is notable for his lack of emphasis on the role of the priest. For Kierkegaard the priest performs three functions. Firstly, in speaking the words "on the night that he was betrayed" the priest draws the congregation into the divine drama and makes them accomplices in the disciples' betrayal of Jesus (CD, 260). Secondly, the priest leads the corporate confession of sin made by the congregation before they approach the altar (CD, 287). Kierkegaard emphasizes, however, that when making this confession the individual is in isolation before God (CD,

---

[15]Because Kierkegaard does not explore how Christ is present in the Eucharistic elements, Hirsch is surely going too far when he claims in his *Kierkegaard-Studien* that Kierkegaard offers the key to understanding the controversial Lutheran doctrine of ubiquitarianism. Emanuel Hirsch, *Kierkegaard-Studien* (Gütersloh: Verlag C. Bertelsmann, 1933) 887.

[16]See the second of *Two Discourses at the Communion on Fridays*, "Love will Hide a Multitude of Sins: 1 Peter 4.8" (WA, 179-88).

290). Thirdly, the priest, or "Lord's servant", is responsible for handing the bread and wine to the believer (CD, 273). Kierkegaard emphasizes, however, that it is not the priest who communicates the blessing to the communicant, but Christ himself (CD, 300).[17]

There is no notion in Kierkegaard's thought of the priest as an icon of Christ and little interest in the role of the priest in the Eucharist. The figure of the priest remains very much in the background in the Eucharistic action, which takes place first and foremost between the individual communicant and Christ himself. Kierkegaard shifts the focus from the priest to the believer. It is not the priest who approaches the altar, but the individual believer (CD, 287), and the words of the priest are hollow if the communicant does not hear *Christ's voice* when the priest speaks.

Assessing Kierkegaard's understanding of the Eucharist is difficult, because he does not provide a systematic, coherent, fully worked out doctrine. This does not mean, however, that he does not have such a doctrine. The emphasis in his thinking about the Eucharist, however, is on the existential, namely on the individual believer's relation to Christ in the communion service. For this reason he does not provide a fully elaborated Eucharistic theology but emphasizes the impact of certain aspects of the communion service on the individual's God-relationship. Central is 1 Cor. 11.23, which Kierkegaard understands to draw the entire congregation into Judas's act of betrayal. These words are not merely a historical description of an event that took place long ago, but make present that event and draw the congregation into that event, not, however, as "poetic" sympathizers with Christ's fate, who sympathize with Christ only in the imagination. Rather, the words connect those who betrayed Christ with people living today: you, too, are a betrayer of Christ. In this way Kierkegaard makes the Lord's Supper contemporary and draws the individual into the divine drama of sin and forgiveness it expresses. It is here that his originality and his contribution to Eucharistic theology lie.

---

[17]There may be an allusion to the priest's invitation to the congregation to receive communion in CD, 281: "Behold, everything is prepared". This passage is reminiscent of the invitation frequently spoken by the priest at Lutheran services after the consecration of the elements: "Come, for everything is prepared, taste and see how friendly the Lord is."

12
The Stage and Stages in a Christian Authorship
Hugh S. Pyper

The title of this paper proved irresistible, although on at least two counts it might have been resisted. Firstly, the pun works only in English, certainly not in Danish, and, secondly, the use of the word "stages" in the discussion of Kierkegaard is very misleading. He seldom used the term, and more often he spoke of existence-spheres or circles. Yet the title sums up quite neatly what I want to explore here, which is the centrality of the idea of *performance* to Kierkegaard's conception of what it is to be a human being and of the relationships between human beings and God. Performance is also a key to his understanding and practice of the avocation of a Christian author.

The title also echoes that of Kierkegaard's article *The Crisis and a Crisis in the Life of an Actress*. This piece, which many have regarded as a relatively obscure and unimportant work, is characterized by Jørgen Bukdahl as "*of such decisive significance for the understanding of Kierkegaard.*"[1] This opinion accords with Stephen Crites's verdict that it "had a significance for Kierkegaard's own life and career as an author, quite independent of the essay's own particular content."[2] Kierkegaard's deep interest in the theater stems from his recognition of the lessons it can teach on communication. The study of *Crisis*

---

[1] Jørgen Bukdahl *Søren Kierkegaard and the Common Man* trans., rev., and ed. by Bruce H. Kirmmse (Grand Rapids MI: Eerdmanns, 2001) 61.

[2] Søren Kierkegaard, *Crisis in the Life on an Actress and other Essays on Drama*, trans. and intro. by Stephen Crites (London; Collins, 1967) 2. I might add here by way of parenthesis that the present paper could be taken as homage to what I have considered, ever since I came across it on one of my earliest forays in Kierkegaard's writings, one of the most illuminating shorter pieces on Kierkegaard: Stephen Crites's introduction to *Crisis in the Life of an Actress*. Many of the ideas developed here have their roots in that introduction, and I only hope that in expanding and reflecting on them I have done justice to the lucid synthesis Crites provides.

helps us to understand the crucial role of the concept of performance, both offstage and onstage, in the overall spectacle of the authorship and ultimately in Kierkegaard's understanding of the anxieties and consolations of being a Christian. The present article seeks to justify these assessments of *Crisis*, as I shall henceforth refer to the work, by going backstage, as it were, in what Martin Thust calls the "marionette theater" of the authorship.[3]

The metaphor works at two levels. Each individual book is a (theatrical) stage set up by its author, pseudonymous or not, where characters or voices enact the drama of existence. In turn, the authors and editors of the individual books themselves become the actors in the theater of the authorship as whole. In a kind of *mise en abyme*, then, the points in the authorship where Kierkegaard explicitly discusses acting, and particularly the role of the actress, give him the opportunity to articulate explicitly his understanding of his own performance as an author and as a Christian.

This may involve going so far as to sneak in the artists' entrance to examine the importance of the figure of the actress in Kierkegaard's work. Given the complex interactions between sexuality and language in Kierkegaard's thought, the figure of the actress allows him to think through with particular clarity the problem of communication between author and reader and between the individual human being and God. As we shall see, this anxiety over performance and the relation between performance and truth in his authorship is also explored in a remarkable play by the Spanish

---

[3]Martin Thust, "Das Marionettetheater Soren Kierkegaards," *Zeitwende* 1 (1925) 18-38. Thust takes as the epitome of Kierkegaard's approach Frater Taciturnus's description of the diarist in "Guilty/Not guilty" as his "puppet" (*Gliedermand*), designed to show a spiritual condition with absolute precision. Thust in effect sees the pseudonyms as standing in the same relation to Kierkegaard as the diarist does to Frater Taciturnus. In Thust's view, these "puppets" are animations of the idea. As such, Kierkegaard's peculiar gift is that they are not bloodless but living. They are animated by Kierkegaard's own personality in that they reflect aspects of subjective rather than objective truth, Kierkegaard's "truth-for-me." Something of his existence is active in them. Yet, insofar as Kierkegaard conceives himself as a 'puppet' in God's master-drama, then Kierkegaard's self, and therefore these derived characters, draw life from the divine life (see esp. p. 21). Thust sees each Kierkegaardian individual as a playactor who plays the role of his own self and who as himself is a marionette in God's great world-theater whose plot is summed up in Christ.

playwright Lope de Vega. The anxiety is the inevitable price of the inescapable need finally to trust the audience as a writer and to trust God as a Christian.

The way in through the stage door of the authorship is provided by a footnote in *Stages on Life's Way* (SLW, 131-2) which pays tribute to one of Denmark's two most admired actresses of the time, Anna Nielsen, the other being Johanne Heiberg, the subject of *Crisis*.[4] This footnote is inserted at a point in the section of *Stages* on "Reflections on Marriage" where the question of women's beauty is being discussed and the issue arises of offering a counter to the idea that the bloom of youth is the important point. Through this footnote, the discussion is turned to the theater in a knowing aside. Is it not in the theater, after all, that this equation of youth and physical beauty is most in evidence?

The point of the footnote is that, Mme Nielsen's example is all the more pleasing in this milieu. Her attraction does not depend on youth. She is always and at every moment true to herself, and thereby she represents the essentially feminine rather than depending on the accidentally feminine for her effects. In this way she is not the victim of time. When she is sixty, she will perfectly portray the grandmother just as she portrayed the young girl "by the dedication that is the pact of pure femininity with the imperishable" (*SLW*, 132), although the very mention of sixty years in connection with a leading actress is coyly apologized for. This talent may not always be appreciated by the spectators who seek a more immediate gratification from the theater, but those who can take a longer, calmer and more discriminating view rejoice in seeing the beautiful when in truth it is before them.

This short but dense footnote represents the intrusion of the

[4]Anne Nielsen (1803–1856) is described succinctly by Janne Risum in her "Towards Transparency: Søren Kierkegaard on Danish Actresses," trans. Annette Mester, in J. Stewart, ed., *Kierkegaard and his Contemporaries: The Culture of Golden Age Denmark* (Berlin: Walter de Gruyter, 2003) as "tall, blond, and gentle with big, blue eyes, a beautiful voice and brilliant diction. Her calm, emotive acting made her the incarnation of the romantic ideal of the Nordic woman: virgin, wife, and mother" (337-8). Robert Neiendam, in his study of the two actresses entitled *Rivalinder: Johanne Luise Heiberg; Anna Nielsen* (Copenhagen: Boghallen, 1955), asserts that no one wrote a deeper characterisation of Anna Nielsen than Kierkegaard in *Stages* when he saw her as "the essential womanhood" (18).

world of the Royal Theater in Copenhagen into *Stages on Life's Way*, which is a book full of adopted characters and staged settings. It is also quite strikingly the only time a real, named contemporary woman appears in the whole of that extensive work. Other women are mentioned, to be sure, but they are either anonymous (Judge William's bride), biblical (Mary Magdalene and Rachel), or drawn from literature (Cordelia, Desdemona and Elvira).

This lack of real, named women is all the more significant since the question of woman is a unifying thread of *Stages*. The speeches at the Symposium, Judge William's reflections on marriage, Quidam's agonizing over his beloved,`` and Frater Taciturnus's urbane reflection on Quidam's diary, all center on women. Crucially, however, it is how men are to perform before women, or more correctly "woman," that is the real issue and the fundamental anxiety witnessed to in *Stages*. The book could be summarized as a series of long, complex and wordy male outpourings about women which occur in the absence of women. It is speech about love and marriage in the absence of any real object, or risk, of love, anxiously rehearsing possibilities with no danger of it becoming reality.

Elsewhere I have drawn on the complex conventions which surround oaths in classical and biblical literature to develop a theory of what I call the "anxiety of utterance."[5] Put simply, I argued that there is a structural similarity between an anxiety that is engendered by language and the anxiety of sexuality which can be seen most starkly in a society which understands the male as the "begetter" of new life. In such an understanding, men can only overcome death by entrusting their seed to the uncontrollable mystery of the woman's body. In that sense, a man cannot infallibly guarantee that he will have a child, whatever his intentions may be.

Analogously, in speech, only by entrusting ourselves to words which by their very nature do not uniquely encode our intentions can we communicate our wishes but also open ourselves to the willful or ignorant misunderstanding of our audience. We cannot guarantee that our words will communicate our intentions any more than men can guarantee that they will have an heir. This analogy

---

[5]See particularly H. S. Pyper, *David as Reader: 2 Sam 12:1-15 and the Poetics of Fatherhood* (Leiden: E.J. Brill, 1996) 186-99.

becomes all the more fraught in the process of writing, where the written by its very permanence both promises immortality ands lay itself open to increased possibilities of misunderstanding as it survives into new and unexpected contexts.

Like actors in rehearsal, or backstage, the men in *Stages* run through obsessively the seemingly endless possibilities of misunderstanding in their commerce with women. Throughout, there is a constant circling round the possible loss or gain to a man of a committed relationship to woman, but underlying that is a deep anxiety over the whole process of the propagation of the self. This is perhaps most graphically epitomized in, but by no means confined to, the well-known exploration, called quite explicitly "A Possibility" (SLW, 276-88), of the man beset by (perhaps delusory) guilt over the prospect of meeting the child he had unwittingly fathered.[6] Even in this scenario, however, the woman disappears from the picture. It is the child, not the mother, that he dreads meeting.

Given this obsession with male imaginings of and speech about woman, it is telling that the only point at which any woman actually appears onstage in the main body of *Stages* is when the participants in the symposium stumble across Judge William and his bride. She remains unnamed, and the conversation overheard between them rather curiously, not to say troublingly, converges on the Danish law on wife beating.[7]

In the context of the almost self-indulgent wallowing in male

---

[6]David Brézis has recently explored the complexity of Kierkegaard's relation to paternal figures and the prospect of fatherhood in his *Kierkegaard et les figures de la paternité* (Paris: Editions du Cerf, 1999) and characterizes a central theme in his work as "Le refus de la paternité": the refusal of fatherhood.

[7]Here I find myself siding with Amy Laura Hall in her *Kierkegaard and the Treachery of Love* (Cambridge: Cambridge University Press, 2002) 146, where she respectfully disagrees with Robert Perkins's more favorable reading of this passage in his article "Woman-Bashing in Kierkegaard's 'In Vino Veritas': A Reinscription of Plato's *Symposium*" in Céline Léon and Sylvia Walsh (eds) *Feminist Interpretations of Kierkegaard* (University Park: Pennsylvania State University Press: 1997) 83-102, 99. Regardless of whether or not the Judge thinks he is joking and whether or not his wife shares the joke or merely acquiesces for the sake of a quiet life, the upshot is that her speech, the only speech by a female speaker in the whole book, is effectively shorn of any consequence, even though her only concern seemed to be the judge's public reputation and her possible detrimental effect on it.

speech that the symposium represents, the way the text deals with the utterances of the Judge's wife is intriguing. She is permitted only to make offers of service to the Judge, encouraging him to drink his tea and offering to warm his dish. When she does venture on a serious point in conversation, it is to say that the judge would have been a much greater man in the world without her. When he condescendingly asks her what her silly idea is, half alluding to Job's characterization of his own wife as "speaking as one of the foolish women do" (Job 12:10), her apparently earnest reply is not even summarized and her husband hums a tune and drums his fingers as she speaks.

When he does deign to answer her, this is what the judge says:

> No, you are not going to make me serious, and you are not going to receive a serious answer; I must either laugh at you or make you forget it, as before, or beat you, or you must stop talking about it, or in some other way I must make you be silent. You see it is a jest, and that is why there are so many ways out. (SLW, 85)

Woman is to be silenced — by ridicule or, if that fails, by violence, not less chilling because it is cloaked as a smiling half-threat. Women's speech is somehow so threatening that it must be silenced at all costs to allow the flow of male speech about the anxiety of reproduction. The link between anxieties over the control of language and the control of women could hardly be clearer.

Anna Nielsen's appearance in the book at all, then, is remarkable. She may be edged out of the text into a footnote, but there she is. It is also highly significant that she is an actress, a performer. In theater, and in literature, the audience overhears the interplay of language, and thus can not only be engaged but also observe the possible predictably unpredictable consequences of language. This makes the stage a forum for bringing to more explicit consciousness these structures of anxiety and to allow anxious possibility to be explored in "play."

The other side of the coin is that for the theatrical performer there is the immediate enactment of this anxiety. All actors know how vulnerable they are to the audience. If the audience rejects or misunderstands the performance, there is little that an actor can do at one level, and yet communication is at the heart of his or her art. The mark of the great actor is precisely his or her ability to command attention and belief with no obvious power of coercion. In this context of the garrulous anxiety of men over their performance before women which forms the bulk of *Stages*, and Judge William's threat of the whip, the woman as performer is a peculiarly unsettling figure. She is both safe, because she is confined to the unreal world of the theater, and dangerous, because she gives voice and body to the unfathomableness of femininity.

This footnote affords us a bridge to the text of Kierkegaard's which is dedicated to analyzing the woman as performer: *A Crisis and the Crisis in the Life of an Actress*. We should now be prepared to believe that this text deals with crucial anxieties within the authorship. The use of the word "crisis" in the title is no accident. What adds to its interest is that this article itself becomes part of the performance that constituted the authorship and becomes caught up in a genuine crisis around Kierkegaard's own anxiety of performance, as the history of its publication demonstrates.

The subject of *Crisis,* as I shall call it for convenience, is the other great lady of the Royal Theater of the time, Mme. Nielsen's rival and complement, Fru Johanne Heiberg.[8] The specific occasion that prompts Kierkegaard to write about her is her reappearance on the stage of the Royal Theater as Juliet in 1847, the first time she had performed the role since her striking debut in it as a sixteen-year-old in 1825. The question then arises: How can she, now aged thirty-seven, measure up to her younger self in this of all roles?

"Inter et Inter," Kierkegaard's pseudonym for this work, explains that the point of this article is to explore aesthetically and psychologically one admittedly very difficult metamorphosis. The more that has been invested in the first phase of a young actress's career,

---

[8]For a wide-ranging assessment of Fru Heiberg's significance in Danish culture, see Bodil Wamberg, *Johanne Luise Heiberg: Kærlighedens Stedbarn* (Copenhagen: C. E. G. Gads Forlag, 1987). Wamberg is less inclined than Neiendam (see n. 7 above) to play up the rivalry between Nielsen and Heiberg. However, in contrast to Nielsen's Nordic calm, Fru Heiberg represented the dark-eyed, passionate, exotic woman. Kierkegaard's interest here is not simply that of the spectator. He had enjoyed a long acquaintance with Mrs Heiberg who, as the wife of the playwright, philosopher and theater director Johan Heiberg, and daughter-in-law of Thomasine Gyllembourg, was at the centre of what Kierkegaard called the "coterie," the small group of leaders of cultured taste in Copenhagen. It is worth noting that the exceptional respect signalled by the fact that Johanne Heiberg was always known even on stage as Fru, rather than Madame, Heiberg required a specific act of legislation by the king.

the more the public will resent the metamorphosis brought about inevitably by time. An actress with less immediate appeal as a young girl may succeed quietly in this, but the public may end up getting angry at the idol.

What will win the audience over, Inter et Inter declares, is its confidence in the control or authority of the performer, and that is predicated on the audience's sense of the infinite resources that the performer can draw on. The audience can relax in the confidence that the performer is equal to all occasions. As in all performance, however, this is a reflexive situation. The clue that such resources exist is the audience's ability to relax in the performer's presence. Confidence is all. The analogy could be drawn with financial matters. A bank succeeds because the customers have confidence in its solvency, not because it actually has the funds to cover its promises in gold in its cellars.

What is missing here is any allusion to the specificity of the dramatic role or the poetic language of Shakespeare's Juliet. It is the being of the actress, not what she says or does, that is all-important to Kierkegaard. Of course, the fact that it is Juliet that she is playing is not negligible.

Here it is fascinating to compare Fru Heiberg' own description of this major moment in her career as recorded much later in her remarkable memoirs "A Life Relived in Recollection."[9] The title of this work has itself a Kierkegaardian ring. Fru Heiberg does mention her first performance in volume one 1 of her memoirs under the title "Confirmationen." The relationship between her playing of this role and her confirmation seems to have struck her. At the same time, no doubt with hindsight, she writes that, as a 16-year-old, "I played Juliet like a child that sings a charming song without knowing about notes."[10] Of her performance in 1838, the one Kierkegaard saw, she writes:

> Juliet appears in the tragedian's first act as a child of 14 years, but one must never forget that she is a 14 year old girl in the South, not the North. In the fourth act there she stands as a fully developed woman, forceful, energetic, not succumbing to the worst horrors,

---

[9]J. Heiberg, *Et Liv gjenoplevet in Erindringen*, 4 vols, 5th ed., ed. N. B. Wamberg (Copenhagen: Gyldendal, 1974).

[10]Heiberg, *En Liv* 1:86.

which could make even a man tremble.[11]

Fru Heiberg argues that a genuinely young girl can play the first part of the play, but cannot rise to the latter scenes. An older actress can bring off the first part with skill, so that she can create an illusion, but the young girl cannot simply use skill to play the fully developed woman since that needs "maturity in the development of art, a true artist, in full possession of all that time, experience and education can guide her with. Every nuance of the lover, the whole scale, leading from the first spontaneous surrender to the heights of demonic passion."[12]

This relates to a remark by the critic Jonathan Bates: "*Hamlet, Othello, Macbeth, Lear*: think of these titles and one thinks first of a character, then of other characters and a story. *Romeo and Juliet*: think of this title and one thinks first of an idea."[13] On a similar theme, Harold Bloom has the following to say:

> Unprecedented in literature (though presumably not in life), Juliet precisely does not transcend the human heroine. Whether Shakespeare reinvents the representation of a very young woman (she is not yet fourteen) in love, or perhaps does even more than

---

[11]Heiberg, *En Liv* 2:163.

[12]Heiberg, *En Liv* 2:163. Here she is echoed almost exactly by another famous performer of the role, Dame Peggy Ashcroft, who writes as follows in John F. Andrews, ed., *Romeo and Juliet: Critical Essays* (New York: Garland Publishing, 1993) 177-82, 180-81:

> My first attempt at Juliet was inevitably agonizing as I was plagued by the idea of it being a "great tragic role." I learnt after that production, in a subsequent one at the Old Vic a year later, that it is essential for Juliet to be a child of fourteen. If that is credible, then her awakening, her passion, her refusal to compromise and, finally, her tragedy take care of themselves.
>
> I know that it has been said that Juliet is an impossible part to play because, by the time an actress is experienced enough to play her, she's too old to look the part. I really think that is nonsense. An actress up to twenty years older than Juliet, if she is really capable of playing the part, is not too old to be convincing. Of course a very young girl, especially on the screen, will be at a great advantage, but she has to encounter a number of technical difficulties. These difficulties are, I would say, two-fold. Firstly, she has to be able to sustain a very long and demanding part on the stage. Secondly, she has to deal at times with extremely complicated verbal fireworks. The part is all simplicity, whereas the language is often complex in the extreme.

[13]Jonathan Bate, *The Genius of Shakespeare* (London: Picador, 1997) 278.

that, is difficult to decide. How do you distance Juliet? You only shame yourself by bringing irony to a contemplation of her consciousness. Hazlitt, spurred by a nostalgia for his own lost dreams of love, caught better than any other critic the exact temper of this scene (II.ii.107-35). He has founded the passion of the two lovers not in the pleasures they had experienced, but on all pleasures they had *not* experienced. It is the sense of an infinity yet to come that is evoked by Juliet, nor can we doubt that her bounty is "as boundless as the sea."[14]

Juliet *is* possibility, and thus relates to the sense of the infinite that is the mark of the great actress in Kierkegaard's account, and the secret of the metamorphosis that Fru Heiberg embodies. One might summarize this by saying that the older actress is no longer lucky in her accidents. She can now truly serve the ideal which requires an inwardness which is not available to the seventeen-year-old. Inter et Inter resorts to metaphors of fire: she becomes calm, warm, glowing.

Fru Heiberg's extraordinary success in her two appearances leads Inter et Inter to distinguish between two forms of metamorphosis. Fru Heiberg's case shows what Kierkegaard calls the "metamorphosis of potentiation" which is the aesthete's touchstone. Kierkegaard contrasts this kind of metamorphosis with the "metamorphosis of continuity", of which Mme Nielsen is the prime example. This is straightforward perfectibility, which is the vindication for the ethical. Importantly, either form of metamorphosis represents the defeat of the power of the years. Either way, the future of the essential actress is secured against the effects of time.

The vital condition is that the actress is in right rapport with what Inter et Inter calls the theatrical "tension" [*Spænding*]. Just as in other spheres, lightness paradoxically comes from weight. Here Inter et Inter cites the way a bird flies as an example. The actress gains lightness from the weight of the theatrical illusion and, crucially, the expectations of the audience. The price for this is that she is free on stage but anxious in the wings. She has elasticity, which becomes anxious in the absence of pressure or tension. Indeed, the greater the powers of the artist, the more her anxiety until she is put in the place of the tension that exactly matches her powers. Inter et Inter

---

[14]In his *Shakespeare: The Invention of the Human* (New York: Riverhead Books, 1998) 91.

concludes, "One of the worst agonies for a person is to have too much elasticity in relation to the tension of the little world in which he lives. Such an unfortunate never comes to feel entirely free just because he cannot obtain sufficient weight upon himself" (C, 313). It is hard not to read Kierkegaard's own experience into this remark. Anxiety is the price of elasticity, of possibility, which is the one thing that can counter time. The ability to change, to be elastic, paradoxically is what allows one to remain essentially constant. It is a question which is at the heart of Kierkegaard's authorship. It is the reason, for instance, he returns throughout his writing to what he called his favorite biblical verse, James 1:17: "Every good endowment and every perfect gift is from above, coming down from the father of lights with whom there is no variation or shadow due to change." This security is the counter to the anxiety of utterance, of performance, and of procreation.

It entails, however, this vital "anxiety in the wings" which is the key to the connection which underlies this essay. Its importance is picked up by Wim R. Scholtens, the editor of the Dutch edition of *Crisis*, which also includes the later short piece on Captain Phister. Scholtens entitles his combined volume *Plankenkoorts en Drankzucht*, which I translate as "stage-fright and dipsomania."[15] Stage-fright is an interesting term in our context. Its plainest sense is the fear of performing, of being before an audience, which clearly relates to the anxieties discussed above, but it can also be taken to mean, perhaps, the fear of being presented with the prospect of moving on between the stages of life. Yet the anxiety is the index of the elasticity that will allow just such a transition.

This key anxiety in Kierkegaard's own authorship is dealt with in the exploration of performance in the little article and then revealingly in Kierkegaard's own stage-fright, so to speak, over publishing it. Kierkegaard's journals reveal his long struggle with himself over this issue. Joakim Garff indicates the importance of this quite starkly when he discusses *Crisis* under the section title "At udgive eller ikke at udgive": "to publish or not to publish."[16] Again, the etymology of the Danish verb is important. Literally, it means to "give out," hence

---

[15] *Plankenkoorts en Drankzucht: Twee Essays over Theater* (Baarn: Ten Have, 1992).
[16] Joakim Garff, *SAK: Søren Aabye Kierkegaard: En Biografi* (Copenhagen: Gads Forlag, 2000) 474.

to publish a book, but it also carries the same second meaning as the parallel English expression: to "give (oneself) out" to be something other than one is. *Udgive* not only means to publish, but also to pretend, or to act.

Here we have a remarkable example of the coincidence between the situation described in the book and the situation of the book itself. Author and actress, publication and performance, come together in a mutually illuminating way. This link is first made clear by the fact that the Anna Nielsen footnote in *Stages on Life's Way* is explicitly recalled in the entries in Kierkegaard's *Journals* when the prospect of publishing this little article is first raised. The existence of that footnote is cited as part of the first reason for publishing the article. "I believe I owe it to Mrs. Heiberg, partly also because of the piece about Mrs. Nielsen at one time" (JP, 6:6209). Fru Heiberg is now to have the balance redressed. There are several good reasons adduced for publication besides this debt to Fru Heiberg, one of which is the desire to "poke Heiberg a little."

A more pressing reason, however, is the impression which Kierkegaard fears may otherwise be received that the interest in the religious in his later writings represents a change in his authorship, whereas, to quote the journal entry, "the nerve in all my work as an author actually is here, that I was essentially religious when I wrote *Either/Or*." Already the connection I want to expand on is made. Just as Fru Heiberg always communicates the essentially feminine, whether as a girl or grandmother, so through all the diversities of Kierkegaard's authorship, the essentially religious persists. The question both the actress and the authorship embody is how the message or relation can remain constant when the messenger and audience are constantly changing.

At this point, however, Kierkegaard decides that on balance the article cannot be published. He reasons that the audience that has been influenced by his later direct and forcible presentation of Christianity may be scandalized by a serialized piece about an actress. In addition, a piece about Fru Heiberg, of all people, would cause much more immediate reaction than any religious book just because of her fame and social position. His careful dialectic might be disturbed. Kierkegaard berates himself for conceitedness.

Now something interesting occurs. A page is removed from the journal and the continuation is as follows:

... it to Gjødwad — and then I left it alone, and become very sick in the afternoon — ah, I would rather write a folio than publish a page.

But now it must come out whatever happens; I will bitterly regret having remained suspended in reflection. (JP, 6:6209)

What could be a clearer indication of the anxiety of utterance incident to the public release of writing? The missing page, as much as the sigh over the effort of publication, is evidence of how deeply Kierkegaard is conflicted over this.

The fact that publication is initially a real and painful cause of anxiety is evident in the journal entries. Indeed, the question of the publication of this little article becomes literally a matter of life or death for Kierkegaard, relating to the deepest roots of utterance and memory. When Kierkegaard does decide the article must be published, he startlingly reveals that what has hitherto prevented him is a conviction that he is soon to die (JP, 6:6211). A posthumous publication has a particular awesome weight, and for his last word to be a piece on an actress would have been a scandal.

Yet for all the anxiety it enacts, a resolution is made in this entry that the article must come out. On further reflection, he realizes that the scandal has become reversed. If the article is suppressed, the problem will be that people will think him so earnest a Christian that he no longer takes an interest in the aesthetic. This too could disturb the whole authorship.

Kierkegaard realizes he has taken himself too seriously, but then has to work through taking too seriously his fault of overseriousness. Another journal entry (JP, 6:6212) shows us Kierkegaard exploring the source of his own morbid reflection and his magnification of this unimportant matter into a horrible reality that reinforces the temptation of inaction. Later entries reflect on the fact that it is precisely in trifles that the trouble occurs because they seem too small to bother God about (JP, 6:6215). The apparent triviality of the article and the disproportion of Kierkegaard's self-analysis in relation to it, which can indeed become rather wearisome to the reader of the *Journals*, are, he realizes, related. The very unimportance of the article lets it catch him off guard, so to speak. This allows an anxiety to surface which underlies all his authorship, but which he can mask in relation to a more serious work.

Even once the decision to publish is made, Kierkegaard's arguments with himself are not over, however. How about publishing the article as part of a collection, to show that the authorship is displayed in every line, Kierkegaard wonders? (JP, 6:6217). In the end, he decides to let it appear separately with a dedication to Heiberg: "To Professor J.L. Heiberg, Denmark's esthetician dedicated by a subordinate esthetician, the author" (JP, 6:6218).

With hindsight, Kierkegaard becomes convinced that the decision to publish the article is really a blessing, in that it will scotch any rumors that Kierkegaard is an apostle. In addition, it may tempt those who have given up reading the later Kierkegaard to peek into his next book: "Perhaps I will get the attention of one or two of them and help him to wound himself" (JP, 6:6223).

What comes through all this debate is precisely a concept of stages, in that the authorship itself has developed, and the author and his audience have themselves developed to a point which might make this little article the cause of misunderstanding, or of deeper understanding. What is fascinating is how much this discussion in the Journals of the publication of the article itself, which takes place "in the wings" of the theater of the authorship, reflects the discussion of performance within the article. Because of its very triviality, Crisis becomes a key moment of self-reflection in the whole authorship.

This is evident in Kierkegaard's final reflection on the whole experience: "It was a good thing that I published that little article and came under tension" (JP 6:6231). As we saw above, the concept of "tension" is vital to the performance of the actress. Does Kierkegaard need to work up this tension by positing this alarming audience and reducing himself to such an anxious state in order to be capable of writing at this level? It seems me that the restlessness and the anxiety offstage in the journals makes possible the urbanity of the little article itself, the price paid by the performer for the sense of security grounded in infinite possibility that wins the audience. I can only speak as one member of Kierkegaard's audience, but it is the sense that he is so sure-footedly ahead of one at every turn that gives his work its fascination and which induces me at any rate to read on even when I feel I am being led through a labyrinth on a tightrope, if I may use such a metaphor. Like the actress, and in her memoirs Fru Heiberg expressly praises his insight in this regard, he is "free on stage and anxious in the wings."

The anxiety in the wings is resolved in the publication as the following journal entry attests:

> N.B. N.B.
>   Yes it was a good thing to publish that little article. I began with *Either/Or* and two upbuilding discourses; now it ends, after the whole upbuilding series — with a little esthetic essay. It expresses: that it was the upbuilding the religious, which should advance, and that now the esthetic has been traversed; they are inversely related, or it is something of an inverse confrontation, to show that the writer was not an esthetic author who in the course of time grew old and for that reason became religious. (JP, 6:6238)

Indeed, Kierkegaard goes beyond that:

> Strange, strange about that little article — that I was so close to being carried away and forgetting myself. When one is overstrained as I was, it is easy to forget momentarily the dialectical outline of a colossal structure such as my authorship. (JP, 6:6242)

What here is Kierkegaard forgetting — or inventing? There are complex debates here over whether the dialectical structure exists except in retrospect or at what point it becomes evident to Kierkegaard himself. Furthermore, he is hard to catch out as ever and is quite aware of the disproportion of his obsession: "In a certain sense, of course, my concern is superfluous when I consider the world of actuality in which I live — for as a matter of fact I have not found many dialecticians" (JP, 6:6242). The audience that he so dreads is one that exists only in his imagination.

Yet of course, there is an audience always, the one woman before whom he constantly performed: Regine. In an important sense, the whole of his complex authorship was a performance before this one reader. This undoubted truth may lead us to neglect the fact that there was also Fru Heiberg, to whom he took care to send a copy of the article when it was republished along with the *Point of View*. His accompanying letter ends:

> Whether it was read at that time [i.e. at the time of its publication in *Fædrelandet*] by many or by only a few — if you did not read it, then it is the author's opinion that it has not reached its destination. But on the other hand, if you have read it — if it was then found to be, if not in perfect, yet in happy accord with your thoughts on that subject, then it is the author's opinion that it has indeed reached its destination." (LD, 390)

For this one article, at any rate, the one reader — "my reader" — in Kierkegaard's sight is Fru Heiberg. Her importance otherwise for him should not be underestimated. Jørgen Bukdahl for one sees Joanne Heiberg as a kind of soul mate for Kierkegaard, the only member of the circle that had the imagination and intensity to understand him, and one who shared his burden of having to live her life in an environment which could not fathom, or had little interest in fathoming, her mental and emotional depths.

I suspect that he is correct in this, but that the situation is more complex. Along with the admiration was there envy? Fru Heiberg had overcome the twin disadvantages of her humble and indeed perhaps illegitimate birth and her femininity to occupy a central place in the intellectual world of Denmark. She had both popular admiration and the admiration of the cultured elite. She played a role in Danish society that Kierkegaard would have loved to play, and yet knew he could not, both for extraneous and internal reasons. He never quite made it into the charmed circle of Heiberg's group and seems to have alternated between cultivating it and despising it in a rather recognizable way. He was aware, too, of the ambivalence of his position as his father's son in Copenhagen. Wealthy merchant he may have been, but Michael Kierkegaard was of humble peasant stock, and Kierkegaard's mother had been a housemaid.

Though the commonplace tag may see Anna Nielsen and Johanne Heiberg as the rivals in the theatrical world of Copenhagen, the truth is that there was another actor on the stage in Denmark and even within the Royal Theater itself. In *Point of View* we have an explicit statement that the Royal Theater becomes the scene not just of Fru Heiberg's performances but Kierkegaard's performance of the role of *flâneur*.

> When I was reading proof pages of *Either/Or*, I was so busy that it was impossible for me to spend the usual time strolling up and down the street. I did not finish until late in the evening — and then in the evening I hurried to the theater where I literally was present only five to ten minutes. And why did I do that? Because I was afraid that the big book would bring me too much esteem. And why did I do that? Because I know people, especially in Copenhagen; to be seen every night for five minutes by several hundred people was enough to sustain the opinion: So he doesn't do a thing:

he is nothing but a street-corner loafer. (POV, 61)

In the introduction to the French translation of *Crisis*, Jean Brun puts the point clearly:

> It is probable that Kierkegaard, who played with his diverse pseudonyms, recognized himself in the theatrical play. Besides, in his own life, was he not acting by seeking to pass himself off in the eyes of the whole of Copenhagen, after the breaking of his engagement, as a cynical dandy? Like the mother who blackened her breast at the moment when the moment has come to wean the infant, did he not seek to blacken himself in the eyes of Regina so that she would turn away from him? In the manner of an actor, Kierkegaard had to step back with respect to the different characters under which he presented himself to the world in order to master their game.[17]

Such passages are evidence of what Steven Crites remarks on as the way in which Kierkegaard's religious motivations could express themselves in a fundamentally theatrical way, which raises the whole issue of religious authenticity. What we have been arguing so far is that the journals show anxiety about publishing the aesthetic work *Crisis* as part of the "restlessness" and "anxiety in the wings" that lies behind the overall public performance of the authorship. However, there is a very pertinent question as to whether the metaphorical distinction between stage and wings, published work and private self-questioning, holds. The journals themselves are part of a wider performance which indeed embraces Kierkegaard's own life as a communicative element of the drama. We could quote a whole series of journal entries that would back this up.[18] The importance of

---

[17]In Søren Kierkegaard, *Oeuvres complètes*, vol. 15, *Discours Chrétiens; La Crise et une crise dans la vie d'une actrice; Monsieur Phister*, trans. Paul-Henri Tisseau and Elsa-Marie Jacquet-Tisseau (Paris: Editions de l'Orient, 1981) xxiii.

[18]As a representative sample of such entries, Kierkegaard makes this theatrical metaphor explicit when he compares Denmark and Germany as "stages" for his authorship: "My whole productivity does not really show up well in so small a theater [Denmark]," he admits, but at least "all the drama contained in my activity as an author over the four and one-half years shows up in a different way. It could not be produced in Germany, for the country is too large" (JP, 5:5904).

On his strategic adoption of roles, he writes "This is how I have understood myself. As long as I was pseudonymous, both the idea of the production and the illusion of the production required that I act outwardly as I did; it was absolutely

Crisis is that here the boundary between backstage and audience is breached, both within the text, which considers the actress in the wings, and in the *Journals* which show the machinery of the performance of the authorship.

What this raises is the whole question of the authenticity of the religious element of the authorship. Is a dramatic presentation of the theological always going to fall foul of the accusation that it is "just" playacting? Are Kierkegaard's wrestlings in the journals or in *Point of View* simply another role that he takes on, with Søren Kierkegaard as yet another pseudonym?

Such a question may not ultimately be answerable since none of his readers can be sure whether or not they are part of the same play. Before God, we cannot hide in the wings or appoint ourselves as audience, far less critic. However, the question of an author's sincerity is one that continues to be pertinent. Kierkegaard's concern over the reality of the theatrical and the tension between religious performance and religious truth is nothing new. It is examined in particular depth by the great Spanish dramatist Lope de Vega. In his play, *Lo fingido verdadero* (translated as *Acting is believing* or *The Great Pretenders*), written around 1607/1608, he dramatises the story of St. Genesius, a pagan actor in fourth century Rome who was called upon to enact his famous portrayal of a Christian martyr to entertain the emperor Diocletian.[19] As Genesius rehearses what he can do to move and entertain the audience by defying the pagan Gods, he hits on the idea of praying for baptism. At that point, an offstage voice announces

---

important to me to do everything to support the illusion that I was not an author. The fact that people nevertheless did regard me as author does not concern me; men are like that and have no aptitude for ideas except for playing havoc with them; but among other things my idea is that this ought not to interfere" (JP, 5:5942).

Kierkegaard was also well aware that this meant that the desire to see behind the scenes of the authorship would bring his life itself under scrutiny, or, to continue the metaphor, would summon him onstage: "And this is why the time will come when not only my writings but my whole life, the intriguing secret of the whole machinery, will be studied and studied" (JP, 5:6078).

[19]Quotations are from the translation and adaptation by David Johnston in *Two Plays by Lope de Vega: The Great Pretenders* and *The Gentleman from Olmedo* (Bath: Absolute Classics, 1992). Genesius may not be a historical character but rather a Roman adaptation of the similar story of Gelasinus of Heliopolis.

Pray to me and you will be saved.
You will not play this role in vain.[20]

Genesius first thinks this must be the voice of another actor, but he is touched by these words; even if they are spoken by an actor, that does not exclude the possibility of a divine intervention. He reflects to himself:

Even if that was an actor
They say that Christ took human form
That this human form suffered death
So that all men could learn to live.[21]

Christ himself is an actor, and the incarnation is in one sense the adoption of a role, Lope de Vega implies. The other actors, we as audience, and eventually the emperor himself, become increasingly confused as Genesius, known for his ability to extemporize, testifies to his own conversion. Is he acting or not? His final renunciation of acting—"I will act no more"—ironically wins Diocletian's greatest applause. Confusion becomes compounded when the actor supposed to play the angel who baptizes Genesius turns up maintaining that he has not yet done his scene while Genesius claims that a real angel has baptized him. At the end of the play, Genesius prays:

My God, you took fact for fiction.
I thought it was a harmless game;
All I sought was Caesar's applause.
I played my part for him so well.
You saw me act out love for you,
You saw this man and pitied him
And sorrowed for his lies and pain,
And you took me at my word
So my little play ends in you.[22]

In the face of this confusion of roles, Diocletian rules that Genesius can continue to play the play to the end if he wishes, but that the martyrdom scene will be a real execution. Genesius dies a martyr's death on stage and is thereafter venerated as a saint.

---

[20]Lope de Vega, *The Great Pretenders*, 72.
[21]Lope de Vega, *The Great Pretenders*, 73.
[22]Lope de Vega, *The Great Pretenders*, 83.

What Lope de Vega brings explicitly into our consideration is the element of performance in the life of Christ and in the incarnation. His complex drama of real and feigned conversion leads to the question of the drama enacted in Jesus' life. It can be read as a conscious or unconscious piece of playacting on the part of Jesus, although the audience in the gospels is highly critical of his portrayal of the Son of God. They have very different expectations of how this role should be played.

At the same time, it can be taken as representing the public playing out of the life of God, God's scandalously vulnerable act of '*udgive*,' of 'giving out.' Kierkegaard's empathetic engagement with the anxieties and joys of the actress is of a piece with his steadfast devotion to the task of elucidating the incarnation. Through considering Fru Heiberg's performance, he is led to a profound struggle with his own role as author, which gives him, and his readers, some further insight into the tension and mystery of divine performance. His authorship, as his life's great performance, is always open to misinterpretation. Like Genesius, however eloquently he pleads his religious motivation, his audience can always interpret his words as another layer of subtlety or extravagance in his performance. In all this, Fru Heiberg as Juliet acts as a metaphor for the relationship of temporally bound and inconstant humanity to the unchanging God and for the trust in infinite possibility that can bring this about. In her own right, she also acts as his audience, both in fact and in Kierkegaard's imagination, which evokes at least one aspect of the complex performance of the authorship. By her reappearance on stage as Juliet, she vindicates the risk of the actor, of the religious writer who knows himself to be different from what he was when younger, and speaking without authority of a God whom he can only serve unworthily. Like Genesius, too, his counterfeit performance may be taken, without his choosing, as real money, to adopt a Kierkegaardian metaphor, and be put to his account.

It is right, then, that the last word should lie with Fru Heiberg herself, whose own voice has been relegated to a footnote hitherto in this paper. Rather unfairly, her response to *Crisis* in her memoirs is sometimes dismissed as simply a repetition of Kierkegaard's thoughts. I suspect this seriously underestimates the intelligence of Fru Heiberg and her capacity as an actress and a producer to reflect on her performance.

After praising Kierkegaard's insight into the joys and anxieties of the actor's calling, Fru Heiberg continues with an intriguing passage about how the role of Juliet took hold of her before the 1848 performance, to the point that she began to think that playing this role was her life's calling. She was then brought to recollect that there is a higher calling than art. "It is an extremely difficult matter in an artist's life to be moderate in one's artistic interests and not to place artistic goals as one's life's highest task, not completely to give way to one's art; but humankind does not have permission to do this. We are bound to a higher goal, a great spiritual struggle . . ."[23] It is one's individuality that is the highest role, she reminds herself.

The lesson that both she and Kierkegaard have learned from her work as an actress and from the crisis that her reappearance as Juliet provoked in both of them is that in the divine theater we are called to act out our selves, in response to the divine performance of the incarnation. This is the lesson that Kierkegaard in turn sought to impart throughout his authorship and that he had to learn again and again as he wrestled with his own anxieties of utterance.

[23]J. Heiberg, *En Liv* 2:162.

13

The Actress and an Actress in the Life of a Critic: Higher Criticism in "The Crisis"

Joseph Westfall

With regard to "The Crisis and a Crisis in the Life of an Actress," Inter et Inter's only published work and Kierkegaard's last attempt at dramatic criticism,[1] it is perhaps best to begin with Kierkegaard's words themselves:

> Yes, it was a good thing to publish that little article. I began with *Either/Or* and two upbuilding discourses; now it ends, after the whole upbuilding series—with a little esthetic essay. It expresses: that it was the upbuilding—the religious—that should advance, and that now the esthetic has been traversed; they are inversely related, or it is something of an inverse confrontation, to show that the writer was not an esthetic author who in the course of time grew older and for that reason became religious. (JP, 6:6238; C, xvi, 420)

Having spent much time worrying over whether he should publish "The Crisis," Kierkegaard seems finally to have resolved that the publication of "a little aesthetic essay" was not only beneficial but necessary to the authorship that he had come to view as essentially religious in nature.[2] Without it, Kierkegaard notes, "the illusion

---

[1]Kierkegaard seems to have penned "Phister as Captain Scipio (in the Comic Opera *Ludovic*)" in December 1848, four or five months after "The Crisis" was published in *Fædrelandet* (*The Fatherland*). Although Stephen Crites takes the careful preparation of the manuscript as evidence of Kierkegaard's intention to publish "Phister" (under the pseudonym, Procul), that it remained unpublished at Kierkegaard's death seems reason to leave the essay among Kierkegaard's posthumous papers—and to consider "The Crisis" the last of the Kierkegaardian dramatic critical works. See C, 329-44, and Crites's editorial notes to Søren Kierkegaard, *Crisis in the Life of an Actress and Other Essays on Drama*, trans. Stephen Crites (London: Collins, 1967) 145.

[2]There is on this point, as on almost every point in Kierkegaard, some debate. In this case, the difference of opinion seems to rest upon the question of Kierke-

would have been established that it was I who essentially changed over the years, and then a very important point in the whole productivity would have been lost" (JP, 6:6238; C, 421). This seems straightforward enough.

Kierkegaard's unpublished accounting of "The Crisis" is nevertheless at least superficially problematic, not least because the short serial newspaper article does not have Kierkegaard as its author, but one "Inter et Inter," a pseudonymous dramatic critic. Kierkegaard is not (at least not clearly) identical with Inter et Inter, and as such what is said of "The Crisis" in Kierkegaard's own unpublished writings ought not be thought necessarily true of or applicable to that work and that other author. Leaving issues of authority aside, however, there is a far more substantive discrepancy of which Kierkegaard's analysis does not take account, and that is the classification of "The Crisis" as essentially aesthetic. While earlier aesthetic works might be interpreted to stand squarely within the aesthetic (as opposed to both the ethical and the religious), if "The Crisis" is a genuinely aesthetic work, it is so only by pushing the bounds of the category of the aesthetic (the "aesthetic stage") so far as to include something akin to the religious within itself. Thus, Inter et Inter is not an unambiguously aesthetic author, as was A in *Either/Or*. Much of what Inter et Inter has to say about drama and actresses would be unfamiliar and antithetical to such an aesthetician-critic of the theater. If Inter et Inter is an aesthete, then he is an aesthete unlike any other.

None of this is to say that Kierkegaard is wrong in his central claim, however, that "The Crisis" plays an important role for the reader in coming to understand the nature and structure of the Kierkegaardian authorship. In this essay, I will suggest a new way of understanding the specific importance of Inter et Inter and "The

gaard's reliability as not only an author, but a critic and interpreter of his own works. For a lively exchange of views on this issue (among others), see J. Garff, "The Eyes of Argus: *The Point of View* and Points of View on Kierkegaard's Work as an Author," trans. Jane Chamberlain and Belinda Ioni Rasmussen, in *Kierkegaard: A Critical Reader*, ed. Jonathon Rée and Jane Chamberlain (Oxford: Blackwell, 1998) 75-102; Sylvia Walsh's reply to Garff, "Reading Kierkegaard with Kierkegaard against Garff," *Søren Kierkegaard Newsletter* 38 (July 1999); and Garff's rejoinder to Walsh's criticisms, "Rereading Oneself," in the same issue of that publication.

Crisis" as indicative of something true, not only of the art of dramatic performance, but also of dramatic criticism—and of a certain sort of dramatic critic. In doing so, I hope to illuminate a previously neglected depth in "The Crisis," Inter et Inter's elevation of his higher sort of criticism above the ethical and ethical criticism. To that end, the three sections below will treat, in turn, (1) the different modes of criticism in the Kierkegaardian authorship that stand in contrast to "The Crisis," (2) the actress as object of Inter et Inter's criticism, and (3) the peculiar nature of that criticism.

Three Modes of Criticism

"The Crisis and a Crisis in the Life of an Actress" is a meditation on the nature of essential genius as it presents itself in the character of an actress, one who first performed the role of Juliet in Shakespeare's *Romeo and Juliet* as a sixteen-year old girl, became a theatrical sensation in Denmark, and then returned to the role as a mature woman of "thirty-one." Inter et Inter leaves the actress of his work anonymous, but it was clear to any contemporary Danish reader of the work that the actress to whom he makes reference was none other than Johanne Luise Heiberg, the renowned actress and wife of the perhaps equally renowned author, critic, university professor, newspaper editor, and all around man of Danish culture, Johan Ludvig Heiberg. As if the fact that Fru Heiberg had performed the very same role of which Inter et Inter writes, once as an ingenue and once again in her maturity as an actress, were not enough for us, it is also the case that, in a letter accompanying a gift copy of his later work, *On My Work as an Author*, Kierkegaard wrote to Fru Heiberg:

> For if you—I request this only for a moment and on behalf of this subject—if you will permit me to say this in all sincerity, that little article has special reference to you. Whether it was read at that time by many or only by a few—if you did not read it, then it is the author's opinion that it has not reached its destination. (LD, 283; C, 456)

This would seem, historically speaking, to settle the matter: Fru Heiberg is the actress. Kierkegaard's intention in this regard could not be clearer, and history could never be more helpful in coming to understand the object of a work of dramatic or literary criticism.

And yet, if we are careful and considerate readers of the Kierkegaardian authorship, then we must keep ever in mind Kierkegaard's own injunction against confusing the pseudonyms with Kierkegaard himself. As for the author of "The Crisis," Inter et Inter never breathes a word about the "true" identity of the anonymous actress of his critical hypothesis. He gives his readers enough, perhaps, to conclude for themselves that the actress in question is very much like Fru Heiberg—perhaps even modeled upon her—but this is something different from saying that Fru Heiberg is the actress under examination in "The Crisis." And thus, critically speaking, Fru Heiberg is *not* the actress. No one is the actress; or, perhaps, in the spirit of A.B.C.D.E.F. Godthaab, we can say that the actress is no one—nothing, a nobody, pure anonym and poetical conjecture.

If nothing else, coming to a basic critical awareness of the difference and distance between Fru Heiberg—a living, breathing, flesh-and-blood woman resident in Copenhagen—and "an actress" of Inter et Inter's title can free us as readers from the prevailing interpretive constraint on readings of "The Crisis," namely, that it is actually about someone—some particular one, whose history and life story should direct and delimit our understanding of Inter et Inter's article.[3] This is important for two reasons. The first of these is that it affords us some distance from readings that bind "The Crisis" and Fru Heiberg so intimately that there can be no distinction between them (the kind of reading that leads Professor Heiberg, husband and aesthetician, ultimately to side with Inter et Inter/Kierkegaard on a question of aesthetics he might otherwise have been prone to dispute).[4] The second and more important reason, however, is that

---

[3]Certainly indicative of this interpretive stance is Janne Risum, "Towards Transparency: Søren Kierkegaard and Danish Actresses," trans. Annette Mester, in *Kierkegaard and His Contemporaries: The Culture of Golden Age Denmark*, ed. Jon Stewart (Berlin: Walter de Gruyter Verlag, 2003) 330-42.

[4]Heiberg's dramatic criticism is more or less Hegelian in its centralization of what Inter et Inter calls "straightforward perfectibility" in the performance of drama, especially tragic drama. For Hegel and Heiberg, the ideal actress for the role of Juliet, then, would be someone with the gifts of a Madame Nielsen, praised for the proper correspondence of her natural age to the roles she performs. Inter et Inter praises Fru Heiberg for an essential genius as an actress that runs counter to what is praiseworthy in Madame Nielsen, and as such elevates Fru Heiberg's theatrical accomplishments to a level he thinks is higher than what Professor Heiberg mistakenly takes to be the highest. Heiberg's praising comments of "The Crisis,"

the anonymity of Inter et Inter's actress makes "The Crisis" something very different from the other works of dramatic criticism in the
Kierkegaardian authorship, of which there are seven: the four essays
on drama in the first part of *Either/Or*; the discussion of farce in *Repe-*
tition; the anonymous newspaper article, "A Cursory Observation
Concerning a Detail in *Don Giovanni*"; and the long footnote on the
actress, A.H.D. Nielsen, in *Stages on Life's Way*. In order better to
understand the peculiarity of "The Crisis," and to get a more complete sense of the Kierkegaardian criticism, we will turn our attention briefly now to these other works.

   Without delving into the details of the aesthete A's dramatic
criticism in *Either/Or* — an inquiry into the difference between ancient
and modern tragedy, a consideration of reflective sorrow in three
tragic heroines, and two dramatic reviews: one of Mozart's *Don*
Giovanni (a perennial preoccupation of the Kierkegaardian authorship), and the other of Eugène Scribe's *The First Love* — we can note
that they share an uncompromising concern for the aesthetic integrity of the dramatic works themselves. To start with the reviews,
we can see that A's criticism of *Don Giovanni* is focused chiefly —
almost exclusively — on the correspondence between the character of
Giovanni and the idea of the musical erotic (EO, 1:57-72); his criticism of *The First Love* keeps its gaze unflinchingly on the correspondence between Scribe's work and the very nature of comedy (EO,
1:263-73). As George Pattison notes, "By taking such contrasting
pieces, Kierkegaard throws the basic criteria of aesthetic judgment
into more vivid relief, namely the correspondence of idea and
form."[5] For A, the idea is ultimately the aesthetic category out of
which the work of art is drawn — in *Don Giovanni*'s case, the musical;

---

published on the overleaf of the first bound edition of the essay seem in this light
to have been written more by Heiberg qua husband than qua critic — but a hint of
the theoretical distance he wishes to maintain from Inter et Inter/Kierkegaard
remains, when he notes that the essay "certainly deserves to be read anew, if for
nothing else, then for the contempt with which it dismisses current incompetent
theater criticism in all its esthetic thinness and moral baseness" (C, 456). In this way,
Heiberg seems reluctantly to offer Danish readers Kierkegaard's little essay — not
because it is (what he takes to be) fine criticism, but because it is (or can be read to
be) such a glowing assessment and vindication of his wife.
   [5]George Pattison, "Søren Kierkegaard: A Theater Critic of the Heiberg School,"
in Stewart, *Kierkegaard and His Contemporaries*, 324.

in the case of *The First Love*, the comic. The form, on the other hand, is the basic structure of the work of art itself — *Don Giovanni* is an opera, *The First Love* a comedic play. (This is the basis for A's famous claim that the character of Don Giovanni only could ever be successfully portrayed in an opera, and that *Don Giovanni* is for that reason the ideal historical expression of the operatic.)[6]

As one might expect, this very same approach to drama plays itself out in the two other essays in which A engages, not in dramatic review, but in more general criticism of the dramatic — that is to say, in the essays "The Tragic in Ancient Drama Reflected in the Tragic in Modern Drama" and "Silhouettes," each of which constitutes a chapter in the first volume of *Either/Or*. In "The Tragic in Ancient Drama," A is concerned with the essence of the distinction between tragedy in its ancient Greek and modern German or Danish forms, a concern A derives undoubtedly from Hegel's similar treatment of the issue in his *Lectures on Aesthetics*. Following Hegel, A is chiefly interested in the character of Antigone, and the focus of "The Tragic in Ancient Drama" is twofold: first, on an analysis of Antigone as she appears in the poetry of Sophocles, and second, on a possible modern Antigone invented by A himself. Ultimately, for A, the difference between the ancient tragedy and its modern variety lies in the relative proportions of two kinds of suffering, sorrow and pain. "In ancient tragedy, the sorrow is more profound, the pain less; in modern tragedy, the pain is greater, the sorrow less" (EO, 1:147-48). Sorrow is a suffering the cause of which comes from without, and must be borne by the sufferer (in the ancient Greek tragic context) in a hereditary manner. Pain, unlike sorrow, contains within it a modicum of guilt — the one who suffers pain instead of sorrow suffers in a guilty way. The difference between the two Antigones, then, like the difference between ancient and modern tragedy, is a matter of poetic form. The brief theory of tragedy propounded in "The Tragic in Ancient Drama" rests entirely upon the tragic poet, whose work must strike the right balance in its portrayal of the idea of tragic suffering.

Similarly, in "Silhouettes," A draws three character sketches

[6]See Sylvia Walsh, *Living Poetically: Kierkegaard's Existential Aesthetics* (University Park: The Pennsylvania State University Press, 1994) 72-73.

from existing works of modern drama. The goal here is to give further elucidation to the idea of sorrow, also addressed in "The Tragic in Ancient Drama," but now with the added distinction between immediate sorrow (of little interest to A) and reflective sorrow (the sort which A and his band of *symparanekromenoi* seem so eager to identify and perpetuate in the poetic world). Such sorrow takes on three different forms, according to each of the three characters A examines in "Silhouettes": Marie Beaumarchais, from Goethe's early tragedy, *Clavigo*; Donna Elvira, from Mozart's opera, *Don Giovanni*; and Margarete, from Goethe's later closet drama, *Faust*. In all three cases, A feels free to modify the original poetic context in which the woman finds herself to suit his task in the essay; and, in each woman's case, the reflective nature of her sorrow springs from the nature of the man by whom she has been seduced.

Marie Beaumarchais's broken engagement with the writer, Clavigo, results in a sorrow reflective because it is from her perspective ever undecided whether Clavigo actually deceived her, or meant to do so if deceive her he did. Donna Elvira's sorrow turns reflective, on the other hand, not in doubt as with Marie Beaumarchais, but in hatred. Elvira knows that Giovanni has deceived her; that knowledge foments in her heart a vengeful passion equal to Giovanni's erotic passion, and for A, Donna Elvira is destined to spend the rest of her life in search of her revenge against Don Giovanni (who came to her in the convent, and thus seduced her into forsaking not only her virtue but her God): "Out of love of him, she has cast away her salvation — if it were offered her again, she would again cast it away in order to avenge herself" (EO, 1:197).

Finally, the reflective nature of Margarete's sorrow has its root in Faust's superiority to her. She is an innocent girl; Faust is a learned man of the world, whose entrance into Margarete's life results in tremendous upheaval, as intellectual and spiritual as it is material. Thus, for Margarete, Faust "was not merely a deceiver, but he was in fact a hypocrite; she has not sacrificed anything for him, but she owes him everything, and to a certain degree she still has this everything, except that now it proves to be a deception. But is what he said less true because he himself did not believe it? By no means, and yet for her it is, because she believed in it through him" (EO, 1:211). Each of the three women becomes for A an example of reflective sorrow, and each is such an example because of the nature of the relationship she has with the male title character of the dramatic work in which she poetically resides. At the center of A's criticism of *Clavigo, Don Giovanni,* and *Faust*—as in the earlier consideration of *Antigone* and *The First Love*—is the correspondence between form (character) and idea (reflective sorrow) essential to the structure of a well-formed poem.

Nowhere in any of A's works, however, is the *performative* aspect of drama central to his critical concern. Following Hegel and Professor Heiberg, A treats drama as a form of poetry—not performance—the culmination of an ideal aesthetic movement from the epic and the lyric into the dramatic.[7] This distinguishes the four works of dramatic criticism in the first volume of *Either/Or* from all of the other works of criticism in the authorship. As a critic, A focuses solely on the dramatic, operatic, or otherwise poetic works—the products of the playwright's or composer's or poet's art—and not, in great contrast to Inter et Inter's criticism, on the performance of them. This is the first mode of dramatic criticism in the Kierkegaardian authorship, a work-focused criticism.

As has been widely noted,[8] the chief concern of "A Cursory Observation Concerning a Detail in *Don Giovanni*" is the performance of the character of Zerlina, with specific reference to the duet between Zerlina and Giovanni in the first act, and perhaps even more specifically, the way in which the actress portraying Zerlina sings a single line—"No, I will not"—in the context of that duet. Unlike the purely aesthetic criticism in *Either/Or,* "A Cursory Observation" rests the entire fate of the opera on the quality of the individual actors' and actresses' performances—not on Mozart's talent for demonstrating the proper correspondence between the fictional character, Giovanni, and the idea of the musical. In contrast A, A. (the anonym-

---

[7]Pattison, "Søren Kierkegaard," 320-21. Hegel and Heiberg disagree as to the relative relation of epic and lyric poetry; A sides with Heiberg against Hegel in situating the lyric as the first stage, and the epic as the second. See Walsh, *Living Poetically,* 33.

[8]See George E. Arbaugh and George B. Arbaugh, *Kierkegaard's Authorship: A Guide to the Writings of Kierkegaard* (Rock Island IL: Augustana College Library, 1967) 284-85; Janne Risum, "Towards Transparency," 334-35; Pattison, "Søren Kierkegaard," 325-26; and my *The Kierkegaardian Author: Authorship and Performance in Kierkegaard's Literary and Dramatic Criticism* (Berlin: Walter de Gruyter, 2007) 147-59.

author of "A Cursory Observation") writes:

> The situation is essentially this: she did not know how it happened,
> but it did, and so she was seduced; and the result of Zerlina's most
> strenuous mental exercise is this: It cannot be explained. This is
> very important for an understanding of Zerlina. Therefore, it was
> a mistake for an otherwise fine actress, Madame Kragh, to sing the
> line "No, I will not" with force, as if it were a resolve fermenting in
> Zerlina. Far from it. She is confused, dazed, and perplexed from the
> start. If reflection is attributed to her at this point, the whole opera
> is a failure. (COR, 30)

Whereas the work-focused critic of *Either/Or* might have considered the character of Zerlina in terms of her placement in the
opera as a young woman to whom Giovanni's seductive interest is
drawn, the careful consideration of Boline Kragh's performance of
the role of Zerlina is something new to Kierkegaardian dramatic
criticism. Although the opera and its performers are perhaps difficult
for a spectator or critic to separate in his or her evaluation of the performance, "A Cursory Observation" is nevertheless clearly engaged
in a different sort of criticism than *Either/Or*. As a dramatic critic, A.
is not A.

Perhaps even more concerned with the performer than A., A
Married Man, in a long footnote to his "Reflections on Marriage" in
Stages on Life's Way, considers Madame Nielsen's merits as an actress
on the stage. Without reference to any specific play or performance,
A Married Man identifies Madame Nielsen's particular gift in her
portrayal of femininity. As he notes, "The actress on our stage who
really portrays femininity — without being narrowly confined to one
aspect of it, without being supported and without suffering under an
accidentality in it, without being assigned to one period of it — is
Mme. Nielsen" (SLW, 131*). And, although this "range is essential,"
according to A Married Man, Madame Nielsen's real triumph is in
her perfectibility as an actress.

> In every period of her life she will have new tasks and will express
> the essential as she did at the beginning of her beautiful career.
> And if she attains her sixtieth year, she will continue to be perfect.
> I know of no more noble triumph for an actress than this — that the
> one person who in perhaps the whole kingdom is most concerned
> not to give offense here dares to mention with confidence, as I do,
> the sixtieth year, which ordinarily is the last thing one should has-
> ten to mention in connection with an actress's name. (SLW, 132*)

What is important here, as A Married Man notes, is the contrast between the beauty and femininity portrayed by Madame Nielsen, and that evident in the more immediately recognized beautiful youth. Contrary to the superficial view, A Married Man notes that, "with the years woman increases particularly in beauty and is so far from diminishing that the first beauty is somewhat questionable when compared with the later" (SLW, 132). Just as women become more perfectly beautiful as they age, for A Married Man, so an actress such as Madame Nielsen grows more perfect in her portrayal of femininity. As a young girl, she could play young characters; and, as she ages, she will be able with equal perfection to play maturer roles, bringing femininity to life for the spectator no less in her performance as the grandmother than in her performance as the younger girl.

Despite his differences from A. A Married Man shares the same focus on the qualities and talents of the performer, and thus, together with A. demonstrates for us another object of criticism and another critical mode. As opposed to the first mode of criticism, A. and A Married Man are not as concerned with the art of the playwright or dramatist as they are with the actor's or actress' art. The second mode of criticism is thus not work-focused, but performer-focused criticism. This, as we will see, bears the greatest resemblance to Inter et Inter's critical approach.

The brief discussion of farce in *Repetition* is perhaps the most difficult to classify, as it is concerned with specific performances of farce in the Königstädter Theater in Berlin, and yet Constantin Constantius goes out of his way not to mention any specific details of those performances. Constantius offers, rather, his observations on the nature of farce (reminiscent of A), the demands it makes of the performers (reminiscent of A. and A Married Man), and the imaginative role required in any performance on the part of the spectators. The performance of farce relies fundamentally upon the participation — indeed, the laughter, according to Constantius — of the audience gathered to view any given performance. As Constantius notes, insofar as the Königstädter performances are exemplary of the nature of farce and farcical performance, the performers "have not deliberated very much on what they will do but leave everything to the moment and the natural power of laughter" (R, 159). While this maintains A.'s focus on the performers—the audience is discussed in terms of its importance for the proper performance of farce—as well as A's focus on the form of the work—the Königstädter performances are used in part to demonstrate the essential aspects of the genre of farce—we might also have here a third, spectator-focused mode of dramatic criticism, to set alongside the work-focused and performer-focused modes we have already identified. Given the brevity of Constantius's critical activity in *Repetition*, however, as well as the interweaving of the spectator and the performer central to farce on his view,[9] it remains an open question whether Constantius's approach is ultimately distinct from what I have called the first, work-focused, and the second, performer-focused modes of dramatic criticism. As it is not essential to the reading of "The Crisis" put forward in this essay, I will not attempt to close this question here.

In our quick romp through the Kierkegaardian authorship, then, we have begun to delineate the possibility of three different modes of dramatic criticism. For the sake of clarity, once again, they are: (1) the work-focused criticism of A; (2) the performer-focused criticism of A. and A Married Man (Procul would fall into this category, as well, if "Phister as Captain Scipio" were to be considered); and (3) the spectator-focused criticism of Constantin Constantius (an admittedly precarious mode). Of these approaches to criticism, only the second mode is anything comparable to the work of Inter et Inter in "The Crisis," and he will consider—but not take—an approach similar to that taken in "A Cursory Observation" and *Stages*.

Two Metamorphoses

It is perhaps easiest to understand the nature of Inter et Inter's criticism in "The Crisis" if we concentrate first on what he takes to be the central notion of the metamorphosis, by way of which his

---

[9]In this, Constantius's understanding of farce is remarkably similar to Nietzsche's understanding of Attic Greek tragedy in *The Birth of Tragedy*, particularly in Nietzsche's discussion of the necessary relationship between the Greek spectators and the Dionysian, tragic chorus. For a nod in this direction, see also Pattison, "Søren Kierkegaard," 325, where he notes that, in the "burlesque theater" wherein Constantius makes his observations on farce, the "atmosphere is positively Dionysian."

hypothetical actress makes evident to the world her essential genius. And it is perhaps easiest to understand the nature of the meta-morphosis of Inter et Inter's central concern by way of comparison with another, "lower" metamorphosis, to which he also devotes some explanatory power in "The Crisis." The two metamorphoses are in fact quite similar from the perspective of externality, but the actresses who have undergone them are inwardly qualitatively different. The first, or lower metamorphosis, Inter et Inter calls the "metamorphosis of continuity," and we have seen something of that already in A Married Man's description of Madame Nielsen in *Stages*. The second, "higher" metamorphosis—the metamorphosis that inspires Inter et Inter's criticism—he calls the "metamorphosis of potentiation."

Inter et Inter does not stray far from A Married Man in his con-ception of the first metamorphosis. The metamorphosis of continu-ity, "closely defined," he writes,

> is a process, a succession, a steady transformation over the years, so that the actress as she grows older gradually changes her sphere, takes older roles, again with the same perfection with which she at a younger age filled younger roles. This metamorphosis could be called straightforward perfectibility. (C, 323)

As we saw in *Stages*, it is a continuous perfection in the performed portrayal of femininity, despite the changes wrought by the process of physical aging and increasing mental and spiritual maturity, that characterizes the actress in this case. As A Married Man notes, "She will portray the grandmother perfectly, once again produce her effect through the essential, just as the young girl" (SLW, 132*). Although she ages, her talent for her art does not diminish, her per-formances are as perfect as ever, and in this sense it can be said of her that she "produced her effect by the dedication that is the pact of pure femininity with the imperishable" (SLW, 132*).

Before moving on to the other metamorphosis, the metamorpho-sis of potentiation, it is important to note that, in the genius actress understood in A Married Man's terms—in terms of what Inter et Inter calls "straightforward perfectibility"—is the concept recog-nition of which makes ethical criticism, or criticism from the ethical perspective, possible. As Janne Risum notes, with particular refer-ence to the discussion of Madame Nielsen, "At a time when the role of the ingenue in the comedies of intrigue was worshipped almost as a cult, Kierkegaard maintained an ethical understanding of the actress' sense of worth and her maturing as an artist beyond the limits set by age and youthful looks."[10] And with specific reference to the metamorphosis of continuity, Inter et Inter writes:

> It has especially ethical interest and therefore will exceedingly please, indeed convince, as it were, an ethicist who, fighting for his life-view, proudly points to such a phenomenon as his victory and, in quiet inner gratitude, calls such an actress his omnipotent ally, because she, better than he and precisely at one of the most dangerous points, demonstrates his theory. (C, 323-24)

Reading "The Crisis" alongside the footnote in *Stages* uncovers a new dimension to the Kierkegaardian dramatic criticism, one that organizes itself along the somewhat familiar lines delineating the aesthetic from the ethical.

Inasmuch as the metamorphosis of continuity takes place in the life of an actress as she develops and changes through time, and yet is evidence of an unwavering commitment to the idea (in this case, the idea of femininity), we find in an actress like Madame Nielsen the same sort of life-view that Kierkegaard found in an author like (the anonymous) Thomasine Gyllembourg and her novel, *Two Ages*, or that Judge William criticized as lacking in his aesthetic corre-spondent, A, in *Either/Or*. In both cases, the ethical is set up against the aesthetic as superior and more complete, and the aesthetic is identified as the root of despair. The Kierkegaardian dramatic criticism seems, then, to share this dynamic — an existential compari-son of alternative perspectives from which to engage the world that falls at least loosely into two categories, stages, or spheres: the aesthetic (A, no metamorphosis) and the ethical (A Married Man, the metamorphosis of continuity). We are thus left with two sets of criteria by which to classify and judge the dramatic criticism, one in terms of the criticism's object (the modes of dramatic criticism), and one in terms of the perspective of the critic (either the aesthetic or the ethical). The first of these is demonstrated over the course of the authorship, but never articulated within it; the second receives its first and only articulation in "The Crisis."

It is interesting, therefore, that Inter et Inter sets the second meta-

---

[10]Risum, "Towards Transparency," 338-39.

morphosis, the metamorphosis of potentiation, in contrast to and above the metamorphosis of continuity. In doing so, Inter et Inter not only offers us an alternative understanding of the essential genius of the actress, but far more importantly, philosophically speaking, he distances himself (and the anonymous actress portraying Juliet throughout his hypothesis) from the ethical. Following hard upon the passage quoted above, in which the metamorphosis of continuity is defined as a process of perfectibility extending straightforwardly through time, Inter et Inter writes, "The metamorphosis, however, of which we have been speaking is the metamorphosis of potentiation, or it is a more and more intensive return to the beginning" (C, 324). Unlike the metamorphosis of continuity, which associates the actress with the imperishable through time, the metamorphosis of potentiation brings the actress into relation with the eternal.

In a lengthy passage in "The Crisis," Inter et Inter sets forth his most succinct definition of the metamorphosis of potentiation, and of the actress who has undergone this metamorphosis. He writes:

> But then in turn an ideality of recollection will vividly illuminate the whole performance, an incarnation that was not present even in those days of the first youthfulness. Only in recollection is there complete tranquillity, and therefore the calm fire of the eternal, its imperishable glow. She has been calmed in the eternity of her essential genius; she will not childishly or plaintively long for the blazing of what has vanished, because in the metamorphosis itself she has become too warm and too rich for that. This pure, calmed, and rejuvenating recollecting, like an idealizing light, will trans-illuminate the whole performance, which in this illumination will be completely transparent. (C, 323)

Unlike the actress of straightforward perfectibility such as Madame Nielsen, who overcomes her increasing distance from physical youthfulness by turning her increasing age to the advantage of her art — playing older roles as perfectly as she played the younger ones — this other actress, the only one truly capable of playing Juliet, according to Inter et Inter, grows younger and younger as time passes. By way of a relation to the idea of feminine youthfulness, such an actress can step into an eternal youth, whereby she not only can perform the younger roles into her own maturity, but she becomes the only actress of any age truly capable of performing those roles.

The distinction drawn between the metamorphosis of continuity and the metamorphosis of potentiation rests almost entirely upon the relationship between recollection and time or, perhaps more accurately, recollection and the eternal. The metamorphosis of continuity — proper to Madame Nielsen and all actresses of straightforward perfectibility — moves in a coherent linear way through time. Her identity as an actress, and the appropriateness of any given role she plays, is simply a matter of the right correspondence between her natural age and the age of the character to be performed. When young, Madame Nielsen plays young roles; when older, maturer characters are played.

Such an actress does engage in a kind of recollection, since it is by way of relation to an idea that she can rightly be called a genius. The idea to which Madame Nielsen relates, however, and that binds her life together as a coherent whole changes as Madame Nielsen changes. Her goal is not to relate to a single idea through time, but always to insure, as George Pattison noted in a different context, a correspondence between the idea and the form. If she can maintain the correspondence, then Madame Nielsen is not only a brilliant actress and a genius to boot — she is in possession of that fundamental element of the ethical and all ethical criticism, a life-view.[11] Importantly, then, when this actress recollects she returns herself to the past, gathering together an understanding of herself as she has passed through time, and striving always to enact the proper correspondence between herself and her work for her age. Always relative to her maturity and her situation in time, Madame Nielsen's life-view maintains the focus of her audience (and her critics) on Madame Nielsen herself — and her recollection is thus always a deepening of her self-understanding and the public's understanding of her self.

---

[11]Sylvia Walsh draws the connection between the life-view ascribed to Madame Nielsen in *Stages on Life's Way* and "the correspondence between the life and art of the creative artist" set forth in *From the Paper's of One Still Living*, as well as the contrast between these and the very different approach ascribed to (an actress very much like) Fru Heiberg in "The Crisis." See Walsh, *Living Poetically*, 184-85. As I have argued elsewhere, there is no such correspondence between life and art in the case of the actress of Inter et Inter's hypothesis. See Westfall, *The Kierkegaardian Author*, 258-59, 268-69.

The actress of Inter et Inter's hypothesis, on the other hand, has a metamorphosis of potentiation, not continuity. Also engaged in recollection—and in relation to an idea—her movement is not backward, into the past, but forward. In the service of the idea, this actress lives *in suspenso*—waiting, as it were, for another opportunity to fulfill her possibility, her potential, as an actress. Thus, while Madame Nielsen recollects herself into the past but, in so doing, keeps the focus on her passage through time and increasing maturity, this other actress' recollection situates her (and her audience, and critics) in the timelessness of an eternal youth—what Inter et Inter calls, once again, "a more and more intensive return to the beginning" (C, 324). The metamorphosis of continuity emphasizes an actress' temporality; the metamorphosis of potentiation, her eternality. Keeping in mind that the actress of Inter et Inter's hypothesis is playing Juliet for the second time, it is perhaps not inappropriate to recall at this point Constantin Constantius's cryptic distinction between recollection and repetition: "Repetition and recollection are the same movement, except in opposite directions, for what is recollected has been, is repeated backward, whereas genuine repetition is recollected forward" (R, 131). In this vein, we might say that Madame Nielsen recollects herself into the maturity of a life-view and the ethical; the actress of Inter et Inter's hypothesis repeats herself into eternity—and, if Johannes Climacus is correct, immanent religiousness or something like it.[12]

---

[12]A full exploration of the relations between *Concluding Unscientific Postscript to 'Philosophical Fragments'*, and "The Crisis and a Crisis in the Life of an Actress" is certainly beyond the scope of the present work. Nevertheless, it is worth briefly noting that, for Johannes Climacus, one thing is essential to both of the border categories, irony and humor: namely, "recollection's withdrawal from temporality into the eternal" (CUP, 1:272). This is not the sort of recollection in which Madame Nielsen engages, a thoroughly ethical means of arranging her life and her performance properly, steeped deeply in her experience of temporality. Rather, the recollection of which Climacus writes is much more like that Inter et Inter associates with the actress of his hypothesis who, in having undergone the metamorphosis of potentiation, draws herself into "complete tranquillity . . . the calm fire of the eternal" (C, 323). Although Climacus never identifies "recollection's immanental withdrawal into the eternal" with immanent religiousness (or Religiousness A) in the *Postscript*, such recollection—recollection of the sort in which Inter et Inter's actress is ever engaged—must ultimately reside for Climacus in either the immanence of that religiousness, or the *confinium* preceding immanent religiousness, that

Siding ultimately with potentiation over continuity, Inter et Inter notes, "in order to *represent* Juliet an actress must essentially have a distance in age from Juliet" (C, 321). With that distance, and a serving relation to the idea of feminine youthfulness, the actress can grow younger. "Of course she will not be young again in the ridiculous sense in which butcher assistants and the public speak of a devilishly pert wench, but only in the sense of ideality will she be young and younger" (C, 319). This is so much and so clearly the case, according to Inter et Inter, that he expresses curiosity at the more common understanding of what is necessary in an actress assigned the role of a young girl. While "butcher assistants and the public" require of her that the actress be young in the physical sense of youth, Inter et Inter is convinced that it is only in relation to the idea of feminine youthfulness — and not participation in the natural fact of feminine youthfulness — that an actress can perform youth.

On this basis, with regard to the actress of his hypothesis in "The Crisis," he remarks, "The most significant assignment given to an actress who relates herself to the idea of feminine youthfulness raised to its most lyrical power is surely the role of Juliet in *Romeo and Juliet*. I wonder if it would ever actually occur to an esthetician that an actress of seventeen years could play Juliet?" (C, 321). If it could not occur to an aesthetician, it could at least occur to a critic — and has, in the form of A Married Man, for whom the appropriateness of a role for an actress has everything to do with the manner in which she relates to her own age (or, presumably, youthfulness). On A Married Man's view, the older actress cannot effectively perform the younger role, precisely because her genius lies in changing her roles as she changes, in perfect accord with and out of respect for the very real passage of time. The ethical criticism of *Stages*, a criticism that searches out actresses like Madame Nielsen who undergo the metamorphosis of continuity as they age, must dispute Inter et Inter's assertion, that an actress must have a distance in age from Juliet if she is to represent her in performance. In his commitment to ideality and the eternal youth of the actress, Inter et Inter breaks definitively with A Married Man and all ethical criticism.

---

is, in humor. Thanks to Robert L. Perkins for drawing this possibility to my attention.

If Inter et Inter is not an ethical critic (as both Risum and Pattison seem to believe he is)[13] then what sort of critic is he? He has already associated himself with the aesthetic, scoffing at the notion that an aesthetician could ever seriously consider a seventeen-year old girl capable of performing the role of Juliet, and this is as good a place as any to begin to understand the character of Inter et Inter in "The Crisis." Shortly after presenting the metamorphosis of potentiation as an alternative to the metamorphosis of continuity, he notes importantly that, "This metamorphosis will completely engage an esthetician, because the dialectic of potentiation is the esthetic-metaphysical dialectic" (C, 323-24). And much earlier in the text, Inter et Inter testifies that, "the author is indeed esthetically convinced that the metamorphosis [of potentiation] is the highest" (C, 307). We began our study with some consideration of Kierkegaard's claim that "The Crisis" is an aesthetic work, and throughout "The Crisis," we find Inter et Inter confirming that classification again and again. As we have already seen, however, Inter et Inter is no ordinary aesthete. If "The Crisis" is an aesthetic work, and yet not in the sense in which A's works are aesthetic, then what sort of aesthetic is appropriate to "The Crisis"? To borrow a phrase from another Kierkegaardian author, we might say that, beyond the aesthetic and the ethical there is a "higher aesthetic" — an aesthetic perspective out of which one such as Inter et Inter could write a higher criticism.[14]

---

[13]Risum, "Towards Transparency," 338-39; Pattison, "Søren Kierkegaard," 328-29.

[14]This, in direct contrast to George Pattison's contention that "The Crisis" falls within what me might call the "ordinary scope" of the aesthetic in Kierkegaard's writings. Pattison writes, "for Kierkegaard, the autonomy of the aesthetic is always circumscribed by other dimensions of or approaches to existence that render the aesthetic questionable. Kierkegaard's practice as a literary critic indicates what was for him the essence of the aesthetic stage: it is the lifeview of the reflecteur who deliberately maintains a critical distance from the immediate object of consciousness in order to judge this object in the light of its relationship to ideality." Pattison, "Søren Kierkegaard," 328-29. On my reading, "The Crisis" throws precisely this understanding of the aesthetic into question.

A Higher Criticism

This higher criticism, as it were, will be a qualitatively different sort of criticism on both sets of criteria we have seen in the dramatic critical authorship. That is to say, Inter et Inter's higher criticism will be both something different from the either/or of the aesthetic and the ethical, as well as something different from the work-, performer-, and spectator-focused modes of dramatic criticism employed in various places throughout the authorship. The higher criticism, as I understand it, will share something of the immediacy of the aesthetic criticism and the reflectiveness of the ethical criticism, and yet will transcend both. This is admittedly a tall order. Nevertheless, it seems also to be at the heart of Inter et Inter's project in "The Crisis."

Perhaps the most basic question one ought to have of Inter et Inter in a reading of "The Crisis" has to do, not with the actress, who is presented clearly and dramatically in Inter et Inter's careful and poetic prose, but with the critic him- or herself. By what indications in the actress or her performance does the critic on Inter et Inter's view identify the essential actress, she who has undergone the metamorphosis of potentiation and lives in an eternal youth? She will, on the surface of things, seem no different from Madame Nielsen or any of the other actresses of straightforward perfectibility. The essential actress is not incapable of performing the older roles, despite the fact that only she, in her maturity, is capable of performing the younger ones. And the public and great mass of spectators are clearly unqualified to guide us in our attempt, seeing as they only and always are in search of the pretty and the pert — not the essential geniuses. Inter et Inter has written himself into something of a circle here, whereby the essential aesthetician is defined as the one who can identify the essential actress, and the essential actress is defined as she who is of interest to the essential aesthetician. Inter et Inter notes that, "if there lived an essential aesthetician at the time and he was asked to appraise this actress or one of her performances, he would no doubt say: No, her time has not really come yet" (C, 314). The definitiveness of the essential aesthetician's assertion is startling, considering the fact that it is as much a claim about the actress in the future — after she has experienced the metamorphosis — as it is about the actress the aesthetician actually can observe and appraise, the actress in the present. In the essential aesthetician's mind, it seems, the essential actress is explicable only in a kind of dissociation from her presence in time.

Moreover, that element essential to the essential actress is, according to Inter et Inter, strictly speaking impossible to articulate. As he writes, "She makes her debut, then, in her seventeenth year. She possesses—well, what she possesses is very difficult to define, simply because it is an indefinable something that nevertheless omnipotently asserts itself and is unconditionally obeyed" (C, 307-308). At the heart of the vision of the essential actress in "The Crisis" is—something indefinable. Although its indefinability does not entail its or the actress' unrecognizability, at least not necessarily, that the element of greatest interest to an aesthetician and observer of the theater in the performance of the actress cannot clearly be defined and stated puts the person interested in learning how to identify an essential actress in something of a bind. Despite Inter et Inter's claim that, in all of its ambiguity, this indefinable something "nevertheless omnipotently asserts itself and is unconditionally obeyed," that omnipotence and unconditionality are clearly only recognizable to the essential aesthetician—all other critics and spectators, as Inter et Inter laments time and again, are after something a bit more definable in an actress. Associated with her eternality, then, is the actress' fundamental inexplicability.

The method or manner by way of which an aesthetician or dramatic critic might come not only to recognize but also to understand an essential actress of the sort Inter et Inter hypothesizes is, then, simultaneously essential to the critic's project and fundamentally unclear. It remains so, throughout "The Crisis." When discussing the tension experienced by the actress, released on stage in her performance, Inter et Inter notes the imperceptibility of the actress' art:

> For every tension can affect in a twofold way; this is the dialectic's own dialectic. It can make the exertion manifest, but it can also do the opposite; it can conceal the exertion, and not only conceal it but continually convert, transform, and transfigure it into lightness. The lightness, then, is invisibly based on the exertion of the tension, but this is not seen, is not even intimated—only the lightness is made manifest. (C, 312)

The essential actress' essential maneuver—the transformation of the weight of the role and the eyes of the audience into lightness — is essentially invisible. No one in the theater, not even the essential aesthetician and critic, can see it occur. If anyone could see it, for Inter et Inter, this would be evidence that the actress was not in fact an essential genius. We are left once again to wonder as to the possibility not only of the actress, but also of the critic who could pick such an actress out of the crowd.

In this way, over the course of "The Crisis," the focus of Inter et Inter's critical inquiry comes to be as much on the critic as it is on the object of the critic's criticism. Although itself a work of dramatic criticism, "The Crisis" does not attempt to criticize or interpret any actual work, performer, or performance. It is, instead, a purely hypothetical, purely ideal examination of the anonymous actress of Inter et Inter's imagination — however much she may seem to resemble Fru Heiberg, to us or to Kierkegaard. Much as Johannes de silentio posits the possibility of the knight of faith without actually attempting to identify one, so Inter et Inter posits the eternally young actress as essential genius, without attempting to give his readers a contemporary or historical example. In a manner of speaking, then, despite its constant discussion of the actress — despite the centrality of the actress in its title — "The Crisis and a Crisis in the Life of an Actress" is criticism without an object, or, perhaps more accurately, dramatic criticism focused, not on the drama, but on itself, on its own critical activity. Inter et Inter thus adds a fourth mode to our taxonomy of Kierkegaardian criticisms, namely, *critic*-focused dramatic criticism.

"The Crisis" is rife with comments critical of the behavior of the dramatic critics of Kierkegaard's day, and seems if nothing else to chide those critics for the superficiality of their interest in drama. Of the criticisms we have seen demonstrated in the Kierkegaardian authorship, only the second mode, the performer-focused mode of criticism, is anything like the criticism of the day in Denmark, and even those works — A.'s concern for the performance of that one line by the actress singing the part of Zerlina, A Married Man's interest in the durability of Madame Nielsen's career, or even Constantin Constantius's conviction that the audience is an essential component in the performance of farce — have something far above and beyond the kind of "bestial" criticism Inter et Inter observes in the Danish newspapers. Interestingly, "The Crisis" never seems to take as its goal the demonstration of the possibility of the essential actress, nor the far more concrete attempt to identify some particular actress as an actress of this magnificent sort (a task that might not have been so difficult, considering how quickly the lines were drawn between his anonymous actress and Fru Heiberg). Rather, Inter et Inter posits the possibility of such actresses, says a great deal about the type, and then chides his fellow critics for failing to search out such women for aesthetic discussion and critical praise. Without ever really engaging in such criticism himself, Inter et Inter demonstrates the possibility of a higher kind of dramatic criticism, philosophically engaged and respectful of the actress as an artist, and yet deeply grounded in the aesthetic rather than the ethical. This last point is an important one since, for Inter et Inter, it is crucial that the actress' triumph be an eternally indefinable aesthetic triumph, and not the successful application of universal ethical categories to drama.

Johannes de silentio announces the importance of the tie that binds a hero to his poet, and it is perhaps not inappropriate to extend the importance of this claim into the consideration of drama in "The Crisis." Bound together forever by her performance and his criticism, the essential aesthetician of Inter et Inter's hypothesis (perhaps Inter et Inter — or Kierkegaard himself) plays the poet to his heroine, the actress of that very same hypothesis (perhaps Fru Johanne Luise Heiberg). Certainly the Heibergs come to see Kierkegaard and "The Crisis" in this way.[15] This relationship, like so many other aspects of Inter et Inter's criticism, locates the fourth mode of dramatic criticism — the critic-focused criticism — squarely within the aesthetic, as Kierkegaard noted in his unpublished writings. And yet, this is an aesthetic that goes beyond the aesthetic, a critical perspective that is somehow above the ethical in a manner that, to this

---

[15]See Howard Hong's editorial notes, as well as relevant quotations from both Fru and Professor Heiberg, at C, xvii; 456. Also J. Garff, *Søren Kierkegaard: A Biography*, trans. Bruce H. Kirmmse (Princeton: Princeton University Press, 2005) 550. Of Prof. Heiberg's publication of Kierkegaard's dedicatory letter to Fru Heiberg (cited above), Garff writes, "Heiberg concluded by recommending Kierkegaard's piece, which he said ought to be read because of, among other reasons, the 'contempt with which he dismisses the incompetent theater criticism of these times, with all its aesthetic shallowness and moral odiousness'." We might contrast Inter et Inter's "aesthetic-metaphysical" higher criticism with precisely the criticism Heiberg deplores.

point in the Kierkegaardian authorship, only faith and the religious have been.

And so, it is perhaps not inappropriate that, in a strange turn of events in the Kierkegaardian authorship, Inter et Inter uses faith itself as a clarifying example of the aesthetic phenomenon of the actress, rather than the more characteristic use of some aesthetic phenomenon as a clarifying example of faith or the religious (as in the works of Johannes de silentio, Johannes Climacus, and often Kierkegaard himself). Shortly after the discussion of the actress' invisible transmutation of weight into lightness, quoted above, Inter et Inter writes:

> In a higher, in a poetical and philosophical sense, the opposite holds true: one becomes light by means of — weight; one soars high and free by means of — a pressure. The celestial bodies, for example, hover in space by means of a great weight; the bird flies by means of a great weight; the light hovering of faith is precisely by means of an enormous weight; the highest soaring flight of hope is precisely by means of hardship and the pressure of adversity. (C, 312)

Instead of understanding this comparison as the diminution of faith, however, it seems for Inter et Inter to function as the elevation of the aesthetic — or, at least, of one form of the aesthetic, what he calls "the aesthetic-metaphysical" and the performance of which I call "the higher criticism": one more articulation, perhaps, of that most Kierkegaardian (and Kierkegaard-like) of characters, the religious poet. Or, perhaps, yet one more stage on life's way.

14

"Drunk"? / "Not Drunk"?
The Dialectic of Intoxication
in "Phister as Captain Scipio" and "Becoming Sober"

Christopher A. P. Nelson

Introduction: The Concept of Intoxication

Generically, the concept of "intoxication" [*Beruselse*] figures and functions throughout Kierkegaard's writings as a ready shorthand for a variety of existential impairments or for existential impairment in general. The author of the dissertation plays upon the rich dispari-ty of the drunken Alcibiades and the Socrates who, according to this same Alcibiades, could drink anyone under the table without ever himself getting drunk.[1] The ethical apologist repeatedly criticizes his

---

[1]CI, 24-25, 41, 47-52, 188-89; cf. Plato, *Symposium* 212d-223a. See the discussion of this juxtaposition in Sylvia Walsh, "Ironic Love: An Amorist Interpretation of Socratic Eros," in *International Kierkegaard Commentary: The Concept of Irony*, ed. Robert L. Perkins (Macon GA: Mercer University Press, 2001) 128-29. It is worth noting here and in connection with what follows that the author of the dissertation is also willing to attribute a kind of intoxication to Socrates specifically — namely, the intoxicating emptiness of negativity (CI, 175*) — and to "the ironist" generally — namely, the intoxicating infinity of possibilities encountered in or occasioned by this negativity (CI, 262). Already in Plato, however, there is a clear enough sense that intoxication is an experience, or rather, a condition that cuts across a variety of existential planes, including the physiological, the psychological, the political, and the religious (see, e.g., *Cratylus* 406c, *Phaedrus* 265b, *Republic* 573c, and *Laws* 637a-674c) — a condition that is arguably all the more potent when, to press the metaphor in a manner that Kierkegaard would doubtlessly applaud, one begins imbibing mixed drinks. Plato even goes so far as to have his "Athenian" recommend a more or less moderated exposure to physiologically induced intoxication as a kind of preparatory exercise for the eventual battle of the self with itself vis-à-vis these other more dangerous kinds of intoxication (*Laws* 649d-650b). In the spirit of Alfred North Whitehead's famous characterization of the European philosophical tradition (Whitehead, *Process and Reality: An Essay in Cosmology*, part 2, chap. 1, sect. 1), one may say that there are really only two substantial footnotes to this item in Plato:

aesthetic counterpart for succumbing to the lure of intoxication.[2] The upbuilding author consistently and coherently warns against the single if multifarious danger of intoxication.[3] And virtually every misguided form of love is pointedly characterized by the Christian deliberator as a kind of intoxication.[4] The verdict appears univocal: intoxication is a more or less vicious but nevertheless somehow alluring existential impairment.[5]

Specifically, however, what is intoxication, or what is it to be intoxicated?[6] The authorship contains two substantial engagements with this particular question, although neither piece was published

---

Kierkegaard on the one hand, and Friedrich Nietzsche on the other. In fact, and insofar as Kierkegaard and Nietzsche have both proven to be perpetually stubborn participants in this tradition, a still more volatile point of reference than the seemingly moderate position espoused by Plato may be the quasi-Platonic and quasi-Christian (and in a very real sense remarkably Nietzschean) Carpocratian heresy, which appears to bear especially upon the question regarding the ultimate significance of intoxication, and about which Kierkegaard displays a profound apprehensiveness (see JP, 1:219; cf. PF, 247; CA, 103; JP, 4:4391; 5:5227).

[2]EO, 2:7, 16, 53, 83, 122, 146, 158, 194. On the other hand, and in whatever guise he appears — e.g., A (EO, 1:41-42, 78), Johannes the seducer (EO, 1:325-26), the young man (R, 190, 205, 221-22), William Afham (SLW, 17-18) — the 'aesthete' appears only too willing to concede the point.

[3]EUD, 37, 70, 80, 89, 111, 192, 201, 212, 215, 257.

[4]WL, 19, 56, 94, 161, 163, 187-88, 298; cf. WL, 428-29, 466.

[5]For a remarkably focused reading of Kierkegaard's authorship in a comparable spirit, see Erik Norman Lindland, *Kierkegaard on Self-Deception* (Ph.D. Thesis, Indiana University, 2004). University Microfilms #AAT 3162279.

[6]For an engaging response to this question in and about the writings of Nietzsche (especially *Thus Spoke Zarathustra*), see Sonia Sikka, "Nietzsche's Contribution to a Phenomenology of Intoxication," *Journal of Phenomenological Psychology* 31/1 (2000): 19-43. Those without the stomach for such an engagement will perhaps find something more to their taste in the analytical discussions of drunkenness, epistemology, and drunken epistemologies in Brian O'Shaughnessy, "Mental Structure and Self-Consciousness," *Inquiry* 15 (1972): 30-63; and Matthias Steup, "Proper Functioning and Warrant after Seven Vodka Martinis," *Philosophical Studies* 72/1 (1993): 89-109. And if one simply cannot decide whether "intoxication" is something to be warmly embraced or coldly analyzed, Michel de Montaigne's "Of Drunkenness," in *Essays of Michel de Montaigne*, trans. Charles Cotton (Garden City: Doubleday & Company, 1947) 95-105, may well hit the spot. This particular edition of Montaigne's essay is worth reading if only for the magnificent accompanying illustrations (also, presumably, of drunkenness) supplied by the compiler of this edition of Montaigne's essays, Salvador Dali.

in Kierkegaard's lifetime: "Phister as Captain Scipio" (PCS, 327-44)[7] and "Becoming Sober" (JFY, 93-143).[8] In both of these works Kierkegaard engages and invokes a dialectic of intoxication according to which the clearest initial indication that one is "drunk" is the very appearance of the maintenance of the appearance of being sober. Among the accidental results of this recognition is a view of the entire authorship as a prolonged and pronounced kind of divine comedy, in and according to which "intoxication" emerges as a particularly telling and uniquely intensified metonym for despair.[9]

---

[7]The text of "Phister as Captain Scipio," trans. Howard V. Hong and Edna H. Hong (hereafter, "PCS"), is included as an "Addendum" in *Kierkegaard's Writings* XVII: *Christian Discourses* and *The Crisis and a Crisis in the Life of an Actress*, ed. H. V. Hong and E. H. Hong (Princeton: Princeton University Press, 1997) 327-44. See also the translation by Stephen Crites—also presented as an addendum to *The Crisis*—in Kierkegaard, *Crisis in the Life of an Actress and Other Essays on Drama*, trans. Stephen Crites (London: Collins, 1967) 107-26.

[8]In addition to "Phister as Captain Scipio" and "Becoming Sober," the authorship contains two broken engagements with this question. The first takes the form of an unwritten book—an "address on liquor" (P, 27)—prefaced by Nicolaus Notabene's "Preface V" (P, 27-30). See Robert L. Perkins, "Reading Kierkegaard's *Prefaces* with 'Continual Reference to Socrates,'" in *International Kierkegaard Commentary: Prefaces and Writing Sampler*, ed. Robert L. Perkins (Macon GA: Mercer University Press, 2006) 125-29; and Stephen Crites, "The Unfathomable Stupidity of Nicolaus Notabene," in *International Kierkegaard Commentary: Prefaces and Writing Sampler*, 33-34. The second takes the form of an unrecorded conversation—a discussion "with regard to the various effects of wine upon consciousness" (SLW, 30; cf. SLW, 556-57)—referenced but unrelated in William Afham's "In Vino Veritas" (SLW, 7-86). See Robert E. Wood, "Two Banquets: Plato's and Kierkegaard's," in *International Kierkegaard Commentary: Stages on Life's Way*, ed. Robert L. Perkins (Macon GA: Mercer University Press, 2000) 49-68.

[9]Having said as much as this—i.e., that "intoxication" is conceived by Kierkegaard as a particularly potent existential impairment and a metonym for the most potent of all such impairments—the elision of Kierkegaard's contribution to the discussion regarding the nature and significance of intoxication in the otherwise astounding treatment of the history of this discussion in Marty Roth, *Drunk the Night Before: An Anatomy of Intoxication* (Minneapolis: University of Minnesota Press, 2005), calls for some comment. Now, to be sure, the fact that Kierkegaard's contributions to this discussion are contained in a pair of posthumously published works that are not exactly among the featured items of Kierkegaard scholarship is arguably a sufficiently mitigating factor. Nevertheless, given the manner in which Roth introduces his study—by reference to a certain "great event in the history of the West," namely, "a shift in the valence of alcohol in the mid-nineteenth century from a register of intoxication to one of addiction" (xiii)—and his provocative

Procul's "Phister as Captain Scipio"

The first substantial engagement with the question regarding the nature and significance of intoxication takes the form of a proposed but ultimately unpublished piece of "drama criticism" titled, "Phister as Captain Scipio (in the Comic Opera *Ludovic*): A Recollection and for Recollection" (PCS, 329).[10] The subject of the piece is the performance of the Danish actor Joachim L. Phister in the character of "Captain Scipio" in the comic opera *Ludovic*, by J. H. Vernoy de St. Georges.[11] The character in question is, among other things, a comic drunk. Or rather, the character is one who is drunk and yet not drunk, being always and only continually half-tipsy. The performance appears to have fascinated Kierkegaard. The question is: Why?[12]

In its final formulation the review of Phister's performance as Captain Scipio was to have borne the pseudonym "Procul" as author.[13] This appellation is perhaps as important as any element of the review itself, inasmuch as it appears to recall the line from Virgil (*Aeneid* 6:258), "*procul o procul este profani*" —a line that is variously translated as "away, away, O unhallowed ones,"[14] far, far away, are

---

hypothesis that "[r]ather than intoxication being used to characterize heaven or ecstasy, ecstasy and heaven were originally carved out of the experience of intoxication" (78) —a reversing of Kierkegaard's reversing of the reverseness—it is regrettable that the appropriately attuned reader is left to imagine what might have been born of this collision had Roth invoked Kierkegaard as an interlocutor.

[10]Following Wood's proposal that "wine . . . is the central metaphor for recollection" throughout the text of "In Vino Veritas" (Woods, "Recollection and Two Banquets," 49), the central theme of "Phister as Captain Scipio" is hinted at already in the work's subtitle, "A Recollection and for Recollection."

[11]See CD, 460n42.

[12]Crites gives the following generally accurate answer already in his introduction to the text: "In the sketch of Phister, Kierkegaard turns to the idea of reflective comedy, showing how the actor exhibits this particular genius in making a stock role in a commonplace comedy into a rare work of comic art." Kierkegaard, *Crisis in the Life of an Actress and Other Essays on Drama*, trans. Crites, 34.

[13]See JP, 6:6292, 6293.

[14]EO, 2:53, 273; CD, 465n81; PC, 5, 23, 61; TM, 345.

the uninitiated,"[15] and "at a distance, you unholy ones."[16] In any case, the basic significance of the name is clear. More than any other pseudonym, the appellation says: I am a false name, a wrong path — look away. Perhaps the admonition is rather like the stereotypical dictum of the police officer charged with crowd control: nothing to see here. The opening of the review appears to suggest as much:

> It may seem accidental and strange to take just a single performance by such a wide-ranging actor as Phister, and if one does take a single performance, then it may in turn again seem accidental and strange to select Captain Scipio in particular. Well, as a matter of fact the latter is accidental, or there is something accidental in it, but so it is and so it must be — least of all is there any intimation of the silly notion that this role is the best, the most splendid, etc. No, there is something accidental in it — namely, "Captain Scipio" is an outstanding performance in what is Phister's greatest strength: reflection — accordingly it is essentially appropriate to make it the subject of a review. The characteristic of the critical review commensurate with reflection is that it concentrates on details, goes into detail; accordingly, with regard to Phister, it is essentially appropriate to make a single performance the subject of a review and of a detailed review — rather than of a general discussion that says very little. The accidental aspect is that precisely this role has appealed to the author. (PCS, 329)

There is something accidentally appealing in Phister's performance as Captain Scipio about which the author finds "a pleasure, a joy, a satisfaction" in writing (PCS, 330). This certain something is the impetus of the review.

Before turning to the elucidation of this accidentally appealing detail, Procul sets the tone of the review. Having identified "reflection" as the greatest strength of the actor, Procul maintains that the review ought to repay the performance in the same coin, as

[15]JP, 5: p.476n159.

[16]JP, 6: p.590n1816. While not reaching as far as Virgil's *Aeneid* for assistance, Crites offers the following assessment: "*Procul*, the pseudonym assumed by Kierkegaard for this article, is Latin for 'afar off' or 'at a distance.' This pseudonym seems to have been chosen with the passage which appears on p. 113 in the text in mind [cf. PCS, 332], which refers to the 'infinitely distant' relationship between the reflective critic and the reflective artist whom he admires, an admiration 'as aristocratically distant as mind can be from mind.'" Kierkegaard, *Crisis in the Life of an Actress and Other Essays on Drama*, trans. Crites, 146n1.

it were. Thus, rather than engaging in either of the typically unreflective modes of aesthetic criticism—"censorious pettiness" at the one
extreme and the "pathology of immediate admiration" at the other
(PCS, 332)—Procul proposes to pit reflection against reflection. A
reflective performance calls for a reflective review. Although the
reviewer is thus released from the bonds of a certain "obligation"
(PCS, 332), the matter becomes arguably all the more earnest
inasmuch as the reflective engagement with reflection "is akin to
undergoing an examination: whether one has understood or not,
whether one knows anything or not" (PCS, 333).

Inasmuch as Captain Scipio is, at the very least, a comic character, the question basically becomes: What is so reflectively funny
about Phister's performance as Captain Scipio? Procul identifies
three elements that contribute to the collective comic effect: Captain
Scipio's "splendid uniform" (PCS, 334), his state of being continually
"half-drunk" (PCS, 333), and what is incidentally apparent in the
juxtaposition of the first two elements, namely, the basic contradiction in his persona between the "military" and the "civilian"
personae (PCS, 335). These elements constitute the playground of
Phister's reflective performance.[17] On this basis, Procul turns his
attention more specifically to the blending of these elements apropos
four points for reflection: "Captain Scipio Standing" (PCS, 336-37);
"Captain Scipio Walking" (PCS, 338-39); "The Lord Only Knows
Whether Captain Scipio Actually Drinks or Not" (PCS, 339-42); and
"In the Second Act of the Play Captain Scipio Accidentally Is No
Longer Drinking" (PCS, 342-43).

With regard to the first two points, the comic effect is mainly
afforded vis-à-vis the splendid uniform. As a military man, or at
least "a man who wears a military uniform" (PCS, 334), one would
fully expect a more or less characteristic demeanor to be manifest in

---

[17]At this point in the review, Procul makes a point of insisting that "one who
has not seen Phister's Scipio," as opposed to one who "has seen and sees Phister
again," is in no position to appreciate the reflective performance (PCS, 334). The
present author by no means counts himself among the initiates who have seen
either *Ludovic* or Phister, much less Phister's performance in *Ludovic*. The most that
can be counted upon in the present endeavor is thus a kind of reflection that is at
least twice removed from the original. But when the issue is precisely one of
reflection, the force of this particular objection is perhaps acceptably diminished.

Captain Scipio's standing and walking. The civilian in Captain Scipio, however, fully violates this expectation. Rather than standing "belly in chest out," the "inadmissibly potbellied" Captain stands, or rather "stoops," "half-cocked" in a veritable reverse "bow" (PCS, 336-37). Rather than walking ahead of the soldiers in a manner befitting one who is to lead and correct others, the Captain comes "bustling, half-skipping," and "hurrying in—behind" (PCS, 338). By themselves, the excessively "military" uniform and the excessively "civilian" mannerisms are perhaps humorous enough to elicit a smile. Pitted together and thus against one another in the same person, however, each one succeeds in making the other appear all the more ridiculous. This is the basic contradiction in Captain Scipio: he is "a civilian-military amphibian" (PCS, 337). From whichever side one happens to catch a glimpse of him, and thus more so than the proverbial fish out of water, Captain Scipio appears characteristically out of character and elementally out of his element. With this much established Procul proceeds to identify that other, incidental and accidental element of Phister's performance as Captain Scipio, namely, the lurking suspicion afforded by the performance that Captain Scipio is actually somewhat drunk. This is the element that so appeals to the author and is the subject of the third and fourth points of the appropriately reflective review.

"The Lord Only Knows Whether Captain Scipio Actually Drinks Or Not" (PCS, 339). But the author obviously has his suspicions. In fact, it is precisely this suspicion around which the whole of the reflective review revolves. It is this that Procul proposes to have understood and to know. From where does this suspicion arise? Is there anything in Captain Scipio that directly testifies to his being intoxicated? Procul eschews this path from the outset: "In a certain sense it is the easiest thing of all, as any esthetician knows, to represent a drunken man, and therefore every actor is able to do it to a certain degree. In other words, being drunk is an incommensurability; there is no specifically designated posture, behavior, etc. that accurately conveys it; the greatest randomness is possible" (PCS, 339). Presumably, Phister has understood this and therefore offers no direct testimony in this regard. Direct testimony is not the principal stuff of which reflective performances are made. Thus, Procul's reflective hypothesis:

But Captain Scipio is not a drunken man. He is such a man who

from the earliest morning hour and at any other time of day—
indeed, even if he were called out at midnight—is continually a
little tipsy, but no more than that. He can manage his affairs as well
as he is usually able to manage them; he does not drink himself
drunk, not even when there is opportunity to do so. One may
rather say that it has become impossible for him to become drunk;
just as the virtuous person reaches a maximum where it is said that
he cannot sin, so Captain Scipio has reached the maximum, he cannot get drunk.[18] We are therefore never entirely sure that this is his
condition, since it may not be seen immediately, at first glance.
(PCS, 339-40)

Thus, according to Procul's suspicion, Captain Scipio is drunk
and yet not drunk, continually half-drunk. The substance of this suspicion itself appears to render the hypothesis all the more gratuitous.
If the state of Captain Scipio is the kind of continual half-drunken-
ness that is both the impossibility of getting completely plastered
and the very semblance of sobriety, whence the richly reflective suspicion in the first place? Procul locates the clue according to the application of a familiar dialectic. Captain Scipio's "condition," his "secret," and his "befuddlement" will be betrayed by his continual and
careful attempts to conceal it (PCS, 340). Thus, "the frequent movement of his hand to his head," "the movement of the hand to the
mouth or in front of the mouth," the "certain rigidity" of "posture"
and the continual standing and landing "on his best foot" (PCS, 341-
42). All of this is a very deliberate something and just enough of a
clue to allow Procul to suspect that Captain Scipio is actually half-
drunk—i.e., continually engaged in the project of concealing his true
condition. The concealment, so to speak, sparks the revelation.
    "In the Second Act of the Play Captain Scipio Accidentally Is No
Longer Drinking" (PCS, 342). And it is here that the author finds

----

[18]In a spirited bout of private correspondence, Robert L. Perkins has suggested
a wholly ironic interpretation of the alleged "saying" that a person could become
so virtuous that he or she could not sin. This seems to be the only plausible interpretation, unless either (a) the happy juxtaposition of "virtue" and "sin" is a careless
oversight on the part of the author, or (b) this juxtaposition is actually the much-
needed clue in the establishment of a kind of Kierkegaardian super-virtue-ethics.
Given an ironic interpretation, the remark presumably pertains to the speculative
pretense of comprehending "virtue" by ascending to the plane of pure thought, at
which point (having reached the maximum) sin becomes an impossibility by definition, as it is a condition uniquely endemic to existing individuals.

confirmation of his suspicion. The dramatic situation appears innocuous enough: "Despite all Capt. Scipio's busyness, he still has not succeeded in apprehending the criminal he has been sent to arrest. In his zeal he makes a vow not to taste wine or brandy before he succeeds in arresting the guilty man" (PCS, 342-43). As far as anyone can tell, the Captain is basically just swearing off an incidental indulgence in something pleasant until the completion of a difficult task. Surely there is nothing to see here. As the act progresses, however, "a kind of depressed listlessness, a kind of *tristitia* is diffused over his figure. Now for the first time he is more like a drunken man; his walk is unsteady, slouching, his arms hang down loosely, his eyes stare, he staggers, his legs refuse to carry him properly, he no longer has a best foot to strike the least posture — and why? Because now he is sober" (PCS, 343). The Captain now and for the first time appears to be drunk, in the very act in which he swore not to drink the least little drop. Procul endeavors an explanation of this development consonant with his suspicion:

> If someone who has been addicted to the continual use of intoxi-
> cating drink without actually being drunk suddenly stops drinking,
> he is for a time in essentially the same condition because of slack-
> ness [*Slaphed*];[19] Indeed, he apparently is almost more intoxicated
> than when he was drinking. Just by using the customary amount
> of spirits, a person of this sort almost seems to be completely sober;
> and when he is one day completely sober, he very likely seems to
> be almost drunk. (PCS, 343)

This is the wittiness of Phister's performance as a man who is continually half-drunk — a condition that is only actually revealed as such when he becomes sober. This is the accidentally appealing aspect of the performance that leads Procul, "many years since [he had seen] *Ludovic*," to repay "a little on the debt" owed to Phister for this reflective performance (PCS, 343).[20] Of course, conceived as a

---

[19]An expression of gratitude is due here, and elsewhere, to Søren Landkildehus for assistance in tracking down various elements in and about the Danish text of the piece on Phister.

[20]Inasmuch as the payment is made in the form a piece of "drama criticism," the characterization of the aesthetician in the hands of a related pseudonym (Inter et Inter) is perhaps only too apropos: "Intoxicated in admiration [*Beundring*] and yet sober in dialectical levelheadedness, he will have eyes for this alone [i.e., "the dialectic of potentiation"] and will understand it as his call [*Kald*] to create room so

discrete pseudonymous persona, Procul may be excused for not rendering *Kierkegaard's* enduring fascination with this reflective performance more explicit. Nevertheless, the former's reflection does provide a remarkably fertile framework for engaging the latter's own reflection on the dialectic of intoxication in the posthumously published discourse, "Becoming Sober."

Kierkegaard's "Becoming Sober"

What is intoxication, or what is it to be intoxicated? The first discourse of the posthumously published *Judge for Yourself!* contains Kierkegaard's most direct engagement with this question.[21] The very title of the discourse is sufficiently indicative in this regard: "Becoming Sober" (JFY, 95).[22] Notwithstanding the shift in authorial tactics

---

that this marvel [*Vidunderlige*] can be seen and admired precisely as such" (C, 324).

[21]For an intriguing anticipation of the position eventually developed by Kierkegaard, see Emanuel Swedenborg's discussion of spiritual drunkenness (*Arcana Coelestia* 1072) in *A Compendium of the Theological Writings of Emanuel Swedenborg*, ed. Samuel M. Warren (New York: Swedenborg Foundation, 1977) 173-75.

[22]In this regard if in no other, it becomes increasingly difficult *not* to hear Kierkegaard reading, in the background as it were, the passage from the "Preface" to G. W. F. Hegel's *Phenomenology of Spirit* in which "the True" is described as "the Bacchanalian revel in which no member is not drunk; yet because each member collapses as soon as he drops out, the revel is just as much transparent and simple repose." Hegel, *Phenomenology of Spirit*, trans. A. V. Miller (Oxford: Oxford University Press, 1977) 27. For a pair of interesting readings of this passage, see Howard P. Kainz, "Hegel on the Bacchanalian Revel of Truth," *Philosophy and Rhetoric* 28/2 (1995): 146-52; and Andrew Haas, "The Bacchanalian Revel: Hegel and Deconstruction," *Man and World* 30/2 (1997): 217-26. Additionally, in what might otherwise seem to comprise nothing but a piece of intellectual trivia, it is worth noting that Kierkegaard leaves off taking (or at least transcribing) notes of F. W. J. Schelling's Berlin lectures (1841-42) at the very point where the latter appears poised at last to embark upon his philosophy of "revelation," having already achieved the basic recognition in his philosophy of "mythology" — "the deeper presupposition of revelation" (NSBL, 400) — that "Dionysus is Occidentalism" (NSBL, 412); cf. NSBL, 403-12. Conceived in this light, Kierkegaard's task consists at the very least in keeping the existential task of becoming sober from being dissolved (as he thought it had been in the systems of both Hegel and Schelling) in the highly intoxicating solutions of "science and scholarship" (JP, 1:1059; cf. TA, 9). Suffice it to say, and whether or not intellectual dexterity in itself should be trusted with the navigation of the problematic, the basic collisions between the three thinkers (Hegel, Schelling, and Kierkegaard) could conceivably be mapped as far as one could

from the earlier pseudonymous works to this, a work that was presumably to have borne the name of "S. Kierkegaard" as author, this is not to say or suggest that Kierkegaard gives anything like an easy answer to the question. Indeed, whether the question is posed in terms of "intoxication" or its conceptual correlate, "sobriety," Kierkegaard manages to confound the matter from the get-go: "The world says of the apostles, of the Apostle Peter as their spokesman, 'He is drunk,' and the Apostle Peter admonishes, 'Become sober'[23] The difference between secularity and Christianity is not that the one has one view and the other another—no, the difference is always that they have the very opposite views . . . what one calls being drunk the other calls being sober" (JFY, 96).

Having thus introduced the thematic of the redoubled and redoubling task of becoming sober,[24] Kierkegaard proceeds to fill in some of the details:

This is Christianity! And the entire relation in the distinction,

reasonably require solely by recourse to what each of them would have us understand by the phrase, "the spirit of intoxication."

Of course, the name of Nietzsche will presumably crop up fairly quickly in any such discussion. See, e.g., David Farrell Krell, "Nietzschean Reminiscences of Schelling's Philosophy of Mythology," *Epoché* 8/2 (2004): 181-93. If a single draught from the flood of Nietzsche's writings may serve to forestall as much of the inevitable discussion as it introduces, the present author can find none better suited to the purpose than the following (drawn from section 48 of *The Will to Power*, and authored sometime in 1888): "Here the experience of intoxication proved misleading. This increases the feeling of power in the highest degree—therefore, naively judged, power itself." Nietzsche, *The Will to Power*, trans. Walter Kaufmann and R.J. Hollingdale (New York: Random House, 1968) 31. That Nietzsche is (here) criticizing the "exhaustion" of the "fanatic, the possessed, the religious epileptic," etc., must not be allowed to obscure the fact that he finds himself (here) compelled to distinguish between "the feeling of enhanced power" — the definition of "intoxication" offered in section 811, also authored in 1888 (*The Will to Power*, 428)—and "power itself."

[23]See Acts 2:13, and I Peter 4:7, respectively; cf. Peter A. Kwasniewski, "'Divine Drunkenness': The Secret Life of Thomistic Reason," *The Modern Schoolman* 82/1 (2004): 1-31.

[24]"In other words, everything essentially Christian is a redoubling, or every qualification of the essentially Christian is *first of all* its opposite" (JFY, 98, emphasis added); see David Cain, "A Star in the Cross, Getting the Dialectic Right," in *International Kierkegaard Commentary: For Self-Examination and Judge for Yourself!*, ed. Robert L. Perkins (Macon GA: Mercer University Press, 2002) 317-19.

spiritually understood, between being sober and being intoxicated is turned around. We began with sensibleness, levelheadedness, and sagacity as being sober, with venturing and venturing to relinquish probability as being intoxicated.[25] But Christianity makes everything new. Thus also here: in reliance upon God, venturing to relinquish probability is precisely what it means to be Christianly sober . . . Whereas, Christianly understood, sensibleness, levelheadedness, and sagacity are . . . intoxication! (JFY, 103)

Thus, in contrast to the putative ideality of sensibleness, level-headedness, and sagacity — i.e., sticking to the facts, probabilistic cal-culation, and the prudential distrust of decisive (i.e., immoderate) venturing — Kierkegaard proposes a model of "sobriety" and "intoxi-cation" that flies in the face of the secular understanding of these conditions. The theme is then developed along two successive lines: becoming sober is "*to come to oneself in self-knowledge and before God as nothing before him, yet infinitely, unconditionally engaged*" (JFY, 104), and "*to come so close to oneself in one's understanding, in one's knowing, that all one's understanding becomes action*" (JFY, 115).[26]

Along the trajectory of the first line, and in stark contrast to the secular conception of the infinite as that which makes one dizzyingly intoxicated, Kierkegaard develops his definition of sobriety point by point: "to come to oneself" (JFY, 104-105) "in self-knowledge" (JFY, 105) "and before God" (JFY, 106) "as nothing" (JFY, 106) "and never-theless infinitely, unconditionally engaged" (JFY, 106-107). It is with regard to this last point that Kierkegaard proposes what is arguably his richest and most telling analogy, regarding a drunken man contemplating a trek across a wide open town square: "But in our thieves' jargon we human beings express it differently; we maintain that we are sagacious, sensible, levelheaded people, that we are sober, and it is precisely the unconditioned that would make us intoxicated. It is like that drunk man's saying 'I am sober, but if I

---

[25]See JFY, 98.

[26]See the discussion of "sobriety" in Paul Martens, "The Emergence of the Holy Spirit in Kierkegaard's Thought: Critical Theological Developments in *For Self-Examination* and *Judge for Yourself!*," in *International Kierkegaard Commentary: For Self-Examination and Judge for Yourself!*, 208-13. See also the suggestive proposal that "becoming sober" is remarkably akin to "dying to" in David Cain, "A Star in the Cross, Getting the Dialectic Right," 321.

walked across that big square, the big square would make me drunk'" (JFY, 114). "This is Christianity's view. It is not the unconditioned that makes one intoxicated, but it is the unconditioned that makes manifest that we are intoxicated—something we ourselves know well enough and therefore sagaciously stick to the finitudes, hug the line of buildings, stay in the alleys, and never venture out into the infinite" (JFY, 114).

Along the trajectory of the second line, and in a manner that cannot but call to mind the perennial ethical "problem" regarding the relationship between knowledge and moral weakness,[27] Kierkegaard continues his critical appraisal of the worldly conception of sobriety: "Here, again, the purely human point of view is naturally of the totally opposite opinion, that precisely this [i.e., allowing one's understanding to become action] is intoxication, whereas what the sagacious, the sensible, and the levelheaded do is sobriety, to take care that one keep one's understanding, one's knowledge, at a proper distance from life, or one's life a proper distance from it, and then not let it gain power over one" (JFY, 115). "And this, precisely this [i.e., that to understand is a pleasure, but to do is an effort], the sensible, sagacious, levelheaded person understands and this is why

---

[27]See, e.g., Aristotle, *Nicomachean Ethics* 1103b, 1146b-47b, 1152a. With respect to Aristotle's likening of moral weakness [ακρασία] to drunkenness in particular, the following entry from the young Kierkegaard's journals is strikingly apropos: "When it is said that in drunkenness men place themselves beneath the animals, there is implicit recognition of a sinfulness which slumbers within man, for otherwise he would merely put himself on an equal level, but now there awakens a hell of impulses" (JP, 1:33). This is a thought that Aristotle *arguably* lacks the (Christian) conceptual resources to think: that there is a quality of character more malign still than the bestial—a quality of character, it should be noted, that is accessed already in the allegedly less malignant quality of moral weakness. Thus, however much Kierkegaard's account of the relationship between knowing and acting may sound like a mere rehearsal of Aristotle, one must exercise caution to avoid prematurely collapsing the position of either one into that of the other. Indeed, several pages prior, in what is either an entirely fortuitous or entirely appropriate maneuver on his part, Kierkegaard equally well recalls the Platonic engagement with this problem (*Phaedrus* 246c-256e) in his figurative illustration of the "royal coachman" and his "horses" (JFY, 107-109; cf. FSE, 85-87), with the *arguably* all important variation that the coachman does not figure as the analogue of the divine element in the soul (as in Plato), but rather as the analogue of the divine itself—i.e., the unconditioned.

he—he is sober—so carefully establishes a chasmic abyss between his knowing, his understanding, which he expounds, and his life; consequently, he is sober" (JFY, 117). To his credit, Kierkegaard then proposes "one more example" of intoxication vis-à-vis the ideal of an unconditional and active engagement with Christianity: the person who, specifically if not essentially differentiated from the visual artist, "wants to muster the full power of language to portray the Savior of the world" (JFY, 121). This too is intoxication. Indeed, if Kierkegaard is to be taken at his word, it is "an extremely dangerous" intoxication (JP, 3:3506).

Inasmuch as the notions of redoubling and reduplication are already in play, it is difficult to think that Kierkegaard is not here thinking of himself.[28] Such a suspicion finds the fullest confirmation in the discourse's conclusion, as Kierkegaard both calls for a confession and confesses, in contrast to the ready wealth of verbal "assurances" to the contrary, that we and he are all basically drunk:

> As for being sober, I am very conscious of not being that, because only *spirit* is sober. But then I do not become totally dazed, intoxicated with the illusion that this toned-down version is Christianity, nor am I drunk with the self-delusion that I, in contrast to this toned-down Christianity in which the majority are living under the name of Christians, am the true Christian. No, I come with the confession . . . This [manner of living] is not being sober . . . this [confession] is not being sober, but it is related to becoming sober. (JFY, 142)[29]

Granting that terms such as "intoxication," "drunkenness," "inebriation" and the like are more or less a kind of generic or even all-purpose shorthand for existential impairment in Kierkegaard's writings, the central problem remains—or, indeed, perhaps only now comes clearly into view. With a proper disregard for the otherwise sound phenomenological postulate that the one who is experientially conversant with a particular existential 'phenomenon' is the

---

[28]Indeed, the fact that the second discourse of *Judge for Yourself!*, "Christ as the Prototype" (JFY, 145-213) consists of what is far and away the most directly discursive treatment of "the Savior of the world" in the entire authorship only serves to highlight the vexingly self-referential dimension of such a line of critique.

[29]Cf. JP, 6:6645.

one most fit to propound its essential character,[30] is it not the height of intoxication to query the drunk (while they are drunk) regarding the nature and significance of drunkenness? Indeed, are not matters made irreparably worse on the heels of the recognition that drunkenness consists in the very proclivity to call sobriety "drunkenness" and vice-versa? Such is the state of the problem in "Becoming Sober."[31]

Insofar as the seeds of the eventual attack upon Christendom are quite obviously sown here in the recognition that, in so many words, Christendom is basically a populace of drunkards,[32] There is a single passage in the attack literature that provides a further clue to the

---

[30]For an example of just such a phenomenological approach to the question regarding the significance of intoxication, see William James, *The Varieties of Religious Experience: A Study in Human Nature* (New York: Penguin Books, 1985) 386-93, 402-405; cf. Abu Hamid Muhammad ibn Muhammad al-Ghazali, *Deliverance from Error*, trans. R. J. McCarthy, in *Al-Ghazali's Path to Sufism* (Louisville: Fons Vitae, 2000) esp. 51-64. (An expression of gratitude is due to Lucian W. Stone, Jr., for assistance in tracking down an acceptable translation of the extended passage from al-Ghazali supplied by James.) On the young Kierkegaard's confessed familiarity with the "experience" in question, see JP, 5:5146; cf. Walter Lowrie, *Kierkegaard* (New York: Oxford University Press, 1938) 117-19.

[31]Paul Martens offers the following note in this regard: "One may wonder how Kierkegaard can see the situation so clearly while admitting his own intoxication. He might counter, however, with the response that the relative sobriety of the situation of grace (which is related to sobriety) provides a vista with a view that can discern the true nature of Christianity and the present age clearly enough to make the claims he does." Martens, "The Emergence of the Holy Spirit in Kierkegaard's Thought," 212n23. However much one might wish that Martens would have expanded upon this insight, one would perhaps do just as well to wonder if Procul has not already said something more than this in what otherwise seems a mere quip: "The Lord Only Knows Whether Captain Scipio Actually Drinks Or Not" (PCS, 339). As the story goes, a comparable concern led Kierkegaard to adopt and defer to a "higher pseudonym" (Anti-Climacus) vis-à-vis the analysis of despair in *The Sickness unto Death* (see, e.g., JP 6:6438, 6446, 6501).

[32]"The world wants to be deceived . . . the world fights to be deceived; it most gratefully rewards with applause, money, and prestige anyone who complies with its wish to be deceived" (JFY, 140). Or again: "as Luther says, the world continues to be like the drunken peasant who, helped up on one side of the horse, falls off the other side" (JP, 3:3724). Or again: "Then 'Christendom' has won the game, a victory that is most fittingly celebrated by a real eating and drinking club, a wild club with bacchants and bacchantes (pastors and midwives) at the head of the hilarity" (TM, 238).

navigation of this conundrum. In the fifth article of the third issue of *The Moment*, "Have the State Check the Accounting, and It Will Soon Be Evident That the Accounting Is Fundamentally Wrong" (TM, 151-52),[33] Kierkegaard proposes a most interesting analogy for the clergy's silent response to his repeated attacks:

> When a man with sedately measured steps walks sedately down the street, one is prompted to think: There is something unusual here. But if one happens to learn that the explanation for this sedateness is that the man is a little tipsy [*beskjenkit*], that this is why (a counteractive measure lest he spontaneously gravitate toward the curb) he has to hold himself with such sedateness, it might be much better for him simply to stagger a little. Perhaps one would smile, perhaps, perhaps not even notice his condition at all, whereas he arouses interest because of his sedateness, does not escape teasing, which becomes more merciless in proportion to his effort to walk more and more sedately. It is the same with the clergy's silence. (TM, 152)

Christendom, according to Kierkegaard, is basically a populace of drunkards with the self-intoxicated clergy at the head. As difficult as this arrangement would appear to render the task of recognizing the "something unusual," however, the matter is really only irreparable for those who will not see the dialectic of the situation through and come to see just how dialectical the true situation is. For, however dangerous it may in fact be to allow one's gaze to be fixed in this direction, the fact remains that the procedure of inverse dialectic—the recognition of the redoubling by virtue of which everything is turned around—by its very nature cuts both ways.[34] It is precisely the "sedately measured steps"—the deliberate maintenance of the appearance of sobriety—that initially betrays the

---

[33]Cf. JFY, 130.

[34]Of course, this is not to say or suggest that every (propositional) conversion in this regard is licit. In other words, inverse dialectic is not and cannot be an all purpose hermeneutical key. If it were, Kierkegaard would be placed in the awkward position of saying that "*whatever* one calls being drunk the other calls being sober" (cf. JFY, 96)—e.g., that when a man stumbles out of a bar, falls laughing into the gutter, and vomits on himself, and the world calls him "drunk," Christianity would be compelled by force of the inverse dialectic to counter, "no, he is sober." The Kierkegaardian 'doctrine' of the stages (immediacy—mediation—immediacy) provides some help in this regard.

drunkard. The full disclosure then comes if only one can get the drunkard to walk out into the open, to confront the unconditioned, or even — in the reflectively humorous words of Procul that become even more so if only they are given a certain metaphoric[35] and ambiguous twist — merely to "vow not to taste wine or brandy before [one] succeeds in arresting the guilty [person]" (PCS, 343). In the mouth of a "Scipio," captain in the papal police force, the words need only be given the twist of ambiguity consonant with the accidentally appealing element of Phister's performance to afford the comic effect: I vow not to drink until I have discovered the true drunkard. Now that is undeniably funny. But when the words are given the further twist of metaphor consonant with the similitude of the dialectic of intoxication in "Phister as Captain Scipio" and "Becoming Sober,"[36] is the matter still so funny?

Conclusion: The Comedy of Despair

Inasmuch as the concept of "intoxication" functions generically as a ready shorthand for existential impairment in Kierkegaard's authorship,[37] the question arises as to whether or not the concept would be particularly suited as such vis-à-vis the most potent of all such impairments: despair. A sufficient number of passages in the authorship suggest that it would.[38] Insofar as Kierkegaard may be

---

[35]That the twist in question is actually better understood as one of metonymy than one of metaphor will become clearer in what follows, apropos the suggested association (as opposed to mere similitude) of "intoxication" and "despair."

[36]For a succinct account of the dialectic of intoxication that informs both "Phister as Captain Scipio" and "Becoming Sober," see JP, 2:2034. For an alternative account of the "dialectics of intoxication" that is strangely if only momentarily akin to that developed by Kierkegaard, see Walter Benjamin, "Surrealism: The Last Snapshot of the European Intelligentsia," trans. Edmund Jephcott, in Benjamin, *Reflections: Essays, Aphorisms, Autobiographical Writings*, ed. Peter Demetz (New York: Shocken Books, 1978) 177-92.

[37]Especially noteworthy in this regard is the diagnosis of the "confused genius" of Adolph Peter Adler as a kind of dizzy intoxication (see BA, 287-93).

[38]See, e.g., EO, 2:194; EUD, 201; FT, 94; SUD, 53, 108; JP, 1:33; 4:4031, 4746. In precisely this vein (see esp. JP, 4:4031), Kierkegaard is entirely willing to attribute a thorough culpability to the "drunkard" (i.e., the sinner) not only for the actions performed while "drunk" but for being "drunk" (i.e., sinful) in the first place. Whether or not this analogue can ultimately afford a sufficiently nuanced

called a "religious poet,"[39] whose more poetic works comprise so many disclosures of one or another form of existential despair, his authorship would thus appear to bear the mark, by definition, of the

---

conception of the theological doctrine of "original sin" (cf. CA, 128, 152), posing the question of culpability vis-à-vis the condition of drunkenness does have some interesting philosophical precedents. Aristotle, as noted above, is explicitly inclined to entertain the question in this regard (*Nicomachean Ethics* 1113b-14a, 1146b-47b, 1151a, 1152a, 1154b). See Randall Curren, "The Contribution of *Nicomachean Ethics* III 5 to Aristotle's Theory of Responsibility," *History of Philosophy Quarterly* 6 (1989): 261-77; Justin Gosling, "Mad, Drunk or Asleep? — Aristotle's Akratic," *Phronesis* 38/1 (1993): 98-104; and Dennis Klimchuk, "Aristotle on Intoxication and Liability," *History of Philosophy Quarterly* 20/3 (2003): 225-43. And while it initially appears ancillary to his main interest in determining the nature of personal identity, John Locke's entertainment of this question (*Essay Concerning Human Understanding* II:27:22 and the subsequent correspondence with William Molyneux) is equally noteworthy. See Henry E. Allison, "Locke's Theory of Personal Identity: A Re-Examination," *Journal of the History of Ideas* 27/1 (1966): 41-58; Paul Helm, "Did Locke Capitulate to Molyneux?," *Journal of the History of Ideas* 42/4 (1981): 669-71; and Henry E. Allison and Nicholas Jolley, "Locke's Pyrrhic Victory," *Journal of the History of Ideas* 42/4 (1981): 672-74.

   To make the association of intoxication with despair as strong as possible, however, the following passage from *Either/Or, Part I* commands some attention: "It [Mozart's music] is intoxicated with erotic love; but, like all intoxication, an intoxication with erotic love can also have two effects, either a heightened transparent joy of life or a concentrated obscure depression" (EO, 1:78; cf. EO, 1:90, 133, 134). A similar distinction is alleged by German Z. Aguilar, "Suspension of Control: A Sociocultural Study on Specific Drinking Habits and Their Psychiatric Consequences," *Journal of Existentialism* 4 (1964): 245-52, between "dionysiac drunkenness" (the stimulation of social intercourse) and "masked suicide" (drunkenness for its own sake). Conceived in this light, and recalling Procul's recognition of the great randomness of intoxication and its consequences (PCS, 339), it would seem that giving the nod to "despair" in this regard is really to neglect a substantial portion of the possible modalizations of intoxication, namely, those that tend in the direction of "a heightened transparent joy of life." Such an objection surely requires a fuller response than that which is or can be afforded here. Nevertheless, it is more than likely that Kierkegaard's response would run somewhat as follows: What the author of "The Immediate Erotic Stages or The Musical Erotic" (EO, 1:45-135) understands by the phrase "transparent joy of life" is actually just one more cleverly disguised and thus anything but "transparent" form of existential despair (see SUD, 25, 26-27; cf. JP, 3:2442). In fact, once spiritual *disorientation* is recognized as the central issue, the rubrics of "despair" and "intoxication" become largely if not wholly interchangeable.

   [39]See, e.g., JP, 1:151; 6:6437, 6511.

tragic. Following the teaser that Plato lets loose toward the end of the *Symposium*,[40] however — a suggestion the significance of which is summarily amplified by the encouraged suspicion that its proponent, Socrates, having stayed awake as long and drunk as much as anyone else, is at last the most wide awake and sober of the entire company — may not Kierkegaard also be construed as a kind of comedian? If one can keep from becoming intoxicated in the occasioned laughter itself,[41] it seems that the answer to this question must be (an inversely horrifying) "yes."

That Captain Scipio, the half-drunk military/civilian amphibian,[42] is a *frenetically* comic character the reader has on the authority

---

[40]"Socrates was arguing with the others — not that Aristodemus could remember very much of what he said, for, besides having missed the beginning, he was still more than half asleep. But the gist of it was that Socrates was forcing them [i.e., Aristophanes (the comedian) and Agathon (the tragedian)] to admit that the same man might be capable of writing both comedy and tragedy — that the tragic poet might be a comedian as well." Plato, *Symposium* 223c-d, trans. Michael Joyce in *The Collected Dialogues of Plato*, ed. Edith Hamilton and Huntington Cairns (Princeton: Princeton University Press, 1996) 574. See Thomas Hanna, "The Compass Points of the Comic and the Pathetic," *The British Journal of Aesthetics* 8 (1968): 284-94; Edmund L. Erde, "Comedy and Tragedy and Philosophy in the *Symposium*: An Ethical Vision," *The Southwestern Journal of Philosophy* 7 (1976): 161-67; Richard Pattison, "The Platonic Art of Comedy and Tragedy," *Philosophy and Literature* 6/1-2 (1982): 76-93; and Michael Platt, "Tragical, Comical, Historical," in *The Existential Coordinates of the Human Condition: Poetic — Epic — Tragic* (*Analecta Husserliana* 18), ed. Anna-Teresa Tymieniecka (Boston: D. Reidel, 1984) 379-99. For a good start on reading Kierkegaard in light of this proposed unity, see John D. Glenn, "Kierkegaard on the Unity of Comedy and Tragedy," *Tulane Studies in Philosophy* 19 (1970): 41-53.

[41]Cf. EO, 1:42-43; R, 161. On the significance of the altogether mystical embrace of "laughter" in the (fortuitously) culminating "Diapsalma" of *Either/Or, Part I*, see EO, 1:8; JP, 5:5371, 5629. On the significance of the category of "farce" — vis-à-vis the proposal of Constantin Constantius that actors in farce must be "intoxicated with laughter" — see George Pattison, "The Magic of Theater: Drama and Existence in Kierkegaard's *Repetition* and Hesse's *Steppenwolf*," in *International Kierkegaard Commentary: Fear and Trembling and Repetition*, ed. Robert L. Perkins (Macon GA: Mercer University Press, 1993) 359-77; and T. F. Morris, "Constantin Constantius's Search for an Acceptable Way of Life," in *International Kierkegaard Commentary: Fear and Trembling and Repetition*, 309-34.

[42]That this is a perfectly suited characterization of Kierkegaard's reckoning of the Danish clergy — the uniform of militant Christianity and the underlying substance of civic Christianity (civilian prosperity) all rolled into one — is perhaps obvious enough.

of Procul (PCS, 339). But who is this "Procul" — and from what is the reader thus being directed "away?" Perhaps the direction is ironic, rather like the direction to "note well" in the name of the author who writes only the most dispensable parts of books (Nicolaus Notabene). Or, inasmuch as there actually remains something worth noting well in the satirical lampoons composed as mere "prefaces,"[43] perhaps there is actually something in particular away from which the reader of "Phister as Captain Scipio" is being directed. Or perhaps, being an aesthetic piece, the name and the review penned under the name mean to suggest both (and more) of these possibilities, with a certain behind-the-scenes editor ultimately deciding that there was too much or not enough of one or the other or both thus resulting in the piece's nonpublication. One might even wonder whether or not leaving the piece for posthumous publication was itself a significant consideration in its nonpublication. And so it goes with "Procul."[44]

Nevertheless, if one is able to look and listen with the right kind of eyes and ears, there is something extraordinarily funny about the human condition reflected in Phister's performance as Captain Scipio, although laughter is certainly not the appropriate response to this most frenzied of frenetic comedies. Ironically, it is perhaps the vestige of this very recognition that discourages most of us from recognizing or even attempting to recognize the comedy. This strangely contagious and highly excited kind of breathing called laughter is not the appropriate response, however necessary it may at times be.[45] Rather, the task is simply to come to recognize, to understand, and to know that which is reflected in the humor — i.e., "the way out" (CUP, 1:516) — and to act accordingly. In other words, this — all of this, the writing, the disclosure of despair in its myriad forms, the discovery of the true drunkard amidst the drunken, and

---

[43]In this regard, see the truly ground-breaking collection of critical essays in *International Kierkegaard Commentary: Prefaces and Writing Sampler*.

[44]On the various plans for the publication and circulation of "Phister as Captain Scipio," see CD, xiv-xv; and *Crisis in the Life of an Actress*, trans. Crites, 145n1.

[45]See JP, 6:6160; cf. JFY, 179. In a related vein, Kierkegaard would doubtlessly applaud the upshot of the physiological diagnosis of "laughter" afforded by René Descartes (*The Passions of the Soul*, part II, article CXXV), according to which laughter never attends the experience of unmingled joy.

even the confession of all of this — *is not becoming sober; but it is related to becoming sober.* Accordingly, the funnier all of *this* becomes the more it cries: *procul o procul este profani* — not back into the half-light according to which all of *this* appears merely tragic and melancholy (the initial manifestation of the transition suffered by Captain Scipio in the second act), but out into the sanctified open where one may truly begin *to act.*[46] That is becoming sober. Accordingly, if a corresponding definition of "intoxication" is still wanted one may say that it is despair, but despair conceived with an emphasis upon the allure that it increasingly exercises over the self-indulgent self, however this indulgence is more particularly modalized, for here "the greatest randomness is possible . . . because here anything goes" (PCS, 339).

---

[46]The striking ambiguity of this imperative "to act" (decisive venturing vs. dramatic performance) is of course subject to a dialectical rendition consonant with the true meaning of coming to know God and to know oneself as nothing before God; see JFY, 185-86.

Contributors

International Kierkegaard Commentary 17
Christian Discourses,
The Crisis and a Crisis in the Life of an Actress,
and the Addendum, "Phister as Captain Scipio"

THOMAS C. ANDERSON is professor of Philosophy, emeritus, Marquette University.

LEE BARRETT is professor of Theology at Lancaster Theological Seminary.

DAVID J. GOUWENS is professor of Theology at Brite Divinity School.

PATRICIA HUNTINGTON is associate professor of Philosophy at Loyola University of Chicago.

LOUISE CARROLL KEELEY is associate professor of Philosophy at Assumption College.

DAVID R. LAW is reader in Christian Thought at Manchester University.

RONALD F. MARSHALL is pastor of First Lutheran Church of West Seattle, Washington.

CHRISTOPHER A.P. NELSON is assistant professor of Philosophy at South Texas College.

DAVID D. POSSEN is a graduate student in the Committee of Social Thought and the Department of Philosophy at the University of Chicago.

HUGH S. PYPER is professor in the Department of Biblical Studies at the University of Sheffield.

MARK A. TIETJEN is assistant professor of Philosophy at the University of West Georgia.

JOSEPH WESTFALL is assistant professor of Philosophy at the University of Houston—Downtown.

MEROLD WESTPHAL is Distinguished Professor of Philosophy at Fordham University.

Advisory Board

Previous Volume Consultants

Volume 1. *Early Polemical Writings*
Julia Watkin, University of Tasmania

Volume 2. *The Concept of Irony*
Ronald L. Hall, Stetson University

Title Consultant for *Either/Or* I and II
George Connell, Concordia College

Volume 3. *Either/Or, I*
David J. Gouwens, Brite Divinity School

Volume 4. *Either/Or, II*
Edward F. Mooney, Syracuse University

Volume 5. *Eighteen Upbuilding Discourses*
George Pattison, Oxford University

Volume 6. *Fear and Trembling* and *Repetition*
Abrahim H. Khan, University of Toronto, *Fear and Trembling*
David Goicoechea, Brock University, *Repetition*

Volume 7. *Philosophical Fragments* and *Johannes Climacus*
Lee C. Barrett, Lancaster Theological Seminary

Volume 8. *The Concept of Anxiety*
Vincent A. McCarthy, St. Joseph's University

Volume 9. *Prefaces* and *Writing Sampler*
Mark C. E. Peterson, University of Wisconsin-Washington County

Volume 10. *Three Discourses on Imagined Occasions*
Lee C. Barrett, Lancaster Theological Seminary

Volume 11. *Stages on Life's Way*
Vincent A. McCarthy, St. Joseph's University

Volume 12. *Concluding Unscientific Postscript
to "Philosophical Fragments"*
Merold Westphal, Fordham University

Volume 13. *The Corsair Affair*
Bruce H. Kirmmse, Connecticut College

Volume 14. *Two Ages*
Merold Westphal, Fordham University

Volume 15. *Upbuilding Discourses in Various Spirits*
Lee C. Barrett, Lancaster Theological Seminary

Volume 16. *Works of Love*
Lee C. Barrett, Lancaster Theological Seminary

Volume 18. *Without Authority*
Lee C. Barrett, Lancaster Theological Seminary
David J. Gouwens, Brite Divinity School

Volume 19. *The Sickness unto Death*
Louis Dupré, Yale University

Volume 20. *Practice in Christianity*
Andrew J. Burgess, University of New Mexico

Volume 21. *For Self-Examination* and *Judge for Yourself!*
David Cain, Mary Washington College

Index